Empires of the Indus

Empires of the Indus

The Story of a River

ALICE ALBINIA

JOHN MURRAY

First published in Great Britain in 2008 by John Murray (Publishers)
An Hachette Livre UK company

I

© Alice Albinia 2008

A CIP catalogue record for this title is available from the British Library

Hardback ISBN 978-0-7195-6003-3
Trade paperback ISBN 978-0-7195-6004-0

Typeset in Bembo by Palimpsest Book Production Limited,
Grangemouth, Stirlingshire

Printed and bound by Clays Ltd, St Ives plc

John Murray policy is to use papers that are natural, renewable and recyclable products and
made from wood grown in sustainable forests. The logging and manufacturing processes are
expected to conform to the environmental regulations of the country of origin.

John Murray (Publishers)
338 Euston Road
London NW1 3BH

www.johnmurray.co.uk

ROBERT MATHERS

(1953–1991)

Contents

Illustrations

Photographs are by the author unless otherwise stated.

Section One

1. Muhammad Ali Jinnah, founder and first Governor General of Pakistan. Pakistan Archives, Islamabad. Photographer unknown.
2. The dry bed of the River Indus.
3. The 'Sheedi' descendants of the freed African slave Bilal, in Hyderabad, Pakistan.
4. Gulabi, a visitor to Bilali house, Badin, Pakistan.
5. Sohni crossing the river. A painting from the Qalandrani Leghari tombs near Johi, Sindh, Pakistan. Artist unknown.
6. Worshippers at the shrine of Sachal Sarmast in northern Sindh, Pakistan.
7. Men and women dancing together at the urs of Shah Abdul Latif, Bhitshah.
8. Khizr at the Water of Life. A miniature painting from a seventeenth-century manuscript of Nizami's *Khamsa* (Five Poems), produced in Isfahan, Iran between 1665 and 1667 and illustrated by Talib Lala, Du'l-Qadari (© The British Library Board, All Rights Reserved: Add. 6613, f.261v).
9. Mohanas, Indus boat-people, arriving at the shrine of Khwaja Khizr, near Sukkur, Sindh, Pakistan.
10. A riverside scene of hell, carved in marble, from the Sadhubela temple, near Sukkur, Sindh, Pakistan. Artist unknown.
11. Uderolal or Zindapir, riding on a palla fish. Painting from Zindapir temple, Sukkur, Sindh, Pakistan. Artist unknown.

ix

Section Two

26. A stone circle, probably an ancient burial mound, near Yasin, Gilgit valley, Pakistan.

27. A prehistoric carving of archers in the hills near Gakuch, Gilgit valley, Pakistan.

28. Potters in a village near the five-thousand-year-old brick city of Harappa, Punjab, Pakistan.

29. Menhirs at Burzahom, Srinagar, Kashmir, India.

30. Girls from Bomoi village, near Sopore, Kashmir, India.

31. A recently discovered upper Palaeolithic rock carving above Bomoi village.

32. A Neolithic hunting scene carved on to a menhir at Burzahom, showing a man and woman hunting a stag. © B. M. Pande/ASI, 1971.

33. A rock carving of a 'shroud' next to the Indus river near the village of Dha, Ladakh, India.

34. Drokpa at their encampment two days' walk from the source of the Indus, Tibet.

35. Senge Khabab, the 'Lion's Mouth': the source of the Indus in Tibet.

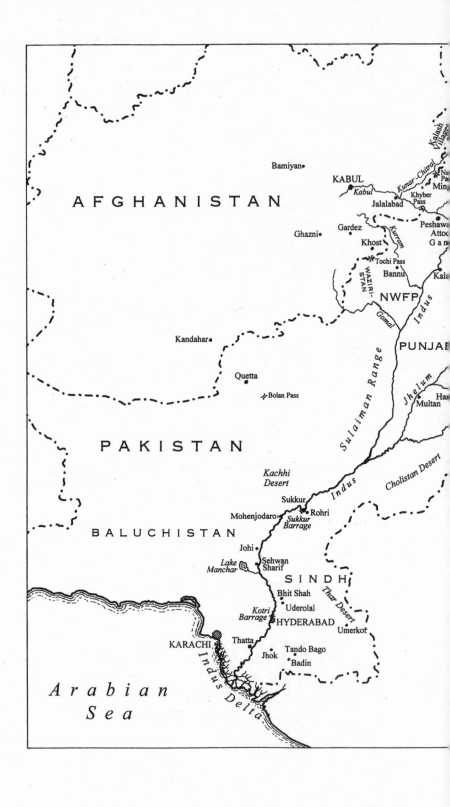

XINJIANG
(CHINA)

NORTHERN
AREAS

Yasin
Gakuch
Gilgit

BALTISTAN

AKSAI
CHIN

Chilas
Nanga
Parbat
Skardu
Pirsar
Ganoks
Kaladaka
Marol
Darbund
Kargil
Dha
Tarbela
Sopore
Mulbekh
Leh
Dam
Srinagar
Alchi
Islamabad
Matho

Taxila

JAMMU &
KASHMIR

LADAKH

Manda
Jammu

Senge-Ali

TIBET

Nankana
Sahib
Amritsar
Wagah
Lahore

Source of the Indus
Senge Khabab
Darchen Mt Kailash/Kangri Rinpoche

INDIA

NEPAL

DELHI

0	miles	250
0	kilometres	400

MAP OF THE
INDUS VALLEY

Preface

IN A LAND where it seldom rains, a river is as precious as gold.
Water is potent: it trickles through human dreams, permeates lives,
dictates agriculture, religion and warfare. Ever since *Homo sapiens* first
migrated out of Africa, the Indus has drawn thirsty conquerors to its
banks. Some of the world's first cities were built here; India's earliest
Sanskrit literature was written about the river; Islam's holy preachers
wandered beside these waters. Pakistan is only the most recent of the
Indus valley's political avatars.

I remember the first time I wanted to see the Indus, as distinctly
as if a match had been struck in a darkened room. I was twenty-three
years old, sitting in the heat of my rooftop flat in Delhi, reading the
Rig Veda, and feeling the perspiration running down my back. It was
April 2000, almost a year since the war between Pakistan and India
over Kargil in Kashmir had ended, and the newspapers which the
delivery man threw on to my terrace every morning still portrayed
neighbouring Pakistan as a rogue state, governed by military cowboys,
inhabited by murderous fundamentalists: the rhetoric had the patina
of hysteria. But what was the troubled nation next door really like?
As I scanned the three-thousand-year-old hymns, half listening to the
call to prayer, the *azan*, which drifted over the rooftops from the
nearby mosque (to the medley of other azans, all slightly out of sync),
I read of the river praised by Sanskrit priests, the Indus they called
'Unconquered Sindhu', river of rivers. Hinduism's motherland was not
in India but Pakistan, its demonized neighbour.

At the time, I was studying Indian history eclectically, omnivor-
ously and hastily – during bus journeys to work, at weekends, lying
under the ceiling fan at night. Even so, it seemed that everywhere
I turned, the Indus was present. Its merchants traded with Mesopotamia

five thousand years ago. A Persian emperor mapped it in the sixth century BCE. The Buddha lived beside it during previous incarnations. Greek kings and Afghan sultans waded across it with their armies. The founder of Sikhism was enlightened while bathing in a tributary. And the British invaded it by gunboat, colonized it for one hundred years, and then severed it from India. The Indus was part of Indians' lives – until 1947.

The very name of India comes from the river. The ancient Sanskrit speakers called the Indus 'Sindhu'; the Persians changed the name to 'Hindu'; and the Greeks dropped the 'h' altogether. Chinese whispers created the Indus and its cognates – India, Hindu, Indies. From the time that Alexander the Great's historians wrote about the Indus valley, spinning exotic tales of indomitable *Indika*, India and its river tantalized the Western imagination.

Hundreds of years later, when India was divided, it might have been logical for the new Muslim state in the Indus valley to take the name 'India' (or even 'Industan', as the valley was called by an eighteenth-century English sailor). But Muhammad Ali Jinnah rejected the colonial appellation and chose the pious neologism Pakistan, 'Land of the Pure', instead. He assumed that his coevals in Delhi would do the same, calling their country by the ancient Sanskrit title, 'Bharat'. When they did not, Jinnah was reported to be furious. He felt that by continuing to use the British name, India had appropriated the past; Pakistan, by contrast, looked as if it had been sliced off and 'thrown out'.

During the two years that I lived in Delhi, I wondered about these things – the ironies, misnomers and reverberations of history. But perhaps, to my sun-baked imagination, it was the river itself that was most enticing. I dreamt about that river, which begins in Tibet and ends near Karachi in the shimmer of the Arabian Sea; I tried to picture those waters, which emperors had built forts beside, which poets still sang of, the turbulent, gold-bearing abode of snake-goddesses.

When at last I reached Pakistan, it was to map these layers of history and their impress on modern society. During the past sixty years, Pakistanis have been brutalized by the violence of military dictatorships, enraged or deceived by the state's manipulation of religion, and are now being terrorized by the West's War on Terror. But Pakistan is

more than the sum of its generals and jihadis. The Indus valley has a
continuous history of political, religious and literary ferment stretching
back thousands of years; a history which Pakistanis share with Tibetans
and Indians. The intertwining of those chronicles, memories and myths
– that is the inheritance of the people who live in the Indus valley.

This book recounts a journey along the Indus, upstream and
back in time, from the sea to the source, from the moment that
Pakistan first came into being in Karachi, to the time, millions of
years ago in Tibet, when the river itself was born. Along the way,
the river has had more names than its people have had dictators.
In Sindh it is called 'Purali', meaning capricious, an apt description of a river which wanders freely across the land, creating cities
and destroying them. Sindhis also know it as 'Samundar', ocean, a
name evocative of the vastness of the river within their landscape
and civilization. For Pashtuns on the frontier with Afghanistan the
Indus is simultaneously 'Nilab', blue water, 'Sher Darya', the Lion
River, and 'Abbasin', Father of Rivers. Along its upper reaches these
names are repeated by people speaking different languages and practising different religions. Baltis once called the Indus 'Gemtsuh',
the Great Flood, or 'Tsuh-Fo', the Male River; here, as in Ladakh and
Tibet, it is known as 'Senge Tsampo', the Lion River. Today, in
spite of the militarized borders that divide the river's people from
each other, the ancient interconnectedness of the Indus still prevails.

The river gave logic to my own explorations; it lies at the heart
of this book because it runs through the lives of its people like a
charm. From the deserts of Sindh to the mountains of Tibet, the
Indus is worshipped by peasants and honoured by poets; more than
priests or politicians, it is the Indus they revere. And yet, it is a
diminished river. The mighty Indus of Sanskrit hymns and colonial
tracts was heavily dammed during the twentieth century. Beginning
with Britain's profit-driven colonization of the lower Indus valley,
and extending through sixty years of army-dominated rule in
Pakistan, big dams have shackled the river, transforming the lives of
human and non-human species on its banks and in its waters. Now
when I think of the Indus I remember the eulogies of Sanskrit
priests, Greek soldiers and Sufi saints. Their words come down to
us across the centuries, warning of all there is to lose.

I

Ramzan in Karachi

1947

'Hell is before him and he shall be given to drink of festering water.'

Qur'an 14.16

A HEAD EMERGES from a hole in the road, dripping with water. Naked shoulders follow, and a naked torso. Arms lift through the water, lean heavily on the tarmac; and with a great effort the man heaves himself out of the sewer and lies on the street, gasping for breath. He is wearing only a pair of white pyjama trousers – now grey and wet. The hole from which he has surfaced swirls darkly with putrid water.

The day is pleasant, and he rests for a moment, in this smart residential area in south Karachi, warming himself in the sun. Minutes pass silently – it is a quiet afternoon in those slow hours leading up to the breaking of the fast at sundown. Eventually, he sits up, lowers himself into the hole again, until the water reaches his navel, then his armpits. Then he takes a deep breath, holds his nose, and ducks down beneath the surface.

I have come across this scene by chance, as I cut home through a housing colony. I am fasting for the first time; I feel weak and tired. The city today was difficult to fathom: even the non-fasters were irritated or wan with collective Ramzan exhaustion. I fainted, in the morning, when the obstetrician in a slum hospital described the baby he had just delivered – 'three whole days the mother spent in labour, being ministered to by a *dai*, an untrained midwife. By the time she was brought into hospital, the baby was dead.' He had to cut it into pieces to pull it out. ('Maternal mortality worries me

I

most, though,' he said, as soon as I came round. 'They die on the potholed road just trying to get here.') At noon, I sat in the British-built law courts – a grand, pillared enclave aloof from the city, where two-thirds of the incumbents were flouting the fast laws.

My last appointment of the day took place deep within a congested north Karachi *basti*, in the tiny turquoise-painted flat belonging to six large hijras. Ayesha, the chief transvestite, was wearing gold lamé and dancing to the music of a Bollywood song when I arrived. The sickly-sweet smell of marijuana lingered in her bedroom as she intro-duced me to her fiancé, a slim young man in a leather jacket. She wiggled her hips briefly to the music, and then related the grim story of how, when she turned sixteen, her guru cut off her penis. (She had drunk four bottles of hooch to numb the pain; and four days later, when they pulled back the bandage, she was sick from the stench.) As I left, she prodded her breasts: 'Give me some money for the operation.'

So by the afternoon, I am eager to return to the house where I am staying on the edge of the sea. Then, seeing a human emerging, almost naked, from a sewer, I think for a moment that I am hallu-cinating from dehydration.

Sitting nearby in the shade of a tree is another man, fully clothed, who has been watching me watching. 'Is he cleaning the sewer?' I ask, pointing down at the water. 'There's a blockage,' the man says. 'It must be a difficult job,' I say. The man wipes the sweat off his forehead with the sleeve of his shirt: 'They've always done it.' 'Who?' I ask, wondering why he assumes that I know who 'they' are. 'The Bhangis,' comes his straightforward answer. 'I am the foreman. Only non-Muslims do this sewer work. It is forbidden for us.'

At the time, I refuse to believe him. But later, when I interview the government officials who control Karachi's hydrology – bringing fresh water in from the Indus lakes and piping sewage out into the mangroves – it is apparent that this is true. By 'Bhangi', the foreman means low-caste Hindus, or low-caste Christian converts – both in India and Pakistan still regarded as 'untouch-able' according to the ancient and immutable Hindu caste system. 'Not one Muslim is doing this job,' the officials say. 'It is an age-old situation, right from the very beginning of Pakistan. This is dirty water. Any spots of sewerage on clothes is difficult when performing prayers.'

After the sewer man re-emerges from the water, I take down his number. Then I hurry back home to wash: the smell of the sewer still lingers in my nostrils, and tonight I am going for *taravih* prayers at the mosque. The Wahhabi-influenced habit of listening to recitations of the Qur'an during Ramzan is, for women, a recent import to Karachi – yet another layer of piety to add to those that already cloak most lives here.

I am not a Muslim, but most Pakistanis take me to be a Christian – and thus one of the *ahl-al-kitab*, people of the book. Early Islam was influenced by the holy scriptures – and prophets – of Judaism and Christianity, and the ahl-al-kitab have advantages in Muslim polities. As believers in one God they might go to Paradise; if they are women they can marry Muslims; they can certainly, according to my Karachi landlady, go to each other's worship-places. Tonight she is taking me with her to the mosque.

At home we eat *iftari* – the food with which the fast is broken. Then I tie my white cotton *dupatta* tightly round my head so that none of my hair is showing and we walk along the seafront to the local mosque. My landlady is deeply and conscientiously religious: in many ways she is the textbook Pakistani. Like most well-to-do Muslims, her family claims blood-ties to that of the Prophet. She has Iranian and royal Afghan ancestry; she grew up in Lucknow (India) and Hyderabad (Pakistan), where her father became a popular Sindhi holy man. She is a polyglot, speaking Sindhi, Pashto, Farsi and Urdu. She prays five times a day; but democracy is futile, Africans are backward, and India is dirty. Army rule is best: only the soldiers can hold the country together. Is she a product of patriotic ideology? Or was patriotic ideology formed by people of her ilk?

The mosque is gaudily strung with fairy lights; hundreds of pairs of shoes line the road outside. Women do not usually go to mosques to pray so the men, as usual, have the spacious main chamber. We are ushered into the courtyard near the toilets. Squeezing on to a prayer mat between a large lady in black silk and a slim teenager in pink floral cotton, out of the corner of my eye I see Arifa, the maid from the seaside house where I am staying. We smile, turn our heads to Mecca (beyond a blank white wall), and in our neat serried rows, start praying. *Allah-u-Akbar*, I chant in unison with the hundreds of voices reverberating around me. As we fall to our knees, press our foreheads to the ground, rise and fall again, I smell sweet female sweat, the fresh aroma of henna. God is great; the feeling of being part of this mass is exhilarating.

There is something soothing, even empowering, in following the crowd, in conforming so closely to a national ideal where every turn of the head, every movement of the body during prayers is prescribed. In the West, to reject religion is a personal matter – society won't even notice. Here, to reject religion is to risk your own life – to trivialize the sacrifices one's parents and grandparents made in emigrating from India – to be seduced instead by the soulless solipsistic materialism of the West. For most Pakistanis, the script of combined religious and national identity has already been written. It was scripted in 1947, when Pakistan was born in the name of religion, and baptized in the blood of those who died trying to get here.

'Great were the sacrifices involved in creating this country,' my landlady whispers to me as we sit down after prayers. And thus whatever peccadilloes Pakistanis commit – however much whisky they drink or usury they indulge in – they exhibit a profound and sincere belief. Exuberant shows of piety are expected. Nearly everyone – generals and aristocrats, fishermen and factory workers – wears religiously acceptable clothes, makes virtuous donations, and brackets every utterance with a holy expression. ('The most zealous upholders of traditional faith,' a scornful Pakistani journalist tells me, 'are the housewives.') As we stand for the recitation of the Qur'an, I catch Arifa's eye. The recitation is in Arabic: neither she nor I can understand a word that is spoken.

It was Ramzan, 610 CE, when Muhammad first became aware that he had been chosen by God as his messenger. As he was meditating in a cave near Mecca, he heard a heavenly presence: 'Recite!' it told him, and Muhammad listened, remembered, and when he reached home dictated what he had heard to his wife and friends. The parts of the Qur'an that date from this era are ecstatic with phrases of mystical elation. But the dictation from God continued in a more prosaic vein over the next twenty-three years, and thus the holy

4

book became by default a historical record, encompassing the growth of Muhammad's persecuted sect, its move to Medina, and its eventual triumph over the doubters of Mecca.

The Qur'an was compiled by the Third Caliph after Muhammad died – not chronologically, but in rough themes, and according to the diminishing length of its 114 *suras* (chapters). (Coincidentally, the arrangement of the Rig Veda, India's oldest Sanskrit text, is analogous to this.) Every word was uttered by Muhammad himself, and no other religion has anything quite like it. Four men wrote up Jesus' mission for him; Buddhism's holy texts were written after its founder's death; Hinduism's canon was composed communally over thousands of years. Muhammad, however, provided his followers with a complete expression of his religious and social intent in one unrivalled volume. The first prose book in Arabic, springing anachronistically from an oral culture, it is poetry mixed with history, combined with legal and ritualistic considerations – guidance from on high on how to behave well. Its tongue-twisting, assonance-activated, verbally dexterous verses are designed to be read aloud.

In the mosque we listen to the recitation of Sura 'Abraham', with its commanding description of Paradise as a garden 'beneath which rivers flow'. This is a persistent theme in the Qur'an. After a lifetime of piety and fasting in the searing heat, 'those who believe and do good' shall enter a riverine paradise, lush and green with heavily laden fruit trees. Rivers resurface throughout the sacred book. In the holy lands of Islam, clean water is a precious resource; to pollute it is an abomination. Rivers are the common gift of God, and should not be sequestered by the few – a pertinent message for a city insatiably sucking water out of the Indus. By contrast, those who go to hell will be forced to drink 'festering water'. Muslims often say that the ablutions required before the five daily prayers institute public and private cleanliness. The very name of the Islamic Republic of Pakistan – which translates as Land of the Pure (*pak-i-stan*) – inscribes this consciousness into the people.

That night, I sit on the strand, watching the families who promenade here after prayers. This part of the seashore is not used by the people who live nearby. The rich swim away from the sewage (but under the eye of a nuclear power station) on private beaches an hour's drive out of the city. For the poor there is Clifton beach, directly in front of my house. Every evening, till late at night, it is their playground. Huge floodlights illuminate the waves, there are ice-cream vendors, angel-faced Afghan boys selling roses, and men offering camel rides. Women come in their burqas or headscarves, with their husbands and children, to stroll on the sand and breathe salt-air sanity into their lungs, away from their cramped apartments for an evening.

Modern Karachi has a reputation as an edgy, brutal city. It has borne the brunt of Pakistan's political paradoxes: martial law; ethnic violence; the sectarian ravings of mullahs. There are riots and shootouts, bomb blasts and kidnappings. Power failures are common; corruption is normal; jumping red lights is prudent. For a city of such extremes, the dove-grey waters of the Arabian Sea often seem like its only solace.

Karachi's social strata radiate outwards from the coast, distinct as a caste system. The aristocrats, industrialists and soldiers dominate the ocean vista. One step back from the salt spray live the tradespeople and petty government employees. Further north still, in ad hoc and illegal low-cost housing colonies, are the working classes. And in the faraway fringes, or in the undesirable interstices, subsist the sewer cleaners.

Distinct, too, are the stories of 1947 that still survive within these strata. Almost every Karachi family has somebody who remembers the beginning of the nation, who was eyewitness to the pain, the trouble or the euphoria of Pakistan's creation. If 1947 was the zero point − a blank state for every citizen − then where has the nation taken them from there? Where did those living by the sea come from, and how did they get there? What happiness or tragedy did Partition visit on those living in the impoverished north of the city? That night, sitting by the sea, I decide to gather Partition memories from these different sections of the city.

An hour before sunrise, Arifa wakes me for *sehri*, the last meal before the fast begins (the opposite, then, of 'breakfast'). By the time we hear the call from the mosque, it is daylight, and the fourteenth day of Ramzan: no more eating, drinking, sucking, chewing, smoking, love-making or tongue-kissing till sundown. Depending on when the new moon is sighted by the clergy (every year, splinter groups

of Muslims, usually those in the North West Frontier Province, celebrate Eid a day earlier or later than the majority of the nation) there
will be fifteen or sixteen more fasts to go.

Later that morning, I meet the sewer man in Clifton again. 'We
sometimes go to the sea where you live, on Sundays,' he says. 'Where
do you live?' I ask; and he explains that his house is in the city's
very newest settlement, right on its furthest perimeter, the straining
apex of north Karachi. 'You work here,' I say, 'so why do you live
so far away?' He tells me that his house – along with those of his
sister, parents and 77,000 other families – was bulldozed last year to
make way for a contentious new road, the Lyari Expressway.

The sewer man introduces me to his sister, who works nearby
cleaning the bathrooms of a rich Hindu family. She is a beautiful,
proud woman, who dislikes the work her brother does. Her husband
cleans the toilets in a north Karachi mosque but she refuses to put
her hands in the gutters. Her Hindu employers think of her as a
Shudra (a Hindu of the lowest caste) and keep separate eating uten-
sils for her – 'but I am Christian,' she tells me in their hearing. Later,
she says, 'The Hindus do just as much *nafrat* [hatred] to us as Muslims.'
(And not just Hindus; even other Christians despise the low-caste
converts. In Karachi's Catholic churches, parallel services are held at
Christmas: one in Urdu in the yard outside for the 'local' Christians,
and one in English in the British-built church for the disdainful,
Westernized Goans.)

'I will take you to meet my parents,' she says that afternoon. 'They
came to Karachi at Partition from Gujranwala in west Punjab.'

We set off after her work is over; but though we leave the sea
when it is not yet dusk, it takes so long to negotiate the length of
the city that it is dark by the time we reach the forlorn outpost
where she lives. By now I have spent a long time in Karachi, exploring
– and in the past few months, my explorations have led me to many
unpredictable quarters. In Clifton – once an imperial 'watering place',
now a high-gloss residential district for high-heeled begums – I have
interviewed politicians by day, and after dark – for Ramzan nights
are ludic – watched children playing cricket in car-lit alleys. In
Defence, an elite housing scheme run by the Pakistan Army, I have
dressed as a man and slipped into an illicit gay party. In Saddar, the

old Hindu-British cantonment bazaar where multicoloured buses wheel and belch, I have wondered at the decaying nineteenth-century mansions hammered out in a rowdy profusion of architectural styles ('Hybridized-Classical, Indo-Gothic, Imperial Vernacular, Indo-Saracenic . . . Anglo-Mughal' is how a Pakistani architect describes it). On Burnes Road, where heroin addicts sit injecting each other in the thigh, I have eaten halwa and haleem cooked by refugees who came here in 1947, bringing their north Indian languages, culture and recipes with them. I have attended a wedding in Lyari, a settlement which dates to the time when Karachi was a Hindu port, the warm, winding streets of which are inhabited by fishermen, along with the descendants of African slaves and the country's dogged Communists. I have dined in the vast concrete colonies of north Karachi, home to UMTs: 'Urdu-Medium Types', as the middle classes have been nicknamed by the snobbish English-speaking kids of Clifton. In the north-west finger of the metropolis, where the gradient of the Delta rises into the steep Baluchi hills, and Pashtuns have settled in this faint imitation of their homeland, I have met shy village mullahs and optimistic teachers. I have driven west, through Karachi's ever-expanding periphery, to the oily workshops where gaudy 'jingle-jangle' trucks come after traversing the country, and further still, to private beaches where the rich and famous throw their parties. I have spent the night in a fishing village on Karachi's easternmost tip. Yet this journey to where the Christian cleaners live, takes me further than ever before through the city's swollen orbit.

Two hours after we leave the sea, when everywhere I have ever been is far behind us, it begins to get dark. We must have travelled twenty-five kilometres from Clifton beach by now – yet still we travel onwards. The bus moves faster, across a shrunken river, past concrete tower blocks where faded washing hangs plaintively from balconies. Soon the settlements thin and peter out. Ahead is a wide dark plain. We have come to the point where the electricity stops. 'Where are we?' I say, for it is as if we have fallen off the edge of the world. As the bus judders on through the dark, fear and confusion grip me intermittently. Eventually I see lights in the distance. Twenty minutes later, the bus comes to a standstill at the mouth of a dirt street lined by large, two-storey houses. The electricity suddenly fades. 'We've arrived,' says the sewer man's sister, and we climb down into the dark.

The sewer man and his sister were given Muslim names by their parents, but she has named her children Arthur, Sylvester and Florence. The children are waiting for her at their grandparents' house, sitting together in the courtyard, illuminated by a paraffin lamp. We sit down opposite them on a string cot and the old couple introduce themselves. As her husband puffs on his hookah, Saleemat Massi tells their story.

'We were married in 1947,' she says. 'At the time, my husband was doing *khetibhari* [farm work] in Gujranwala.' They had only been married a few months when there arrived in the village first one, then two, then a stream of Muslims from across the border. Finally the day came when the landlord sent a message: there was no more work, they had better get out. 'So,' says Saleemat, 'we came to Karachi.' But the situation here was no better. They had no patrons or credentials, and every job was taken. There was only one difference: city dwellers needed sewer cleaners. 'We worked together in the gutters,' says Saleemat Massi. 'With Pakistan we began this dirty work. The Muslims gave jobs to their own kind. What did Quaid-e-Azam do for us?'

Quaid-e-Azam, Muhammad Ali Jinnah, flew to Karachi (his birthplace, and Pakistan's new capital) on 7 August, a week before British India was partitioned. At the time, Karachi was a tidy, quiet town; and the place where the Christian cleaners live now was a distant patch of scrubland in the desert. That year Ramzan also fell in August, and the long days and short nights of summer made the holy month of fasting particularly difficult. But Jinnah, who paid no heed to religious ritual, did not spare a thought for Islamic abstinence either. His hazy idea for a new country had suddenly come to fruition; the borders were about to be drawn; and all he had to do now was render some order from the bedlam.

Some commentators maintain that Jinnah was taken by surprise when the British conceded his demand for a separate state for Muslims – was he using the idea of a separate Muslim homeland as political leverage, a bargaining tool? Had he banked on British and Congress pride in an undivided India? All agree that he was dismayed by the eventual British settlement – the poisoned chalice of a divided Punjab and Bengal – a 'moth-eaten, truncated' Pakistan, itself separated by a thousand miles of India.

Suave Louis Mountbatten, eager to assure himself a dashing role in history, had accepted the job of Indian Viceroy in February 1947 on one condition: that by June the following year, Britain would be out of India. The post-war Labour government – anxious to disburden Britain of its empire – gave the green light to the Viceroy's hectic schedule. Mountbatten arrived in India in March. In June he made the startling announcement that India was to be divided – not next year as he had agreed in London, but in *ten weeks' time.* ('The date I chose came out of the blue,' Mountbatten recollected many years later. 'Why? Because it was the second anniversary of Japan's surrender.') He then appointed Cyril Radcliffe – an 'impartial' British lawyer, that is, one with no knowledge of India whatsoever – to oversee the dissection of the country. In July, the two men drew lines on the subcontinent's maps, Mountbatten ensuring that India got Calcutta, several Muslim majority provinces in the Punjab, and access to Kashmir. In August, loath to spoil a good party, Mountbatten delayed the announcement of the noxious new borders until two days after Independence was declared. Only once he had made his speeches, had his photo taken and received his thanks, could the killing begin.

There had been problems throughout 1946 – religious rioting in Calcutta, a heightening of Hindu-Muslim tension – and Jinnah himself had warned that the partition of Bengal and the Punjab would have 'terrible consequences': 'confusion . . . bloodshed'. If the historian Ayesha Jalal is right – that Jinnah never wanted an impermeable division of India, that it was Congress which insisted on it – then 1947 can only be viewed as a tragic blunder. Perhaps, had Jinnah been able to predict that hundreds of thousands of people would lose their lives, he might have called the whole thing off. He certainly never imagined that such a massive transfer of population would be necessary; he had not conceived that the borders would be drawn so indelibly, or so bloodily. He had not packed away a single silk sock from his mansion in Bombay or his colonial bungalow in Delhi (fondly imagining weekend retreats to India with his equally naive sister Fatima). Until the very last moment he seems to have had in mind a vague cohabitation of dominion states; he even seems to have convinced himself that the nation he had won for Muslims would be a realm where religion didn't matter. 'You are free,' he said three days before Independence in a speech that has become the mantra of Pakistan's embattled secularists (and conversely is excluded from editions of Jinnah's speeches by the pious), 'you are free to go to your temples, you are free to go to your mosques . . . You may belong to any religion or caste or creed – that has nothing to do with the fundamental principle that we are all citizens and equal citizens of one State.'

Jinnah himself had many non-Muslim friends, and very little religious sensibility. His family were Ismailis and his father, Jinnahbhai Poonja, was a Gujarati hide dealer (whose own parents came from a village not far from that of Mahatma Gandhi's). Moving to Karachi in the wake of the colonial economic boom, Jinnahbhai quickly rose from being a small-time merchant to a prosperous banker (an aspect of Jinnah's antecedents never mentioned in state-sanctioned biographies). So Jinnah grew up in Kharadar, at the seaside gate of the long-vanished Hindu fort, under a British dispensation, in a town run by Hindu and Parsi merchants. His family was a rare exception to the rule: that in Sindh, Muslims were either rural landlords or penniless peasants.

Jinnah had begun political life in Bombay, where he already worked as a successful lawyer. At first, he was an ardent nationalist and member of the Indian National Congress. He joined the Muslim League in 1913, seven years after it was founded, and soon became known as the 'ambassador of Hindu-Muslim unity'. But by 1930, he had grown disillusioned with Indian politics, and in particular with Gandhi. By collaborating with the post-war Khilafat movement, a pan-Islamic campaign to reinstate the Caliph, and winning the support of the Muslim clergy, Gandhi, Jinnah felt, was inciting and encouraging religious frenzy. Despite his political success and national renown, Jinnah renounced politics entirely and retired to London.

He was persuaded to return in 1934, by which time several different permutations of the Muslim state he would eventually create had already been mooted. But he still refused to whip up religious passions, continued to drink whisky, eat ham sandwiches and dress like a Brit. In 1937, he gave a speech in which he described Indian Muslims as 'a nation' apart from Hindus; nevertheless, of the twenty distinguishing categories that he mentioned – culture, language, architecture – not one was explicitly religious. When a holy man wrote to him suggesting he go to Mecca, Jinnah replied that he was far too busy. In 1947, according to Mountbatten, Jinnah even scheduled a lunch party to celebrate Independence though Ramzan wasn't yet over: such a faux pas would have been an outrage to the pious and his advisers had to cancel. If Jinnah's faith existed, it was of the lapsed variety. The depth of popular religious passions was his fatal blindspot.

In 1947, to Jinnah's distress, religious violence, not triumphant celebration, inaugurated Independence. As he sat in the Governor General's house in Karachi, each new day brought fresh tales of bloodshed from the Punjab. Ten million men and women walked out of their ancestral village homes, forced east or west by the fact of their religion. Between 200,000 and one million people died in the ensuing religious frenzy – an official body count was never made, and thus the figures vary widely, with the British at the time estimating up to 500,000; Winston Churchill accusing Mountbatten of killing 'two million Indians'; and later commentators in India and Pakistan putting the tally as high as two or even three million dead.

Nobody since has been able to explain the gargantuan scale of the tragedy; why Sikhs and Hindus slaughtered Muslims, why Muslims butchered Hindus and Sikhs, why villagers who had lived peacefully as neighbours turned on each other, why women were raped and abducted, why children were separated from their parents. In 1947, with the help of sectarian volunteer armies – Muslim, Sikh and Hindu storm-troopers secretly trained and drafted in for the purpose – massacre spread like contagion. Every refugee who survived had a terrible tale to tell, and a deadly grudge to bear.

The stories told by those who lived through 1947 are generally difficult to relate and painful to hear but they have become integral to Pakistan's image of itself. And so, one evening after iftar, I take a taxi north from the sea, to meet a woman who survived the carnage of the Punjab Partition. Zohra Begum is an old woman now, who sits surrounded by her daughters and grandchildren in a large, cool house on a quiet street where boys are playing cricket. She came to Karachi in 1947 as someone who had lost almost everything – family, possessions, peace of mind. Her memories of that time are vivid and agonizing, and as I listen to her speak, and then hear her protest, 'Why are you asking all these questions?', I remember the importance of forgetting, if grief is not to be overwhelming. 'But it is also important for us to hear these things,' her daughter tells me later.

In 1947, Zohra was just sixteen years old. One evening, she came in from the fields to find her girl cousins lying dead on the floor, their tongues and breasts lying beside them. She allowed her Hindu servant to take her by the hand, and left the village for ever. At the time, Zohra was, by her own admission, 'an uneducated village girl'. Married at fourteen, widowed at fifteen – now with a six-month-old baby – she had no idea what was happening when Partition was declared. In fact very few Muslims in Jalandhar expected that this district of the Punjab would go to India: Radcliffe's Boundary Award took them by surprise. Prakash, the family's Hindu servant, saved Zohra's life by smearing *sindoor* in her hair as if she were a Hindu bride, binding the child to her chest, and professing to be her husband.

Barefoot, covered in dust, with no headscarf, Zohra was delirious by the time they arrived at Atari station on the border. 'The world had gone mad,' she says. 'Muslims were fighting each other to get on the train; mothers were throwing their babies on to the tracks and escaping.' Prakash found a space for them both next to the scalding engine. The twenty-minute journey took two days; Hindus kept stopping the train and killing Muslims; there was no food, no water. 'It was like Karbala,' she says.

Like a miracle, Zohra's brother was waiting for her at the station in Lahore. He had been coming there every day since 15 August, calling his sister's name in the hope that she might have made it through the mayhem. He took her to Karachi, where they lived in tents on the edge of the city. Prakash converted to Islam.

Later, Zohra's brother made enquiries about the fate of the extended family. The men had been killed; the women had either been killed or abducted. He even made the difficult trip to India to try and bring the abducted women 'home' – but they were Sikhs now, married with children. It was too late for reunions: Pakistan was a foreign country.

For women like Zohra, who had witnessed hell, Jinnah became a hate figure. He had forced Pakistan upon them; he had flown to this '*jungli*' (uncouth, dirty) new country in the comfort of an aeroplane; he had allowed all the best places to go to India. And he had wrenched women like Zohra apart from the Hindu-Muslim culture she loved – on this point she is insistent – and into the arms of this miserable, overcrowded city.

Descending on Karachi from north India in 1947, Jinnah's central government made an unpleasant discovery – Pakistan had drawn the short straw. India had inherited the imperial capital, grand buildings and a robust political infrastructure. Karachi was a provincial seaside town in Sindh, British India's smallest state. It had so little Muslim history that when, five days after Independence, the new nation celebrated its first *Eid-ul-fitr* (marking the end of Ramzan) the government realized to its embarrassment that while the city boasted a Parsi fire temple, Jewish synagogue, churches of most Christian denominations and some of the oldest temples in the subcontinent, there weren't enough decent mosques to accommodate the immigrant aristocracy (the mosques in the filthy labourers' slum of Lyari were out of the question). In August 1947, the ruling class squeezed into the Eidgah (where Muslims assemble for Eid prayers). By 1948 the Eidgah had become a refugee camp. That year, Eid prayers were held in the park.

Pakistan really was 'starting at zero' (as Jinnah's *Times* obituary later put it). According to the terms of the Partition divorce settlement, the spoils of British India – money and arms, paper clips and pencils – were to be divided three to one, with Pakistan receiving the smaller share. But after Delhi was convulsed by murder and looting, the clerks who should have stayed behind to divide the spoils fled for their lives. For years, Pakistan battled India (with mixed success) to be granted the food, furniture and files that were its due. In 1947, with next to nothing from which to build a nation, the government cashed in its foreign reserves and was bailed out in gold bullion by the Nizam of Hyderabad in south India. The central government ministries were housed in barracks and hastily constructed hutments; memorandums were written along the edges of newspapers; thorns were used for paper clips; ministers voted for a reduction in their salaries. The Muslim League newspaper, *Dawn*, spoke of 'an inevitable period of austerity'. But morale was high, and the patriotism needed to build a country from scratch invigorating.

In 1947, Hameeda Akhtar Husain Raipuri was a young mother whose story, I find when I meet her, illustrates well the noble ambitions of the Pakistan movement. Today she lives ten kilometres north of the sea, in a large post-Partition housing colony – impenetrably large, its tree-lined streets numbered according to an idiosyncratic system that even my taxi driver cannot fathom. He stops, reverses, and swears under his breath several times before we reach our destination. At last a servant comes to the gate, and leads me through the house to a room at the back overlooking the garden, where Hameeda Begum is sitting on her bed, writing; she is composing her memoirs in Urdu. A servant is despatched to bring me tea and biscuits. I sit on a long, low wooden divan, and listen as she reminisces.

She came to Karachi at Partition with her family from Aligarh – that bastion of Muslim scholarship in northern India. Her father wrote popular Urdu detective novels; her husband had a PhD in Sanskrit drama; her family is the quintessence of India's Urdu-speaking elite 'with its famous syncretic culture, neither wholly Muslim nor Hindu . . . floating upon society like an oilslick upon water', as the historians Ayesha Jalal and Anil Seal describe it in an essay entitled 'Alternative to Partition'. Why did she leave her pluralistic life in India? Was she spurred on by Muslim League rhetoric, or disturbed by Hindu sectarianism? 'Neither,' she says. 'The time came when our Hindu neighbours felt they could no longer protect us, and so we were left with no option.'

As the wife of a civil servant in the Education Ministry, Hameeda's introduction to Karachi was comparatively orderly. The train that brought her from Delhi was one of the first to be attacked; but it was full of government employees, and thus was well defended by the army. 'A gentleman was waiting at the station in Karachi with the keys to our flat in Napier Barracks,' she says; 'another was holding out a ration card.' So the family settled into their new country, full of hope.

Then the refugees began arriving – physical proof of the stories of murder, rape and looting which had filtered through from the Punjab, of the 'madness that the two countries did to each other'. Leaving her young children at home with the servants, Hameeda Begum enrolled in the women's wing of the Pakistan National Guard. She was given a course in nursing by the army and put to work in the emergency first aid camps. She ministered to the semi-dead – the refugees who arrived without clothes, without food, without limbs; some came on stretchers, others limped in on foot. With up to a thousand new patients a day, 'there was no time to think.' For a young mother in a new town it was hard work – but at least she was doing something.

Hameeda's husband, meanwhile, was growing increasingly disillusioned by the corruption involved in rehousing the refugees. Within a few months of Independence it became clear that Karachi's population had doubled in size. Rich industrialists and bankers – those whom Jinnah had personally invited to help launch the nation – flew in from Bombay. Businessmen, craftspeople and entrepreneurs arrived en masse from India's United Provinces. Some 44,000 Muslim government employees – tea boys and peons, civil servants and politicians; their spouses, parents and children – took the train from all over India and came to Pakistan. Naturally, they hollered for housing, they camped in Karachi's schools, they filled up its lovely green spaces with their clamorous existence.

Rumours began circulating of the dishonesty and sleaze emanating from the Rent Control and Rehabilitation Department. Government servants had been caught taking bribes; rich citizens were buying accommodation chits off desperate refugees; Muslims were living in houses from which Hindus had been forcibly evicted. A marital as well as national crisis was brewing. Hameeda had brought their residency papers with her from India – the family had owned a large house in an upmarket area of Delhi and was due something of equivalent size in Karachi. She presented her papers to the housing authorities, and they gave her the right to a commodious residence on Bunder Road.

But when she returned home and showed her husband the family's rightful compensation, he was furious. The corruption in the housing authority, he felt, was compromising the integrity of Pakistani society. He ripped up the paper and, like many other decent and worthy Pakistanis, sacrificed his family's comfort to the ideal of a high-minded nation.

Sixty years later, almost all of Hameeda's descendants have spurned the chaos of her adopted homeland for the relative safety of Dubai, the United States or England. As I leave that evening, she is sitting serenely with her silver *paan* box on her knee, listening quietly as her son practises the sitar.

For five months following Partition, Pakistan's leaders consoled themselves with the fact that Karachi had not seen any of the rioting that had disfigured Delhi, India's blood-soaked capital. Sindh had been allocated to Pakistan undivided. The Hindus hadn't left. The outlook seemed peaceful. There was one intractable problem. The city was brimful with people. Something had to give.

On 6 January 1948, nearly two hundred Sikhs arrived in Karachi en route to India, by train from Nawabshah, a small town in Sindh. The Nawabshah administration sent a message to Karachi: the Sikhs were to be transported directly to the docks. In the confusion some-body forgot to relay the communication; or maybe the error was deliberate. That morning, the Sikhs – wearing the bright turbans distinctive of their faith, and thus for many Muslim migrants symbols of the terrible Punjab riots – were taken to the *gurdwara*, the Sikh temple in the centre of Karachi. It was the chance the refugees had been waiting for. They surrounded the gurdwara, stoned it, and set it on fire. Throughout the city, massive, apparently spontaneous rioting erupted. Hindus – hitherto secure in their homes and mixed-faith neighbourhoods – now took refuge in their temples; Muslim refugees, on many of whom the same experience had been visited a few months before in India, occupied their abandoned houses. M. S. M. Sharma, Hindu editor of a Karachi paper, claimed that the rampage was organized by disgruntled Pakistan Secretariat clerks. Whoever was responsible, wrote Sri Prakasa, first Indian High Commissioner to Pakistan, from now on 'no Hindu had the courage to continue there.'

Sindh had been championed as a paradigm of inter-faith harmony.

Following the riots, the government estimated that three thousand Hindus a day were taking their belongings down to the docks, and purchasing a passage to India. The Indian Government launched 'Operation Evacuation'. Jinnah, who had witnessed Nehru's sense of disgrace at the carnage in Delhi, admitted that the 'refugees have blackened my face'. He was 'the most shocked individual in Pakistan', Sharma wrote later. But Sharma also knew that Jinnah had to be careful: Partition had visited tragedy on countless Muslims, and many refugees read his conciliatory words to the 'minorities' as betrayal. The government issued statements lamenting the Hindus' departure, but it did little to stop them going.

Pakistan had been viewed by many north Indian Muslim businessmen as a golden opportunity; if Sindh's famously rich and 'venturesome' Hindu mercantile class left for India, they could fill the vacuum. Hindu moneylenders were hated by Sindhi Muslim landlords (a Sindhi version of *The Merchant of Venice*, written in 1890 by Mirza Qalich Beg, cast Shylock as a Hindu). For both the opportunistic business class and the indebted landed gentry there was much to gain from Hindus leaving. The riots of 6 January – intentionally or not – provided the answer.

Dawn, by now Pakistan's foremost English-language newspaper and the government's media mouthpiece, played a major role in fomenting a climate of suspicion and ill-will, causing Hindus to feel like outsiders in their country, which in turn hastened their departure. In January 1948, it complained that Hindus were seen on the decks of their departing boat, shouting '*Jai Hind!*' (Long Live India) and flinging their Jinnah caps into the sea. In February, it bemoaned the government's policy of restoring stolen property to Hindus: 'the only chance they will avail of,' it whined, 'is to fleece the Muslims.' In March it gave a sinister gloss to Jinnah's request that Hindus must 'cooperate as Pakistanis'. In April, it successfully backed a motion to overturn the statute enshrined in Karachi Corporation's pre-Partition Convention, that the mayor should be elected alternately from among the Muslim and non-Muslim communities. In May it endorsed the sacking of the Hindu editor of the *Sind Observer*. In June it maintained that Hindus were emigrating 'only to spite Pakistan'. In July, when Hindus began returning – Sindhi refugees having found themselves unwelcome in many areas of India – it questioned the government's 'wisdom in letting these non-Muslims' back into the country. In August it alleged that Hindus were 'pouring' across the Sindh border to disrupt Pakistan. In September it termed the refugees 'Hindu deserters'.

Many of these tactics mirrored those being employed by provincial Indian newspapers. But *Dawn* – founded by Jinnah and representing the views of national politicians – should have been more circumspect. By the end of 1948, four-fifths of Sindh's Hindu population – up to a million people – had emigrated to India.

Within a month of the riots, the government realized to its alarm that something entirely unexpected was happening: among the fleeing Hindus were the city's sweepers and sewer cleaners. *Dawn* began publishing letters and articles by outraged residents of Karachi, who regretted, cajoled and complained: 'Asia's cleanest city' had become an unhygienic disgrace. The streets – washed every day during the British administration – were littered with stinking rubbish; the *nalas* (streams), which once ran with such clear water that young boys could swim or fish in them, were becoming rancid sewers. There were enough jobs for two thousand cleaners, and not enough people to do them.

Throughout February 1948, the Government of Pakistan printed a daily three-page review in *Dawn* of the policies and achievements of each of its ministries since Independence. It was the turn of the Interior Ministry on 23 February:

> Lately, in view of the apprehended blow to the social and economic structure of the province as a result of the wholesale migration of depressed classes, the Government of Sind have [*sic*] been compelled to take legal powers to slow down the migration of such persons who in their opinion constitute the essential services of the province.

'Depressed classes' meant low-caste Hindus and Christian converts. 'Essential services' meant sweeping and sewer cleaning. Pakistan was not living up to the purity of its name, so the government was answering the chorus of demands for a cleaner capital city with a form of social apartheid.

In 1948, Hindus reacted with horror. Sri Prakasa, the Indian High

Commissioner, scheduled a meeting with the Prime Minister of Pakistan to complain: 'surely God did not create the Hindus . . . to clean the roads and latrines of Karachi!' But 'who,' the Prime Minister purportedly replied, 'would clean the streets and latrines of Karachi in case they did not come back?' One of Gandhi's major campaigns had been for every class and caste to clean their own toilets. But in Pakistan, the attitude of the ruling class appeared to be that huge swathes of the population were second-class citizens.

The fast has not yet broken when I arrive at a government-built accommodation block in Saddar, home to many of the Hindu sweepers who opted to stay in Pakistan. By chance, by mistake, I arrive in the middle of a funeral. The body of a ninety-year-old sweeper, cloth wrapped, marigold strewn, is lying under a fan in a room on the ground floor, where a priest is singing prayers. Outside, sitting under a cloth canopy in the courtyard, are his friends and relatives – all of whom worked, or still work, for the government as sweepers, sewer cleaners or sanitary inspectors.

As the sweeper's sari-clad daughters stand around his body weeping, an argument breaks out in the courtyard between the older sweepers and the younger generation, over the extent of the discrimination still practised today in Pakistan. An old man wearily expounds his view that ancient Brahmin enmity is to blame for their woes. A younger man, dressed in a crisp shirt and trousers, responds angrily that there is 'no impediment, our community is going ahead'. Another man interrupts, saying that many of their children, at least, have acquired slightly better employment, as chambermaids in five-star hotels or toilet cleaners in air-conditioned shopping malls. At last the old pandit speaks. An emaciated man with a loud clear voice, he recalls how Jinnah ordered their leader, Magsi Bhagwan, to go to India and bring the sweepers back. 'Jinnah said to Magsi Bhagwan, "Your people must not go to India. Those that have gone must come back to Pakistan. We will give you whatever you need, housing, employment, education for your children."'

The pandit turns to me. 'There is nothing wrong with this job,' he says. 'I have seen Scheduled Castes in your Europe.' (He is refer-ring to the fact that there are cleaners in the West; that we too have an underclass to do our dirty work.) 'Even Muslims do this cleaning when they go abroad. But they wouldn't do it in Pakistan, all the same. Especially not the Mohajirs.'

What the Mohajirs would and would not do was the nub of the problem. 'Mohajir' is an Arabic word meaning migrant. It has a religious connotation, denoting the faithful who followed Muhammad to Medina from Mecca in 622 to escape religious persecution. Many of the north Indian Muslims who came here in 1947 as refugees gave themselves this name in order to evoke the suffering they had undergone for the sake of Pakistan. They felt that they were entitled to some compensation – a house vacated by a Hindu, a job with the central government, a perk of some description.

For many refugees, there was safety – as well as cultural continuity – in numbers. Barely 6 per cent of Karachi's population spoke Urdu – the Mohajir tongue – before Partition. But in 1947, so many refugees came to the city, it was the Sindhis, Baluch and others who were obliged to learn the immigrants' language, not vice versa. Whole streets of old Delhi – teachers, merchants, schoolchildren – decamped to Karachi. For months leading up to Partition, the newspapers in India had been full of small ads offering the exchange of like-for-like businesses, shops or residences in the neighbouring countries. For many refugees, especially the young ones, the transition from one country to the other was relatively painless. For Mohajir businessmen, it was often far easier to get lucrative contracts here than it had been in India. In Pakistan, some migrants got very rich, very quick.

But Pakistan did not visit such fortune on everyone. By 1948, Sindhis were rapidly coming to the conclusion that they had gained least from the country's creation, and they began to resent the wholesale takeover of their homeland. *Dawn* sensed this resentment and scolded the indigenous inhabitants: 'If Pakistan had not been established, where would Sindh and the Sindhis have been?' Sindhis and Mohajirs were begged to desist from 'jealousy and bickerings' and to 'live as brothers'. As for the refugees from the Punjab, everyone should understand that they had 'suffered greatly' and should not be judged collectively on the abysmal behaviour of some 'bad characters'.

But as it was with the people, so with the government. For

immigrant politicians from India, there was one stumbling block to the smooth consolidation of power: the incumbent Sindhi adminis-tration, run by Muhammad Ayub Khuhro. A rural Sindhi landlord, Khuhro was also a consummate politician. He had wide experience of the Muslim League (he had been in local politics from the age of twenty-one); he had very close links with his local constituency, and Sindh was his power base. Unfortunately, he fell out with Jinnah over the issue of whether or not Karachi should be separated from Sindh – a suggestion to which the entire Sindhi administration was opposed. On 26 April 1948, Khuhro was dismissed for 'gross corrup-tion and maladministration'. The charges levelled against him were so numerous that the case began to look ridiculous and the govern-ment dictatorial.

But the Pakistan Government, it seemed, could not stomach dissent. On 15 June, six weeks after Khuhro's arrest, the (unelected) central government placed G. M. Syed – another forthright Sindhi politician – under house arrest. Six days later, an official at the American embassy wrote in a confidential letter to Washington that the Pakistanis 'continue to lean on the authoritarian props on which the British Raj rested . . . present authoritarian methods of govern-ment will become standard operating procedures.' It was a disturbingly accurate prophecy of the trouble to come.

Hamida, Muhammad Ayub Khuhro's formidable daughter, lives in Khuhro Apartments, a tall, imposing block surrounded by palm trees in Clifton – the smartest part of Karachi. Hamida Khuhro is an establishment figure in Pakistan, and she speaks to me, in her pleasant, picture-filled drawing room, from the vantage point of the nation's elite. The Khuhros did all right from Pakistan in the end. Muhammad Ayub Khuhro was too powerful (or too popular) to be kept out of power for long; his 'dutiful' daughter became a professor of history, wrote a book clearing his name, and followed him into politics. But Hamida has no qualms about speaking plainly of the 'mess' that Pakistan has become. Although, unlike other Sindhi aristocrats, she does not feel nostalgia for the Raj, she nevertheless blames the Pakistan Government for encouraging a 'dangerous decline in admin-istrative standards'. Above all, she indicts Jinnah as the architect of Pakistan's 'authoritarian culture'.

For Hamida, as for many of Karachi's inhabitants in 1947, Pakistan was a nasty shock ('a Himalayan blunder', as one disillusioned Mohajir tells me glumly). Her father himself 'would never admit that it was wrong' but Hamida, as a child, bewailed Pakistan's creation. She was eleven years old in 1947. The 'sleepy' seaside town, with its empty beaches, sturdy stone architecture and child-friendly tramline, had been her nursery – and she, scion of the local nobility, was the centre of its world. Then Partition happened. Overnight, 'comfortable, secure' Karachi was whisked away, and in its place arose a city of never-ending crises, of desperate, wailing humanity, of ambitious Delhi politicians and their glamorous, socialite begums. Khuhro remembers her Hindu school-friends disappearing with no explanation to India, and the Mohajirs who took their place bragging about the 'exotic and exalted' Indian cities they had come from. Far worse than these childish squabbles was the grim discrepancy that emerged between the Muslim League's grandiloquent vision of an Islamic homeland and the tawdry reality of Pakistan, with its 'squalor and insoluble problems'. The nation that was to have swept them off their feet with its devout Islamic vision and its streets paved with gold, proved dysfunctional from the start.

As a brand-new country, Pakistan was searching for meaning. Its government-appointed scribes immediately began rewriting Indo-Muslim history in a manner befitting the new homeland; but heroes were needed and everybody looked to the founder of the nation. Even before his death, Jinnah was promoted as the national ideal: selfless, self-regulated – and Islamic. Today, children all across the country learn their 'Alif, Bay, Pay' beneath a poster called 'National Heroes' which shows Jinnah leading an army of peasants towards the promised land. The real Jinnah has been conveniently forgotten. Ardeshir Cowasjee, the outspoken Parsi columnist of *Dawn*, shows me a photograph of Jinnah snapped in a rare, informal moment: impeccably clad as usual in a Savile Row suit, crouching on the lawn with his dogs (dogs are deemed unclean in Islam), a cigarette clamped in his smiling mouth. Cowasjee claims that this photograph also hangs in the President-General Musharraf's office. How ironic, then, that most Pakistani citizens are only acquainted with the officially sanctioned Jinnah: straight back, poker face, top to toe in what is deemed to be Islamic dress.

Jinnah may not have manufactured the image bequeathed to the nation but he certainly consented to his own beatification. In 1938, he agreed with his colleagues that henceforth he should be known in the imperial manner as Quaid-e-Azam (Great Leader). Opening the State Bank of Pakistan in 1948, he travelled to the ceremony – so the state-authorized biographer wrote eulogistically – in 'one of the old Viceregal coaches . . . the escort wore the startling red uniforms of the bodyguard that had accompanied the Viceroys, in the grand old days before Partition.' He encouraged the grouping of power around him, doing nothing to moderate his acolytes' treatment of him as a quasi-king. It was almost as if Jinnah had forgotten that the fight for independence was not just about freedom from foreign rule, it was also about freedom from totalitarianism. Then again, it was precisely from a fear of democracy – the voting power of majority Hindus, and the dread that Muslims, as a minority in independent India, would be disenfranchised – that Pakistan had come into being.

In those months after Independence was declared, Jinnah was faced with the conundrum of his own making – a safe haven for Muslims, yet one which he must save from being Islamicized by the mullahs. It required a fine legalistic mind to guide the new country to political stability. It also required time. By now Jinnah was dangerously, secretly ill with tuberculosis and lung cancer. Ensconced in the grandeur of the Governor's House, isolated from his people by his hauteur and perilous state of health, well aware of the unscrupulous and opportunistic nature of the politicians who surrounded him, he must have felt that he had little choice but to put in place, as soon as possible, measures to safeguard the continued existence of his nation.

As a lawyer, he knew the importance of a written constitution. His sister, Fatima, later described how it became his highest priority. 'He worked,' she wrote, 'in a frenzy to consolidate Pakistan.' But in June 1948, less than a year after the state's creation, Jinnah retreated to the hills. He was dying. Three months later, on 11 September, he was flown back to Karachi for emergency treatment. The ambulance sent to meet him from the airport broke down on the way home. For an hour, he lay on the roadside next to a refugee camp, on the outskirts of the city that he considered synonymous with his person. He died that night – if not a broken man, then a profoundly disillusioned one. He had wanted an undivided Punjab and Bengal; he had hoped to win Kashmir and Junagadh; he had fought for the moral high ground. His people, by 1948, were homeless, disorientated and angry. The central government was quarrelling with the Sindhis; the Mohajirs with the locals; the country as a whole with its neighbour.

Everybody who remembers Partition remembers the hysteria and weeping when Jinnah died. The country went into mourning for forty days. Forty issues of *Dawn* were printed with a thick black border. The official cause of death was 'heart failure' (tuberculosis was considered a shameful slum disease).

Jinnah died; and his country – much to the world's surprise – lived on. India gleefully anticipated Pakistan's swift and dramatic demise. But there was too much to gain from keeping this querulous infant alive. As *Dawn* wrote regally, 'The Quaid-i-Azam is dead. Long live Pakistan!' And the Prime Minister, giving voice to another fragile paradox, declared: 'I believe that my nation is a living one and will sacrifice its life for defending and maintaining Pakistan.'

After Jinnah's death Karachi continued to grow like an unruly child. By the end of the twentieth century, it was the fastest-growing city in the world. As workers poured into it from all over the country, housing colonies and industries mushroomed. Civil amenities planned by the British filled to bursting point – then burst completely. Sewage and effluent seeped into the Delta, poisoning the water and killing the mangroves. On Karachi's sandy beaches and crowded streets, new and old ethnicities, languages and cultures confronted each other.

Still Karachi grows. Still more water is drawn from the Indus. And still the sewer people immerse themselves in the flux of the city's fetid streams, segregated and exploited, indispensable and despised.

2

Conquering the Classic River

1831

'The Indus is a foul and perplexing river.'
Lieutenant John Wood, 9 February 1836

AT THE END of Ramzan, the morning after Eid has been celebrated with 'religious fervour throughout the country' (as *Dawn* writes year after year), while the rest of Karachi is sleeping off yesterday's overeating, I go down to the harbour. I have a date with a fisherman. His name is Baboo.

A wizened man in a blue knitted bonnet, Baboo assumes an air of profound gloom when I first ask him to ferry me from Karachi (the old Indus Delta, where Pakistan began), along the mangrove coast, and up the river to Thatta (the major port in the region until British times). 'But there is no water,' he says in an Urdu thick with the lilt and cadence, music and sorrow, of Sindhi, his mother tongue. 'No water?' 'The Punjabis take all the water. Between Hyderabad and the Delta the river is dry. The only water is *namkeen* [salty; sea water].' He scratches his head and looks up at the sky. 'If you want to go to Thatta you should go by bus.' He unwraps a packet of *gutka* – a perniciously cheap chewing tobacco – and folds it into his mouth. He swallows. He spits. 'Or taxi.' He seems thoughtful. 'What about a plane?' He smiles hugely. 'That would be *zabardast* [awesome].'

'But I want to go through the Delta by boat,' I say, and turn to go. Baboo calls after me: 'I will take you as far as we can go.' 'How far is that?' 'Along the coast to the mouth for 150 kilometres. The sea comes up the river for a hundred more. After that the water is so low my boat won't make it.' His despondent expression returns: 'It will take at least two days to get that far by boat. Or three . . .'

Only two days. The journey from the Delta to Karachi took the East India Company two hundred years.

We sail out of Karachi, amid a throng of painted wooden fishing boats, on a bright November morning. Baboo's crew of five strip off as soon as we clear the harbour and lounge on the deck in their thin cotton trousers, mending nets, singing in Sindhi, or laughing among themselves (most likely at my expense). But Baboo remains fully clothed as the sun beats down on the boat. He sniffs morosely, peers into the distance, and every now and then furnishes a dismal prognosis of our progress.

I quickly discover why his boat was the cheapest on hire in Keamari: it is as decrepit as its owner is forlorn. Over the next two days, as the propeller breaks, the fan belt snaps and the engine floods, Baboo's crew mend almost everything with a few blobs of spit and a small ball of string.

The crew – three teenage boys and two hardened uncles – are all related, all from one village in the Delta. None of them ever went to school. Ali Nawaz is seventeen and can't even spell his name. As we sit conversing on a pile of nylon fishing nets (I have become inured to the whiff of fish), Ali Nawaz watches curiously when I write down what he says in my notebook. He laughs when in the middle of the day – the sun is high in the sky, the water alluring, and the fishermen have been in and out of the river all morning – I jump off the boat (fully clothed of course) into the cool brown water. I watch him too, when he swims out with the nets to catch our supper. We watch each other and wonder.

Ali Nawaz's family comes from the river – from the Indus-fed Kinjhar lake that now supplies Karachi's fresh water. As the lake dried up, so did the family's trade, and they were forced out to sea in search of fish. The river was kind; life at sea is tough. Fishermen like Baboo sometimes spend ten days at a stretch out of sight of land. The unlucky ones stray into Indian waters – to be clapped in jail for years by over-zealous coastguards. Then there is the inclement weather. Ali Nawaz's elder brother was drowned during the 1999 cyclone – none of these small wooden boats have life jackets, radios or flares – and they never found his body. So it is with the stoicism of lack of choice that Baboo and his men float for days on the surface of the Arabian Sea, hauling up the nets every two hours and packing the catch into ice in the hold.

When their ancestors fished the Indus, Ali Nawaz's uncle tells me, they worshipped Uderolal – the Indus river saint – but after moving out to sea they felt obliged to switch spiritual allegiance. These days they call themselves the sons of Moro (the mythical Sindhi fisherman who was swallowed by a whale). Once a year they make a pilgrimage to the shrine of Pir Datar, the most popular saint in the Delta, whose *urs* (death-anniversary celebration), gratifyingly, is on the same day as the Prophet's birthday.

Neither Baboo nor his crew are in a hurry. The hard work will begin once they have dropped me on the banks of the Indus somewhere upstream. So we proceed at a leisurely pace, winding slowly in and out of the Delta creeks that stretch between Karachi and the mouth of the Indus, stopping to mend broken parts, or so that I can pee behind a screen of mangroves. Every two hours they reheat some sweet milky tea; for lunch Ali Nawaz fries up some pungent, flaky white fish in a coriander paste; and we swap some fish for shrimp with a passing boat, and dine that night on jheenga omelette. The coastal route is well frequented, almost a school run: people from the Delta islands pass us on their way to Karachi; smarter fishing boats than ours draw up alongside and share our dinner; a boat with a rigged-up sound system playing pirated Indian film songs tows us for three hours after Ali Nawaz drowsily allows the propeller to drop into the thick mud of a creek and a blade snaps off.

The Indus in the Delta is slow, serene and wide. It is thick and brown with the silt that has nourished the land it traverses, and which here in the Delta gives birth to the amphibious mangroves. With their gnarled branches and protruding roots, their shiny green undergrowth and dull, tarnished leaves, these sweet-salt trees resemble a crowd of old fishermen, gossiping eternally on the banks of the river, noting its floods and ebbs, as it fades and swells.

So many things break – so many hours are spent idling in the backwaters – that it is late afternoon when we reach Keti Bunder (a wretched little port rendered practically defunct by the desiccation of the river) and dark by the time we get to the main channel of the Indus. Baboo had planned by now to be three hours further

north, in the mouldering town of Kharochan (the 'Venice of the
Delta', I was told by a friend in Karachi, who had evidently never
been there). Instead, we spend the night on an island in the Indus.

It is pitch-black when we arrive, and the village is absolutely silent,
in the manner of places without electricity. I take off my shoes and
strap my bag on to my back; Ali Nawaz balances a plank from the
edge of the boat, and one by one we step down through the mud
and into the dark. Three sleepy men with their heads wrapped in
scarves come down to meet us. We are invited to spend the night
in a large low building – the school, I am ashamed to discover in
the morning (all Sindhi schools double as guest rooms and meeting
halls; some don't see any use as schools at all). A child brings water
for us to wash our feet, and then we sit sipping tea in the candle-
light, as the men exchange sombre news in solemn voices. Amidst
the unfathomable Sindhi, I hear a name that I recognize. 'Yes,
Alexander Burnes came here on his tour of the Delta,' Ali Nawaz
says, translating for me into Urdu what the men have said about the
nineteenth-century East India Company servant (and spy). 'The Delta
was great once,' Baboo tells me.

In the morning, only boys arrive for lessons at school. Girls spend
all day fetching water from the hand pump half a mile away. A year
ago the government built a large reservoir on the edge of the village
– but they never filled it. Heavy irrigation upstream means that *mitha*
(sweet; drinking) water is scarce downstream in the Delta; the water
that surrounds them is *namkeen*, saline. I am taken on a tour of the
village. We walk up the mud street, in and out of its identical wooden
huts (a bedroom with ventilation flaps, a lean-to kitchen and bathroom). The village is so poor that it is spotlessly clean: there is no
rubbish (none of the usual blue plastic fluttering from bushes, dusty
sweet wrappers or litter of silver cigarette papers); nothing is bought,
nothing is disposed of. I cannot see any animals (the tea we drank
last night was sweet but milkless); the adults look weary, defeated;
the children look malnourished.

We squelch back through the mud to the boat. It is a coldish
morning and the wind is whipping up the water, but Baboo has
a sudden surge of enthusiasm: he wishes me to see the Ozymandias
metropolis of his childhood. Soki Bunder is now a mile-long mud

flat, fringed with mangroves, much like any other in the Delta. But it holds a secret. *Soki* means rich in Sindhi – and sixty years ago, Baboo says, it was a town famous throughout the Arabian Sea for its fine textiles and wealthy traders. Baboo's mother was brought here as a child to be treated by one of Soki Bunder's famous *hakims* (doctors); his grandmother is buried in the now-buried graveyard. There is nothing left; the sea has carried all but the foundations away.

The mud is smooth and dense, and we stub our toes on the worn golden sandstone slivers, which is all that remains of the headstones. Baboo crouches reverently in front of his grandmother's grave, muttering prayers. Further ahead, he points out the remains of the bazaar, the hundred-horsepower rice mill, and the courthouse. We gather round a small squarish brick foundation. 'A washroom,' says Baboo. 'A *masjid*,' says one of his crew. 'A temple,' says Ali Nawaz's uncle. 'The Delta was great once,' Baboo says again. 'Before Partition, Sindh was a rich and prosperous nation.'

From Soki Bunder we sail upstream to Kharochan, one of the few functioning towns left in this decaying island world. The jail – once the pride of the place – is falling down. The grove of date palms has been killed off by the salt which the land sucks in from the coast. A lunatic called Monday stitches nets all day and unpicks them every night. Men sit outside the dispensary, sipping tea and lamenting the state of their heritage. When I stop to buy some sugar-cane candy from the grocer's shop, an old man in a dirty shirt and thick black grimy glasses shouts at me, gesticulating angrily. 'What is he saying?' I ask. 'He is mad,' says Baboo without listening. 'He thinks the British were bad.' But the doctor disagrees: 'He is praising your people.' 'Why?' I feel embarrassed. 'The Raj dispensed good justice,' the doctor says. 'Look at us now,' puts in a fisherman. 'Everything was cheap in British times,' Baboo concurs. 'Japanese sugar was ten paise a kilo!' says an octogenarian farmer. 'But why did the British send our Hindu brothers away to India?' says the doctor; and Baboo thumps the table: 'And why did they let the Punjab steal our Indus?'

As we sit together in the gathering dusk, I think how dramatically this ancient river has changed in the past few decades. Imagine the disbelief, had you told the British officials, who coveted the Indus from the early seventeenth century, that one day this darkly swirling river would actually run out; had you prophesied then that the exhaustion of this river in the twenty-first century would be in part the legacy of their irrigation projects. For three hundred years after the British first saw it, the Indus was the 'mighty river', capricious, frustrating, desirable. Nobody could have guessed that one day, down here in the Delta, there might be no fresh water left.

Sir Thomas Roe was the first ambassador from England to the Mughal court, sent there at the East India Company's behest. In his first letter home to the Company, written on 24 November 1615, he alerted them to commercial prospects on the 'commodious' 'River Syndhu'. Over the next five years, Roe often mentioned the 'famous' and 'very requisite' Indus, the waters of which were navigable, whose inhabitants wove some of the finest cloth in the region. But alas, as he put it plaintively in 1618, 'We must wring it from Portugal.' In 1613, the Portuguese had threatened to burn Thatta's port if the English were allowed to trade there. They controlled all European commerce from the Delta, and the East India Company, which had only been granted its charter by Queen Elizabeth in 1601, was not yet powerful enough to take them on.

By 1635, however, the English had beaten the Portuguese from Bombay and negotiated a more favourable position at the Mughal court. As yet, they had nothing to sell which the Indians wanted to buy. Roe had cringed with embarrassment after his goods were rejected:

> all those guilte glasses on paste, and the others in leather cases with handles, are soe meane, besids so ill packt, that noe man will except [accept] of them of guift, not buy; they are rotten with mould on the outside and decayed within . . . your pictures not all woorth one penny . . . Here are nothing esteemed but of the best sorts: good cloth and fine, rich pictures, they comming out of Italy over land . . . they laugh at us for such as wee bring.

For now, all was in India's favour. The English were prepared to pay hard silver for Sindhian cloth. As the Company merchants wrote to London in 1636:

of all sorts of Indian goods none are in such request as those of Synda nor finde more reddie vend, as being in reguarde of their substance and coullers most requireable.

The Company's initial efforts to establish a depot at Thatta, however, were scuppered by the 'depredations' of an English pirate, William Cobb, which 'disgraced us from thence'. But by 1639 the affair had 'overblowne' sufficiently to allow the Company to settle some traders at Thatta. Back in London, the Directors urged their merchants to 'continuate that Scinda residence', for 'the goods received from thence are the flower of the whole parcel.'

It was Company cost-cutting that resulted in the depot's closure in 1662 (along with those at Agra, Ahmedabad and Basra). Almost a hundred years later, in 1758, the Company tried a second time, opening another warehouse to export red and white rice and doing a slow trade in English crimson velvet and woollen cloth of the most sombre colours: 'clove, cinnamon, purple, and the dark greens'. The Kalhoras, a local family who had just wrested control of Sindh from the Mughals, paid tribute to an Afghan conqueror partly in Company woollens.

But the Kalhoras did not trust the British, whose position in India had strengthened considerably by this time, and in 1775 they evicted the Company merchants. Soon afterwards, the Kalhoras were succeeded by the Talpur family as rulers of Sindh, and again the British tried to return. This time it was local Hindu merchants – founders of 'Crotchy' (Karachi), now an up-and-coming port – who placed an embargo on the presence of the British there. But in the end the Talpur family gave in to Company entreaties, and Nathan Crow was sent as the British Agent to Karachi and Thatta.

By now the British wanted their agent to act not only as a broker of trade but also to spy for the Company. The Talpurs were highly suspicious, spying on Crow in their turn, and monitoring his correspondence, social life and exports. In May 1799, a few months after Crow arrived in Karachi, Tipu Sultan, the great Muslim leader of south India, was defeated and killed by a British army. Immediately afterwards, Muslim powers from all over the region – Kandahar,

Muscat, India – wrote to the Talpurs warning them of British perfidy. In 1800, Crow was expelled.

For the East India Company, Sindh was proving to be a fractious and intractable province. This baffled British merchants, contrasting as it did with the situation elsewhere in India, for by the eighteenth century the British had acquired land revenue rights all over the subcontinent – and an army. With gunpowder, ships and ledgers, they had founded Madras (1639) and Calcutta (1690), conquered Bengal (1757), subdued the French (1763) and the Marathas (1775–1818), and taken the Mughal town of Delhi (1803). By the dawn of the nineteenth century, the British had become the de facto kings of India. Yet over in the western wing of the subcontinent – in the intransigent Indus valley – the stubborn natives refused to cede their freedom. Excluded from Sindh by the Portuguese in the early seventeenth century, thrice evicted from Thatta thereafter, 'British intercourse with Sinde,' as James Burnes commented bluntly in 1831, 'has been rare, and for the most part unsatisfactory.'

The men who ran the East India Company were classically educated. They knew – through their reading of Arrian, Strabo and Pliny – that for Alexander of Macedon, reaching India (or the Indus valley) was the pinnacle of his world conquest. The author of *The Periplus of the Erythraean Sea*, a Greek navigation manual, had called the Indus 'the greatest of all the rivers that flow into the Erythraean Sea'. Pliny the Elder described the Indus (*Indus, incolis Sindhus appellatus*: 'the Indus, locally called Sindh') as the western boundary of India (*ad Indum amnem qui est ab occidente finis Indiae*). For a Company keen to endorse its presence in the Orient with regal analogies to the glorious Alexander, acquisition of the 'classic river' came to seem like the natural (indeed, indispensable) corollary to the attainment of India proper.

There were some basic obstacles to taking Sindh. By the early nineteenth century, the British still knew astonishingly little about the Indus valley. All was hearsay. For five centuries now, England's poets and playwrights had described India's two major rivers. The wondrous Ganges, with its large 'fysshes', was first mentioned in a Middle English version of the *Alexander Romance*. The Indus – India's namesake – was evoked by Andrew of Wyntoun in his early fifteenth-century *Original Chronicle*:

betuix Ynde and Paradiss
Mony dissert landis lyiss . . .
Out of a hill callit Calkasus
The watter is rynnand of Indus,
And efter that watter, as we fynd,
The kinrik is callit of Ynde.

It was in the seventeenth century, however, that the Indus and Ganges both became popular as symbols of eastern exoticism. King James I of England mentioned the 'orientall Indus' and its 'cristall streames' in an unpublished poem. 'To meet old Nereus, with his fiftie girles / From aged Indus laden home with pearles', wrote Ben Jonson in a masque he put on for Twelfth Night in 1626. 'Thou by the *Indian Ganges* side / Should'st Rubies find', answered Andrew Marvell in 'To His Coy Mistress' (*c.* 1646). While the Ganges was always emblematic of lush eastern glamour, the Indus was versatile, and several playwrights twinned it with the Nile, to suggest the vast expanse of Asia. The Indus could evoke the alien mystery of India, or the history and politics of classical civilization.

Nevertheless, knowledge of where the Indus actually flowed was vague at best. In his letters home, Sir Thomas Roe had repeatedly pointed out the 'falseness of our maps', which showed the Indus emptying itself into the sea at the Bay of Cambay in Gujarat. A century later, Company maps were barely any better. Cartography was one of the great advances of the European Enlightenment but when the French cartographer Jean-Baptiste d'Anville began publishing his 'map memoirs' of India in the mid–eighteenth century, he relied on the Ancients, Mughal and Persian histories, and contemporary European travel memoirs. D'Anville never visited India, and he was perfectly honest about the paucity of his sources. He apologized that although he personally viewed the Indus as the most important of India's boundaries, '*la première connue*' (the first known) of its rivers, the fact remained that it had not been explored by Europeans in recent years, and thus current knowledge of it was – he regretted – woefully imprecise.

Britain's chief cartographer in India, James Rennell, travelled to Bengal to survey the province between 1765 and 1771. Nevertheless, when he drew up his all-India map after his retirement, he too relied on literary sources (and in particular records of the Company's military manoeuvres and marches) to fill in the gaps. Large areas, including the Indus valley, remained *terra incognita*.

In 1774, the coast was at last mapped by a Company squadron. At least until 1831, however (when the Company surveyed the Indus as far as Attock: about half its length) maps of the Sindh region were compiled mainly from guesswork. And while the river's 'furiously rapid' mountain course was charted in 1842 by G. T. Vigne, the British never managed to map its source, and for a long time they thought the Indus rose in Kashmir.

If cartography was an imprecise art, the East India Company's murky impression of the river was clarified somewhat by the accounts of pioneering travellers. In 1638, for example, an Englishman called Henry Bornford managed to sail from Lahore to Thatta in a flat-bottomed boat. But it was the free merchant and adventurer, Captain Alexander Hamilton, who gave the Company most hope, for his *New Account of the East Indies*, published in 1727, attested that the Indus was navigable 'as high as *Cashmire*'.

Hamilton was scornful of the 'Tribunal of Map-travellers', whose 'Stock of Knowledge is all on Tick'. His detailed description of 'the Mogul's Dominions on the River *Indus*' – far from being an awed account of the river's classical history – addressed its practical advantages. 'This Country,' he wrote, 'abounds richly in Wheat, Rice and Legumen . . . they never know the Misery of Famine, for the *Indus* overflows all the low Grounds in the Months of *April, May* and *June*, and when the Floods go off, they leave a fat Slime on the Face of the Ground, which they till easily before it dries, and being sown and harrow'd, never fails of bringing forth a plentiful Crop.' (Even now in Sindh the fertile *kaccha*, the land along the riverbank, can yield three crops in a good year.) Moreover, Hamilton wrote, certain stretches of the river were able 'to receive Ships of 200 Tuns'. This optimistic intelligence would inspire East India Company officers, eager to exploit the Indus for trade and agriculture, throughout the nineteenth century.

Hamilton's guide to the river's commercial potential was matched in importance, for the Company, by George Forster's much-read

Journey from Bengal to England (1798). It was Forster who popularized the potent concept that 'The Indus forms a strong barrier to
Hindostan on the west . . . Armies at all times have sustained difficulties and damage in crossing the Indus.' For a Company now
anxious to defend its Indian territory from attack by hostile mountain tribes – or more likely, rival European powers such as Russia –
Forster's notion of the Indus as a military barrier was a decisive
factor in the Company's advance towards the river.

Then again, the very fact that the river's natural defences had been
breached in the past was also a source of great anxiety. As one
Company servant wrote, 'It has been remarked that the difficulties
attendant on the invasion of India, *must* be estimated, because that
Country, *has* been successfully invaded.' It was this fear which encouraged the East India Company to stake a claim over not merely the
Indus but the countries beyond it too – Sindh and Afghanistan.

In 1830, the first step towards the annexation of Sindh was made
with the compilation of an Indus intelligence dossier. This, the
collected 'Memoranda on the N. W. Frontier of British India and on
the importance of the river Indus as connected with its defence',
set out Britain's two chief concerns – the case for invading Sindh,
and the fear of a Russian advance on India. By now, the Company
had come to terms with most powers along the river. In 1809, it
had made a tribute agreement with the Sikhs east of the Indus.
Negotiations with the powers to the west had begun as early as
1800, in response to the feared advance of Napoleon towards India
(he had just taken Egypt). Embassies were despatched to Persia, and
then to Afghanistan. This left Sindh – a small but strategic province
on the lower Indus. Ruled by the Talpur family, without a well-
trained standing army, Sindh was considered to be the weak spot.

Sindh's rulers knew this. They were also aware that the English
were a deceitful race; and for as long as they could, they pursued a
policy of isolation: kicking out the Company's merchants when they
got too overbearing, and only grudgingly acceding to the slippery
terms of the Company's treaties.

The first such treaty, signed in 1809, was extremely short. Its sole
aim was to keep out the 'tribe of the French': it was not the guarantee of trading interests which the Company hoped for. In 1819,

when the Company took the adjacent province of Cutch, it hoped that trading rights in Sindh would follow; but as James Burnes wrote, those 'haughty and jealous chieftains . . . viewed the extension of our Empire in this direction with distrust and apprehension'. If commercial advances into Sindh were to be denied the Company, then outright conquest was the only answer. Happily, Sindh – the 1830 Memoranda made this quite clear – would be an easy province to conquer.

In the manner of most preludes to annexation, the Memoranda drew attention to the 'tyrannical principles' by which Sindh was governed. The moral case for invasion was established with details of the bigotry and 'debauchery' of the Sindhian rulers. Among Sindh's crimes, the Memoranda noted that 'much of the fertile and cultivatable ground' along the river had been deliberately left barren as hunting ground for the Talpur rulers. A 'mild and beneficial rule', this document slyly concluded, would be the best thing for the people.

The Memoranda outlined the ease with which an attack could be launched. In practical terms, the 'only Fortifications of Sinde worthy notice are Hydrabad and Omerkote'. Politically, all that was needed was a quick dose of 'divide and rule': 'the disjointed texture of the Sindian Force and Government . . . would afford us ample means of coercing any refractory chiefs, and of converting many into grateful allies.' The purpose of this speculative endeavour was to secure the Indus, navigation of which was crucial 'in case of such an event occurring of vital consequence to the defence of the country'. The event in question was the feared invasion of British India by Russia.

The latter half of the Memoranda addressed this apparently pressing problem. The soldier-experts differed as to its gravity but they all concurred that controlling the Indus was key to British India's security. Sir John Malcolm admitted that 'Russia has entertained, and still entertains, designs of invading India.' But he believed that the Russian Treasury could not sustain an invasion on such a scale, through such sparsely populated, inhospitable terrain. Sir John McDonald was more alarmist. He advised sending spies to acquire 'an accurate knowledge of the nature and resource of the territories, immediately west of the Indus; the fords, the ferries, and Military features of that great boundary of our Empire'. So the Company urged itself onwards with the phantasmagoria of '30,000 Russians' creeping through the Hindu Kush towards India.

The immediate result of the Memoranda was that an enthusiastic young officer, Alexander Burnes, was sent to navigate the Sindhian and Sikh courses of the river. Given the 'jealousy' of the Talpur rulers, the true purpose of the trip – to survey the river's width, depth and suitability for navigation, and to examine the defences of the Sindh forts along its banks – was concealed. A ruse was found. Ostensibly, Burnes was to use the river as a means of taking five dray horses to Maharaja Ranjit Singh one thousand kilometres upstream in Lahore. (These are 'Horses of the Gigantic Breed, which is peculiar to England', Burnes boasted in a letter to the Sikh ruler.) Under cover of this Trojan present, he would explore the river, and augment Britain's knowledge of it, which at the moment was so 'vague and unsatisfactory'.

From the beginning of his journey, young Burnes was fired with zeal for his mission. Adroitly, he negotiated with the various Talpur rulers, who, guessing (correctly) that 'we were the precursors of an army', at first refused to allow him to travel by river to Lahore. For three months they placed him under boat arrest in the Delta, denying him fresh water. The Talpur at nearby Thatta answered Burnes's pleas with letters in which 'he magnified the difficulties of navigating the Indus, and arrayed its rocks, quicksands, whirlpools, and shallows, in every communication; asserting that the voyage to Lahore had never been performed in the memory of man'. Burnes must have known this was a lie; but he took the exaggerations seriously, henceforth considering himself an Indus pioneer. He also used this time to explore and map the winding Indus Delta. Eventually, when he could brook no more delay, he travelled overland to Thatta to meet the ruler in person and persuade him to give in.

It is probable that the Talpurs' change of heart was due to the thorough search which their soldiers made of Burnes's luggage as he waited in the Delta. They were looking for arms – there were none. To their cost, they failed to appreciate the significance of the modern 'surveying instruments' which Burnes was carrying with him.

Now that he was no longer considered a threat, Burnes was given special treatment. He had travelled through the Delta in a flat-bottomed skiff, but from Thatta onwards he was lent the Talpurs' state barge. He floated upstream, dining on goat stew prepared by the royal chefs, and innocently admiring the splendid countryside – soon to be part of Britain. It was only at night, under cover of darkness, that he unpacked his instruments, and carefully noted, calculated, measured. In his ensuing 'Memoir on the Indus and Punjab Rivers', Burnes proclaimed the river perfect for trade and ripe for annexation:

> The British Govt. may without difficulty command the navigation of the Indus . . . the insulated fortress of Bukkur is alone an important position – by securing that . . . the British would command the whole navigation into a most fertile country.

Naturally, the Company bosses were delighted. The following year – using the threat of conquest by Maharaja Ranjit Singh in the Punjab – they coerced the Talpur rulers into signing new treaties providing 'for that portion of the Indus which flows through Sinde being thrown open to all merchants and traders'. There would be two more treaties, in 1834 and 1838, each more favourable to British interests than the last. As early as 1837, Burnes was able to write: 'The haughty Lords of SINDE have been indeed humbled . . . we have at last . . . secured our influence on the Indus.'

Buoyed by his success, Burnes had in the meantime persuaded his superiors to support him in a still more ambitious journey. He left India in 1832 and travelled across the Indus into Central Asia, disguised as an Armenian merchant. It was an adventurous sequel, and on his return to England in 1834, Burnes wrote up his two expeditions as a three-volume work, *Travels into Bokhara*. Burnes had a popular touch, and his Indus exploits, in particular, caught the imagination of Britain.

A central theme was the parallel between Burnes's own exploits and those of his namesake, Alexander the Great. Burnes began with the frankly inaccurate claim that he was 'the first European of modern times who had navigated the Indus'. He went on to assert coyly that in Lahore, 'we were daily informed that we were the "second

Alexander", the "Sikunder sanee", for having achieved so dangerous a voyage.' Above all, he emphasized the latent power and potential of his Indus mission:

> As we ascended the river, the inhabitants came for miles around to see us. A Syud stood on the water's edge, and gazed with astonishment. He turned to his companion, as we passed, and in the hearing of one of our party, said, 'Alas! Sinde is now gone, since the English have seen the river, which is the road to its conquest.'

In London, Burnes and his journey became the talk of the town. He was feted in every salon; nicknamed 'Indus Burnes' in the press, and granted an audience with the King at Brighton. The French and English Geographical Societies awarded him medals, the Asiatic Society of Paris applauding the 'luminous line' he had drawn 'across the obscurest region of Asia'. The media were equally enthusiastic: 'The Indus; with the Ganges, folds as it were in an embrace our mighty empire of British India,' trilled the *Monthly Review*; 'The ancient ALEXANDER descended the Indus and its tributaries from Lahore to the ocean, the modern ALEXANDER ascended,' purred the *Spectator*. The book was a huge success for its publisher, John Murray, selling out immediately. It was reprinted in 1835 and 1839, and over the next twenty years was translated into German, Italian, French and Spanish.

Underlying the romance and adventure of Burnes's book was an economic proposition: that the Indus should be 'opened' for trade and navigation. Burnes had done his reading on this subject, and he was particularly inspired by William Robertson's *History of America*, which established, in a general sense, the commercial and prospecting possibilities available to clever European pioneers in a 'virgin' land. The steamships used in North American freshwater navigation were an inspiration to East India Company officers, and the Indus led a fertile existence in their imaginations as an Indian Mississippi or Hudson.

Between them, Malcolm's Memoranda and Burnes's *Travels* held out the tantalizing promise of the Indus to a Company greedy for territorial aggrandizement. As Burnes hinted, the Indus was a catch in itself, but it was also the high road to greater glory. Indeed, Burnes's splendidly assured prose, and the deceptively simple westward trajectory that his book recommended, must be held partly responsible for the first of Britain's disastrous forays into Afghanistan.

After the raptures which greeted the publication of Burnes's *Travels*, it was not long before Auckland, the Governor General, promoted him as the Company's Political Agent in Kabul. During his second residence in Kabul, Burnes became obsessed with the notion that the arrival of 'Vilkivitsch', a Russian agent, presaged a Russian-Afghan invasion of India. But the letters he sent to Calcutta urging the government to conciliate Dost Muhammad, King of Kabul, were ignored by Auckland, who instead sanctioned an invasion of Afghanistan.

Auckland gave his reasons: the Afghans, he proclaimed, were plotting to extend 'Persian influence and authority to the banks of, and even beyond, the Indus'. Of course, this hypothetical intrigue was simply the mirror-image of Auckland's own designs. The force which left India in the autumn of 1838 was named after a land the British did not even yet own. The Bombay and Bengal armies were rechristened the 'Army of the Indus'.

When the soldiers began their westward march – thus breaking the Talpurs' ban on the transfer of military personnel and stores across the Indus in the 1834 Treaty – Burnes's words were on everybody's lips. Most of the officers had read *Travels into Bokhara*, and his images buoyed them through the deserts of Sindh, across the 'noble' Indus, and into the Bolan pass. Here the rations ran out, 'Belochees' with rifles began picking off soldiers and camels, and as one officer put it, Burnes had duped them with his 'flowery imagination'.

The landscape of Baluchistan – its dry, sandy valleys and high barren hills – was unfamiliar to the British. Hundreds of soldiers died from starvation. When they eventually reached the 'bleak' and 'barren' country of Afghanistan – so far removed from the *'fairy land'* which they had been led by Burnes to expect – and stormed the towns of Ghazni and Kabul, they were shocked by the cold and unfriendly reception they received from the local population. The soldiers had been led by their officers to expect rapturous, thankful crowds; the virgins of Kabul, they thought, would strew their way with flowers. Instead, as memoir after British memoir attests, the

Afghans appeared ungrateful – even angry – at the efforts the British had gone to in deposing their ruler. By 1840, the Army of the Indus was thoroughly disillusioned.

Back home in England, however, the invasion was applauded as a triumph for the new imperial Victorianism. Alexander the Great, wrote one commentator, merely 'meditated the invasion of India . . . but the conquest of that country was destined for a nation almost unknown in the days of Alexander'. The new queen, Victoria, knighted Burnes, and the other key players, for services to her empire. The Houses of Commons and Lords gave votes of thanks to the Army of the Indus, and Sir John Hobhouse delivered a patriotic speech in which he extolled the army's 'bold and brilliant achievement' of bringing 'civilization' to the 'banks of the Indus' – for the first time since the 'great Alexander' marched his army down the river.

The euphoria, however, was short-lived. In November 1841, the ousted Afghans retaliated. The first victim of the coup was the young hero Burnes himself. As the 'Khans of Caboul' wrote in a letter to their allies:

> stirring like Lions, we carried by Storm the house of Sickender Burnes . . . the Brave Warriors having rushed right & left from their ambush, slew Sikender Burnes with various other Feringees of Consideration . . . putting them utterly to the sword, & consigning them to perdition.

So much for British understanding of the Afghans. The army fled in confusion. Of the 4,500 soldiers and 12,000 camp followers who left Kabul in January 1842, only one man reached safety in Jalalabad. A handful of officers and their wives were taken hostage. Everybody else was killed – by Afghan snipers, by starvation, or by the cold.

As news of the disaster trickled into London and Calcutta, attitudes to Auckland's Afghan venture shifted. The Court of Directors of the East India Company, it now emerged, had always been 'strongly opposed to the war' and the 'inexpediency of interfering with the states beyond the Indus'. Sir Henry Fane, commander-in-chief of the army until 1838, had apparently resigned out of distaste for the 'injustice' of the Afghan expedition. He was said to have warned in 1837: 'Every advance you make beyond the Sutlej to the westward . . .

adds to your military weakness . . . Make yourselves complete sovereigns of all within your own boundaries. *But let alone the Far West.*'

The government, forced to defend the army's action in the House of Commons, needed a scapegoat. They chose the late lamented Burnes. In speeches to the House, Lord Palmerston and Sir John Hobhouse now hinted at Burnes's misjudgement and folly. In the official parliamentary 'Blue Book', Burnes's reports and letters were edited to suggest that he had urged – rather than opposed – the fatal invasion. Charles Napier, the future conqueror of Sindh, joined the chorus: 'the chief cause of our disasters is this – When a smart lad can speak Hindostanee and Persian, he is *made a political agent,* and *supposed to be a statesman and a general.*'

But even this rearguard action could not relieve the sense of British disgrace. The new Governor General, Ellenborough, badly misread the public mood when, in 1842, he sent a second force to sack Kabul and Ghazni. In an overt incitement to anti-Muslim feeling, he wrote an open letter to the 'People of India' in which he depicted the war as historical retaliation for the invasion of Hindu India by an eleventh-century Afghan, Sultan Mahmud of Ghazni. The army was proud of having despoiled the Sultan's tomb, Ellenborough declared, for now 'The insult of eight hundred years is at last avenged.' Ellenborough even ordered that the sandalwood gates of the Somnath temple in Gujarat, taken to Afghanistan as a victory trophy in 1025 by the Sultan – 'so long the memorial of your humiliation' – should be returned to India.

In Britain, this was seen for what it was – a cynical attempt to stir up religious passions and justify a brutal Afghan invasion. In India, few Hindus took much notice at the time, though it became an emotive issue much later, around the time of Partition. (Later still, it was discovered that the gates were not Gujarati at all, but Egyptian.)

Having proved the power of British arms, Ellenborough then ordered the army back to India. He issued another proclamation explaining that the government was 'Content with the limits Nature appears to have assigned to its empire'. Nature's limits now apparently included 'The rivers of the Punjab and the Indus'. Having dealt with the Afghans, Ellenborough was moving on to the Sindhis.

Sir Charles Napier – a sixty-year-old General who had never been to India but wanted to make some money before retirement – was contracted to wage the war. Napier arrived in Sindh in the autumn of 1842. He sailed up the Indus by steamer, reading Burnes's book, and writing silly, threatening letters to the Talpurs as a prelude to battle:

> but as there are two sides of your river, so there are two sides of Your Highness' arguments. Now the Governor-General has occupied both sides of Your Highness' river because he has considered both sides of Your Highness' arguments.

Napier waited impatiently on the Indus for the Talpurs, whom he portrayed as villainous immigrant despots – they came from neighbouring Baluchistan – to be tricked into betraying the trading terms of their treaty. At last, in February and March 1843, he fought two decisive battles. The Talpurs were preparing for a family wedding, and their army was disorganized, so the British won easily by bombarding the riverside forts from armed steamships (a dry run of Britain's colonization of Africa by gunboat). Napier arrested the Talpurs, confiscated their country, and packed them off down the river on a pension. The loot from the fort in Sindh's capital, Hyderabad, came to a million sterling.

The conquest of Sindh received almost universal condemnation in India and England. The Indian newspapers savaged the invasion; in England, *Punch* displayed its disapproval with the Latin pun *Peccavi* (I have sinned/Sindh). The Secret Committee of the East India Company called for an investigation. In 1844, unconvinced by Ellenborough's defence, the Committee had him recalled to England. As for the army, if in 1841 it had retreated to the Indus with its tail between its legs and its military reputation in tatters, by 1843, public approbation had rarely been so low.

It would take the 'Mutiny' of 1857 to reignite support in Britain for Company policy. Concomitantly, the critical 'loyalty' displayed in 1857 by Sindh, the newly-annexed Punjab, and the recently 'pacified' Afghan powers, did much to rehabilitate the reputation of the trans-Indus provinces in the popular British imagination. Now nobody could deny that conquering Sindh – as Charles Napier famously said – was 'a useful piece of rascality'.

One of the most damning indictments of the Kabul interlude had come from Charles Masson, a British army deserter turned explorer and spy, who in 1842 published a character assassination of Burnes. Masson asserted that Sir Alexander had misread the Afghans and the Russians; hinted that he was unduly fond of local 'black-eyed damsels'; and poured scorn on the 'primarily commercial' goals of Burnes's second journey up the Indus. Playing on British complexes about being known as a 'nation of shopkeepers' by Oriental princes, Masson jeered that the Afghans had wholly disparaged Britain's eagerness to sign trade treaties. In fact, the picture was more depressing than even Masson imagined.

Seven years before, in 1835, having signed a trade treaty with the Talpurs, the British grandly 'opened the river'. But while local tradesmen had long used the river as a trade route, the British had difficulty in persuading Indian merchants to do so. Thus in 1836, four Company employees – Carless, Leech, Wood and Heddle – were despatched to test Burnes's earlier assertions. These men, mostly engineers by profession, showed that navigating the Indus was far more problematic than had hitherto been expected. As a comparison of maps made in 1817 and 1837 showed, the Indus was highly unstable, subject to frequent flooding and changes of course, especially at its mouth. The first sixty miles of river from the sea were deemed unsuitable for 'boats drawing more than four feet of water'. Merchants had long since 'abandoned the Indus and they now use the camel to transport their wares'.

At the top of the surveyors' list of solutions to this problem was the introduction of steamboats (following the American model). In 1836, therefore, Wood and Heddle triumphantly sailed into the mouth of the Indus, and 'had the proud satisfaction of unfurling our country's flag . . . from the first steam-boat that ever floated on its celebrated waters'. But Wood also voiced his anxieties: 'The Indus,' he wrote bleakly, 'is a foul and perplexing river.' In 1838, he criticized the prospectus for a steamboat firm which the East India Company had attached to its *Abstract* on the Indus, calling it 'crude' and 'erroneous'. It is 'suited', he wrote, 'to the equable streams of the New World, but not applicable to the ever-changing channels of our Indian rivers'. The Indus – low in autumn, flooded in springtime by mountain snowmelt – waxed and waned like no other river these men had ever seen.

After he had conquered Sindh, Napier pursued the 250-year-old

British ambition of trading up and down the Indus, regardless of the setbacks. In his 1846 'Memorandum on Sind', Napier described how 'the Merchants at Kurrachee now cry out for Steamers up the River'. Attesting that 'of every *seven* vessels coming down the river . . . *six* are either lost altogether, or the goods destroyed', he begged the Governor General 'to make over 4 of the War Steamers on the Indus to the Sinde Government, for mercantile purposes'. But Napier's frustration merely indicates the attitude of the government in Calcutta – acquisitiveness had by now given way to apathy. Sindh was a poor, provincial backwater, and the image of the Indus – glamorized in Greek histories, the *Alexander Romance* and Renaissance poetry, talked up in Company despatches and best-selling travelogues – was very different from reality. It took another ten years for Napier's promised steamboats to arrive. And then, in the 1860s, river navigation was rendered redundant by the railways.

At first, administrators clung to the notion that the Indus was 'peculiarly suited to the combined system of railways and steamboats'. By 1861, passengers on the thirty-eight-day trip from Marseilles to Multan (on the upper Sindh–Punjab border) were taking boats from Europe to Karachi, where they caught the train up to Kotri near Hyderabad, and from there took an Indus steamer.

But the new railway soon proved so fast, efficient and popular that river transport began to look old-fashioned – not to say dangerous. By 1867, *Our Paper*, a bi-weekly published from Karachi, was referring to steam navigation as 'the problem which has for the past twenty years been puzzling the ablest naval architects that have ever come into this country'. While the Scinde Railway reported ever-increasing traffic and revenue, the Indus Flotilla reported shipwrecks, and the death of its passengers.

W. P. Andrew, chairman of both the Indus Steam Flotilla and the Scinde and Punjaub Railways, now petitioned the government to build a line from Sindh to the Punjab: 'the shallow, shifting, treacherous nature of the river Indus,' he wrote, 'makes it inefficient, uncertain, unsafe, costly.' The government agreed and, in 1878, a line was opened running right the way through Sindh, along the banks of the river – thus ending for ever the ambitions of a succession of Company servants, from Sir Thomas Roe to Sir Charles Napier.

Men like Burnes had portrayed the Indus as a lucrative windfall, and that it did not immediately make the Company rich was a disappointment to colonial officers. For decades, accountants juggled the books, offsetting Sindh's deficit with profits from the opium trade in China. Napier had begged the government for money to build the infrastructure – roads, harbours – which Sindh desperately needed. But projects like these were time-consuming, expensive and slow to realize returns. Even the railways – which turned Sindh from a 'difficult' province into a 'regular' administration – did not make the country wealthy, just easier to manage.

Back in 1727, Alexander Hamilton had lauded the extreme fertility of the silt-rich Indus valley. In the end, it was irrigation that rescued Britain's conquest of the Indus from financial disaster.

After the Company conquered the Punjab in 1849, the British began work on an Indus valley canal system. The Kalhoras, Talpurs and Sikhs had been competent canal builders but the British planned to improve the existing seasonal canals, while also installing perennial irrigation to bring arid areas under cultivation. This was a new area of technical expertise. Over-irrigation from canals in northern India had caused waterlogging and salination, rendering the land agriculturally unfit, so the British knew of the potential dangers. The building of dams – mandatory if large amounts of water were to be saved for year-round use – were known to cause a host of structural and siltation-related troubles. But in 1878, famine broke out in north India, and so the government hurried through the Punjab irrigation proposals. Creating fields out of scrubland had many advantages on paper. It increased agricultural production to feed the growing population; and it dealt – by eviction – with the untaxable nomads and bandits who used the desert for low-intensity grazing or refuge from the law.

By 1901, four of the five rivers of the Punjab had been 'canalized' or dammed. Grain poured out of the Punjab, feeding hungry mouths in India, and transmitting new taxes to London. The Punjab became a 'model province' in British India: productive and peaceful.

But Sindh was more difficult to manage. The river, receiving the combined force of the Punjabi and Afghan tributaries, was liable to flooding. With no large canal-irrigation projects yet in place, massive amounts of river water were thus flowing 'improvidently' down-stream without being used. As the Report of the Indian Irrigation Commission stated regretfully in 1903, '60 per cent of the surface water will still run to waste in the sea.' The British, now eager to supply Lancashire's cotton mills with raw material, began to examine how to irrigate Sindh's rainless deserts.

Some Cassandra-like Sindhis looked in alarm upon both the irri-gation projects under way upstream in the Punjab, and those planned for Sindh. (If the level of water went down, they feared, navigation would be harmed; the impact on fishing and agriculture was not even considered.) But British officials dismissed these concerns, believing that there was more than enough water to go round. A site was chosen for Sindh's first barrage, at Sukkur in the north of the province, and after some delay, work began. By 1932, the barrage was complete.

The Sukkur barrage changed Sindhi society for ever. Huge areas of wasteland were turned into fertile agricultural regions, almost overnight. Grain and cotton exports, in turn, helped make Karachi into a world-class port. Landowners and administrators lavished praise upon this, the biggest irrigation project in the world. The British, when they left India in 1947, crowed that they had transformed Sindh from a desert into a surplus province. Only the farmers of the Delta looked upon Sukkur askance.

By enabling the storage of huge amounts of river water, and viewing each drop that went out to sea as 'wastage', what the engineers had ignored was the need for plenty of fresh water downstream in the Delta, in order to maintain a healthy balance with the salt water from the sea, and thus to safeguard the unique ecosystem of the mangroves, shrimp beds, fish and farmers.

The Delta lands, it is said today, were once 'the richest' in all Pakistan'. But the British did not see it like this. Alexander Burnes had spent three frustrating months waiting in the Delta, and he depicted it harshly, as a barren, unpeopled land. The image stuck. Almost a century later, the influential Sindh *Gazetteer* noted the idio-syncrasies of the Delta's cultivation methods, and the fact that rice (but only rice) grew abundantly. With its frequently flooded paddies, shifting settlements and semi-nomadic farmers, the 'unhealthy' Delta did not fit the picture of a viable or desirable agricultural model.

For the British, who wished to transport grain quickly into northern India, it made better economic sense to develop Punjab and upper Sindh than to defend the strange agrarian culture of the mangroves. Where Britain led, with its infrastructure-heavy, intensive irrigation projects, Pakistan followed.

The need to build more dams on the Indus was brought home forcibly to Pakistan on 1 April 1948 – exactly eight months after Independence, and the morning after the Arbitral Tribunal closed. (This was the body convened to adjudicate on Partition disputes.) On that morning, India blocked off the canals that led from its land into Pakistan. It was the start of the sowing season, a whole harvest depended on this water, and India could not have chosen a more devastating way of demonstrating its superior strength and bargaining power.

The incident did not go unnoticed in North America, where the new World Bank was based. In 1951, David Lilienthal, former head of the Atomic Commission, toured India and Pakistan, and in August he wrote up his researches in a magazine article, in which he identified the Indus water controversy as one of the most serious issues facing the independent countries. More contentiously, he linked it to the nascent Kashmir dispute. Arguing that the copious amounts of river water that flowed out to sea simply had to be diverted and distributed properly, Lilienthal suggested building dams all along the river. On 20 August 1951, Eugene R. Black, President of the World Bank, wrote to the Prime Ministers of India and Pakistan, enclosing a copy of Lilienthal's article and offering the Bank's 'good offices' for the development of Indus infrastructure 'along the lines suggested by Mr Lilienthal'.

As a confidential British Foreign Office memo written on 1 November 1951 revealed, Mr Lilienthal had 'recently become a partner in Lazards' – an international financial advisory and asset management firm – and thus his 'main interest at present' is 'that there should be a lot of money in it'. Despite the baseness of these profiteering motives, the British read and commented on all the Bank's correspondence, and so the plan was hatched for the division of the Indus basin – a 'riparian Iron Curtain'.

Pakistan, in its turn, began building the Kotri barrage, just north of Thatta. This dam, like those that followed, was supposed to solve the country's problems. But while it indeed facilitated the mass production of cash crops, Kotri also began the trend of the next sixty years: growing debt to Western banks, experts and construction firms. Pakistan is not alone in its mania for large hydraulic structures as the answer to its food and water shortages. Nor is it alone in discovering that over-irrigation leads to salination of agricultural land upstream, and the rapid death of river deltas. Following the construction of the Kotri barrage in 1958, the Delta shrank from 3,500 to 250 square kilometres. With barely any water flowing south to the sea, salt water was sucked into the mangroves. The fields of red rice turned to white salt encrustations, and the farmers had no choice but to turn to fishing.

'The farmers here voted against the Sukkur barrage,' Baboo says as we stand together in the graveyard of Soki Bunder. The old men at Kharochan agree: 'After Sukkur opened, farmers became fishermen,' says the doctor. 'And with Kotri, then all the rice fields went saline. After that there was Tarbela [the biggest dam of all, just north of the Punjab]. But nobody would listen to us that the Delta needs more water.'

As Baboo's boat chugs slowly north from Kharochan, dolphins arc through the water – not the famous blind river dolphins of upper Sindh but ocean mammals that have wandered into this salty river from the Arabian Sea. We sail as far as we can in Baboo's feeble boat but there comes a point when this once large and magnificent river is too shallow and perilous for a fisherman to risk his vessel. Towards evening, the propeller snags on something once again, and snaps. As day turns to night, we float back down the river to a place where Baboo had seen a village. As Ali Nawaz walks inland to ask for accommodation, we sit in the silent boat, rocking gently backwards and forwards under the stars, listening to the river's murmurings. It is impossible now to make the journey that generations of fishermen, merchants and foreigners – including the Alexanders Macedon, Hamilton and Burnes – once made along the Indus.

I spend that night in another forlorn Delta village, and early the next morning, begin a slow journey north along the riverbank by taxi, stopping whenever possible to walk down and check the level of the river. A ration of water is allowed downstream from Kotri during the spring and summer sowing seasons, and also during times of high flooding upstream, but now that it is autumn, all that is left are a few pools of standing water: stagnant and undrinkable. At Sondoo, a small village near Thatta, the riverbed blows pale white sand into my eyes, and the grey strip of water is just a few feet deep. I watch as a bullock cart, and then a line of camels, cross the river, and finally I too take off my shoes and paddle across the mighty Indus.

Further north, just below the Kotri barrage, the local authorities use the glorious Indus as a conduit for sewage. There is no flow below the dam (contravening the technical specifications and compromising the dam's structure, according to the engineer who fifty years ago helped design it). The fishermen whose families have fished here for centuries show me their catch: fish so exhausted by swimming in sewage, they lie weakly in the water, barely moving. 'We danced for joy when the government let down water last summer during the floods,' Fatima, a fisherwoman who has lived here all her life, tells me. 'Then the river once again dried up. We have sent this water in bottles to the Senators in Islamabad, and said to them: "Would you drink this?"'

It is the same everywhere in Sindh: peasants, farmers and fisherfolk protesting about water shortages; almost daily, in some small town or village, an anti-dam march. In the once-illustrious city of Thatta, on the banks of the once 'commodious' River Indus, I attend a water rally. A thin old man stands up, thrusts his hands into the air, and sings a song in Sindhi:

> Musharraf you big cheat,
> Shame on you a hundred times,
> Pakistan has bowed before America,
> And you are trying to rape our river.

But the army-run government, far away in northern Punjab, does not listen to farmers from the Delta. Money lies in the cotton fields of Punjab and northern Sindh – and the power to control the country resides in a centralized irrigation policy dictated one hundred years ago by imperial engineers.

3

Ethiopia's First Fruit

1793

'The state of my Sheedi brothers in Sindh pierces my heart like thorns.'

Muhammad Siddiq 'Mussafir', *Ghulami ain Azadi Ja Ibratnak Nazara* (Eye-opening Accounts of Slavery and Freedom), 1952

IT IS DECEMBER, the rumbustious Muslim marriage season is in full parade, and one night soon after I arrive in Thatta, I find myself in a van, heading east from the Indus along small country roads to attend a village wedding. The warm desert land through which we drive is dark and quiet, the stars are sharp in the sky, and the full moon bathes the fields in a cold white light – which is just as well, for the van's headlights are broken. The other three women in the car, clad in black burqas, sing shyly: Sindhi folksongs about passionate lovers and misbegotten trysts.

The sexes are segregated at the wedding, and by the time we arrive, the women are singing inside the house. But I am led to the yard in front, where the men are dancing in a circle by the light of a bonfire. By now I have been to many Pakistani weddings – over-long processions of overdressed guests carrying overladen plates. Nothing, therefore, has prepared me for this. The men are dancing around a chest-high wooden drum, their bare feet thumping the ground as the drummer's hands move faster and faster. '*Ya Ali!*' they cry, in praise of the first Shia leader. The light from the bonfire flickers across their flowing white robes, dark skin and tightly curled hair. I feel as if I have strayed across an East African rite. And indeed, that is exactly what this is.

These are the Sheedis, descendants of slaves taken from Africa to

Sindh by Muslim traders. 'They are dancing the *leva*,' says Iqbal, the Sheedi friend with whom I have come here tonight. 'Our ancestors brought the leva with them from Zanzibar.' The leva has been danced by Sheedis in an unbroken cultural tradition ever since the first slaves landed on these shores in the seventh or eighth century. They call their distinctive, four-footed drum the *maseendo*, or *mugarman*, and it too is a relic of their African inheritance.

That night, as the mood grows wilder, the men scatter red-hot coals on the ground, and step across them. 'Did Sheedis convert to Islam after arriving in Pakistan?' I ask Iqbal's uncle, who is watching nearby, now too old to join in. 'But we are the original Muslims,' he says, and relates the story of how, thirteen centuries ago in Arabia, the Prophet Muhammad's first male convert was Bilal, a tall Ethiopian slave with a sonorous voice. 'And our Prophet honoured Bilal,' Iqbal's uncle says, 'by asking him to call the faithful to Islam's first prayer.'

Bilal is a famous figure in Islamic art: often represented standing on the sacred black stone cube of the Ka'ba in Mecca and cupping his hands to his mouth (in those idyllic days before loudspeakers). And so, watching this forceful, joyous dancing, I wonder at the irony that despite Bilal's role in Islam's early history, Sheedis should be ignored by their co-religionists, regarded by other Pakistani Muslims as *jahil* (ignorant) and *jungli* (wild) on account of their African genes. Little has been written on their history and culture by Pakistan's intelligentsia. During the past sixty years there have been some famous Sheedi musicians, footballers and boxers; but no politicians, land-lords, generals or clerics – the traditional holders of power in Pakistani society. Instead, the majority of Pakistan's one million or so Sheedis still live in the small towns and villages to which their ancestors were brought as slaves, and the majority still work as labourers.

The next morning, I stand in Iqbal's office in Badin town – which doubles as a Sheedi meeting-place and tea-drinking stop – looking at the photograph which hangs there of a tomb. Garlands of red roses have been draped along the grave; the pale yellow stone, now badly chipped, was once carefully chiselled with sharp architraves and floral swirls. Before the tomb is a chubby toddler dressed in a white shalwar kameez, his skin dark and smooth as a lychee stone.

The photograph was taken in Hyderabad eighteen years ago. Today, the small boy, Awais, is by my side: still wearing a shalwar kameez, but twenty years old now, and six feet tall. As for the tomb, it has changed beyond recognition, blandly renovated to reflect its incumbent's new fame as the hero of Sindh's freedom struggle. Nowadays it is enclosed within a concrete shed, and the yellow stone flowers have been smoothed grey with cement. On the black and white placard propped up against the stone is a clue to the tomb's new importance. It reads:

Shahid Sindh General Hosh Mohammed Sheedi ko khirayitah Sindh
(Martyr of Sindh, General Hosh Muhammad Sheedi, Sindh salutes you)

General Hosh Muhammad Sheedi was killed on 24 March 1843, in the final, bitter confrontation between the Talpurs and the British. He was buried where he fell, on a battleground north of Hyderabad, and for over a hundred years his grave stood untended and unnoticed by the local population, next to those of the other battle dead, including the British. Then, in the mid-1980s, when Sindhi nationalists were searching their history for indigenous champions to unite them against the immigrant Urdu-speaking Mohajirs, somebody thought of honouring the last anti-imperial defender of Sindh. Hosh Muhammad was seized upon and promoted as a local hero.

What the Sindhis didn't seem to notice was that, like their Mohajir enemies, Hosh Muhammad was of immigrant descent too: from Africa.

Little is known about Hosh Muhammad Sheedi's life. He was born a slave into the ruling Talpur family, joined the Sindhi army and was quickly promoted to General. When the British invaded, and the Talpur forces in upper Sindh capitulated, it was Hosh Muhammad who rallied Sindh's army in the south with the patriotic cry, '*Marveso marveso par Sindh na deso*: I will fight and fight but I will never give up Sindh.' In a country where, since 1947, not one Sheedi has become an army officer, the story of Hosh Muhammad's rise from slave to army commander is a damning testament to the fact that before British rule, African slaves were highly regarded and given positions of power.

Today, Lower Sindh, or Lar, the land between Hyderabad and

Thatta, is the home of South Asia's largest African-descended population, and by the time Hosh Muhammad Sheedi died, it had been
at the centre of a maritime trade, in black slaves and other goods,
between Africa and India for centuries. The people of the lower
Indus valley were trading with Mesopotamia five thousand years ago
and with Africa since at least the time of Pliny (in the first century
CE). The slave trade itself was age-old within Africa; but it was Arabs
who, even before the time of the Prophet Muhammad, first developed the trade out of the country. Then came Islam, with its
single-minded conquests and trans-oceanic merchant networks, and
the business spread from Arabia to the Iberian coast, from East Africa
to South Asia.

Islam had a complex relationship with slavery. As in the Bible,
slaves were an important part of the Qur'an's social system –
Muhammad himself sold the Jewish women of Medina into slavery
– and the Qur'an, which has a rule for everything, scripted a strict
code regarding their treatment. Slaves were not objects, but human
beings, and they were to be considered as part of the family. Although
the East African slave trade was vicious and brutal, even in the cruel
nineteenth century it appears not to have reached the extremes of
the Christian-run Atlantic trade from West Africa to the Americas.
One reason for this may have been that sellers and buyers were
Muslim. In Islam, good treatment of slaves incurred heavenly benefits for the owner. Freeing a 'believing slave' was regarded as so pious
that it negated the sin of killing a Muslim accidentally. Prophet
Muhammad set the example, venerating Bilal with the nickname –
in terms a trifle patronizing to Bilal's homeland – 'the first fruit of
Ethiopia'.

As a result of this close and paternal relationship between owner
and slave, Islamic societies, wherever they grew up, made slaves a
central feature of society. Slaves were not just a silent underclass,
as in ancient Greece or the Americas, but often became an elite,
with responsibility as soldiers, advisers or generals, and power over
free persons. From the ninth century onwards, slave armies and
administrations became one of the defining characteristics of Islamic
polities.

The armies of Islam recruited slaves widely from wherever Muslim soldiers marched – lower Sindh, the Eurasian steppes, Africa. Africans, in particular, became extremely popular in Muslim states, from Spain to Persia. The tenth-century Baghdad Caliph had seven thousand black eunuchs (and four thousand white ones). African women were renowned as good cooks; the eunuchs were trustworthy servants. Then there was the aesthetic consideration: being surrounded by black servants made the master's complexion seem paler. Black slaves served a similar role in Europe, where, as one English writer put it in 1675: '[A Towne Misse] hath always two necessary Implements about her, a Blackamoor, and a little Dog, for without these she would be neither Fair, nor Sweet.'

As Islam's reach into Africa deepened, and the number of black slaves being exported to Arabia increased, so did Arab racism about Africans. Some historians trace this to the revolt by black slaves working in the mines and plantations of Mesopotamia, in 883 CE. But in his last sermon the Prophet made the dubious point that 'no white has [priority] over a black except in righteousness' – and perhaps it was this that licensed Arabs to export two million sub-Saharan slaves between 900 and 1100.

Like the Christian slave traders – who ransacked the Bible in search of passages denigrating blacks – Islamic traders found justification in the 'Hamitic hypothesis' that Noah had cursed his son Ham to have black-skinned descendants who would be forever the servants of non-blacks. The Arabs also adopted the racism of the places they conquered. The Zoroastrianism of Persia pitted light against dark in a manner that easily mutated from the abstract to the epidermal; pejorative categories such as '*barbara*' were enlisted from the Greek; and Arabic translations were made of the works of Galen, the Roman physician who wrote that the black man had a 'defective brain'. Important Muslim thinkers such as al-Masudi and Avicenna seem to have taken his words seriously. It is the sight of a black slave topping his fair queen which prompts King Shahryar's uxoricide in *The Thousand and One Nights* – the juxtaposition between black and white became a favourite aesthetic of Arabic literature.

When the first Muslim-Arab army arrived on the shores of Sindh in 711 CE, it arrived with plenty of African slaves, and these stereotypes intact. But in India – a continent with a huge variety of human skin types – the polarity could not function so smoothly. India had its own dark-skinned population and its own non-African slaves. Arab prejudices were at times reinforced by local conditions, at others dissolved.

Four centuries later, when Islam expanded permanently into India, immigrant Muslim kings – themselves descended from Turkish slaves – ruled over a native population of Hindus. Now it was the Hindu who became negatively associated with blackness, in comparison to the fair Turkish warrior. While Jewish and Christian commentators had assumed that the slave children fathered by Ham, Noah's unlucky son, were Africans, Ferishta, the Persian historian, now added the peoples of 'Hind' and 'Sind' as well.

The Indians, in their turn, sometimes found the colouring of their conquerors abhorrent. A Kashmiri Hindu recoiled in horror on beholding the pale Ghurid ambassador, a Muslim from Afghanistan:

> it was almost as if the colour black had shunned him in fear of being stained by his bad reputation . . . so ghastly white he was, whiter than bleached cloth, whiter than the snow of the Himalayan region where he was born.

The difference in skin colour between the ruling Muslim kings and the native population persisted through the Mughal era, such that when European travellers began exploring India in the seventeenth century, they understood the word 'Mughal' to mean white: 'The word Mogull in their language is as much [as] to say the great white king,' wrote Robert Coverte in 1612.

India's immigrant Muslim rulers, meanwhile, considering Africans more loyal than indigenous servants, encouraged slave galleys to bring ever more Africans to India in fetters. In direct contrast to the Atlantic slave trade – where huge numbers of African men were purchased to work on the sugar plantations in the Americas – Asia, which already had a large agrarian population, needed twice as many women as men. Presumably these African women were used as concubines, servants, wet nurses and cooks. But the record is silent about what happened to them (an example, perhaps, of the far greater assimilation of the slave race here than in the Americas).

Elite male Africans, however, were highly visible. In Delhi, the convention of African slaves being given positions at court reached its dramatic climax in 1240 when Razia – the city's first and only female sultan – was deposed for having an affair with her Ethiopian slave minister, Yaqut.

Razia, herself the product of a Turkish slave dynasty, was an unusual woman who refused to marry, wore 'manly garb', and rode a horse, all of which shocked the conservative clergy. It was her extramarital affair with an African slave, though, which led to her deposition. In the early fourteenth century, Ibn Battuta, a Moroccan trader and writer who stayed in the city after her death, repeated the Delhi gossip, that 'she was suspected of relations with a slave of hers, one of the Abyssinians, so the people agreed to depose her and marry her to a husband.' Africans could hold places of honour, but there was a line beyond which they were not allowed in tread. Yaqut was executed.

Nevertheless, after Yaqut there were many more African slave rulers in India. A fourteenth-century Sultan of Delhi had a black vizier who was elected governor in eastern India. The governor's adopted black son then became an independent ruler who struck his own coinage. Throughout the fifteenth century there were black slave soldiers all over India, from the Deccan to Bengal. Two hundred years later, the Portuguese sailor João de Castro noted that Ethiopian soldiers were proverbially reliable throughout the country, and that Indian armies were always commanded by Africans. In the early seventeenth century, Malik Ambar, a slave from Ethiopia, grew so powerful in central-southern India that he assembled his own army and successfully defeated the Mughal emperor Akbar's attempt to take over the region. (In Lyari, I was even told that the south Indian ruler, Tipu Sultan, was a Sheedi.) And in 1858, when the British besieged mutinous Lucknow, they found themselves being fired upon by the Nawab's richly dressed African eunuchs, whose 'skill, as marksmen', wrote William Russell, war correspondent for *The Times*, 'caused us great loss'.

In Mughal India, Africans were also sailors of repute. Ibn Battuta had already observed that they were renowned as the 'guarantors of safety' on the Indian Ocean, and as late as the seventeenth century, African admirals worked for the Mughal empire on prestigious salaries. Janjira, an island near Bombay, was colonized by African sailors in 1100 and they continued to control much of the trade off the west coast for the next six hundred years. In the seventeenth century, the Marathas in western India attempted unsuccessfully to defeat them; and it took the British until the early nineteenth century to stop the African presence hampering their colonial designs. Seth Naomal, the Hindu trader who helped the British take Karachi, referred to the period of 'Shidi rule' in Bombay – indicating that Africans wielded not inconsiderable power, in local memory at least, as late as the nineteenth century.

Early English travellers remarked upon the phenomenon of African influence in India with some awe. In 1698, John Fryer noted that Africans were offered some of 'the Chief Employments' in India; 'Frizled Woolly-pated Blacks', he wrote, were given 'great Preferments'. In 1772, John Henry Grose remarked that Ethiopian slaves were 'highly valued' by Indo-Muslim rulers 'for their courage, fidelity, and shrewdness; in which they so far excel, as often to rise to posts of great trust and honor, and are made governors of places'. Since many Muslim kings in India were themselves from slave dynasties, Grose observed, they treat their African slaves with 'great humanity, and bind them to faithful and even affectionate service, by their tenderness and next to parental care of them'. But during the nineteenth century, after the British took over the running of large parts of India, this legacy was suppressed. 'European historians,' E. Denison Ross observed in his *Arabic History of Gujarat* (1910), 'have failed to attach significant importance to the part played by the Habshis in the history of that country.'

This is borne out by British ethnographic writing on Sindh. When the British began to explore what is now southern Pakistan, they found that along the coast 'no family of any consideration was without male and female slaves, and the greater number of Sidis, or negroes, came from Muscat.' Freeing the slaves of the Talpurs – whom the British had just evicted – was repeatedly presented as colonialism's justification, its great moral crusade, a distraction from the crime of conquering the country.

With Britain as the ruling administration, however, the perception of Africans worsened. Richard Burton, the traveller and explorer, was a young soldier in Sindh during the early days of British rule there. In 1848, he wrote a report for the Bombay Government in which he noted under the section *Slaves* that 'Formerly great numbers of Zanzibarees, Bombasees, and Hubshees (Abyssinians) &c. found their way into Sind . . . All of them are celebrated for their thievish, drunken, and fighting propensities.' Three years later, in his book on Sindh, *The Unhappy Valley*, he described a Sheedi dance at the Muslim shrine at Manghopir (now in north Karachi). The 'bevy of African dames', he wrote, have 'uncomely limbs' and dance with 'all the grace of a Punjaub bear'; the men howl 'like maniacs' and drum with 'all the weight of their monstrous muscular arms'. Burton's prejudices surfaced again in his book, *Sind Revisited* (1877), in which he dismissed the African admirals of Janjira as 'pirates' and 'sea-Thugs'.

Burton's jottings were typical of the unpalatable British colonial reaction to Africans in India. Where an Indian might have associated an African aristocrat or slave with the long history of African presence there, British imperial servants – seeing them as threats, or perhaps simply as cogs in a racist colonial endeavour – voiced prejudice and suspicion. The British abolished slavery, but it is possible that one of the effects of a hundred years of British rule was the decline in status of black people in India.

This deterioration is evident in the way the word 'Sheedi' – which has no plain etymology in Arabic or any Indian language – was interpreted over the centuries. In the eighteenth century, John Henry Grose explained that 'Siddee' was the title given by Indian Muslim rulers to those Ethiopian slaves whom they had elected as governors – an honorific. But Burton's 1851 spelling of the word – 'Seedy' – is innately uncomplimentary; and in 1877, when he used the variant spelling 'Sidi', he implied that it was a term of abuse. In Sindh today, most people will tell you that Sheedi means 'black' or 'African' or even 'slave'. One Western academic has speculated that it derives from the Arabic *shaydâ*, 'fool' or 'senseless'. Al-Habsh, a semi-defunct Sheedi cultural group in Hyderabad, perhaps embarrassed by the negative connotations attributed to the word, claims in a Sindhi-language pamphlet that it means nothing at all. In Badin, however, Iqbal's uncle gives me a proud and evocative etymology. Sheedi, he says, is a mutation of the Arabic word *Sahabi*: friend or companion of the Prophet. This is contentious, for an association with the Prophet is generally the privilege of Sindh's social and religious aristocracy. But the Sheedis think of themselves as the kinspeople of Bilal; and it was to him, after all, that the Prophet said '*Ya Sahabi*', my companion.

Even after the British conquered Sindh and banned slavery, the trade persisted. As late as 1890, when Alexander Baillie wrote his book on Karachi, an English boat captured a man-of-war with twenty-five slaves on board. In his autobiography, the Hindu merchant Seth Naomal recalled how he had offered to find four thousand fighting men from Zanzibar to supplement British troops in Karachi during the 1857 'Mutiny' in north India. Whether the Zanzibaris were slaves or mercenaries, he didn't say. But his comment is an example of just how closely Sindhi and Gujarati traders like Naomal were involved in the trade as middlemen, and had been for centuries.

Whereas Africans were assimilated by Islamic societies, there was no place for them in Hinduism, and very few African slaves became Hindus. Anybody outside the caste system – especially one with dark skin and tightly curled hair – was a *mleccha*, a barbarian. Today, as any Indian or Pakistani mother with a daughter of marriageable age can tell you, the northern subcontinent is a morbidly skin-colour conscious society. Thus 'Fair & Lovely' skin-lightening cream is available all over Pakistan, in villages beyond the reach of tarmac and buses, in even the most scantily stocked tea-shacks. In the Classified Ads section of India's national newspapers, girls and boys of 'fair' or 'wheaten' complexion are demanded and proffered. '*Gori gori gori*' (fair-skinned girl) sing the heroes of Bollywood films; and girls all across Pakistan sit up and take note.

I vividly remember the first time I saw Bollywood playing racism for laughs. Six years ago, I was sitting in the Eros cinema in Delhi watching *Hadh kar di apne*, a Bollywood B-movie, with an Indian friend, when on to the set lumbered two parody Africans. Clumsily made up in black face-paint and Afro wigs, they towered menacingly over the diminutive Indian actress and attempted to rape her. Her screams brought the rotund Indian hero running to her rescue, and as the audience cheered, he threw the Africans to the ground and kicked them into submission. The hero and heroine swooned into each other's arms and exited back to the main narrative; the 'Africans' disappeared as suddenly as they had come.

In the Bombay film industry, stereotypes of primitivism have long been a staple. Song and dance routines use African or Indian 'tribals' as objects of parody and exoticism. Even in the twenty-first century, 'Africans' (usually blacked-up Indian actors) make pantomime appearances. Pakistan's cinema industry is currently even cruder; but the films made there are generally so bad, and Bollywood's dominance of Pakistan's cable TV channels so complete, that they play to near empty houses.

More popular in Pakistan than Lahore's own movies is the 1983 film made by the Indian director Kamal Amrohi of the Razia Sultana story. Watching a pirate copy bought in Karachi's Rainbow Bazaar, I am bemused to see that the Punjabi film star Dharmendra was cast as Yaqut the Ethiopian. During the course of the film, Dharmendra's famously pale complexion waxes and wanes. In tender love scenes, he is fair and lovely as usual; only when his character is angry or anxious does his skin colour darken. It is almost as if the film-makers could not countenance a black romantic lead – only a black character as victim or threat. Towards the end of the film, Razia's minister denounces her relationship with Yaqut as a 'blemish on Turks. We Turks are white. Our blood too is white. Turks will never agree to an alliance with a black. This Turk girl thinks that Yaqut is a human being.' The film was presumably meant as a critique of such racism, but with its ambivalent portrayal of Yaqut it did little to counteract the Bollywood stereotype.

Bollywood's pale-hued aesthetic, of course, is merely a reflection of India's ancient prejudice. The Sanskrit law books of classical Hinduism, and those of the Jains and Buddhists, proscribe contact between the upper and low 'black' castes. In the nineteenth century, when European scholars began translating India's oldest Sanskrit text, the Rig Veda, some read into it a primordial clash between the immigrant authors (the *arya*, hence Aryans) and the indigenous population. In his *History of India* (1920), Vincent Smith canonized this image with a description typical of imperial racism that contrasts the colonizing Aryans ('tall, fair, long-nosed and handsome') with the 'aborigines' ('short, dark, snub-nosed and ugly').

The Rig Veda theory has long since been discredited, partly because this ancient text is simply too obscure and abstruse to deliver neat hypotheses, but also because the Europeans appeared to be reading their own racism and colonizing project into a literature arguably innocent of such intentions. Even in the nineteenth century there were some scholars who were by no means sure that the references to the enemy's 'blackness' meant their skin. Could the authors of the Rig Veda be referring to the clouds, or the night, or the 'spirits of darkness'? Perhaps they were asking their god to chase away the rain clouds from their grazing pastures. But the damage had been done: the clash of skin colour predicated between two sectors of India's population invaded the national psyche. With ancient Hindu skin-colour consciousness, immigrant Muslim superiority and British racial stereotyping, attitudes to skin colour in India were never simple.

It is unsurprising, then, that in south India, where the population speak non-Sanskrit-based languages and skin tone is generally darker than in the north, a movement has grown up portraying Indian history in those old colonial terms, as a clash between white invaders and black aborigines. The 'Dravidians', as they call themselves in the south, draw explicit parallels between their own perceived plight two thousand years ago, and those of African slaves in the Americas. A controversial Internet polemic, *The Bible of Aryan Invasions*, calls upon 'Dravidians all across the world . . . to realize that their suffering at the hands of Caucasoids did not start in the eighteenth century with the rise of plantation slavery in the South, but dates back several centuries and started with the Aryan invasion of India'.

If Indian racism was rooted in the caste system, and reinforced by British colonialism, then it would follow that the creation of an independent, caste-free Islamic country in 1947 should have simpli-fied life for Sheedis. But many of the Mohajirs who migrated into the country at Partition considered themselves to be of Turkish, Arabic or Persian stock, and the racism with which they regarded the indigenous populations – the more populous Bengalis far away to the east of India, as well as the local Sindhis – is well documented. And so, while as Muslims in an Islamic country the process of assimi-lation should have been fairly easy for Pakistan's Sheedis, because of their African features they were often treated with derision.

Today, Sheedis are divided on the issue of their African descent. In Sindh – where a 'Black Power' movement briefly flourished in the 1960s – Sheedis are proud to be black; proud, as Iqbal says, that their physical appearance links them to a worldwide community of 'African brothers and sisters'.

But things are different for the Negroid Makrani population along the Baluchistan coast, west of Karachi. Initial scientific research on a small sample group of these people showed a weak link – 12 per cent of paternal Y-chromosomes – to sub-Saharan Africa. (If it is true, however, that women were the subcontinent's slave majority, and that 'mixed' Sheedis often have a non-Sheedi paternal heritage, analysis of maternal mitochondrial DNA would have made more sense.) Whatever their exact genetic make-up, the Negroid Makranis who have intermarried with local tribes, taken local names and adopted local customs, prefer to forget, ignore or deny their ancestors' origins. Partly, this reflects the extent to which they have been assimilated into Baluchi society. But it is also symptomatic of the stigma that Negroid features carry in this society.

In Karachi, a Baluch-Sheedi friend, Khuda Ganj, offers to help me investigate the city's African history. He takes me on the back of his turquoise Vespa through Lyari, where he lives, to meet a local journalist. 'His mother,' says Khuda Ganj, 'was a Sheedi. Maybe he can tell you about Sheedi culture.' Khuda Ganj's own interests lie more with economic than racial emancipation. 'Fifteen years ago my house was a Communist cell,' he shouts back at me as we veer round a corner, swerve to avoid a chicken and skim across an open sewer.

We arrive at the aptly named Mombasa Street, where the journalist lives, and are ushered into his office. But it soon becomes clear that the journalist does not consider himself to be a Sheedi, despite his maternal heritage. He quickly loses his temper with my questions. 'We never use the word "Sheedi",' he says. 'Culturally, linguistically, these people are Baluch. In Sindh they call themselves Sindhis. African culture has no relevance. Some people have a vested interest in being "Sheedi" in order to get government benefits. This is their racket. Why are you studying these things? Why are you highlighting black people? I am fed up with black issues.'

Dismissing my question about Mombasa Street with an impatient wave of his hand, he says: 'This whole area of Lyari is called "Baghdadi". My people migrated from Baghdad, Syria, the Middle East. Not from Africa.'

I climb back on to Khuda Ganj's scooter, and we drive on, to visit another friend of his, a Communist party member with pictures of Che Guevara all over his sitting-room walls. 'You must go into the interior,' the Communist says (meaning rural Sindh, as it is known to city-dwellers). 'In Badin town you will find Sheedis who are proud of their African heritage. There you can meet the descendants of Muhammad Siddiq, a Sheedi writer and educationalist known to his community by his pen-name, "Mussafir".'

So it is that early one morning I eventually take my leave of the fisherpeople I have been staying with in Thatta, and drive east through the threadbare settlements which line the road into the desert. My taxi arrives at high noon in Badin, a town of such pleasing diminutiveness that donkey carts and horse-drawn victorias are the only public transport and the Mubarak Bakery (with its salt-sweet cumin-flecked biscuits, bottles of pop and bundles of soap) is the smartest shop. It is in Badin that the modern network for Sheedis has converged under the auspices of the Young Sheedi Welfare Organization (YSWO), run by Iqbal and founded by Faiz Muhammad Bilali, a tall serious advocate, with a face as grave as his wife's smile is wide.

YSWO was started twenty years ago to improve the educational prospects of Sheedi children in the area. Back then only thirteen Sheedi children in Badin district went to school. (Iqbal was one of them.) Recently, and it is a measure of the community's success, YSWO has broadened its mandate to include any deprived social group in the vicinity, and there are plenty of those. In particular, it supports the Muslim and Hindu villagers whose livelihoods were ruined after the infamously expensive and faulty Indus drainage canal burst its mud banks in 2003 and poured industrial effluent and sewage all over their fields and homes. Here in Badin, the Indus is not known for its fecundity. It is known, rather, for its lack: for the impoverished trickle of water supplied to farmers through concrete canals, and for the hellish deluge of waste water that passes through the district on the way to the sea. (And thus each Badin home, including ours, receives diluted sewage as drinking water.)

When I arrive in Badin, I plan to be away from Thatta for a day. The Sheedis at YSWO, however, assume that I am staying throughout the marriage season – or at least until all girls of marriageable age in the office have been betrothed. They present me with a red tie-dyed shalwar kameez, see off my taxi driver, and I am ushered along the town's back streets to my new accommodation. 'But all my spare cash is in Thatta,' I say to Iqbal. 'We can lend you some money,' he says. 'Is there anything else you need?' Thus begins my residence in Badin, one that will last for five weeks, until the start of the Islamic month of Muharram.

I am to stay in the house of Faiz Muhammad Bilali, with his family of forty-four people: stepmother, siblings, spouses, offspring, and offspring's offspring. Faiz Muhammad is the eldest of three brothers, each of whom has a different surname, after the famous Africans of early Islam. Faiz Muhammad is 'Bilali' (from Bilal), his middle brother is 'Qambrani' (after the slave freed by Ali) and the youngest is 'Sheedi' (friend of the Prophet).

It is in this house that that I discover just how fundamental family relations are to people's lives in Sindh. Every time a visitor or friend from town is introduced to me, the varying degrees of separation from the Bilali house are laid out like a map – 'my uncle's wife's brother's daughter's husband'. If the house is the focal point of the social lives of forty-four people, the calm centre of this whirlwind is the grandmother, Addi Vilayat, whose own name means literally 'Sister from Abroad'. She sits all day in the large central courtyard, preparing food, drinking tea and greeting newcomers, as her three daughters-in-law and all their children swirl around her. Some of the household's women work as housewives; others pull burqas over their heads and walk through the streets of Badin to school, to their jobs in the Young Sheedi office, or to a women's sewing centre. The men come and go. At mealtimes they hover like hungry, forgotten ghosts – though once I witnessed a young father cooking his children dinner (a thing as rare in Pakistan as a free and fair election).

On my first day in the house, a thin mattress is unrolled from the pile on the verandah and laid out for me in the room where Addi Vilayat and four of Faiz Muhammad's daughters also sleep, between the wardrobe (where the girls' gold and silk wedding trousseaux are locked away) and the bathroom door, such is the pressure for space in this ever-expanding house. Then these teenage and twenty-something women sit me down in the shadow at the edge of the courtyard, so that our toes dabble in sunshine, and explain. 'Sheedis,' they say, using the English phrase, 'have *gender-balance*.' Men are known as 'the husband of so-and-so', not the other way round. Children can opt to take their mother's family name. 'My husband and I,' says Baby, a whip-thin woman coiffed in spangly combs and clips, 'live here in my parents' house.' Her husband is the ghostliest of the ghosts: he shares Baby's room, three doors down from mine, but in the weeks that I spend in the house, I never once meet him.

Elsewhere in the world, the proverbial cheerfulness of black people – the 'happy-go-lucky singing-dancing Negro' – has been derided as a stereotype, but it is in similar terms that Faiz Muhammad's daughters describe themselves to me. 'Leva is very important to us,' they say. 'It came from Africa. *Humein dukh nahin lagta* – we never feel sorrow – only laughter. Sindhi culture is so sad and gloomy; there are too many problems for women – *karokari* [honour-killing], dowry – but there is nothing like that here. We manage to ignore these things and be happy.'

Nevertheless, this is also a house of divergent, sometimes conflicting, interests. Faiz Muhammad Bilali has worked all his life for the social emancipation of his people, and is emphatic about the importance of the link between Sheedis and Africans elsewhere in the world. 'All our education and improvements in status are due to the work of Mussafir,' he says, referring to the man I was told about in Lyari. 'He instructed us to be proud of our African culture. Our grand-fathers used to know some African words. We still have our mugarman drum and songs. We support the West Indies in cricket and have read Nelson Mandela's book in the Sindhi translation. Muhammad Ali, *America ka King Luther* [Martin Luther King], Booker T. Washington, Kofi Annan: we think of these American Sheedis as our brothers. But the Sheedis in America went ahead, and we lagged behind. If it hadn't been for social injustice, Sheedi people would have risen higher. This is our great sadness.'

His middle brother, however, who spent many years working as a government clerk, has recently become a pious Wahhabi Muslim.

For the Wahhabi and his children, this purist form of Islam is their most important social marker. Every morning I am woken before dawn, as the Wahhabi marches around the house, banging on each dormitory door to wake the family for prayers. (Every morning the women in my dormitory roll over and go back to sleep.)

For some of the Wahhabi's eight children, Africanness is a source of shame, not pride. Ever since the youngest daughter was eleven years old, she and her sisters have been using skin-lightening cream; they aspire to transcend the boundaries of Pakistani society by changing their skin colour. Their brother, who has a comparatively lucrative job on a nearby British Petroleum oilfield, set the example by marrying a fair-skinned non-Sheedi girl: 'I do not want to be ashamed of my wife wherever I go,' his cousins tell me he said. There is general exclamation among these girls when I say that 'Sheedis' in America and Europe call themselves 'black': 'To us it is an insult.' They look up to Michael Jackson, a 'world-famous Sheedi', but also a Sheedi who has successfully obliterated his African image.

Although Faiz Muhammad's daughters are proud of their blackness, even they at times succumb to the monolithic Pakistani ideal of beauty. When the eldest daughter comes to be married, every evening for weeks leading up to the ceremonies, she bleaches the skin on face, hands and feet (those parts of her body which will be visible beneath her wedding garments). A pale bride is an obligation for the family – even if everyone knows it is fake. 'It is only for the marriage photos,' she says apologetically; 'otherwise I will be laughed at for my blackness.'

All month, in preparation for the wedding, the girls strut around the courtyard, practising Bollywood dance songs. Although Faiz Muhammad speaks enthusiastically about the mugarman drum, there are no plans to have one at his daughter's wedding. Nor will they be dancing the leva, as at the village wedding I went to with Iqbal. The family does not own a mugarman drum. Nobody in Badin does. 'You will have to go to Tando Bago to find one,' says Iqbal. Then he adds: 'You can visit the tomb of Mussafir while you are there. It is as important for Sheedis as that of Hosh Muhammad in Hyderabad.'

Rural Tando Bago – a village thirty kilometres to the north-east – is at the other end of the spectrum from Sheedi social advancement in urbane Badin. Here there are old men and women who can still remember words and songs in African languages; who play the mugarman; and who tell stories of their ancestors' journeys. Yet the caste system is entrenched: Tando Bago's Sheedis work only as labourers, and live in Kandri Paro, a ghetto set apart from the houses of their fair-skinned employers.

I drive to Tando Bago with Kulsoom, Iqbal's wife, who was born there. The houses in Kandri Paro are small and cramped, made of tumble-down brick, and without the spacious courtyards found in the rest of the village. They open directly on to the street: the women sit at their front doors, peeling vegetables and calling out to their neighbours. It does not take long to find the one man in Kandri Paro with a mugarman. He plays it for me, but half-heartedly: the buffalo skin on the top is ripped, and it will take them months to raise the funds to repair it.

Kulsoom leads me along the main street to visit Tando Bago's oldest and most venerable resident. Mianji Phoota claims to be one hundred years old. He sits bolt upright outside his rickety brick house, with its unkempt thatched roof, on a sagging charpay bed. Kulsoom and I sit on a charpay facing him. 'Our community began,' he says, 'with a wife and husband who came from Africa as slaves. All they had was a drum. They don't know where they had come from, only that they had been bought by the Talpurs. The wife was made the wet nurse of the Talpur children. They were our ancestors.'

From the neighbouring house, octogenarian Papu calls out: 'My people knew where they came from – Zanzibar.' Later she says, 'In those days blackness was a sign of poorness.' Sheedis inter-married only with the other poor castes: the Mallahs (fisherpeople), the Khaskeli (labourers), the Katri (dyeing caste) and Kori (cloth-makers); hence the 'mixed' Sheedis, like Iqbal's wife, with their straight noses and lighter skin. 'But we say that as long as your hair is curled you are a Sheedi,' says Papu, stroking Kulsoom's coiled locks.

Papu's assertion, that her ancestors came from Zanzibar, is matched by several academic studies linking East and Southern African culture with the subcontinent's Sheedi communities. A North American musicologist found that an African family in the Deccan, India, sang an old folksong identical to one she had recorded in Tanzania. There are some known Swahili-language survivals among the 'Black Sidis' of Gujarat in India; and Sheedi tribal names from Sindh, recorded by Richard Burton in the nineteenth century, have been linked to Swahili-speaking tribes. The four-footed mugarman drum, unique in the subcontinent, is considered to be a relative of the *ngoma* drum from Zimbabwe. Even Mali enters the picture. In Lyari, Khuda Ganj played me the music of Ali Farka Touré, which has recently become popular with Sheedis there because its rhythms are considered similar to those played by Pakistan's famous Sheedi musicians such as the late Bilawal Beljium.

Kulsoom tries to encourage Papu to speak in African *boli* (language). 'When I was little our elders would talk like this,' she says: '"*Makoti*" meant bread, "*magera*" meant money. "*Magera hakoona*," they would say when someone was going down to the shops, "There isn't any money."' (Some of these words are pure Swahili – *kate*: 'bread'; *hakuna*: 'there is none'.) Instead, Papu begins to sing. It is a song in Sindhi about a woman called Mai Maisira:

> *Mai Maisira bagh banaya,*
> *Lima archaar le*
> *Heman manga hera thera*
> *Heman manga re.*

In Gujarat, Mai Mishra is revered by Sheedis as a saint, a woman who travelled from Africa to Mecca to India with her two brothers to do what they were unable to do, and defeat a demoness. But the story seems to have been forgotten in Pakistan. When Kulsoom asks Papu, 'What does the song mean?' the old woman pulls her printed cotton shawl over her head, and says, 'Nobody can remember.'

I have also come to Tando Bago to find out about Mussafir, the writer and teacher whom Faiz Muhammad Bilali, and all other vocal Sheedis in Badin, call 'the true liberator of our community'. Faiz Muhammad was awarded a place by Mussafir at the high school he ran in Tando Bago. 'He allowed my parents to get into arrears with the fees of four annas a month,' Faiz Muhammad has told me. 'We Sheedis owe everything to Mussafir. He not only gave us a good education, he gave us awareness. Without him we would still be working in the fields for the Syeds.'

Mussafir lived and died in Tando Bago, and Kulsoom and I walk to the overgrown village graveyard to visit his white-and-blue-tiled tomb. Nobody from Kandri Paro has time to come with us. 'Where are his descendants?' I ask as we leave; but their answers are non-committal: 'They have gone away to Hyderabad city.'

That night, Kulsoom and I travel back to Badin. As soon as we reach home, I ask Faiz Muhammad: 'Please may I see Mussafir's books?' But Faiz Muhammad turns his palms upwards in a sorrowful gesture – he no longer owns any. Nor are there any, I discover the next day, in the local library. Iqbal eventually finds a first edition of Mussafir's influential 1952 study of slavery in one of his cupboards, but it has been nibbled down the right-hand margin by mice, and warped by the monsoon. Nevertheless, I have been told enough now to know that this book – printed on crumbling yellow paper, in cramped Sindhi script – is the key to understanding the evolution of Sheedi culture. We slowly begin work on a rudimentary transla-tion. Days pass, and then one day Ali Akbar, who works in the office, sees me bent over the fragile volume. 'Do you want to meet Mussafir's son?' he says. 'He is married to my sister.' I look up in astonishment: it is as if I have been let into the Sheedis' inner sanctum. At last, the chance to meet somebody with memories of Mussafir – the archi-tect of Sheedi identity, the man whom all Sheedis credit with 'bringing our people up'. In a state of some excitement, I board the bus to Hyderabad, Sindh's former capital, one hundred kilometres away to the north.

I have been to the city several times, but never to this convoluted old quarter with its streets too tiny for cars to pass along, lined by black drains dotted with piles of rubbish as bright as marigold garlands – coriander stalks, milk sachets, mango skins (waiting there, I find out later, for the proud Hindu sweeper who calls himself 'Flower' to come by and collect them). As we approach the house, I hear rhythmic, hypnotic singing coming from the mosque. It is a sound that I will get to know well over the next few weeks – a dirge for Muharram, the month of mourning for Shias. Bazmi, Mussafir's only son (his one daughter is dead), lives with his two wives and their nine children in a modest, sparsely furnished house; a sanctuary of cleanliness and light at the end of a long claustrophobic alleyway.

When we arrive at the house I am shocked to discover that Bazmi cannot speak, read or write. For years, he worked as a teacher and poet, but a decade ago he suffered a stroke that left him unable to communicate verbally. We sit in his bedroom exchanging gestures and words of frustration and sympathy. Bazmi sends his daughter Ani – a slender, self-composed woman who, like her parents, is working as a teacher – to unlock his library. 'My father wishes that he could tell you the stories and histories of our Sheedi people,' she says, interpreting Bazmi's wordless grunts and hand signals for me. 'He is sorry that he cannot talk to you about my grandfather. But these,' she hands me two books, 'contain some of our family history.'

Bazmi's original library was kept in the village, but it was destroyed by a cyclone, and almost all the copies of his father's works were lost. Today, only one library in Pakistan contains a copy of Mussafir's study of slavery, and it seems that only Bazmi owns an edition of Mussafir's autobiography. I look at the two books Ani has placed in my hands. They are like a forgotten memory, or a fast-fading dream; the vestiges of a history that may soon be entirely lost.

Bazmi's two wives and four daughters, surprised and pleased to meet somebody who wants to know about Mussafir, invite me to stay; and grateful for the chance to talk about the history of black slavery in Pakistan, I accept. During the three weeks that I spend in Bazmi's house, Ani and her sisters work on me in significant ways: by the time I leave their house to travel on up the river, my sartorial disarray has been corrected by tactical purchases from the Silk Bazaar; I have been taught how to cook a simple dal with lemon; I know that Ani wears her burqa to visit the tailor but not when she walks to college; and I understand more about the priorities of an educated but economically straitened family in Pakistan. I also have a deeper understanding of the world of good, well-behaved, God-fearing Muslim girls.

I make friends with Ani on the very first night, as we sit up together, reading Mussafir's autobiography. Bazmi normally keeps his books locked away, too sad even to look at them now that he cannot read, and Ani has never been given the chance to explore her family's history. She is as apprehensive as I am about what her grandfather's autobiography might contain. Like all Mussafir's books, the autobiography was written in Sindhi, and like all of them, it has never been translated into Urdu, English or any other language before. But by midnight – with Ani reading the book in Sindhi, rendering it into Urdu, and me writing down the English translation – we have managed to read Mussafir's tale of his father's transition from slavery to freedom, with which the autobiography begins.

'Mussafir' was Muhammad Siddiq's pen-name – the word means 'traveller': a veiled allusion to his own father's forced emigration out of Africa. Both Mussafir and Bazmi were born when their fathers were extremely old. Encapsulated in Mussafir's autobiography, then, is the history of the past two hundred years – 'from the time of slavery,' as Mussafir writes, 'to the time of freedom'.

Mussafir's father was born in Zanzibar in approximately 1793. When he was five or six years old, his entire family was killed by a rival tribe and he alone sold into slavery. He remembered being taken down to the sea by the victors and put on to a ship. Eventually the ship docked at Muscat on the Arabian coast, where a trader, Sheikh Hussain, bought the whole human cargo. The Sheikh sold on every other slave except Mussafir's father – 'and that,' wrote Mussafir, 'was his good luck'.

The Sheikh gave his Zanzibari slave boy a new and significant name: Bilal. (Presumably this also marked the moment of Bilal's conversion to Islam.) Two years later, Sheikh Hussain sold Bilal to a trader from Sindh, who took him by boat along the coast and up the Indus to Thatta. There he was bought by a stonemason who had just been commissioned to build a fort for a member of the ruling Talpur clan, in Tando Bago (a building which later became Mussafir's high school). Once they arrived in the village, the stonemason sold Bilal on to Hour Ali, a childless nobleman.

So began Bilal's life as a Sindhi. For the first time since leaving Zanzibar, wrote Mussafir, 'my father was happy'. Hour Ali's wife educated Bilal, teaching him how to fast and pray. When Bilal grew up, Hour Ali purchased an African woman to be his wife.

Then in 1843 the British banned slavery. Hour Ali freed Bilal, but he was so fond of his former slave that he built him a house at the bottom of his garden and asked him to stay. By now, Bilal was fifty years old. He was elected leader of the local Sheedi *panchayat*, the community's decision-making body, with seven nearby villages under his charge. The only vexation was that of issue: his wife had given birth to eighteen children, all of whom had died in infancy. Soon afterwards, his wife died too. When he was sixty years old, Bilal married again, and his second wife had twelve children in her turn. Of these only the youngest survived. This was Mussafir.

The story that Mussafir tells of his father's life is full of hope, luck and triumph. Mussafir, too, led a fortunate life. Born in 1879, when his father was eighty-six years old, he made friends as a child with Mir Ghulam Muhammad, heir of the local Talpur clan. Together, they changed the social prospects of Badin's Sheedis. Mir Ghulam had no children and plenty of money, and Mussafir persuaded him to open a school for Sheedis – including, for the first time in Pakistan's history, education for Sheedi girls.

Mussafir felt the sufferings of his people deeply. In his 1952 book on slavery, published in Sindhi as *Ghulami ain Azadi Ja Ibratnak Nazara* (Eye-opening Accounts of Slavery and Freedom), he described how 'Sheedis have suffered such persecution that all the windows of tenderness and kindness were closed to them.' The book is a polemic, informed both by the 'shivering and miserable tales of slavery' that Mussafir heard first hand from his elders, and by his own wider reading on the global slave trade.

The history of black people in America was a big influence on Mussafir. He wrote about abolitionists such as William Wilberforce, and included moving histories of the American slave leaders, Frederick Douglass and Booker T. Washington. Sheedis in Pakistan, he pointed out, should be grateful: 'it is a fact that the cruelty and hatred which was suffered by the Sheedi slaves of America, was not endured by Sheedis in Sindh.'

The stories that Mussafir collected from his people, however, could hardly have been more distressing. One particularly horrific account was related to him by two slaves from Tando Bago, who escaped mutilation, forced cannibalism and death in Muscat. They described being shunted into a slave factory, where the healthiest males were picked out and killed in front of the other slaves by a blow to the head. Their bodies were placed in huge cauldrons, and cooked to extract a 'special medicine', and the discarded flesh was given to the remaining slaves to eat. The two men from Tando Bago were saved from death when a guard took pity on them, feeding them a handful of salt to bring on sickness. Instead of being killed, they were sold to a trader from the Indus.

Other Sheedis told more mundane stories of ritual humiliation. A woman in Tando Bago described to Mussafir how, as a young woman, she was made to stand all day with a pot of food on her head so that her master's favourite camel could eat without bending down its head to the ground. Most Sheedis toiled 'severely' in the fields, regardless of the weather. A few lucky ones – such as Mussafir's father – chanced upon a kind master. Contrary to the academic picture of Hindu slavers, Mussafir stressed that Hindu businessmen cared for their slaves with particular 'softness and kindness'.

Because he was poor, Mussafir ghost-wrote books for a rich businessman but altogether twenty-five books were published under his own name: texts on Islam, translations of Urdu and Farsi novels, a biography of the Sindhi writer Mirza Qalich Beg, and a book, *Sughar Zaloon*, about wise women.

It was his book on Sheedis, though, which made him well known. It was a bold endeavour, and it ended with a series of appeals – to the Sheedi community, to Pakistan's Muslims, ministers, newspaper editors and educationalists – proposing an agenda to lift Sheedis out of poverty and illiteracy. The Prophet showed respect for Sheedis, wrote Mussafir, and so should every Muslim in this country.

Mussafir's emphasis on education as a means of social emancipation has been a blessing, but it has also caused a rift between Mussafir's descendants and the Sheedis in Tando Bago. Like his father and grandfather, Bazmi was the Sheedi's community leader. In the 1970s, he coined a slogan in Sindhi, *Paro ya Maro*: Read or Die. Sheedis are renowned in Sindh as musicians, wrestlers and dancers; they also make a trade as comics, or 'joke-masters' at weddings. Bazmi felt that this was demeaning – he wanted Sheedis to be known for more than just sport or entertainment – and so he held a meeting at which he urged them not to work as servants in other people's houses, not to 'eat without invitation to weddings' (that is, not to go as hired dancers, or to queue up for the free food), and to educate their children. The other Sheedis grew angry. 'Our fathers were slaves,' they said. 'We are poor and need to work as servants. What is the point of educating our children?' This, at least, is how Mussafir's granddaughter Ani tells it to me. But perhaps the Sheedis of Tando Bago also felt frustrated by Bazmi's dismissal of their music, their leva, their African culture.

In Tando Bago, there was mutual incomprehension between the Sheedis and their leader and eventually Bazmi moved his young family away to Hyderabad, protesting that the rural Sheedi community was not making enough effort to emancipate itself from its slave background. But he remained head of the panchayat and Sheedis, Ani says, would often ring and consult him. Then, ten years ago, a disagreement arose over a plot of land belonging to the community. Bazmi believed that it should be used to build a high school. Others wanted a marriage hall. Still more argued that the land should be sold because they needed money. The discussions were acrimonious, and that evening, when Bazmi returned from Tando Bago, he had a stroke. When he recovered, he found himself unable to communicate linguistically; literacy, the one thing that he had always seen as the route to social improvement, had left him.

Ani tells me this troubling story of her father's stroke, with difficulty, after I have been staying in Bazmi's house for some weeks. Since their father's illness, she and her sisters have not returned to Tando Bago. Instead they have immersed themselves in a quiet interracial city life: they study diligently, take part in neighbourhood prayer groups, and are attentive aunts to their young nieces and nephews. They are serious, sweet women, aloof from the preoccupations with cosmetics and husbands that trouble most other Pakistani girls of marriageable age. Only in their father's disability does the sad memory of a community's distrust of itself linger.

One afternoon in late December I am sitting on the terrace in the cold winter sun reading the English translation of Mussafir's book on slavery, prepared for me by a friend of Bazmi's son-in-law. I have reached the final section.

At the end of his book, Mussafir laid out the remedy for his fellow Sheedis' ills – illiteracy, poverty and lack of social cohesion. He called for his people to organize themselves, to educate themselves, and to be good Muslims – but above all to embrace African culture. The mugarman drum, he wrote, was not incompatible with Islam, as some clerics had been complaining. Quite the contrary; the Prophet himself, Mussafir claimed, used to take his favourite wife Ayesha to listen to the mugarman being played. Every nation, he pointed out, has its own 'spiritual instrument' which 'they use for worship and also for the entertainment of their souls'. The Pashtuns have their *rabab*, the Arabs their *duff* and the English their piano. For Sheedis there is the mugarman. Old Sheedis would listen to the beat of the drum and weep, remembering the lands they had been snatched from. When the drum was played and the dancing began, the 'old language' would come back to them. Mussafir urged Sheedi parents to play the mugarman to their children, to teach them the old language, and to pass on the African culture they had inherited. Sheedis should not feel 'shame and disgrace' when playing the mugarman. Their 'ancestral instrument' was a 'weapon' for building Sheedi solidarity – one of the principal things, he felt, that Sheedis had lost since the time of freedom.

For Mussafir, the time of 'freedom' was not 1947 but 1843 – when the British took over. It was a happy time, for Sheedis were so grateful for their liberty that they worked with enthusiasm, formed vigorous social networks, and even though they had few possessions, were always 'dancing and laughing' (contrary to Richard Burton's characterization of emancipation being 'to them a real evil'). Because of their 'joyous nature', they were called '*Sheedi Badshah*' by other Sindhis. Though meaning literally, 'Sheedi is King', for Mussafir it described the Sheedi people's elation in their freedom:

> Most of the rich men observed their joyful nature with jealousy, because now they could not force them to work by threatening them with swords or sticks.

Bazmi's two wives have come upstairs to sit with me on the terrace while I read. Zubeida, Bazmi's first wife, was just twelve years old when she married, and she remembers her father-in-law well. She has often told me what a serious and pious Muslim he was. So I ask her: 'Did Mussafir talk about "Sheedi Badshah" with you?' 'With me?' She shakes her head ruefully. But Zarina, Bazmi's serene younger wife whom he fell in love with and married long after his father died, has read all the books in her husband's library. She smiles briefly and says: 'Haven't you heard of the Mombasa Art Club?'

The next day Ani and I take a rickshaw to Jungli Sheedi Paro, where Vikee Jackson (real name Khuda Baksh) is waiting for us. It is clear from Vikee's chosen name where his musical tastes lie; but the name of the house is a throwback: it was named so one hundred years ago, in memory of the journey from wild jungly Africa. In the sixties, Vikee Jackson's father founded the Mombasa Art Club here. We have come to listen to Vikee sing a song written in Sindhi by his father and uncle.

When we reach the house, Vikee apologizes: he has no mugarman, he will have to beat the rhythm on the tabletop. We sit down opposite him, and now that we are inside the house, Ani pulls back her burqa. I watch her as Vikee begins to sing. As she listens to the song, her beautiful serious face breaks into a smile, and I smile too, when she translates it for me from Sindhi into Urdu:

> *Sheedi Badshah, hum Badshah*: Sheedi is King, I am King,
> Where he puts his foot, there is peace.
> Our lips are like the parrot,*
> And we are proud of our nose.

That evening, Ani and I walk back home together. 'When you get married,' I say, 'they can sing that song at your wedding.' Ani laughs. I cannot see her face beneath her burqa, but I know that she is pursing her lips and frowning. 'I am not waiting to get married,' she says. We walk on in silence, down the lane where the donkeys that haul loads around Hyderabad are brought at night, their backs gashed and bleeding, to be stabled. As we reach the tailor's shop at the top of her alleyway, she turns to me and says: 'But you are right about one thing: I will sing that song.'

---

* In the subcontinent the parrot is proverbially a wise bird (and the owl dim-witted).

4

River Saints

1718–1752

'Every wave is filled with rubies, water perfumed with musk,
From the river waft airs of ambergis.'

Shah Abdul Latif (1689–1752)

ALL ALONG THE riverbank in Sindh, in the desert and on hill-
tops, next to springs and by lakes, there are shrines of Sufi saints.
Countless holy men have wandered along the river in the past eleven
hundred years; 125,000 alone are said to be buried in the yellow
sandstone necropolis at Thatta; and villages, fairs and pilgrim communities congregate thirstily around their tombs. Sufism is the mystic
vein that runs through Islam: Sufis themselves preach the oneness of
humanity, and the shrines of saints are indeed the one area of Sindhi
social life where all faiths, politics and ethnicities – Sheedis and
soldiers, Communists and Hindus, peasants and dictators – are
welcome. But given this choice, the saint revered by Iqbal Sheedi,
his friend Fida, and thousands of other Sindhis, is the icon of radical
social reform, Sufi Shah Inayat. It is Shah Inayat who in the early
eighteenth century founded an agrarian commune in Jhok, staging
a rebellion against the landowning system with the slogan *Jo kheray
so khai tehreek* – 'those who sow should eat'.

Shah Inayat's stand against the aristocracy is remembered tearfully
in Sindh today as a movement before its time. In order to initiate
me into what they consider the best of Sindhi culture, Iqbal, Fida
and I drive to Shah Inayat's urs, the death-anniversary celebration
held every year at his tomb, with Mashkoor, a cheerful poet of limited
means and a boundless ardour for Sindhi music and history. As we
bump over the dusty road to Jhok, a village in that indeterminate

hinterland between the Indus and the desert, Mashkoor tells me that Shah Inayat's movement was a precursor of the French Revolution: 'He was the world's first socialist. Before the French and before Marx. But because of the nature of Sindh at the time, his message didn't spread. That is our tragedy.'

This notion is repeated the same evening by a member of Shah Inayat's family, Sufi Huzoor Bux, a man whose bare village home (or rather, male guesthouse) has become a pilgrimage place for Sindhis disgruntled with the state, with the army, with the Punjabis, and with the *pirs*, the holy men. We join a group of men sitting in a circle around Sufi Huzoor Bux in the dark (this small village has no more than a passing acquaintance with the national grid). 'If only the world had listened to Sindh and come to our help, we could have changed society,' says Sufi Huzoor Bux. 'Shah Inayat was a big socialist Sufi but his message has been manipulated according to other people's interests.' Shah Inayat was a political thinker, he says. Not like those fraudulent Sufi leaders who sell black threads to poor peasants.

Sufi Huzoor Bux has been banned from attending the urs or even entering the shrine by his cousin, the Sajjada Nasheen, or Guardian of the Shrine. The ostensible reason is the disrespect implied by Sufi Huzoor's claim that the family are not Syeds, but of non-Arabic, tribal Baluch lineage. The criticism goes beyond the charge of pretentiousness, however. The Sajjada is a landlord. As on other Sindhi farms, his 300 *haris* – landless labourers – are forced to give him half the crop they have grown, in rent. The landowner buys the other half off them at non-negotiable prices (generally below the market rate). If the money they make from the crop does not cover their living expenses, they borrow money off the landowner on extortionate terms and go into debt. For illiterate labourers, it is a perilous system. There are currently approximately 1.7 million haris in southern Sindh alone, most of them in 'debt bondage'. Whole families are enslaved to landlords, and the debt is passed down through the generations, growing as it goes. It is exactly this system that Shah Inayat protested against. It was exactly this protest which lost him his head.

At first, Shah Inayat's stand was only of local concern. After he invited peasants in to farm his land for free – thus establishing what one Sindhi historian calls 'the first commune of the subcontinent' – the neighbouring Syeds, growing jealous of his popularity with their serfs, appealed to the Mughal governor of Thatta for help. Local pirs, who had lost *murids* (devotees) to Jhok, added their voice to the call for Shah Inayat to be dealt with, and an attack was sanctioned. Initially, the dispute seemed to go Shah Inayat's way. His peasants defended Jhok, the attackers retreated, and when Shah Inayat complained to Delhi that several of his dervishes had been killed, the Mughal court ordered that land should be given by the killers in compensation. So the commune grew larger, and yet more peasants arrived at Jhok, eager for remission from the grim cycle of their landlord-owned lives.

The local gentry in nearby Thatta, used to seeing the peasants in penury, were outraged by the social revolution being fomented in this remote and insignificant village. A poet with aristocratic sympathies wrote a verse complaining of the comfortable life lived by the lower orders, which ended with a call to arms: 'Sindh will have no rest as long as the enemy sits in Jhok.' Then in 1716, a new Mughal governor was appointed in Thatta, and the nobles seized their chance. They convinced him that the faqirs of Jhok would overrun the Mughal empire – and the governor took their concerns seriously. He alerted the governors of Bukkur, Sehwan and Multan, the three other important trading towns along the Indus, to the possibility of Sindh-wide rebellion, and wrote to Delhi, asking for troops. An army assembled.

The soldiers besieged the Jhok commune for two months. The nobles wrote letters to each other in excitable Persian boasting of how 'with cannonballs and gunpowder the stones of the citadel of the evildoer will fly through the air like the cotton-flakes of the cotton-carder and the lightning sword will put fire into the harvest of his life'. But to the army's surprise, the faqirs were resilient, and so, finding it difficult to prise Shah Inayat out of his stronghold, the army finally tendered peace and invited him to talk terms. His safety was guaranteed by a local noble, Yar Muhammad Kalhora, on a copy of the Qur'an. But it was a trick. Shah Inayat was seized, tried, and executed on the seventeenth day of the Islamic month of Safar, 1130 AH (7 January 1718). His head was sent to Delhi.

This is all that can be gleaned from the sparse contemporary material on Shah Inayat – three letters written by his Kalhora and Mughal enemies, one favourable history composed in Persian by the poet Qani forty-four years after the event, and two virulently hostile histories. But if the archives are meagre, oral history is rich in poignant stories of this lost utopia. '25,000 faqirs died,' says Sufi Huzoor, 'the army that surrounded Jhok was like ants.' The siege lasted 'six months'; the Mughal army burned the commune's records after Shah Inayat was beheaded; and as the saint's decapitated head travelled to Delhi, it recited a long poem, *Besar Nama* (Book of the Headless).

Apart from the death-defying *Besar Nama*, Shah Inayat left no other mystical poetry, and no statement of his philosophy. But every Sufi has a *silsila* – literally, the 'thread' that affiliates them with a particular Sufi school or master. Shah Inayat, unconventionally, had two silsilas; and there are other indications, too, that he was not entirely conformist in his religious thinking.

According to Qani, the poet from Thatta, Shah Inayat left Sindh when he was still a young man, to travel through India in search of a religious guide. He went to the Deccan, and then to Delhi, where he found a teacher who was so impressed with his Sindhi pupil that he followed him back to Thatta. There, pious local theologians – who had been campaigning to banish 'pagan' practices from Sindhi Islam, and in particular to outlaw the Sufi dance parties at Makli – branded them both heretics. The usual reason given is that Shah Inayat's teacher had prostrated himself in respect before his pupil – humans should only prostrate themselves before God. But as we sit listening to Sufi Huzoor Bux speak of the Jhok commune, Mashkoor whispers to me through the dark: 'Shah Inayat was also a follower of Sarmad.'

This intriguing report links Shah Inayat to the most unorthodox Sufi tradition in India. Sarmad was a Persian-Jewish merchant, who had journeyed during the early seventeenth century to Thatta on business. There he fell in love with a beautiful Hindu boy, Aabay Chand. Thatta was in its heyday as the cosmopolitan riverside centre of Sindh's cloth trade, and according to Fray Sebastien Manrique (a fretful Portuguese friar who visited in 1641), 'So great indeed is the depravity in this sink of iniquity that . . . catamites dressed and adorned like women parade the streets, soliciting others as abandoned as themselves.' Sarmad and Aabay Chand travelled on to Delhi, where, if their homosexuality (and Aabay Chand's Persian translation of the Pentateuch) went unremarked, Sarmad's nudity did not. But it was his insistence on uttering only the first phrase of the Muslim creed, 'There is no God', which brought down on his head the clerics' wrath. When they pressed him to finish the sentence with the crucial words, 'but God', Sarmad declined, saying, 'I am fully absorbed with the negative connotations: how can I tell a lie?'

Heretics were two a paisa in India, but Sarmad attracted the devotion of the Emperor's son, and this led to his death. Dara Shikoh, heir apparent of the ruling emperor Shah Jahan, had a deep interest in syncretic Islamic-Hindu traditions, and even had the sacred Hindu Upanishads translated to satisfy his curiosity. Aurangzeb, his younger brother, considering Dara Shikoh to be both a heretic and the impediment to his own imperial glory, had him assassinated in 1659 after a dramatic river-battle on the Indus, and Sarmad was executed soon afterwards for blasphemy. After his death, Sarmad was referred to reverently as the 'Mansoor of India' – a reference to Mansoor Al-Hallaj, a Sufi saint who wandered along the Indus in 905, and was executed in 922 on his return to Baghdad because his sermons were too esoteric.

Shah Inayat was only seven years old when Sarmad was killed. Nevertheless, during his visit to Delhi twenty years later, he met Sarmad's disciples and visited his grave. From Sarmad, says Mashkoor, Shah Inayat learned to disregard human laws, laugh at fasts and prayers, and avow in the face of clerical protest that '*Hindu-Muslim ek hi hain*' (Hindu and Muslim are one). There is little actual evidence that Shah Inayat thought any of these things, but the fact that these iconic images of him live on in Sindh is enough. Shah Inayat's status as the ultimate rebel endures.

The hero, then, not only of every anti-feudal protest but also of a thoroughly anti-fundamentalist kind of Sindhi Islam, Shah Inayat has come to embody Sindh's distinct brand of nationalism – politically socialist and religiously syncretic. G. M. Syed, the late father of Sindhi nationalism, dedicated a book to Shah Inayat: 'He sacrificed everything which he possessed and waged a war against religious prejudices.' But

Sindh, too, deserves an accolade. In all India, Sindh has the longest history of continuous Muslim-Hindu interaction, and it is significant that the Sufi trio who lost their heads on account of their non-conformity – Al-Hallaj, Sarmad and Shah Inayat – all spent some time here.

Shah Inayat may be dear to the hearts of Sindhi socialists, but the immediate effect of his execution three hundred years ago was the rise of the local family which led him to his death – the Kalhoras. Having shown their strength in quashing the uprising, they soon augmented their hold on Sindh and became its overlords. With Shah Inayat died Sindh's hope of land reform.

Land distribution under the Mughals was based on the *mansabdari* honours system – land was leased to the nobles and reverted to the state on the incumbent's death. The Kalhoras, by contrast, rewarded the loyalty of pirs and Syeds by granting them land outright. The result was a feudal system that was augmented by the Talpurs, and set in stone legally by the British (who needed their collaborators in the countryside to be powerful). Partition increased the economic power of the landowners because many of the Hindu moneylenders to whom they were indebted fled for their lives to India. 'Feudalism' is a highly contested term in modern India and Pakistan, but the form of landownership that exists in Sindh today, whatever name it goes by, keeps the peasantry illiterate, poverty-stricken and hopeless. The landlords, who are also the politicians, dictate rural voting via a network of agents. A rural agent explains it to me quite openly: 'In exchange for access to the politician, which is vital for me in securing my children and relatives local government jobs, I make sure the villagers vote the way I say.' 'If they don't?' I ask. 'If they don't, we send in the *ghoondas* [thugs].' The haris suffered in Shah Inayat's day, but modern democracy has disenfranchised them once again.

The Kalhoras who inaugurated this system are nevertheless lauded as patriots by the state, for during their half-century of rule they freed Sindh from the shackles of the declining Mughal empire, improved agriculture by digging canals, and promoted the arts at court. Persian poetry thrived under the Kalhoras. (When they were finally usurped, in 1782, it was their former disciples – the Talpurs – who defeated them, naturally.)

After talking with Sufi Huzoor, we walk up the dirt road to the shrine, past the noisy, colourful stalls selling mango juice, elaborate hairpieces for women, bangles and milk-sweets. It is a different world inside the gates. Most Sufi shrines are relaxed places but here there is a cultish air of order. We step between neat flowerbeds and surrender our possessions to rigorous, security-concerned attendants. During the public concert held in the presence of the Sajjada Nasheen, men and women are seated apart (the men getting the flower garden in front of the stage, the women making do with loudspeakers in a muddy paddock).

This is the closest that most people get to the Sajjada – seeing him from a distance as he sits on a hay bale to signify his 'poverty'. In all the years that they have visited Jhok, Iqbal and Fida have never once met him. In Sindh these men (they are always men) are treated like gods, expect royal respect and generally meet only with rich devotees, politicians – or foreigners.

We send a message to the Sajjada, and permission to see him is quickly granted. As we climb the steps of the white marble complex set back from the tomb, my friends mutter between themselves about its opulence. Sufis value poverty but the building is infused with the cool glamour of a Saudi Arabian sheikhdom. It is entitled – apparently without irony – Kaseri Qalandar, 'Palace of the Wanderer'. The Sajjada himself – dressed in dazzling white – has four wives, a sign of immense wealth in Pakistan. The first is his relative (an arranged marriage), the second is French ('I like to dominate her,' he tells me provocatively), the third lives in the capital, Islamabad, and the fourth is special and kept in a 'secret location'.

The Sajjada openly admits to being a 'landlord', that scourge of his ancestor. He says he owns 1,400 acres (the legal limit in Pakistan is 150 irrigated or 300 unirrigated acres); and that if the people are poor it is because the Punjabis and the army have taken all the jobs. Sindh's problems were caused by the 'criminal, wanted people' who came here at Partition; peasant rights are not a concern. Instead, what exercises him inside his palace is 'male-female separation'. 'Man is like fire, woman like cotton,' he says by way of explanation; and if I am mystified at the time by the cottonwoolliness of this statement, later it strikes me as logical that the male belief in purdah should increase incrementally with the number of wives you keep. In the centres he has established in England, Germany, Africa and India, this is the Sajjada's primary goal. 'There are many young girls in London,' he says to me that evening, 'who have stopped eating pork and wearing bikinis.'

It is sad that the message of a great Sufi reformer has come to this, and Fida and Iqbal are disillusioned. But the lesson I learn in Sindh is that the descendants of saints are universally unreliable. Some sajjadas boast sweetly to me of their expensive Italian clothes, fleets of Mercedes cars, and credit cards from American Express. Others describe the 'small, boneless djinns' they have communed with or talk of the devilishness of their fellow sajjadas (competition for rural devotees is intense). All demand *izzat* – honour and respect – from their illiterate peasant followers. The devotees who visit the shrines are expected to give money, livestock or even their children in life-long service to the sajjada. There are lurid stories about the *droit de seigneur* that sajjadas exercise over the pretty daughters of their murids; and one sajjada points out to me his murids' children, whom he has taken in as unpaid workers for life, as they serve us tea. It is a form of voluntary slavery, a measure of the Sindhi peasantry's economic desperation – and an indication of their spiritual devotion.

I question the Sajjada on the contradiction between the message of Shah Inayat and his own position as a landlord. 'If Shah Inayat was alive today, what would he say about the state of Sindh? The peasants are still poor, there are still big landholdings . . .' But the Sajjada simply smiles: 'Shah Inayat is alive. Whatever I am saying, Shah Inayat is saying. I am Shah Inayat.'

Mashkoor alone does not seem perturbed by the Sajjada's words. 'These sajjadas are all the same,' he says afterwards. 'They are feudals.' He is not here for the politics. He is here for the music.

The descendants of saints may bear little or no philosophical resemblance to their forebears; the devotion extended to them by a disenfranchised peasantry may be wholly bemusing; but there is one thing that makes the shrines inspiring places: the music. The death-anniversary parties of the most popular saints bring together the best musicians from all over Sindh.

After being relegated to a field during the daytime concert, women have of course been banned altogether from the sixty-five musical performances being held simultaneously this night in the grounds of the shrine complex, the *dargah*. But as an unveiled foreigner I am not really a woman, and so with exultant Mashkoor in the lead we wind from one musical gathering to another, listening to flautists from northern Sindh, to old men playing the *surando* (a stringed violin-like instrument), to dancers leaping and jumping as they pluck the one-stringed *yaktora*. In a small tented space at the far end of the dargah is a singer from Umerkot, the desert town where Emperor Akbar was born. He is seated on the ground, playing the accordion with accompaniment from a tabla player, and singing poetic compositions from all along the Indus – those of Bulleh Shah (an eighteenth-century Punjabi disciple of Shah Inayat), of Aijaz Shah (a Sindhi poet), and even the newly-minted love-song of a student of pharmaceuticals to his beloved university of Jamshoro. As each performance draws to a close, the audience fills the night air with its untranslatable cry of appreciation: '*Wah wah!*'

We leave Jhok Sharif at dawn. Sufi Huzoor Bux is waiting for us in front of his house. He is in defiant mood. 'Raag and music is very nice,' he says, 'but it is nothing more than escapism. It does not provide the poor with those things they are lacking.'

I ponder this comment over the next two months, as I travel up the Indus from shrine to shrine. Sufi Huzoor Bux's characterization of music as escapism is true, but the peasants of Sindh have much to escape from. Apart from providing free musical concerts and holidays to the poor, shrines also give refuge to the repressed. In cities where nightclubs, dancing and intoxicants are banned, a shrine's Thursday night Qawwali provides a legal party. At the shrine of Abdullah Shah Ghazi in Karachi, working- and lower-middle-class men dance in groups around small fires, flirting with hijras, and smoking marijuana. Further north along the river, inside the magnificent shrine of the maverick thirteenth-century saint Lal Shahbaz Qalandar, the drumming at dusk looks like a rave, as women (some shrouded in burqas, others with their long hair loose and tangled with sweat) swing their upper bodies to the beat of the enormous kettledrums, fling their heads back and forth, and expend as much pent-up energy as they can before collapsing on the ground, exhausted. In Hyderabad, at Makki Shah's tomb in the middle of the crumbling Kalhora-built fort, the Kaccha Qila, purdah-bound women of all social classes give even fuller vent to their emotions. They come to scream and shout and tear their clothes and beat their breasts in the women-only open-air enclosure formed by two of the fort's slowly disintegrating brick walls. Every time I visit Makki Shah's tomb, women are running backwards and forwards under the trees, uttering wordless shrieks, or rocking themselves frantically in a corner. A young housewife whom I meet at Makki Shah explains to me that she comes here every month or so, 'when I feel my djinn taking control of me'; she had arrived this morning, and now, at three in the afternoon (after a day of running and screaming), she felt better and was about to go home. (Months later I have my own experience of being unremittingly cooped up, in a Pashtun village home. As the family watch, I take the servant's bike and, cycle round and round the courtyard in a bid to ride out my frustration, remembering the women from Makki Shah.)

Some women at this shrine are clearly suffering from serious mental-health problems but, for the majority, the shrine provides temporary respite from their poverty, repression and lack of autonomy. Surveys conducted in Pakistan by international medical journals corroborate this impression: over half the population of low-income housewives suffer from anxiety and despair. Proper mental health care for Pakistan's lower classes is non-existent, and for the ill, sad and lonely, shrines are often their only recourse.

Each shrine, then, serves a slightly different function: Makki Shah for the mentally unhinged; Sehwan Sharif for the repressed ravers; and Sachal Sarmast for the lovers of ecstatic poetry. But it is at Bhitshah, the home of Shah Abdul Latif, that all these are combined, and it is here that I experience the greatest musical and social event in Pakistan.

Shah Abdul Latif was twenty-eight years old when Shah Inayat was executed, and perhaps because of this he never challenged the feudal powers directly. However, his outlook was demotic and he expressed it linguistically, in sung poems that have woven themselves into the soul of Sindh. As a Sindhi professor of literature tells me, it was he 'who made Sindh live. After the Indus, Latif.'

Until Shah Abdul Latif began composing poetry, Muslim poets and saint-versifiers in India wrote in Persian. The antecedents of this language were grand (Rumi, Hafiz), its metaphors imported (nightingales, roses), and both the poet's persona and his subject (the Beloved) were courtly and male. Shah Abdul Latif, like Luther, spoke to the people in their own tongue. He read and quoted Rumi just as he read and quoted the Qur'an, but his subject matter was entirely local. He sang of farmers and fisherfolk, camels and crocodiles, the seasons and the stars – the very being of peasant life. It was the Indus, though, the river at the heart of Sindhi life, which was the silent protagonist of many of his songs. In the eighteenth century, the Indus was used far more than it is today – for travel, for transport of goods, for recreation as well as for irrigation – and Latif describes it in all its moods: its high waves and whirlpools and treacherous quicksands, the boats that sail upon it and the pilgrims and merchants that traverse it. He journeys, in his songs, out through the Delta and on to the high seas, across small creeks and freshwater lakes. Water is a blessing and rain, like the Prophet, is *rahmat*: Divine Grace. But the river is also dangerous, and crossing it is an allegory of the torturous passage from life to death.

Latif's *Risalo* (the generic name in Sindh for a collection of poetry) is divided into thirty *surs* (song chapters), most of which retell the stories and legends that have been recounted along the banks of the Indus for generations. Perhaps Latif's most significant departure from the Persian tradition was to follow the indigenous Indian custom of having female, not male protagonists. It is women's voices that are heard in his songs. In a land where women are inhibited and curtailed by tribal notions of honour and quasi-religious concepts of purdah, the attention that Latif paid to women was revolutionary.

The poems begin just as the heroine is struggling with the great moral trial that defines her and which represents on an allegorical level the Soul's yearning for God. Every Sindhi villager knows how to sing the songs of Latif, and often, as I sit in a Sindhi village with the stars in the indigo sky the only light, the warm breeze blowing across my skin, the rustle of maize in the fields and the lowing of buffalo the only other sounds, listening to a farmer singing 'Sur Sohni' or 'Sur Sassui', it is easy to mistake the centuries and be cast back to the dark night when Sohni drowned in the tempestuous, treacherous Indus.

A potter's daughter, Sohni was married against her will to her cousin, but she had always loved Mehar, a merchant who took up buffalo-herding and pipe-playing to woo her. Every night, Sohni crossed the river to meet him. One night, her sister-in-law, having observed her assignations, substituted the fired pot that Sohni was using as a float, for an unbaked one, and when Sohni plunged into the river as usual, the waters of the Indus soaked into the soft clay and the pot dissolved in midstream. Latif begins his poem at this moment, as Sohni is being swept to her death:

> Pot in hand, trust in God, she enters the waves;
> Her leg in the dogfish's mouth, her head in the shark's,
> Bangles twisted, hair drifting through the water,
> Fishes, big and small, crowd around her
> Crocodiles waiting to devour her.

The Indus is also central to the story of Sassui, Latif's other favourite heroine, a Hindu orphan discovered in the Indus by a Muslim washerman, and brought up as his child. When she grows up, Sassui falls in love with Punhu, a Baluch noble who pretends to humble birth in order to woo her. His aristocratic family is enraged by this folly and abducts him one night while Sassui is sleeping. Latif recounts Sassui's long journey on foot in her lover's wake across the Baluchistan desert, where she dies, far from the Indus lands that were her home.

In the desert west of the Indus are several constellations of eighteenth-century graves, the last resting-place of many of the Kalhoras, and their murids, the Talpurs. These pale, sand-coloured tombs, with their huge onion domes and thin cupolas which now rise eerily isolated from the desert, enclose like sentinel fingers a rare and delicate portrait of eighteenth-century life in Sindh. But they are so remote that I would never have found any of them were it not for the headmaster of a local school, the only man in the district who knows where they are; and they are so dispersed that it takes three days to visit them all. After hours of driving through the desert, a cluster of domes shimmers into view in the distance. Sometimes we find five, sometimes ten, sometimes twenty thirty-foot-high domes in one group, silhouetted against the pale blue sky in silent grandeur, and around them, scattered like pebbles, scores, or even hundreds, of smaller stone tombs.

This is an abandoned land, for the farmers were long ago encouraged to forsake the traditional irrigation provided by the hill torrents and migrate east to the dam-managed Indus green belt. The headmaster gestures to the sand that stretches endlessly in every direction, as far as the eye can see. 'This area was once lush and fertile,' he says. We cross a long earth ridge. 'This is the Kalhoras' old canal system,' he says. 'It once irrigated this entire area. But today we cannot even do what the Kalhoras did in the eighteenth century.' He bends down and runs some sand through his fingers. 'Only camels can survive here now.'

Blasted by the desert's searing heat, I step inside a tomb. There is a clapping of pigeon wings, and I gasp as I look around. Inside is a torrent of colour and life. Frescoes cover every inch of the curved walls and domed ceilings. In the corners, and trailing along the architrave, are spiky-topped pomegranates, purple aubergines and plump yellow mangoes. The ceiling is a dense swirl of ochre, blue, red and green flowers. The borders between the pictures are filled with animals, fish and birds: pelicans with stripy fish in their beaks, monkeys climbing a date palm, amused-looking cattle.

The main compositions on each of the four walls depict local eighteenth-century folklore, history and society. Religion is represented by mosques, rosaries, water pots for ablutions and Qur'ans laid open on stands with the words flying up from the pages into the air like a spell. There are illustrations of domesticity: a husband and wife sit together on a charpay, a sword and musket laid carefully under the bed; a mistress is fanned by her maid. There are pictures of the outside world: a boat sails along the Indus; men stalk tigers; a camel treks slowly through the desert. High up on the wall of one of the tombs, a fierce battle is being waged between sword-wielding horsemen and warriors on elephants. Everywhere is evidence of the vanished water that once kept these people, plants and animals alive. The tombs stand here in the sand like an unheard prophecy – a bleak warning to a country where agricultural land is rapidly disintegrating into salt marsh or desert sand.

Like the river, the tombs are unprotected, and this rich culture is on the verge of being lost. In Europe such a treasure would sustain an entire tourist industry. Here, they stand in a windswept desert, blown by the sand, visited only by the occasional porcupine, or tomb raiders who mistakenly dig up the graves in the hope of finding treasure (the Kalhoras never buried goods with their dead). Islamic attitudes to the representation of humans wavered, and in eighteenth-century Sindh there was clearly little anxiety about human depiction (not to mention 'male-female separation') – but unfortunately several of the faces, especially those of the women, have recently been scratched out by iconoclasts intent on imposing their own censoriousness on the past. The structures, too, are falling apart. Cracks run doggedly through every dome, and in many of the grandest, the summits of the domes have collapsed, letting in the sky.

Of all the scenes painted on these walls, the most moving are those taken from the songs of Latif. Sassui is here, desperately pursuing the abducted Punhu along the riverbank. Sohni clasps a pot to her bosom as she swims across the river, chased by a crocodile and a shoal of fish. Her husband stands on one side, twirling a rosary in his fingers; on the other, waiting amidst his herd of buffalo, is Mehar, holding his reed pipe. In the modern heat of the desert, pictures like these augur the disappearance of the Indus that once nourished this verdant eighteenth-century botany, was the source of these fat (now virtually extinct) palla fish, and provided the tranquil-menacing scene for Latif's *Risalo*.

Every year for three days, these eighteenth-century scenes are also memorialized in music during Shah Abdul Latif's urs. Men and women, villagers, townspeople, city professionals, Sunni, Hindu and Shia, come from all over Sindh to Bhitshah, the village north of Hyderabad which Latif made into his musical retreat. Every night of the year, from dusk to dawn, local musicians sing the entire *Risalo* in front of Latif's shrine. During the urs the village of Bhitshah opens its arms wide and welcomes crowds of devotees, each with their own camp kitchen, tents and fire, each with their own team of singers. Throughout the village, inside the shrine, along the narrow streets, into the fields beyond, the music of Latif fills the air.

Latif invented an instrument, the tambooro, and a new musical verse, the *vai*. His songs, with their female protagonists, are recited by groups of male musicians in a raw, haunting falsetto. They are technically difficult to sing, and the Sindhi is archaic and hard even for native speakers to understand. But there is something in the completeness of their form, or the sincerity with which they are sung, that makes them understandable to everybody.

I wander all night, as circles of spectators form and disperse – around a hijra dancing with tinkling bells on her ankles, around a flute-player sitting on the ground, around dancers gaudily enacting Latif's stories with gestures as well as words. In Latif's mud-walled *chillah*, the room where he sat and meditated, black-clothed musicians from the local village are quietly practising 'Sur Sohni'. In the street beneath the devotee-crowded house of the Sajjada Nasheen, faqirs are smoking marijuana together and catching up on each other's news. In the space before the shrine, drums are being banged for the ecstatic dancing of the *dhammal*. At Bhitshah, the best of Sindhi society has assembled. There is freedom here, during the three days of music and celebration; a stubborn resilience to Pakistan's social hierarchy and religious homogeneity. Perhaps because the social organization is dominated neither by the Sajjada Nasheen – as at Jhok – nor by the government (official events are held at the other end of the village), the atmosphere is that of a carnival or medieval mummers' fair.

On the morning of Latif's death-anniversary, the Sajjada Nasheen puts on Latif's cloth cap and cloak and progresses towards the shrine, as his urban devotees weep. That afternoon, a group of youthful green-turbanned missionaries with wispy beards run towards the shrine chanting '*Allah-hu, Allah-hu*'. Late that night, through the noise of the urs, I hear the beat of a mugarman, and run towards the shrine, to find that a party of Sheedis has transfixed the crowded courtyard with their energetic crouching and jumping, as they dance towards Latif's tomb to the pounding of their tall wooden drums. All of Sindh is here, and everybody has a place.

The non-sectarian harmony indulged at Bhitshah would appal the newly-conservative, Wahhabi-ized sections of society. Late one night, I meet a Baluch journalist who tells me that he comes here every year, 'leaving my middle-class prejudices behind in Karachi'. He wrote an article about the urs once, the first line of which was cut: 'A Hindu untouchable family sleeping in the Sunni mosque of a Sufi shrine dominated by Shias.' I walk into the mosque to check, and it is true: in the prayer hall I step over sleeping families, men and women. It is as if society has suspended its usual pettiness and comprehended this mosque for what it is: a space to accommodate devotees. On the second night, I stray into an annexe of the shrine and find a host of government officials from the Auqaf Department, which deals with religious affairs, sitting around a gigantic green pile of small-denomination rupee notes, all mixed up with pink rose petals, as they sleepily count the money that has been donated by pilgrims. (Officials say that a well-attended urs can bring in 'Rs30 lakh' – £30,000.) I spend a second night listening to musicians singing the *Risalo*, and at dawn return to the Syed-house where I am staying with relatives of the deceased saint.

The Syed women are still dressed in black, because Muharram, the month of mourning for the Shia heroes, has only recently ended. They never leave the house; they never clean or cook – their murids do that; they just sit all day long in their lacquered wooden swings, rocking backwards and forwards and gossiping, like plump spiders in a web.

It seems perverse that the women should remain inside while this pageant celebrating their ancestor swells on their doorstep. But when I talk to Latif's relatives – including the Sajjada Nasheen – I discover that they do not consider him to be an inclusive and all-welcoming Sufi. For them, he was 'a Shia through and through'. Wishing to claim him for their own particular sect, some of Latif's relatives regard the unregulated urs with ambivalence. While the literary festival in the village celebrates Latif as a poet, and the masses revelling outside regard Latif as the ecumenical voice of Sindh, for the Sajjada Nasheen the *Risalo* is primarily a religious text – a Sindhi version of the Qur'an. In most Muslim homes, the Qur'an is set apart from other books, such is its sacred importance. But in the Sajjada's house, the *Risalo* is actually placed on a par with Islam's holy book. Both texts are wrapped in gilt cloth and laid like babies – like the Baby Krishna – in a cradle.

Whatever Latif was, his *Risalo* is not the work of a dogmatist. It contains few tenets of any kind, whether Sufi, Shia or Sunni. It is certainly the work of a Muslim – but no more stridently than Shakespeare's plays are coloured by Christianity. Just as Shakespeare has been called a Protestant, Catholic, atheist, and the inventor of romantic love, so, according to the Sindhi historian Hussamuddin Rashdi, the same fate has befallen Latif:

> Shah was the crown of the Sufis, Shah was a folk poet, Shah was the master of ragas, Shah was a patriot, Shah was a Congressman, Shah was a Muslim Leaguer, Shah was Rumi, Shah was Goethe . . . in short, Shah is the medicine for every illness.

Shah Abdul Latif has always been as beloved by Sindhi Hindus as by Sindhi Muslims, and every year Hindu scholars from India are invited to the government-sponsored literary festival, held during the urs. Latif himself spent some three years in the company of Hindu yogis, and he praises them in his poetry:

> I find not today my Yogi friends in their abodes;
> I have shed tears all the night, troubled by the pang of parting;
> The Holy Ones for whom my heart yearneth, have all disappeared.

(These verses are also interpreted as a secret dedication to the martyred Shah Inayat.) Latif's *Risalo*, then, exemplifies the easy spiritual interaction that exists between the two faiths, an easiness that has been acquired after centuries of cohabitation. This legacy is an irony in a country based on the separation of Muslim and Hindu, and it is wonderful that this syncretism has survived.

With its piecemeal structures of authority and idiosyncratic attitude to canonical religions, Sindh is a fecund place, and there were periods during the past millennium when the closeness of Hinduism and Islam even resulted in the two faiths' identification with each other. In the holy book of the Ismailis, a breakaway sect from Shiism that arrived in Sindh in the ninth century CE, the Prophet Muhammad, or alternatively his son-in-law Ali, is hailed as the tenth avatar of the Hindu god Vishnu. At the time, Ismailism was under attack from Sunni hardliners as well as recalcitrant Hindus, and in order to conceal their religion from suppression, they developed a way of camouflaging their missionary activity in Hindu forms. This, at least, is how Shias have always explained away these potentially heretical doctrines: as a form of *taqiyya* – the legitimate concealment of one's inner faith in order to escape persecution – or as a method of canny proselytization, of making their preaching acceptable to the Hindu ear. (The early Jesuit missionaries in India practised a similar form of 'accommodation' when they dressed like *sadhus* – Hindu holy men – and called themselves Brahmins from Rome.)

But the holy texts of the Ismaili Satpanthi community, published around 1757 and stored in their headquarters in Karachi, do not give this impression. The sacred *Dasa Avatara* begins conventionally with an exegesis of the ten avatars of Vishnu. By the ninth incarnation, however, conventional Hinduism has warped into surreal burlesque, as a maverick 'Buddha' – bandy-legged, facially deformed, Persian-speaking – preaches to Hindus that the Prophet Muhammad was the avatar of the Hindu god Brahma. Buddha persuades the Pandavas – heroes of the ancient Sanskrit epic, the Mahabharata – that they should violate their religion by killing a cow. The Pandavas become his converts, and they parade down to the bazaar wearing the head and legs of a dead cow as hats. There, the dismembered cow's parts turn to 'glittering gold crowns' and the anger of the Brahmins in the marketplace to envy. They too rush to wrap themselves up in the cow's intestines. Anyone who believes, the *Dasa Avatara* claims, will go to Amarpuri, the jewel-filled Eternal Abode.

This is an extremely transgressive text, which breaks the major taboos of Islam, Hinduism and Buddhism. Yet until recently, the Ismaili Satpanthi community in Karachi would sing it 'standing up', on all festival occasions, to the tune of 'Kedara' – the raag which Shah Abdul Latif used for his Muharram poetry.

Obviously, to an orthodox Muslim, the notion of reincarnation is anathema. But in Sindh, as the Sajjada of Jhok demonstrated, such ambivalence is common; how different is the Hindu philosophy of reincarnation from the idea that an eleventh-generation grandson of Shah Inayat might actually *be* Shah Inayat? Muhammad is lauded by Muslims as the last and greatest of all the prophets. If you include the Hindu 'prophets', then Muhammad is also the last and greatest of the avatars of Vishnu. Seemingly irreconcilable ideas merge by the simple osmotic process of being in close contact with each other.

Many of the proselytizing saints who arrived in Sindh from Iran or the Middle East gave their mission a boost by putting down roots in ancient Hindu places of worship, or even by allowing themselves to be identified with Hindu gods. Sehwan Sharif, where Lal Shahbaz Qalandar's tomb is located, is the site of an important Shiva centre. The name Sehwanistan, as it was known until recently, derives from Sivistan, city of Shiva, and the modern faqirs still dress like Shaivite yogis, in torn clothes, with matted hair. Lal Shahbaz Qalandar also used to be called Raja Bhartari by Hindus; and when I visit his shrine I see, flashing in red neon Urdu script above his tomb, the words *Jhule Lal*, one of the many Hindu names for the god of water. At least until the nineteenth century, it was believed by Muslims and Hindus that the Indus waxed and waned according to Lal Shahbaz Qalandar's whim.

Time and again during this journey up the river I find that the Indus is still – as it has been for centuries – a place where people, ideas and religions meet and mingle. In a desert, a river is an innate hub, crossing-point and natural resource, and with so many people congregating around its waters, neither Hinduism nor Islam managed to retain its original purity. There never were many Brahmins in Sindh – the centre of Hinduism, its clergy and texts, shifted to the Ganges two millennia ago – and cults always multiplied and thrived here. One of these is the Daryapanthi sect, whose adherents revere the Indus itself. Even today, the Indus is worshipped by Muslims as well as Hindus at two places in Sindh: the village of Uderolal near Bhitshah, and much further north, near the famous riverside town of Sukkur.

I arrive at Uderolal at dusk. As I climb down from the bus I can hear that the *mela*, the fair, has begun: through the loudspeakers mandatory to any subcontinental religious event, *bhajans* – Hindu devotional songs – are being chanted; and in the background is a steady wall of noise, the coming and going of pilgrims. The Muslim-occupied village of Uderolal rises out of the plain, a cluster of simple rural houses collected here for no other reason than that the Indus once flowed nearby. Then I turn the corner in the road and see the massive Mughal fort, with its five-foot-thick walls, which enclose a mosque, a temple, and the tomb of a man whom Muslims call Shaikh Tahir and the Hindus call Jhulelal or Uderolal – and whom everybody calls Zindapir (Living Saint). Today it is Zindapir's birthday.

To the Hindus, the tomb actually represents Zindapir's *asthana*, his seat, for he never died, he is a god; to the Muslims he was a great saint born in 952 CE. The Muslim legend – related to me by the Muslim Sajjada Nasheen – is elastic: it stretches across seven centuries. Fished as a baby, Sassui-like, from the Indus, Zindapir was brought up by Hindu parents, but his great spiritual power was only exposed by chance during his childhood, when (two hundred years later, technically) four thirteenth-century Muslim saints – Lal Shahbaz Qalandar and his friends – met him as he was playing ball by the Indus. Realizing that his *shakti* ('power': itself a Sanskrit-Hindu word) was being stifled by his Hindu upbringing, they readopted him. Four centuries passed, however, before Zindapir really made his mark, after he convinced the puritanical Emperor Aurangzeb to cease his oppression of Hindus. He thereby stands as a classic figure in the harmonious coexistence of Sindh's Hindus and Muslims.

In 1938, perhaps encouraged by separatist demands elsewhere in British India, the Hindus and Muslims who worshipped here quarrelled. 'The Hindus put a *bhood* [ghost] on the shrine,' says the Muslim Sajjada, and pulls out of his wallet a much-folded document. It is a copy of the British-stamped court order dating from 1938, which settled the debate over which community – Hindu or Muslim – could pocket the donations accruing from the mela. The colonial court decided in favour of the Muslim landlords, and ever since then every rupee deposited in the collection boxes during the mela is taken by the Muslim Sajjada.

The court also ruled that the Hindus should have separate facilities for eating, sleeping and worship, and so a complex was built adjacent to the fort, enclosing Zindapir's sacred well. Any money that Hindu pilgrims leave there goes to the Hindu Sajjada, currently a woman known as 'Mata' (mother). The net result of the firman was a loss of income for the Muslims.

Despite this division, nobody ever suggested establishing two different festivals, and the birthday party in Zindapir's honour is still held on the date of Cheti Chand, according to the Hindu – not the Muslim – calendar. The Sajjada Nasheen may be sulking in his guesthouse, Mata may lurk beside her holy well, but the fort belongs to pilgrims of both faiths.

The shrine is undergoing extensive renovation, financed by a Hindu merchant from Karachi. As always in Pakistan, the old but interesting is being destroyed to make way for the shiny new. Frescoes – painted, at a guess, a century ago, by somebody with eclectic tastes: there are Dutch windmills, Chinese willow-pattern boating scenes as well as Mughal-esque vistas – have already been disfigured probably beyond repair by the whitewash splashed on to the domed ceiling, and will soon disappear altogether under the onslaught of expensive marble and mirrored tiles.

As I am circumambulating Zindapir's tomb with the crowd, a Hindu family arrives, bearing a traditional green Muslim cloth, inscribed with Qur'anic verses, which they drape over the tomb in thanksgiving. In the adjacent room, devotees are queuing up to pray to a roomful of Hindu images. In the room next to that are the graves of the four Muslim Shaikhs who – according to the Hindu legend – granted Zindapir the land, free of charge, on which to build a temple in the tenth century. Outside in the courtyard is a tree the branches of which are hung with pieces of coloured cloth, the wishes of supplicants of both faiths. (The tree grew from the cast-off toothbrush of Zindapir, who, whether Hindu or Muslim, established admirably high standards of dental hygiene.)

I have been invited to the Hindu-only festivities by Diwan Lekraj, a member of the Evacuee Trust Property Board set up after Partition to protect the monuments of the absent 'minorities'. Diwan is a Hindu, but he is almost indistinguishable from the Muslims around him. There is nothing in his dress (shalwar kameez) or his language (Urdu) or his car or his house to draw attention to his 'minority' faith. Perhaps the horrors of Partition taught Pakistan's Hindus that it was wiser thus. Or maybe there really is not much to distinguish them after all, as the story of Zindapir's two faiths suggests.

From Uderolal it is a long journey north along the Indus Highway to Sukkur, Zindapir's other shrine in Sindh. Standing as it does on a tiny island in the middle of the river, this is the smallest, least frequented and most pleasing of all Sindh's Sufi enclaves. With the town of Sukkur on one side, Rohri on the other, and the larger island of Bukkur a few feet away across the water, the shrine exists in watery isolation, a nonchalant synthesis of all Sindh's cultures, suspended dolphin-like above the river, in contravention of time's gravity.

The Indus is at its narrowest here, hemmed in by limestone, and unlike all settlements to the south, which are constantly in danger of being flooded, comparative riparian stability has given these towns a chance to luxuriate in their semi-aquatic character. Mohanas, Indus boat-people, still live on the river in wooden sailing boats. All day long, flat-bottomed skiffs float past Zindapir's island, carrying workers to the vegetable plantations upstream, or pilgrims to the island shrine, or sacks of rice and bags of spice from the bazaar to the shrine's kitchen. During the urs at a shrine on the Rohri side of the river, even I am awarded my own Sufi silsila: '*Zabardast kism ka naam,*' I hear the Sajjada's son remark to a friend when he hears what I am called: An amazing kind of name. And he spells it out, making the last two letters sound like the Urdu word *se*, 'from', thus giving it an Islamic etymology: *Ali-se*, from Ali, the Sufi father of them all. ('He's spared you the expense of a family tree,' a friend jokes later when I tell him: 'Now that you're a Syed, where are your murids?')

The Sajjada's son also tells me that until recently, palla fish would swim up the river from the sea in order to salute the panoply of Indus river saints at Sukkur. Every Sindhi has emotional memories of the palla, *Tenualosa ilisha*, or *hilsa* as it is known in Bengal: one of the herring family, and in Sindh the ancient symbol of a vanished riverine paradise, its national dish, and now endangered (because dams on the river prevent it from migrating up and down the Indus to spawn). South of the shrine, and visible from Zindapir island, is the cause of the palla's demise: Sukkur barrage, the dam built by the British in 1932 to feed a network of irrigation canals. The barrage has vastly increased the agricultural potential of Sindh – but it has also trapped the blind Indus dolphin upstream of Sukkur. Resident here since the river was formed millions of years ago, this glorious mammal is only now facing extinction.

Islands are an intrinsic part of the character of these towns. A majestic, white marble Hindu temple dominates the southernmost island in the river. Between it and the shrine of Zindapir to the north, is the island fort of Bukkur, the most important military settlement in this region until British times. Of these three islands,

Zindapir's shrine to the north is the smallest – there is barely space for Zindapir's smooth stone asthana, a few palm trees, and a hut made of leaves under which the faqirs sit all day, preparing *bhang*, the thick marijuana infusion that they politely tell me is 'green tea'. And yet for centuries this little piece of land in the middle of the Indus thronged with Sindhis who gathered here to reverence the river.

I spend many days on Zindapir's island, talking to the faqirs, easily the most laid-back Pakistanis I ever meet. They have their own stories about Zindapir's origins, but despite the historical dates assigned to the stories by folklore, it is impossible to tell how old the cult of the river saint really is. There is a theory among some Muslims today that the Hindu story was only concocted after Partition; but colonial-era biographies of Zindapir, written by Sindhis, disprove this. The Hindu variant simply gives a human face to the primordial worship of the river and may have its roots in Rigvedic times, or before. The Muslim option is comparably ancient in terms of the history of Islam, for few other saints claim to have arrived here earlier than 952 CE.

The Zindapir faqirs give their version of the story a clever plot-twist by declaring that the saint who appeared on the island was Khwaja Khizr. This person, whose name means 'Mr Green', is found all over the Islamic world, usually in association with water cults. His antecedents are mysterious, for while pious Muslims (such as the new Sajjada Nasheen) maintain that he is a Qur'anic prophet, in fact Khwaja Khizr is never mentioned by name in the holy book. He was inserted after the event by the writers of the Hadith (sayings of the Prophet) as the hitherto nameless friend of Moses.

This was the start of – or perhaps a subsequent means of justifying – Khwaja Khizr's ubiquity in the Islamic world. Richard Carnac Temple, a civil servant in nineteenth-century British Sindh, researched, but never published, a monograph of the saint, entitled *Zinda Peer: Everliving Saint of India*. Khwaja Khizr, he wrote, is 'known to every child from Morocco to the Malay Peninsula, the helper in all trouble of whatever kind, and at the same time the bogie par excellence, and the most widely known of all the modern sea and river godlings or saints'. In Muslim versions of the *Alexander Romance* – the medieval legends of Alexander the Great, popular in both Europe and Asia – Khwaja Khizr became the eponymous hero's friend, accompanying him on a quest for the Fountain of Eternal Life. This, Khizr discovered by chance when a dried fish he was carrying fell into a spring and he watched amazed as his lunch flicked its fins and swam away. Khizr drank deeply from the spring, and hurried away to fetch Alexander, but by the time they returned the spring had disappeared (luckily for mankind, or else Alexander would even to this day be marching round the world, conquering random countries according to his whim). Instead, it is the 'shy and retiring' Khwaja Khizr who lives on. The patron of travellers, the helper of those in dire need, he manifests himself to those who call upon him in sincerity.

His first recorded appearance in Sindh occurred in 952 CE, when a Delhi merchant was sailing downriver with his daughter, a girl whose uncommon loveliness came to the attention of the local Hindu raja. The wicked man attempted to ravish her, but the girl called upon Khwaja Khizr, who diverted the Indus from flowing past the raja's capital at Alor, and instead landed the boat safely on the island in the river. (The current Sajjada Nasheen, who has spent his life working for Pakistan's infamous, all-powerful Water And Power Development Authority [WAPDA], feels duty-bound to point out to me that while it is true that the Indus changed course several centuries ago, as an engineer he is unable to confirm that this occurrence was Khwaja Khizr's own creation. Even Qur'anic prophets who have drunk deeply from the elixir of eternal youth have their limits.)

In Sukkur, Hindus and Muslims worshipped together at Zindapir's island shrine until the late nineteenth century. The 1874 *Gazetteer of Sindh* attested to the non-antagonistic character of the common worship there; but by the time the 1919 *Gazetteer* was published, the Hindus had moved off the island.

When I ask the Sajjada Nasheen to explain the reasons for the community's rift, he tells me that during the 1880s, the Hindus brought a case against the Muslims, arguing that the absence of a tomb on the island meant that it must always have been the worship-place of an immortal Hindu god. The Muslims countered that there was no tomb because Khwaja Khizr is still alive. The colonial court, called upon to determine in law exactly what the worship-place on the island represented, awarded priority to the Muslims, and so the Hindus placed a light on the water, and built a new temple where it came ashore. If you stand on Zindapir's island you can see the large, yellow-painted Hindu temple across the river. Any traces of the original temple that might once have stood here on the island were eradicated in the flood of 1956, which also destroyed the mosque, the 'throne of serpents' and the large silver-plated gates. All that the river left behind, fittingly, was the smooth stone of the saint's asthana.

I am keen to read the court documents that the Sajjada has spoken of but unfortunately his barrister cousin, so I am told, recently gave them away to some foreign visitors whose names he cannot remember. Nor can he recall whether they were in English, Sindhi, Sanskrit or Persian. The barrister thinks that there might be another copy in the Civil Court, a stone's throw – or at least a short boat ride away – from Zindapir's island; and so we go there together.

The British-era court is a quaint construction, the only building on top of a riverside hill, built there, presumably, to protect it from the ravages of the angry masses (or the angry river). I meet the female magistrate, who, with her lipstick and waved hair, is perched incongruously upon this crumbling edifice of another era. She kindly gives us permission to search through the records. But they are in a terrible state: three months ago a series of explosions (apparently random detonations of confiscated and forgotten armaments) destroyed the north side of the building and tragically killed the Head Clerk 'who knew everything'. Though we search through all the bundles from the 1880s we fail to find the judgement.

For the British, who were ruling Sindh at the time, the Zindapir dispute was of limited local importance, and direct notification of the community's religious divorce was apparently never sent to London. The affair only surfaces twice in British records. The first is in a Public Works Department Resolution of 1894, determining that the land which the Hindus have squatted across the river from the island is of no use to the government, and can be sold to them, the 'Jind Pir fakirs', for Rs1,000. The second is in the 1919 *Gazetteer of Sindh* where it is noted that 'about twenty years ago . . . the Hindus abandoned their claim and set up a shrine of their own to Jinda Pir on the Sukkur bank of the river'. In addition, amidst the papers that form the notes and manuscript of Richard Carnac Temple's book on Zindapir, I came across a typed transcription of this passage from the *Gazetteer*, on to which Temple had pencilled a date: '1886'. This tallies with the Sajjada's memory of the judgement. But neither Temple nor the *Gazetteer* revealed the original causes of this dispute.

Hindus still go every Friday to their temple to worship Zindapir – but they have no idea when the temple was built (there are apparently no records there either) nor of the court case that led to the split. Above the entrance to the inner part of the temple is a painting of Zindapir, royally clad in blue and crimson Mughal dress, a green turban on his head, riding along the Indus on a palla fish. On Friday night, I follow a group of male Hindu worshippers through the temple and down some stone steps to an underground cave where a light is always kept burning and Indus water laps at our feet. Singing bhajans, the men light butter lamps and take them back up to the main river, where they are placed in little paper boats. The *diyas* float away through the night, luminous pinpricks on the inky-black water, faint memorials.

One of the contributing causes of the Zindapir rift seems to have been Hindu reactionary piety. In 1823, when the Nepali missionary Swami Bankhandi arrived in Sukkur, he found that the Hindus had forgotten their ancient lore, and he made it his express mission to 'awaken' them to the sacredness of the river. He also wished to wean them away from their attachment to Sufi shrines. To that end, he colonized Sadhubela island in the middle of the river, the perfect location for such an isolationist enterprise (and a direct challenge to Zindapir's shrine, a mile upstream).

At the time, Hindu reform movements elsewhere in Sindh and India were encouraging widow remarriage and other modernizing trends, but in Sukkur the management of the Sadhubela temple believed such projects would 'undermine the entire Hindu social organization'. Sadhubela's focus was on the entrenchment of ancient Hindu values. (The priests even tried to resurrect the Kumbh Mela at Sadhubela, claiming that 'in ancient times' this gigantic Hindu gathering was held here, not on the Ganges, that the Buddhists had eradicated the practice two millennia ago, and that Muslims had stifled its revival.)

Sixty years after Swami Bankhandi's missionary project began, Hindus forsook Zindapir's shrine altogether. Over the next century, the Sadhubela temple management undertook a series of ambitious building projects on the island, funded by Hindu 'chiefs, grandees and rich merchants', with the aim of articulating in expensive white marble their community's division from the Muslim majority. (Where boats dock at the temple, two white marble tableaux still illustrate to worshippers the options before them: one shows a river of naked, drowning sinners – some being skewered and roasted, at least one a Muslim saying *namaz*; adjacent to it is a scene of the righteous: fully clothed, queuing meekly to get into heaven.) The white marble was complemented, in the early twentieth century, by a flurry of devout publications about 'Uderolal' – as Zindapir was now known to Hindus. In 1924, a book was published in English on the history of the Sadhubela temple, and another in Sindhi, Gurumukhi and Sanskrit on the holiness of the Indus. All efforts – architectural, literary, financial – emphasized disparity.

Sitting a little mournfully upstream on the near-deserted island shrine of Khwaja Khizr, the Muslim Sajjada is quick to admit that it is the Muslims who lost most from the Zindapir dispute: 'Now very few people come to the island,' he says. 'The Hindus were the richest and they made a separate shrine and the Muslims are poor and then in the flood of 1956 everything was swept away.' He has brought with him a copy of his family tree, to illustrate to me how 'my Arabic family merged over time with the local culture'. The family tree begins, of course, with Adam and descends via the first Caliph. But during the eighteenth century the Sajjada's ancestors shed their religious titles and took quintessentially Sindhi names such as 'Nimbundo'. They became, he says, 'true Sindhis'.

As the Muslims had nothing to gain from the Hindus leaving, and the Hindus wished to reclaim their original lost purity, it seems likely that the Zindapir dispute was prompted by an internal Hindu reform movement. Yet the more I search through Sukkur's monuments, records and memories, the more I wonder why it was that the colonial court allowed a community that had worshipped together for eight hundred years to be divided; why it conspired in rendering legalistically unequivocal that which had been harmoniously amphibious. It was with incidents such as these that the Pakistan movement was nurtured, and with hindsight, the dispute over Zindapir does seem to be a precursor of Partition. Perhaps what the colonial court fostered here in the 1880s was a classic case of divide-and-rule. As I sit under a palm tree on the island, watching the wooden boats with their voluminous white sails floating past, and observing the already stoned faqirs mixing themselves another drink of bhang, it seems lamentable that short-term separatist sentiments were allowed to prevail over hundreds of years of shared culture.

Mohanas, Indus boat-people, still live on the river, near both Khwaja Khizr's shrine and the island temple of Sadhubela. The unmechanized wooden boats they navigate along the Indus – propelled by sails, rudders and poles – are identical in outline to boats etched on to the five-thousand-year-old seals of the Mohenjodaro city civilization. The Mohanas are a direct connection to the prehistoric Indus river cult, and if anybody has the answer to the mystery of its origins it is they. In 1940, the magazine *Sindhian World* reported that 'the special duty of Zinda Pir is to help the Indus boatmen in the flood season.' Even today, faqirs on the island, and the Mohanas who live here, all say that Zindapir is the '*pani ka badshah*' (Water King). He lives under the water and the river flows '*unke hukum se*': according to his rule and pleasure.

In the last sixty years, the Mohanas' lives have changed significantly. Dams have curtailed the distance they can travel by river, and road-building has created competition in the form of the multi-coloured trucks which now transport most goods around the country. Mohana spokesmen also blame General Zia's Mujahideen days in Afghanistan for exacerbating Sindh's heroin and Kalashnikov culture and rendering the river unsafe. All these changes have taken them further away from the water. Even now, the wild, wooded kaccha lands along the riverbank are the domain of powerful landlords and their bandit henchmen, and most Mohanas are afraid to travel far up or downstream from Sukkur. Recently, though, a few Mohanas have begun making the eight-day journey north to collect timber from the kaccha lands again. On the riverbank opposite Sadhubela, enormous wooden sailing boats with crescent-shaped prows are once again being built to do this work. Every day for a week I come to the riverside to watch the boat-building and then, when the boat is ready, arrive to find the Mohanas throwing a party: sailing the boat out into the water and diving into the river from the prow.

The Indus boat-people have four family names: Mohana, Mallah, Mirbah and Mirani. 'When fishermen wear white cotton and carry currency notes, then they are Mirani,' a Mohana who lives near Khwaja Khizr's island tells me. Miranis are rich; they no longer live on boats. Today, most Mohanas aspire to be Miranis: to send their children to school, to move off the river and into a pukka home. The further Mohanas live from the river, the more orthodox is their Islam – and the faster their belief in the power of the river, and in Zindapir, dissolves.

But there are still Pakistanis for whom the power of the Indus, and the power of Islam, coexist. Early one morning, I am sitting on the riverbank opposite Khwaja Khizr's shrine, drinking tea with a family of Mohanas, when I see a woman standing in the river. She has just had a bath in the quiet channel between Bukkur and Khwaja Khizr's island, and her clothes and long dark hair are wet and tangled. She wrings her hair out, pulls on dry clothes, and then she calls on one of the Mohanas to row her out into the middle of the river. Pervez, a young Mohana whose job it is to ferry pilgrims from Bukkur the short distance to Zindapir's island, offers to take her, and I watch as she climbs into the boat and sits in the stern. Pervez stands at the prow, pushing off from the bank with a long wooden pole, and the boat moves slowly out past the edge of the island. As they reach the main channel of the river, the woman stands up suddenly in the boat, and throws a bundle of cloth into the river. It twists on the surface in a blur of red and gold, before sinking into the river. Then the woman kneels on the edge of the boat, collecting water in a bottle.

'What were you doing?' I ask her when they return. Pervez speaks for her in Urdu: 'Her child is sick; we went to the middle of the river where the water is purest.' He adds what he has told me before: 'Our Indus water is worth four of your *namkeen sarkaari* [salty government-bottled] water.' He is laughing at the perplexed expression on my face when the woman interrupts.

'*Darya main phenkne se sawab milta hai*,' she says: You throw it in the river in order to get a blessing.

'Throw what?' I ask.

'The Qur'an,' says Pervez.

'The Qur'an? In the river?' I am shocked. Even now, after coming across such a plurality of practices fusing Islam and ancient river worship, the idea of flinging the holy book into the belly of the river seems incredible. I begin to ask another question, when the woman looks up at me scornfully from the boat.

'*Aap parne, likhne walli hain,*' she says, '*aur nahi samjhi hain.*'

You can read and write – and still you do not understand.

5

The Guru's Army

1499

'Lord, Thou art the mighty river,
Thou knowest and seest all things.
How can I, a poor fish, know
Thy depth and thy expanse?'
                Guru Nanak (1469–1539)

GHOSTLY RIVERS HAUNT the Punjab – rivers dammed and
diverted; vanished rivers sung about in Sanskrit hymns; rivers
where Sikh gurus were enlightened and died; rivers flowing like
moats past Mughal forts; rivers traversed by Afghan and Macedonian
adventurers; rivers over which nations do battle.

Punjab means 'five waters'. The five rivers of the name are the
tributaries which flow westwards to the Indus from India – the Beas,
Sutlej, Ravi, Chenab and Jhelum – defining and shaping the fecund
agricultural land they water. Where the five rivers join the Indus,
Hindus wind the number five into their rituals. 'Five rivers, five
prayers, five saints,' a Hindu lawyer tells me, 'and five lights burning
in our temples.' In the Punjab, the peasant Sufi cult of Panj Piriya
venerated the five Shia heroes. For the Sikhs too, whose homeland
is in the Punjab, *paanch* – five – became a holy number. 'I am composed of five elements,' sang Guru Nanak, the founder of Sikhism.
The last Sikh guru, Gobind, chose five brave Sikhs to inaugurate his
militant Khalsa movement, and then gave the larger Khalsa community five distinctive symbols of their Sikhdom. It is a cultural lacuna
that in modern-day Punjab three of the five rivers have been dammed
into non-existence.

If Pakistani Punjab is haunted by its departed rivers, it is also haunted by its departed Sikhs. In 1947, Sikhs from west Punjab abandoned Pakistan for India. The new map gave India the Sikh headquarters at Amritsar but other major pilgrimage centres – such as Ranjit Singh's tomb in Lahore and Guru Nanak's birthplace, which the Indians had argued should be made into 'a sort of Vatican' – went to Pakistan. Since then, Sikhs in India have added a regretful clause to the *ardaas*, their formal litany:

> Bestow on the Khalsa the beneficence of unobstructed visit to and free management of Nankana Sahib and other shrines and places of the Guru from which the Panth has been separated.

They console themselves with Guru Nanak's aphorism that 'union and separation are part of the pleasure and pain of life.'

Although very few Sikhs remain in this Islamic Republic, monuments and memories of the Sikh era still punctuate the landscape. There are Sikhs in Peshawar on the border with Afghanistan, where gurdwaras, Sikh temples, are crumbling. In Quetta, further south along the Afghan frontier, I stay on a street, Gordat Singh Road, named after a nineteenth-century Sikh philanthropist. And in the Punjab there are the Indian Sikhs, who come here on pilgrimage.

On a quiet Friday morning in February, just before I leave Sindh behind and travel north to the Punjab, I am standing in the Hindu library on the island of Sadhubela in Sukkur, admiring the luminously coloured nineteenth-century paintings of Hindu gods and goddesses that have been preserved here. I can see the divine lovers Radha and Krishna, elephant-headed Ganesh, and even Zindapir (skimming over the Indus on four palla fish). But the biggest, most resplendent and prominent paintings are of a white-bearded man sitting cross-legged on the ground and listening to his disciples. 'Who is that?' I ask the young Hindu librarian. 'Our Spiritual Master,' the librarian says, 'Guru Nanak Sahib.'

Most Hindus in Sindh are *Nanakpanthis*, followers of Guru Nanak. The boundary between Sikhism and Hinduism is less defined in Sindh than elsewhere in the subcontinent, and during the 1881 and 1891 censuses, Nanakpanthis could not decide whether they were 'Hindu' or 'Sikh' and gave different answers each time. To this day in Pakistan, many temples and gurdwaras are combined in a way that

Right: Muhammad Ali Jinnah, founder and first Governor General of Pakistan, with his dogs. This snapshot contrasts with the official portraits of Jinnah in austere Islamic dress.

Below: The dry bed of the Indus, a river so heavily dammed that villagers in southern Pakistan can drive their bullock carts across it.

Above: The 'Sheedi' descendants of the freed African slave Bilal in Hyderabad, Pakistan. Bilal's grandson Bazmi is sitting in the centre, with his two wives behind him. On Bazmi's right is his daughter Ani, who helped me translate her grandfather Mussafir's family history.

Left: Gulabi, a visitor to the home of some Sheedi activists in Badin, southern Pakistan.

Right: Sohni, the folk-heroine of Shah Abdul Latif's eighteenth-century *Risalo*, crossing the river to meet her lover. This much loved story was rescoed on to the domed ceiling of a neglected eighteenth-century tomb belonging to the Qalandrani Leghari family in the desert near Johi, Sindh, Pakistan.

Below: Worshippers at the shrine of Sachal Sarmast in northern Sindh, Pakistan.

Above: Men and women (and hijras) dancing together at the dhammal held at dusk during the urs of Shah Abdul Latif in Bhitshah.

Left: Iskandar – Alexander the Great – and an angel watching the Islamic prophets Ilyas and Khizr drop their dried fish lunch into the Water of Life. (Persia, seventeenth century.) Khizr, a figure of Islamic mythology, is associated with water shrines and cults all over the Indian subcontinent, including those at Uderolal and Sukkur on the River Indus.

Mohanas, Indus boat-people, arriving at the shrine of Khwaja Khizr, which stands on an island in the Indus near Sukkur, Sindh, Pakistan.

A Hindu vision of hell as a river: this marble tableau adorns the Sadhubela temple, on an island in the Indus downstream of the island shrine of Khwaja Khizr.

This Hindu painting of the Indus river-god, Uderolal or Zindapir, riding on a palla fish, hangs at the entrance to the Zindapir temple in Sukkur.

Guru Nanak, the founder of Sikhism, bathing: a scene from the *Janamasakhi*, Guru Nanak's biography, illustrated by the Indian artist Alam Chand in 1733.

Sikhs bathing at the Golden Temple in Amritsar, Punjab, India.

An illustration to the Persian
translation of a French infantry
manual, commissioned in Lahore
by the French officers of Maharaja
Ranjit Singh's army in order to
train Punjabi soldiers in European
fighting techniques.

A sixteenth-century
illustration of Sultan
Mahmud of Ghazni
kissing the feet of the
sleeping Ayaz, his
slave-lover. The
romance between
Mahmud and Ayaz
became an iconic
theme in Indo-
Persian culture.

Emperor Akbar giving thanks for a military victory on the banks of the River Indus. This illustration from the *Akbarnama*, the official history of Emperor Akbar's reign, is believed to show an event which took place in 1572. The artist appears to have added the Attock fort, which was built in 1588 a few years before the *Akbarnama* was completed. This anachronism may have been warranted by the fort's strategic importance in guarding the Mughal empire from attack by enemies beyond the Indus.

This photograph of Sami-ul-Huq, who is now a Member of Parliament in Pakistan, shows him holding a Kalashnikov in one hand and a Qur'an in the other. It hangs in his guest quarters next to the madrassah he runs in Akora Khattak, North West Frontier Province, Pakistan.

is not the case in India (where Hindu-Sikh relations deteriorated seriously in the 1980s, and Sikhs still protest against the 1950 Indian Constitution which defines them as a Hindu sub-caste). In Sukkur every temple has a room set aside for veneration of the Adi Granth, the Sikh holy book. The boatman who rowed me across the river told a story which intertwines Sikh and Hindu traditions: according to local legend, Guru Nanak came to Sadhubela 'to talk with Varuna, our God of Water'. (Hindus in the 1920s, by contrast, claimed that he came to scold the Muslim guardians of Zindapir's shrine.)

'The Sikhs have got it all wrong,' the librarian says. 'Guru Nanak did not mean for a new religion to be created – just like he did not believe that Hindus and Muslims should be separate. He was a Hindu reformer.'

Guru Nanak was born in 1469 to high-caste parents in the west Punjabi village of Talwandi, now called Nankana Sahib in Pakistan. As an infant he displayed all the usual proclivities of mystics: periods of silence, an aversion to education, sudden numinous pronouncements. Sent first to a Hindu priest for primary education, then to another for a grounding in Sanskrit, and finally to the Muslim maulvi for lessons in Persian (the language of court and administration), Nanak surprised each of them in turn with his special spiritual erudition. He also tried several careers before becoming a professional mystic. He worked as a shepherd – a bad one, for he allowed the sheep to escape; as a shopkeeper – he gave away rations to the poor, and finally as a clerk for the local Nawab.

Then, early one morning in 1499, as he was bathing in a river, he vanished. Distressed, his family and friends searched for him for three days. The Nawab ordered the river to be dredged, but to no avail. At last, on the fourth day, Nanak mysteriously reappeared. He did not say where he had been – later Sikh hagiographers maintained that he had disappeared to heaven to commune with God – but whatever had happened, it was clear that he had changed. His first action was to give away his clothes. Then he spoke, saying, 'There is no Hindu, no Muslim.' The people whispered that his time in the river had curdled his brain. But Nanak shrugged off the rumours, and from this moment onwards – to the despair of his in-laws – he embarked on a quest for spiritual harmony.

Until Nanak's nativity, Talwandi was a modest, run-of-the-mill hamlet between two rivers. Four and a half centuries later, when I visit Nankana Sahib, I traipse around six different gurdwaras commemorating every detail of Nanak's famed childhood. There is a gurdwara where he was born, another where he went to school, a third in the alley where he played as a child, a fourth near the tree he sat under, a fifth in the field where he tended buffalo, and a sixth marks the spot where he was shaded from the sun by a cobra.

There is also a sacred tree, an empty concrete *sarovar* (bathing tank) – and several thousand Sikh pilgrims from India. The Pakistan Government allows carefully monitored pilgrimage groups from India to visit three holy places: Nankana Sahib, Lahore and Panja Sahib in far western Punjab. The visits are scrutinized down to the last detail – 'even our hotel room numbers are written on our visas,' an old Sikh lady tells me. As I sit talking with Sikh pilgrims on the lawn outside Nankana Sahib's impressively large, yellow-painted, domed and pinnacled central gurdwara, they point out their Pakistani Intelligence minders – uncomfortable-looking men lounging on the grass not quite out of earshot, sipping sticky soft drinks.

In a large pre-Partition house opposite Nanak's birthplace, I meet another of Pakistan's hybrid breeds. Tall, strapping Pathan Sahab – as he is known to his neighbours – wears a dark red Sikh turban, yet he hails from Parachinar, one of the 'tribal agencies' that border Afghanistan. In 1947, Punjabis massacred each other as they migrated in different directions to their respective new countries, and this is why it is with some trepidation that Indian Sikhs tour Pakistan today ('Security is tight, in case of bad elements'). But the Pathan or Pashtun Sikhs – those born in the Frontier Province bordering Afghanistan – did not go to India at Partition. Again and again I am told that 'the Muslims protected us.' 'They held jirgas,' says Pathan Sahab, 'and the tribal elders decreed that we should stay.'

This triumph over sectarianism has not endeared the Pashtun Sikhs to their Indian guests. Despite their shared religion, the Sikhs of Pakistan and the Sikhs of India do not embrace each other as brothers. 'We are Pashto-speaking, they speak Punjabi,' explains Pathan Sahab; adding, apologetically, 'We were rustic village people when we came here from the Frontier. Our women did purdah, we were uneducated.'

The Indian pilgrims tend to agree. 'There are language problems,' says a young teacher from Jalandhar; 'Pakistan is small, its cities are small,' adds a businessman from Chandigarh; 'This country has got very behind educationally,' says a salesman of electronic goods. They seem to regard the Pashtun Sikhs as eccentric, un-pukka, slightly embarrassing imitations of themselves. 'They are *sahajdhari*,' someone whispers: uninitiated.

The Pashtun Sikhs are probably a legacy of Ranjit Singh's huge nineteenth-century empire, which, in the Maharaja's own words, extended 'to the limits of the Afghans'. It is possible that they are descendants of converts made by the sixteenth-century Sikh missionary, Bhai Gurdas, who travelled to Kabul. They may even be offspring of those Pashtuns whom Nanak met on his voyages west of the Indus. But a month later, in the Afghan town of Ghazni, I meet a small Sikh community of cloth traders, and they tell me that 'We Sikhs came here from India with Sultan Mahmud.' This is unlikely, for the iconoclast sultan died 439 years before Guru Nanak was born (he did, though, have an Indian contingent in his army). But the comment, inaccurate though it is, reflects once again the interleaved histories of the Indus valley. Everybody's story jostles with everybody else's, and the image of the five rivers, winding like the fingers of a hand through the Punjab, illustrates the alternate convergence and division of the state's tangled history.

For a religion that grew up in the land of five rivers, it is natural that Sikhism should have water at the heart of its rituals. There are many legends about Nanak's watery experiences in rivers, lakes and oceans – he made the dry wells of Mecca brim with water, converted the Muslim river saint Khwaja Khizr, and was led to God through a pool of water in the south Indian desert. Every Sikh pilgrimage involves imbibing, bathing in, or giving thanks for the cold river water that fills the gurdwaras' tanks. Sikhs in the Indian Punjab are forever undressing and submerging their bodies in these cool dark 'pools of nectar'. At Baisakhi, the spring festival, they decorate cauldrons of water with flowers in gratitude for the annual mountain snow-melt. The tank of the Golden Temple in Amritsar 'lies in the heart of this great [Indus] river-system', say the Sikh authorities; it symbolizes the 'future confluence of world-cultures into a universal culture' and represents a five-thousand-year-old continuity with the communal city baths of the Indus Valley Civilization.

'But we cannot bathe at Guru Nanak's birthplace,' the Indian Sikhs at Nankana Sahib complain. The holy bathing tank is dry. '*Pani ka masla* [water problems],' says Pathan Sahab. Brittle brown leaves blow across the tank's concrete base and no pilgrim deigns to go near it. The lack of water is a symbol of the Sikhs' own absence.

But Pakistan does possess some holy Sikh water. Panja Sahib is the second most important Sikh site in the country, commemorating a spring that Guru Nanak created for his followers. When a local Muslim saint refused to let Nanak drink from a hilltop fountain, and rolled a rock down to squash him, the Guru put out his hand to stop it and water gushed out. The place is still sacred to both faiths. Muslims climb the hill to the shrine of the implacable saint, and Sikhs perambulate around the fish-filled sacred pool at the bottom. The water here is so delicious that Emperor Akbar cried 'Wah wah!' on tasting it (the name of nearby Wah Cantonment immortalizes this moment). I even meet a canny Muslim businessman who is developing a bottling plant at Panja Sahib to export vials of holy water to the Canadian Sikh diaspora.

Panja Sahib, which stands on the lip of the frontier with Afghanistan, is 'proof', says Pathan Sahab, 'that Guru Nanak visited my native place, that we Pashtuns are original Sikhs too' – although, if his many biographies are to be believed, there was barely anywhere that Guru Nanak did not travel to. After he emerged from the river in 1499, he lived a peripatetic life for the next two decades. In sixteenth-century India, one way to search for life's meaning was to run away and join the faqirs. Nanak took with him his best friend, a low-caste Muslim musician called Mardana, and like Sufi qalandars or Hindu yogis, wanderers in search of the Truth, they roamed all over India together.

According to Sikh tradition, Nanak and Mardana made four major journeys, following the points of the compass as far as they could go in each direction. They went east, to the Hindu holy places at Mathura, Benares and Prayag (Allahabad); south, to the Buddhist headquarters of Sri Lanka; and north through the Himalayas to the hallowed mountain of Kailash in Tibet where the Indus rises. Finally, they disguised themselves as Muslim hajjis – pilgrims – in leather sandals, blue pyjamas and bone necklaces, and took a boat west – to Mecca, Medina and Baghdad. 'Proof' of this journey, too, exists at Nankana Sahib, where a gold-plated gazebo inside an enormous, incongruously polished and expensive glass case encloses a cloak embroidered with Qur'anic verses, the Caliph's farewell gift. (Indian Sikhs, however, who have a cloak of their own in India, regard it as a fake.)

Nanak is also one of the few people who has journeyed along the Indus both near its source in Tibet, and south through the Punjab and Sindh to the sea. What did such restless itinerancy denote? Later, with the benefit of hindsight, Nanak would sing of how

> Religion lieth not in visiting tombs
> Nor in visiting places where they burn the dead
> Nor in sitting entranced in contemplation
> Nor in wandering in the countryside or in foreign lands
> Nor in bathing at places of pilgrimage.
> If thou must the path of true religion see,
> Among the world's impurities, be of impurities free.

If it did anything, travelling cured Nanak of attachment to religious frippery. He had visited all the important pilgrimage places of Hinduism, Buddhism and Islam, and rejected them all. Henceforth, the geographical centre of his spiritual life was the Guru – that is, himself. He returned to the Punjab, bought some land on the banks of the River Ravi, 'donned worldly clothes', and articulated what it was he believed in.

Guru Nanak had become a purist. When pressed, it became clear that there was not much in other religious systems that he endorsed. He did not believe in asceticism – his disciples were supposed to participate fully in the world, while leaving time in the early morning and evening for meditation and prayers. He did not believe in reincarnation, avatars or caste – as a child he famously refused to wear the Brahmin sacred thread that his father tried to force upon him. He also lost caste – deliberately, presumably – by crossing the *kalapani*, the 'black water', the sea, during his voyage to Mecca.

He criticized the decadent ruling powers. Over the previous five hundred years, the Punjab had borne the brunt of raids by Afghan kings, Muslims who often used religion to justify invasions of India. Lying directly on the route from Kabul to Delhi, the Punjab's granaries, orchards and herds were regularly pillaged to feed Muslim soldiers on the move. During Nanak's childhood, north India was ruled by the Lodhis, Pashtun kings, whom he later characterized as hopelessly decadent. But they were paragons of virtue compared to the man who usurped them, Babur from Uzbekistan – the first of the Mughal emperors – who conquered north India in 1526. Guru Nanak encountered Babur's army at first hand – hagiographical stories tell of how he was ordered to grind wheat like a slave until Babur recognized his virtue and released him. But Nanak himself spoke of Babur only to censure him:

> His hordes are perpetrators of sin . . .
> Propriety and laws have gone into hiding
> Falsehood comes to the fore.

If Babur caused chaos in the Punjab, Guru Nanak made it his mission to give his people something to live for. He rejected the caste-bound Brahmins as 'butchers' and the Muslim kings as Satanic exploiters, and centred his sect around Punjabi identity itself. He wrote all his poetry in Punjabi, and while this has inhibited the spread of Sikhism outside the Punjab, it also defined the community and fostered its sense of nationalism. In his 1963 *History of the Sikhs*, Khushwant Singh described Guru Nanak as 'the first popular leader of the Punjab', and put the esteem in which he is held down to his fine Punjabi verses.

The hymns of Nanak, and the nine Gurus who came after him, together form the Adi Granth, the Sikh's holy book. Singing the Adi Granth, or listening to it being sung, is the supreme form of worship for Sikhs. But just as the Sikh bathing tanks in Pakistan are empty, so the gurdwaras echo with silence. 'At Amritsar,' says an old Indian pilgrim I meet, 'hymns are sung all day, every day, by musicians seated inside the Golden Temple itself.' 'It is a full-time, non-stop, twenty-four-hour concert,' says another. 'You must go to India. Sikh worship there is a long melodious musical.'

For decades, crossing the border between India and Pakistan has been fraught with difficulty. But as I reach Lahore, an Indo-Pakistani détente is announced, and in the wake of political goodwill follow new bus, train and plane services. In Lahore I join a busload of Pakistani businessmen and a clutch of families nervously anticipating reunions with their relatives in Lucknow. Pakistanis secretly pine for the grandeur of the India they lost at Partition, and those who can afford to, make up for decades of separation in trips across the border. But although I journey to and fro between the countries several times over the next month, the only Indian tourists I meet are Sikh pilgrims. Nationalist propaganda in India is a powerful force and most Indians have no reason to travel to what they consider a dangerous, fundamentalist nation. The one Indian returnee on my bus is an Ayurvedic herbalist with a suitcase full of the 'forty different plants' – liquorice from Afghanistan, gum from Quetta, leaf syrup from Swat – that for thousands of years have been gathered from the mountainous country west of the Indus.

At Wagah, I step across the artificial line that slices the vast culti-vated Punjabi plain in two, and begin searching for differences between the countries. Are the roads better in India? Is it really dirtier and poorer (as Pakistanis often say)? Does it feel freer? I laugh at myself, remembering the Indian writer Manjula Padmanabhan's description of the journey she made from Pakistan to India as a child in 1960. Sitting on the train, waiting for the shining home-land she had heard so much about to appear from the gloom, she eventually asked – 'When are we going to get to India?' Her little heart sank when she was told that they had been travelling through India for the past two hours.

As I am standing, lost in this reverie, and waiting for the Pakistani soldier to check my passport, a truck from India reverses up to the border. Pakistani porters in blue shirts rush over to unload the cargo: huge sides of beef (too sacred to be eaten in India; cheap meat for poor Muslims). 'Such nice Urdu,' say the Pakistani customs officers. 'Very nice Hindi,' says the woman at Indian customs ten minutes later. 'Sharab? Beer?' I am asked as I step into India by the Sikh owner of a tea-stall, wise to the thirst of those returning from the Land of Prohibition. The bus for nearby Amritsar arrives, and I sit at the back behind a man in a peacock-blue turban, savouring the freedom from being confined to a special women's section. The bus passes through green wheat fields, and as we approach the suburbs, I see a long line of small shops advertising 'Pig Meat' and 'Whisky'. In the city centre I stare open-mouthed at the Sikh women, zooming through the traffic on scooters, sacred daggers slung around their waists.

The omnipresence of Sikhs here is a grim reminder of the reason for their absence over the border – and of the ghoulish way that some Pakistanis commemorate this absence. Pakistan Army officers tell 'stupid Sikh' jokes; school textbooks describe Sikhs as 'murderous butchers'. *Larki Punjaban* (Punjabi Girl), a film released in 2003 by Pakistan's veteran film-maker, Syed Noor, depicts a drunkard Sikh father who chops off his nephew's arm with a meat cleaver, and tries to murder his daughter when she falls for a Pakistani Muslim. When I ask Rukhsana Noor, the film-maker's wife and scriptwriter, to explain this bigoted representation, she tells me simply: 'Hindu-Muslim marriage in Pakistan is impossible.'

Syed Noor's film transposes on to Sikhs all the worst stereotypes about Muslims – violence, religious intolerance, mistreatment of women. Yet despite the two religions' mutual distrust, Islam profoundly influenced Sikhism. ('Islam,' writes the historian of the Indian and Pakistani armies, Stephen P. Cohen, transformed 'Sikhism from a pietistic Hindu sect into a martial faith'.) During the lifetime of the first five Sikh Gurus, there was no antagonism between Muslims and Sikhs – who, after all, are monotheistic. Guru Nanak's *Japji*, the Morning Prayer, begins with a statement of faith close to the Muslim creed:

> There is One God
> His name is Truth
> He is the Creator
> He is without fear and without hate.

Emperor Akbar – perhaps atoning for the sins of his grandfather Babur – asked for copies of this, and other Sikh hymns, to ascertain whether or not they were anti-Islamic. Pleased with what he read, he extended royal patronage to the Sikh community in the form of a land grant. The Sikhs dug a tank on this land for pilgrims to bathe in, and later a temple was constructed within it – the foundation stone of which was laid by a Muslim saint from Lahore, on the invitation of Arjun, the fifth Guru. (This was the Harmandir, one day to be nicknamed – after Maharajah Ranjit Singh smothered it in bullion – the Golden Temple.)

The period of Sikh-Muslim harmony came to an abrupt end with Akbar's death. Jahangir, the new emperor, had always been suspicious of non-Muslim sects, and of the Sikhs in particular. 'For years,' he wrote in his diary, 'the thought had been presenting itself to my mind that either I should put an end to this false traffic, or he [the Guru] should be brought into the fold of Islam.' When Jahangir's son Khusrau rebelled from his father, he was sheltered by Guru Arjun in Amritsar. Jahangir needed no further excuse: 'I fully knew his heresies,' he said of the Guru, 'and I ordered . . . that he should be put to death with torture.' Arjun was taken to Lahore, and tortured till he could no longer stand. He died of his wounds as he was bathing in the River Ravi.

Over the next hundred years, state repression by the Mughals gave Sikhism its final and definitive form. To combat the armies despatched to the Punjab from Delhi, the Sikhs perfected the art of guerrilla warfare. At first, they lived in soldier communities, singing heroic ballads instead of peaceful hymns; later, they lived like bandits, pillaging Afghan and Mughal baggage trains. Alarmed by Sikh separatism, Emperor Aurangzeb had the ninth Guru executed.

For Sikhs, the death of two of their Gurus at the hands of the Muslims was not just an unmitigated tragedy. It compelled the tenth Guru, Gobind, to recognize two prosaic truths. First, that violence should be met with violence: 'When all other means have failed, it is permissible to draw the sword,' he wrote to Emperor Aurangzeb. Second, that his people needed more than the spiritual wisdom of their leaders. They needed to feel they were a people apart – neither Hindu nor Muslim – with special rules, a rigid organization and an instantly recognizable uniform.

In 1699, Gobind called a meeting of Sikhs during the spring festival of Baisakhi. Here, he announced the formation of a militant new group, the Khalsa. Instead of Nanak's *kirtan* (hymns), Sikhs were now to be identified by five visible symbols of their power: *kesh* (uncut hair tied up in a turban), *kangha* (comb), *kach* (shorts), *kara* (steel bracelet) and *kirpan* (sword). He also announced that the Adi Granth would succeed him as the eleventh and final Guru. From now on, Sikhs were to be led, not by the few, but by the rule of the collective, by their communally scripted holy book, and by the social cohesion of the Khalsa.

The attempt to give the Sikhs unity saved the movement from disintegration. Moreover, with Emperor Aurangzeb's death, and the subsequent collapse of the Mughal empire, there was opportunity for regional powers to assert their independence from Delhi. In 1799, exactly one hundred years after the Khalsa was founded (and three hundred years after Guru Nanak emerged from the river), a one-eyed teenager called Ranjit Singh conquered the Punjab and established the first Sikh kingdom. The Gurus had sown Punjabi nationalism through their Punjabi-language songs, Sikh rules of attendance, and regional consciousness. Ranjit Singh marched into Lahore proclaiming himself not just a Sikh leader, but a pan-Punjabi patriot – one who celebrated Hindu festivals, married Muslim wives, and kept at his court ministers of all religions. Guru Nanak had criticized the ruling power of Kings but Ranjit Singh declared himself Maharaja.

By the time the British began making plans to annex the Indus, Maharaja Ranjit Singh was the most powerful and flamboyant ruler in western India. The letters that Alexander Burnes wrote to his commanders in Calcutta are telling for the envy that seeps through every page. The British may have been in control of large swathes of India, but they were paltry penny-pinchers in comparison to the lavish style of native rulers. The court of Ranjit Singh, Burnes wrote, 'realized every notion of Eastern bounty and grandeur that we imbibe in early life'. The elephant mounts of the 'English Gentlemen formed a sad contrast to the burnished, glittering, gold-howdars of the Seikhs'. The British gaped in astonishment as the Maharaja introduced them to his 'Regiment of Amazons' – seventy female dancers dressed as men in yellow silk. With 'covetousness' they gazed upon the Maharaja's massive Koh-i-noor diamond that had belonged to Taimur, ravager of the Punjab, and was engraved, Burnes wrote, with the names of Aurangzeb and the eighteenth-century Afghan Ahmed Shah. The

Maharaja then scattered the tatty British group with gold dust and for two days afterwards the entire party, loath to wash, was distinguished 'by their glittering and bespangled faces'. Never was the stark disparity between the British and an indigenous power clearer.

Burnes himself saved the gold-embossed letter of welcome that the Maharaja sent him, with its polite Persian phrases expressing gladness at the alliance between the Sikhs and British ('friendship, the reservoir of pleasure in the garden of happiness'). After Burnes's death it became a token of Oriental splendour in London, and his brother had great difficulty in getting it back from the various ladies who clamoured to see it; 'Runjeet,' he wrote to Burnes's publisher, 'seems to be a great favourite with the fair.'

Ranjit Singh ruled the Punjab by coming to an accommodation with the Muslim population. For the anarchic decades preceding his reign, Muslims and Sikhs had traded insults – the Afghan armies desecrating the Golden Temple's tank with dead cows, the Sikhs using Aurangzeb's mosque in Lahore as a stable. When he became Maharaja, Ranjit Singh made some efforts to smooth away the differences. He had two Muslim wives, a Muslim foreign minister and Muslim courtiers. In his army there was a Sikh cavalry, Muslim artillery and Muslim and Hindu infantry. Even the architecture of his holiest structures was a diplomatic amalgam of Mughal and Hindu designs. A Pakistan social studies textbook from the 1980s told schoolchildren that:

> Muslims and Hindus are completely different in their way of life, eating habits and dress. We worship in mosques. Our mosques are open, spacious, clean and well-lit. Hindus worship inside their temples. These temples are extremely narrow, enclosed and dark.

Ranjit Singh's Golden Temple – with its dome, spires, wide-open spaces, 'Sanctum Sanctorum', sacred water and holy book – seems designed to confound such prejudice.

Throughout the subcontinent there are high- and low-caste temples and churches, but in Sikh gurdwaras, as in Islam, all classes worship side by side. At Amritsar, menial tasks such as mopping and sweeping are performed – not by low-caste Hindus, as they would be almost anywhere else – but by Sikh volunteers. Guru Nanak particularly stressed the importance of the *langhar*, the communal kitchen, and the only sound that can compete with the hymns being sung in the temple, is the clatter of steel plates being washed and stacked. Day and night, Sikh volunteers cook, serve and clean, and thousands of people turn up to eat the holy fast food that they serve. Even here though, caste has not disappeared. The Sikh Gurus only ever married within their own caste, and today there is still an impermeable division between the Jat Sikhs – high-caste landed farmers and business people – and the low-caste converts to Sikhism, called Mazhabis.

At Nankana Sahib the Sikh pilgrims had spoken to me in reverent tones of the Golden Temple's 'constant music', and coming from Pakistan I am anticipating Qawwali-style revelry. But this is no frenzied Sufi shrine. There is no mystical dancing, not even any modest head-waggling. Indian Punjab gave the world the boob-jiggling bhangra and giddha, but inside the Golden Temple not one Sikh is moving to the beat. The experience is shared, yet self-contained; the aesthetic of music and food, gold and water, is designed to be soothing on the ear, stomach, eye and soul. From the middle of the pool of water the gleaming, shimmering gold-plated temple rises. White colonnaded walkways surround it on all four sides. Pilgrims circulate barefoot, stopping to listen to the hymns, to sleep, or to take a holy dip.

One of the main points of coming to Amritsar is to bathe. The men strip off out in the open, down to their underpants, and plunge into this soup of gold. Women go into a covered section. Sikhs emphasize that all faiths are welcome in their temple, and so when a Sikh lady from Southall beckons me in, I follow after her. It is an odd experience, after so many months of covering every inch of my skin from view, to stand completely naked in a pool of holy water, surrounded by other naked women. I would be wary, too, of immersing my body in this water – holy rivers in India are generally sluggish with sewage – had I not been told of the rigorous water purification system recently installed here. Amritsar's name means 'ambrosial nectar' and in recent years the Golden Temple management has taken this description literally.

A genial Sikh member of the Gurdwara Management Committee takes me on a day-long tour to witness with my own eyes the 'world-quality filtration system'. In the basement of a building behind the Golden Temple, the massive, brand-new plant is humming to itself. 'The water purification system is two years old and imported,' he says, pointing to the MADE IN USA sticker on the side. The water circulates three times around the complex, before it is transported across the city by canal to a sand filtration tank. Later that afternoon, we walk there together, out of the stampede of the city to a quiet lane where water rushes through an underground reservoir. This tank, in turn, feeds five other gurdwaras: each thus blessed with a full, deep pool of precious river water.

The abundance of water is not just symbolic. It is this very commodity – sucked out of the Indus and poured on to the land – which made the Punjab rich: the canal system that every ruler upheld in the name of taxation; the irrigation-fed land reclamation of the British; the post-colonial water disputes between Pakistan and India; the gold necklaces purchased by rich farmers to hang around the necks of their plump Punjabi wives. I think of Gobind's taunt to Aurangzeb: 'I shall strike fire under the hoofs of your horses, I will not let you drink the water of my Punjab.' Land as rich and fertile as this needed soldiers to defend it.

Guru Gobind formed the Khalsa and did battle with the Mughals. Maharaja Ranjit Singh had a French-trained standing army which in 1827 did what no Punjabi army had yet done, and prevented an army of Afghans from crossing the Indus. The British had to wait until the Maharaja's demise before invading, but when they did, Ranjit Singh's military became the backbone of their own pan-Indian army. Even after the British left India, the Punjabi Sikh contingent has remained an unassailable force in the region. In Pakistan, particularly, the powerful triangle of Punjabi water, wealth and military prowess controls the country.

Under British colonial rule, the Sikh – and Punjabi – reputation for martial valour did not decline; if anything, it was enhanced. Barely a decade after the British conquered the Punjab, Indian soldiers in northern India mutinied. The Punjab, however, did not rise; instead, many Sikhs in 1857 fought for the British against their fellow Indians. Britain responded by recruiting large numbers of Punjabis to the army, considering them the finest of India's 'hardy' races. 'All Sikh traditions, whether national or religious, are martial,' stated an army recruitment manual in 1928. During both World Wars, up to half the Indian Army was comprised of Punjabis; Punjabi Muslims dominated, followed by Sikhs. Even now, in a classic statement of Raj nostalgia, a Sikh veteran of the British Army tells me, 'Still today, every Sikh would lay down their life for the Britishers.' Official Sikh policy now, however, is to denigrate collaboration with the British. The Temple Management distributes a free booklet stating that the British tricked Sikhs into believing that the imperialists 'were allies of the Khalsa, come to Asia in fulfilment of a prophecy of the Guru'.

In the nineteenth century, the link between the military and the Punjab was assured by the British policy of granting a plot of irrigated land to soldiers upon retirement. This soon became the principal incentive for joining up. In western Punjab, the British built a network of irrigation canals, precisely in order to increase the land available. West Punjabi nomads were evicted from the grazing grounds, and 'surplus' populations brought in from central India. (Much of the bitter violence at Partition was a fight to retain, or claim, this valuable land.)

In a direct continuation from the colonial era, it was Punjabi military men who assumed power in the independent nation. For over half its life, Pakistan has lived under army rule – an army that is still three-quarters Punjabi. With Punjabi ex-servicemen taking jobs in the civil sector, Punjabi farmers taking more than their fair share of Indus water, and army farms and businesses buying up land and power all over the country, every Pakistani who is not Punjabi complains of Punjabi imperialism.

From 1953 onwards, the post-colonial Indian state began to address the imbalance of Punjabis in their army by recruiting from areas, like Tamil Nadu and Gujarat, that the British had not considered 'martial' – and by ceasing to recruit Sikhs. Pakistan, however, maintained the colonial status quo. To this day the lack of recruitment from outside the Punjab creates an imbalance of power – and it is a policy with a dangerous history. In 1971, discrimination against Bengali soldiers contributed to the secession of East Pakistan as Bangladesh (the other factor was West Pakistan's racist annulment of the election after it was won by a Bengali). Yet even after losing half the country and suffering humiliating defeat in a war against India, the army has continued to consolidate its Punjabi interests. Pakistan – say Sindhis and Baluchis – 'is a country run by and for Punjabi soldiers'.

Travelling through the irrigated croplands of the Punjab to Lahore, I meet a good many Pakistan Army officers, including several generals who have worked with both of the last two military dictators. But it is during the taxi ride south from Lahore to Nankana Sahib that I come to understand why the army is such a compelling career choice for ordinary Punjabis. The driver tells me that both his father and grandfather were landless peasants from western Punjab. He himself spent five years in the army, during which time he was trained as a clerk and driver, and given a firearms' licence. This has enabled him to work since then as a secretary, taxi driver and security guard, and even now he and his family receive free medical treatment (this in a country with severely impaired public health care). If, like his brothers, he had stayed in the army until retirement, he would have been given some land or cash as well. '*Faida to hain*,' he says emphatically: There are many advantages. He pulls a piece of paper out of the glove compartment and hands it to me. It is a leave certificate. He stole a big pile of them before he was discharged, and now he fills one in whenever he travels out of Lahore. 'Guarantee,' he says: if the Police think he is a vacationing soldier they do not dare ask for bribes. The army, then, functions for its members like a bootleg welfare state. (It functions for the officer class as a guarantee of luxury and privilege.) No wonder that Pakistan's soldiers guard the institution so jealously – even to the extent of deposing elected politicians.

Punjabis dominate the army, and the army has a monopoly over the country's natural resources. In 1960, thirteen years after the religious and social division of the Punjab at Partition, India and Pakistan signed the Indus Waters Treaty. The three eastern rivers – the Ravi, Sutlej and Beas – went entirely to India, which promptly dammed them to channel every last drop of water into irrigation. Pakistan's Punjab was given the Indus, Jhelum and Chenab, and it has appropriated and guarded these rivers, making them the muscle and centre of the country. Even now the ramifications of the Indus Waters Treaty create cross-border tension: in 1999, India announced that it was damming the Chenab, one of Pakistan's three rivers, just before it crossed the border. No Pakistani politician can forget April 1948, when India cut off Pakistan's irrigation canals at the start of the sowing season. The Indian dam, given the go-ahead in 2007 after the World Bank appointed a neutral expert to arbitrate on its justness, is supposedly for hydroelectricity but Pakistan fears the capability that its neighbour now possesses: of unleashing the weapon of water deprivation.

It is a weapon, say Sindhi farmers, that is already being used against them by Punjabis. As Sindh receives very little monsoon, farmers rely on the state to deliver water to their fields. With over 80 per cent of Pakistan's cropland requiring irrigation, water is a powerful political tool. The Pakistan Government, like the British colonial government before it, has invested heavily in the irrigation infrastructure, by which means they are able to control society. Sindhis claim that the dams built since Partition have been designed (by the army) so that Punjabis can take the lion's share of the water. Nobody who has visited the Delta and seen the trickle of water which is all that remains of the river there, could disagree.

Dams also have powerful advocates in the capital because of the lucrative kickbacks they provide for politicians, bureaucrats and engineers. (For this reason, bribes to get into WAPDA, Pakistan's water management department, are the highest in the country.) Local development analysts have long argued that Pakistan needs less capital-intensive, technology-heavy, foreign-expertise-reliant irrigation systems. Dams, they say, are highly wasteful of water, time and money (international consultants push local costs up by 40 per cent; international tenders by another 300 per cent; water resource management is the second-largest contributor, after defence, to Pakistan's foreign debt). What is needed instead, they say, is better management of local water resources and more effective irrigation systems.

The Indus is also a river prone to heavy silting, so dams do not last long here. The gigantic Tarbela dam, constructed in the 1970s, has grown so thick with silt that it is forecast to be entirely inoperable by 2030. Even the fickle World Bank, which for the first sixty years of Pakistan's existence urged dams on developing nations, has come round to the view that they do more harm than good.

But Pakistan's lack of water in relation to need is now the priority, and the government considers dams to be the only answer to the problem. The President, General Pervez Musharraf, who nine years before his coup wrote a paper in London on South Asia's water security, has put his moustachioed military clout behind the building of dams, and in particular Kalabagh on the Punjab–Frontier border, the most contentious dam of recent times – condemned both by Sindhis, who fear that even less water will come downstream, and by people from the North West Frontier Province (NWFP), whose land will be flooded. Some of the more pessimistic Pakistanis predict that the double stranglehold of the Punjabi Army on both politics and water will push the country into a second civil war.

As he lay dying in 1539, Guru Nanak's final words were of his birthplace. 'The tamarisk must be in flower now,' he said; 'the pampas grass must be waving its woolly head in the breeze; the cicadas must be calling in the lonely glades.' Nanak was grateful all his life to the Punjabi landscape. Its rivers and trees, animals and birds were a constant inspiration to his poetry:

> Worshippers who praise the Lord know not His greatness,
> As rivers and rivulets that flow into the sea know not its vastness.
> . . .
> As the Chatrik bird loves the rain
> And cries for a few drops to slake its thirst
> As the fish gambols in the waters,
> Nanak is athirst for the Name of Hari.
> He drinks and his heart is filled with joy.

Nankana Sahib today is a dry and dusty place. During Nanak's lifetime the village stood in the middle of the 'Nilianwali Bar', the forest of blue deer, but within years of the British taking over the Punjab, neither trees nor deer were left. The woods disappeared, uprooted to make way for the huge wheat and rice fields. Babur hunted rhinoceros in the jungles of northern Punjab; Sikh outlaws took refuge in the *lakhi* (a central forest of a hundred thousand trees); and up until the late nineteenth century, 'lions, tigers, leopards, panthers, bears, wolves, hyenas, wild boars, nilgai' roamed through the Punjab's forests. British irrigation projects (and trigger-happy officials) eliminated the lions and tigers, and Pakistan's pesticide-fed, dam-led, intensive agriculture projects have exterminated all the rest. Of all the lands along the Indus, the Punjab has changed most in the past two hundred years.

Deforestation has obvious short-term gains – with mechanized agriculture, the bigger the fields, the bigger the return. But trees keep the land supple and moist – and deforestation can create deserts. Downriver from Nankana Sahib are the desiccated remains of Harappa, a city from the third millennium BCE, which despite its extraordinary sophistication, collapsed and perished probably because its citizens over-exploited forest and water supplies – a stark provocation to sustainable resource use, though one blithely ignored by modern Pakistani landlords.

And thus at Guru Nanak's birthplace, where Pakistan-despising pilgrims are unable to bathe in the sarovar, it is dust which they take home with them to India as a sacred souvenir. In the hallway of the central gurdwara, I pass a woman crouched on the floor, pulling back the mats that have been laid there and squirrelling away the dust in a twist of paper. 'What is she doing?' I ask a man in a sunshine-yellow turban. He bends down and scoops up some dust in his fingers: 'We regard the dust of Nankana Sahib as holy,' he says, and drops it on to his tongue like sherbet.

That evening I return to Lahore, and pay a last visit to the Dera Sahib Gurdwara. Here, standing on the edge of the red-light district, between Emperor Aurangzeb's sublime sandstone mosque and the royal fort, encircled to the north by the waterless River Ravi, is the shrine of Maharaja Ranjit Singh.

Sitting in a tiny office near the Maharaja's tomb, sipping sweet milky tea, is a Sikh who fled from Pakistani Punjab to India at Partition, and fled back again in the 1980s. Manmohan Singh Khalsa shares a name with the Indian Prime Minister, but he dismisses his namesake as a 'puppet'. A member of the guerrilla army that led a 'terrorist' campaign for Khalistan, an independent Sikh state, Manmohan Singh claimed asylum in Britain in the 1980s after the Indian Army stormed the Golden Temple. Declared a wanted man by the Indian Government, Lahore is the nearest he has been to Amritsar since then.

'*Khalistan Zindabad* [Long Live Khalistan],' Manmohan Singh says, and laughs: 'In India they would put me in jail for saying that.' (The Pakistan Government, by contrast, welcomed – even armed – Khalistan fighters.) He is unrepentant about losing his Indian homeland. 'I could not live in Occupied Punjab,' he says. 'In Pakistan Sikhs have more freedom. Sikhism was born here. Maharaja Ranjit Singh ruled from Lahore. Muslim and Sikh culture is the same.' In London, he has founded the World Muslim-Sikh Foundation to celebrate 'our common language, customs and tribal background'. 'What about Partition?' I ask. He frowns. 'That nafrat was caused by Brahminism, the black spot on Asia.'

'If Sikhs are so happy in Pakistan,' I say finally, 'why are there no Sikhs in the army?' I am thinking of the ultimate irony: that the Pakistan Army, which has its roots in Sikh martial traditions, has never conscripted a single Sikh. But Manmohan Singh has a triumphant answer. 'General Pervez,' he says, 'is very good for Sikhs.' He tells me how he talked with Musharraf for 'three and a half hours' after the General became Dictator. 'I said, "Take Sikhs in the army." He said, "OK." And now there is a Sikh, the first in Pakistan's history. He joined two months ago. A young boy from Nankana Sahib.'

Manmohan Singh sits back and drains his cup of tea. It is dark outside, and the last prayer of the day is being called from the Badshahi Masjid. We sit and listen in silence, for the mosque is famous not only for the vastness and perfection of its red sandstone court-yard but also for the beauty of its muezzin's voice. 'The first Sikh soldier in the Pakistan Army . . .' says Manmohan Singh, and I add: 'From the village where Guru Nanak was born . . .' As we sit in the dark, listening to the azan, I wonder when the converging rivers will divide.

6

Up the Khyber

1001

'Once the water of Sind is crossed, everything is in the Hindustan way.'

Emperor Babur, *c.* 1526

LEANING OVER THE rampart of Attock fort on the banks of the Indus, I look across the river, contemplating the contrasts. Behind me are the Punjabi plains, regimented army cantonments, women in rainbow-hued headscarves and men with well-trimmed moustaches. Ahead are the blue Afghan hills, frontier towns, Kalashnikov-clutching smugglers, and women in burqas. Even the river maps the confluence of these worlds. Below me, the Kabul river streams in from the west, brown with silt and turbulent with Pashtun intrigue; the Indus flows in from the east, icy-blue with glacial mountain snow-melt. For a few hundred yards after they join, the brown Kabul and blue Indus flow side by side; only once the water has passed in front of Attock fort, do the colours merge. It is here that generations of Indian generals have stood, keeping watch over this crossing, wary of Afghan invaders.

Babur, like other medieval Muslim adventurers who galloped down from Samarkand, across Afghanistan and through the frontier passes, had long cherished the idea of conquering India. In 1526, after several unsuccessful attempts, he broke through the defences and defeated the Sultan of Delhi. For a Central Asian nobleman in search of a kingdom, India, as Babur saw it, offered two supreme rewards: 'it is a large country, and has masses of gold and silver.'

Only once he got there did he discover that the people were plain, the architecture abysmal and the conversation paltry. There weren't even any musk melons, candlesticks or horses. 'Hindustan is a country that has few pleasures to recommend it,' he wrote dismissively in his memoirs. But while Babur's friends quickly grew sick of the heat and dust and begged to return to their homeland, the new Emperor was adamant. The future of his dynasty lay east of the Indus:

> Give a hundred thanks, Babur, that the generous Pardoner
> Has given thee Sindh and Hind and many a kingdom.
> If thou have not the strength for their heats,
> If thou say, 'Let me see the cold side,' Ghazni is there.

And so, with Afghanistan – chilly Ghazni – on the distant horizon as solace for the homesick, Babur moved to the plains of north India, and made Delhi the centre of his kingdom. For the next three centuries India would be ruled by emperors whose grandsire was an Uzbek.

Babur was not the first Muslim king to cross the Indus, and where he trod many more would follow. The Lodhis whom he had usurped from the throne of Delhi were a Pashtun family, and Humayun, his Kabul-born son, barely lasted a decade before he was usurped by an Afghan, Sher Shah Suri. Humayun's son Akbar learned from his father's mistake: beware of men from Kabul.

Modern Afghanistan is an ethnic mix of Hazaras, Tajiks, Uzbeks and Pashtuns (Pathans or Pakthuns, the ungovernable tribesmen from both sides of Afghanistan's eastern border). But when Babur and his descendants referred to 'Afghans' they meant the Pashtuns – entirely different stock from the Mughals. Babur's mother's family were Mongols descended from Timur and Genghis Khan, and his father's side was Turkish. Babur was conscious of his heritage, and he bequeathed an iron principle to his descendants – out-and-out suspicion of Pashtuns. Babur's grandson Akbar in turn spelt it out to his followers: on no account were these 'brainless', 'turbulent' and 'vagabond' people to be made governors, given major army commands or senior bureaucratic posts. Even their wives were to be excluded from royal weighing ceremonies (when the monarch's weight in gold was given away to the poor). 'It is a rule in the Mughal empire,' wrote the seventeenth-century Venetian traveller

Niccolao Manucci, 'not to trust the race of Pashtuns.' The Persians got the top jobs, the Turks ran the army, Hindus looked after imperial finances. Only the Pashtun-Afghan tribesmen were routinely passed over for promotion. (The stereotype of Pashtun unruliness, it is tempting to think, originates with the Mughals.)

In the 1580s, Akbar began building a big red sandstone fort at Attock, on the Punjabi side of the river. Looking out towards the land of the Afghans, the fort was designed to defend Akbar's empire from his scheming half-brother in Kabul. It was named 'Attock Banaras' to twin it with 'Katak Banaras' fort on the eastern extremity of India – and it was placed on this riverine 'boundary', wrote the court historian Abul-Fazl, as a 'noble barrier' between 'Hindustan and Kabulistan . . . for enforcing the obedience of the turbulent'. The fort was the perfect symbol of how far – in half a century – the Mughals had travelled from their Central Asian past.

Nor has the fort lost any of its Mughal symbolism in the past sixty years: requisitioned by the Pakistan Army as a maximum-security detention centre and military court, Asif Zardari, Benazir Bhutto's husband, was incarcerated and Nawaz Sharif, the Prime Minister whom President-General Musharraf deposed, was tried by the army here. As I am standing looking over the wall of the fort's Begum Sarai, I hear a shriek, and turn to see a teenage Pakistani soldier running towards me, waving his gun. 'This is army property,' he says as soon as he gets his breath back, 'and forbidden to outsiders. Get out before my seniors catch you.'

Emperor Akbar managed to contain the Pashtun threat through constant vigilance along the Indus. But in the vastly expanded Mughal empire of the seventeenth century, the peace could not last. During the reign of Akbar's great-grandson Aurangzeb, Pashtun resentment turned to war.

Emperor Aurangzeb was a Muslim zealot: he quickly gave up the pluralistic practices of his grandsires, abandoned the royal fashion for celebrating Hindu festivals and culture, instituted regulation trouser- and beard-length – his modern incarnation is the Taliban. Since roughly the time that Sultan Mahmud, the warring Afghan, invaded their country in the eleventh century, the Pashtuns have been Muslim. But where Islamic law clashes with Pashtunwali (the Pashtuns' unwritten code of conduct) it is tradition, not religion, that prevails. 'I am a drinker of wine,' wrote the great Pashtun poet, Khushal Khan Khattak, 'why does the Priest quarrel with me?'

Khushal Khan Khattak, a Pashtun chief from a village near the Indus, was not shy of making his disgust with Emperor Aurangzeb public:

> I am well acquainted with Aurangzeb's justice, and equity,
> His orthodoxy in matters of faith . . .
> His own brothers, time after time, cruelly put to the sword,
> His own father overcome in battle.

(Even Aurangzeb's venerable ancestor did not escape Khushal's scorn. 'Babur, King of Delhi,' the poet pointed out, 'owed his place to the Pashtuns.')

In 1664, Aurangzeb despatched a contingent of the imperial army west of the Indus to deal with this impertinent rebel, and Khushal was at last brought in chains to India. But four years later, on his release, Khushal returned home unrepentant, and rallied the Pashtuns to rise up against the Emperor. The Mughal army could manoeuvre effortlessly in the open plains of Hindustan but in the rocky terrain of the Frontier it was no match for Khushal's guerrilla tactics. Aurangzeb camped for two years at Attock, trying to raise the low morale of his troops: 'against no people,' wrote Khushal's Victorian translator, 'did he make more strenuous and futile efforts.' Like the Army of the Indus, the Coalition of the Willing, and the Pakistan Army, Aurangzeb's men could make no headway against the Pashtun rebels holed up in the Afghan mountains. Like his frustrated successors, where warfare failed, the Emperor turned to bribes. He bought off one of Khushal's sixty sons – that was enough. Khushal died heartbroken, a fugitive far from home. His dying wish was to be buried where 'the dust of the hoofs of the Mughal cavalry' would not light upon his grave.

Khushal was a prolific author and while he may have lost the war of swords he won the war of words. He wrote over three hundred and sixty works – poems about the Frontier's rivers and mountains; treatises on falconry, turbans and medicine; a travel book in verse; a prose autobiography. In particular, he wrote about women. Kama

Sutra-like, the *Diwan* (his collection of odes) enumerates the carnal qualities of women from different Pashtun tribes; it boasts of his prowess (fifteen women a night); it eulogizes the author's 'organ' and dispenses sex tips to eager young boys. In the current repressive climate, the sex bits have become an embarrassment for Khushal's family who recently tried to get them excised from his oeuvre, and a poetic anomaly for the Pashto Academy at Peshawar University which is unable to teach them, let alone discuss them, for fear of the repercussions. Yet they exist – a poignant reminder of life before the mullahs took over.

It is odd then that, despite his pious proclamations, persecution of Shias, and model theocracy, Aurangzeb has never really become a hero for Pakistanis. Some textbooks state gratefully that he upheld the 'Pakistani spirit'. But in general, notwithstanding his Islamic huffing and puffing, Aurangzeb (who even endowed some Hindu temples) is a little too *Indian*. The heroes Pakistani rulers love – the ones they name their ballistic missiles after – are the medieval Afghan idol-breakers and Hindu-killers. Of these the first and most illustrious is the eleventh-century Sultan Mahmud of Ghazni.

Like the Mughals after him, Sultan Mahmud was a Turk, on his father's side. But his mother was an Afghan from Zabul, and this has allowed both Afghan and Pakistani Pashtuns to claim him as one of their own. Mahmud's father was a slave. Yet the son became – as a maulvi in Afghanistan later puts it to me proudly – the 'first President of our country'. He was not a Pashtun; and yet the Pashtuns love him.

Mahmud grew up in a borderland of overlapping worlds. His forefathers came from the Turkish steppes; he was born in Ghazni, 150 kilometres south-west of Kabul; his religious life was dictated by Arabia, and his culture by Persia. All these spheres were equally important. He studied Arabic, picked up Persian, and spoke Turkic at home with his slaves. His mother's birthplace became his kingdom; his father's nomadic people provided the backbone of his army; the Sunni Caliphate in Baghdad gave his rule religious authority; Persian poets imbued his court with glamour. As if this was not enough, Mahmud himself added another ingredient to this intoxicating mix: India.

Other Muslims had reached India long before Mahmud. Muhammad bin Qasim – seventeen-year-old nephew of the Caliph – invaded Sindh in 711. Arab traders probably built mosques along the south Indian Malabar coast before that. But the journeys that Sultan Mahmud made across the Indus were far more significant than these minor incursions.

When Sebuktigin, Mahmud's father, arrived in Ghazni at the end of the tenth century, it was little more than a village. There was one strategic advantage: proximity to India. In good weather it took barely a month to reach the River Indus. For Mahmud, a small energetic man with a wispy beard and endless enthusiasm for going on journeys, this was like striking gold. During his thirty-year career as a jihadi, Mahmud marched into India twelve, thirteen, or even seventeen times 'on the path of Allah'. By 1030 he had managed to wage religious war – if not annually, as he had hoped – at least every other year, by following the tributaries of the Indus down to the river and into India. Sometimes he took the difficult, northern Khyber pass road (if he wished to fight the Hindus near Peshawar). Once he went south to Kandahar and through the deserts of Sindh to Gujarat to destroy the stone lingam – sacred symbol of Lord Shiva's penis – in the Somnath temple. But the most direct path to the Indus was east, through what is now north Waziristan, currently Al-Qaeda's favoured base in Pakistan.

India made Sultan Mahmud's career. The country was rich. The people were Hindus, so plunder and murder could be legitimized as jihad against the polytheist infidel. Mahmud made a speciality of looting Indian towns with massive temples, and he always (except when his baggage was washed away in the Indus) returned laden with booty.

Thanks to jihad, Mahmud's territories expanded. Ghazni was transformed into a dazzling imperial city. Foreign ambassadors came to gawp at the jewels – diamonds 'as big as pomegranates' – laid out on carpets in his palace. Volunteers flocked to his army to become *ghazis* – holy warriors. Mahmud himself was invested with the highest religious dignities from the Caliph in Baghdad: a robe of honour, permission to call himself 'Sultan', and a clutch of honorific titles for posterity: 'The Guardian of the State and of the Faith'; 'The

Lustre of Empire and the Ornament of Religion'; 'The Establisher of Empires'. It is difficult to gauge the impression that Mahmud made on India at the time. But India's impact on the Islamic world was instant and phenomenal.

Ever since the dawn of Islam, India – vast, rich, exotic – had posed a problem for Muslims. In the Hadith, the sayings of the Prophet, Muhammad himself aspires to conquer it: jihadis who fight against India, he is said to have avowed, 'will be saved from hellfire'. The famous Moroccan merchant Ibn Battuta described how the pre-Islamic prophet Sulayman (Solomon) travelled to a mountain in Sindh, looked down into India and saw nothing but darkness. India was black and wicked – but it possessed great material and intellectual treasure. Arabs had been profiting from the Indian spice trade for centuries. Indian scholars visited Baghdad in the eighth century, and Arabic translations were made of important Sanskrit texts on astronomy, philosophy and medicine.

In the early eighth century, when Muhammad bin Qasim arrived on the coast of Sindh, Al Hajjaj, the Caliph, ordered him to cooperate with the local Hindus – 'give them money, rewards, promotions . . . give them immunity [*aman*],' he wrote. Immunity made the Hindus into the *dhimmi* – the 'protected', like the Jews and Christians. Henceforth, to have fought them would have been *fitna* (internal strife), not jihad. Nevertheless, there was no explicit Qur'anic justification for this stance. It was thus an issue open to interpretation.

Three hundred years later, when Sultan Mahmud wished to make his name and fortune, the Hindus and their idols became a legitimate cause for warfare. Mahmud presented his raids on India as victories for Sunni Islam – and the Caliph agreed. ('The King,' wrote the historian Ferishta, 'caused an account of his exploits to be written and sent to the Caliph, who ordered it to be read to the people of Baghdad, making a great festival upon the occasion.') Yet five hundred years later still – when Emperor Akbar was on the throne in Delhi – the juridical pendulum swung back again. Abul-Fazl, Akbar's chief historian, wrote with great distaste of Sultan Mahmud's misplaced iconoclasm. 'Fanatical bigots representing India as a country of unbelievers at war with Islam,' he thundered, 'incited his unsuspecting nature to the wreck of honour and the shedding of blood and the plunder of the virtuous.' Even in Sultan Mahmud's day, there were Muslims who took this view. The most important of these was Alberuni.

In 1017, Mahmud – as was his wont in the summer months when the Indus was impassable – turned his attentions north-west to the independent country of Khwarizm (in modern Uzbekistan). He invaded it, annexed it, and returned home to Ghazni followed by lines of prisoners. Among them was a man named Abu Raihan Alberuni, an astronomer, philosopher and mathematician. Alberuni had already read widely about India in Arabic translations of Sanskrit texts, but he had never been there. Over the next thirteen years, as Sultan Mahmud's field of war in India expanded steadily eastwards, Alberuni travelled in his wake – not fighting but talking, not killing but learning. Alberuni had a deep regard for Indian thought – and the book that he published on his return was a scholarly master-piece.

At the very same time that Al Utbi, Sultan Mahmud's secretary, was eulogizing jihad against the Indians, Alberuni was learning Sanskrit, conversing with pandits, and compiling a systematic record of Indian thought. He had to tread carefully. He was writing a book about one of the greatest civilizations in the world – from the court of an orthodox Sunni iconoclast. 'This book is not a polemical one,' he wrote in his Preface, and insisted, 'I shall not produce the arguments of our antagonists in order to refute such as I believe to be wrong.' 'My book,' he wrote emphatically, 'is nothing but *a simple historic record of facts.*' Some scholars interpret his *History of India* as intended to disparage Sultan Mahmud's campaigns in India. But it is difficult to tell. 'Mahmud utterly ruined the prosperity of the country, and performed wonderful exploits,' Alberuni wrote, 'by which the Hindus became like atoms of dust scattered in all directions, and like a tale of old in the mouth of the people.' Is this praise, or disapproval?

Alberuni spent several years in India, teaching Greek philosophy and being taught Hindu concepts in return, and he seems to have come to the conclusion that Hellenic and Indian thought, despite their polytheistic trappings, essentially boiled down to a monotheistic system. He drew favourable comparisons between Hindu religious concepts

– such as creation – and those in the Qur'an. Later he admitted that although he developed a 'great liking' for the subject, he found it hard going at first, especially as 'in that respect I stand alone in my time'. Moreover, there was plenty in Hinduism which he found opaque; 'the Hindus entirely differ from us in every respect,' he wrote on the subject of religion; 'we believe in nothing in which they believe, and vice versa . . . They are haughty, foolishly vain, self-conceited and stolid.'

Of course, Alberuni's book was ample proof that India had much to be vain about. Even Sultan Mahmud could not help but be affected by the country's grandeur. Mahmud is said to have so admired the stone architecture of temples in Mathura that he found himself unable to destroy them. Having sacked the temple of Somnath, 'the beauty of its inhabitants, its alluring gardens, flowing rivers and productive soil' tempted him to settle there (his soldiers wouldn't hear of it). He pardoned a Hindu king, Nunda Ray, on account of an extremely flattering poem the Hindu sent him. He even had a coin minted with Arabic on one side and the *kalma* (Islamic creed) translated into Sanskrit on the other – which, shockingly, described the Prophet Muhammad in strictly non-Islamic terms as an 'avatar' of God. Maybe the great iconoclast himself anticipated Emperor Akbar's rampant eclecticism.

'India' was a populous country and in contrast to the notion later peddled by Europeans – that the Hindus, effeminized by the ener-vating climate, were easily conquered by hardy mountain Muslims – the armies Mahmud found himself up against were formidable. Al Utbi calls the Indian soldiers 'obstinate opponents' and Mahmud clearly developed a grudging admiration for them. Indians were highly prized as mercenaries: Mahmud had a Hindu division in his army, who lived in a special Hindu quarter in Ghazni, and he used them to devastating effect against heretic or rebel Muslims. (In Zarang they sacked the Friday mosque, killed all the worshippers within it, and murdered some Christians as well.)

Mahmud also learnt from Hindu battle formation. In addition to their redoubtable numbers, the Indians had a tactical advantage – elephants. In an age of spears, bows and maces, the elephant ('head-strong as Satan') was a coveted weapon and there was something of an arms race to possess them. Mahmud claimed elephants as booty from Indian kings, he gave them as rare presents to honoured friends, and he counted them as carefully as he weighed his enormous diamonds. They were also used to intimidate his enemies. Firdawsi, author of the *Shahnamah* (Book of Kings), is said to have fled Ghazni in disguise after the Sultan vowed to have him trampled to death by elephants. Even the Caliph was threatened. 'Do you wish me to come to the capital of the Caliphate with a thousand elephants,' he shouted at the Caliph's ambassador, after the latter had refused to give him Samarkand, 'in order to lay it to waste and bring its earth on the backs of my elephants to Ghazni?'

Even more frightening than India's elephants were its rivers. Nowhere could have been more different from the dry highland steppes which Mahmud was used to than the lush green mosquito-ridden Punjab. Rivers – crossing them, drowning in them, fighting battles upon them – became a major motif of Mahmud's Indian invasions, and one which he never entirely mastered. His army waded across them (the Sultan on an elephant, his generals on horseback) and if the rains were heavy, or a campaign mistimed, the river could scupper everything. Rivers were not a natural part of Mahmud's military expertise. Al Utbi described the end to one campaign, when the Sultan 'returned to Ghazni in triumph and glory . . . but as his return was during the rains, when the rivers were full and foaming, and as the mountains were lofty, and he had to fight with his enemies, he lost the great part of his baggage in the rivers, and many of his valiant warriors were dispersed.' To medieval Muslim historians, the Punjab was the land of the 'seven dreadful rivers'. None was more dreadful – none more 'deep and wide' – than the Indus.

Mahmud's adversaries were not stupid, and whenever possible, they used the Indus against him. The Punjabi king, Anandpal, refused to allow Mahmud to cross it in 1006; Daud, the Karmatian 'heretic', hid on an island in the middle of it; and the Jats – determined river people, probably ancestors of the independent-minded Sikhs, who knew the river's every bend and quirk – harassed Mahmud's army incessantly as it marched wearily north along it on its return from Somnath in 1026.

It was perhaps the final indignity of being pursued by the Jats that gave rise to the story of Sultan Mahmud's last battle – fought on the Indus. All his other campaigns were conducted on dry land with elephants and maces; yet in 1026 the field of battle switched to the river. Mahmud built 1,400 boats, each equipped with a triple spike – one spike sticking out of the prow, two on either side – with which he pierced and sank the Jats' 'four-thousand-strong' fleet. The story was written up by Mahmud's historians as his swansong, for he never went back to India. By 1030 he was dead.

Sultan Mahmud's descendants had neither his energy nor his wanderlust, and the Ghaznavid dynasty soon petered out. But for Central Asian noblemen like Babur a precedent had been set. Sultan Mahmud of Ghazni had shown the way – and over the next five centuries, hordes of Muslims followed him. As Babur wrote, clearly delineating a genealogy of holy warriors, 'From the time of the revered Prophet down till now three men from that side have conquered and ruled Hindustan. Sultan Mahmud *Ghazi* was the first . . . I am the third.' The Pakistan Army, in turn, has cast itself as Sultan Mahmud's heir in anti-India aggression, naming its new ballistic missile 'Ghazni'.

By the time I am shooed from the walls of Attock fort by a Pakistani rifle, an idea has taken shape. Despite (or perhaps because of) the dangers that every sensible and informed Pakistani warns me of, I feel a need to travel back to – as Babur put it – 'the cold side', to see the homeland of these invaders, and to understand from this vantage point what it was that drew them across the river.

On a jaunty spring morning a week later, I am in a car at Torkham, the Khyber crossing between Pakistan and Afghanistan. In the six months that I have been in Pakistan, I have never been so excited as by this hackneyed rite of passage: *going up the Khyber*. I collect my entry stamp, look around me at the piles of used car parts (doors, gear sticks), at the women in their pleated blue burqas, at the wide open sky above my head. It is an eight-hour drive to Kabul, through well-watered plains fringed by the Tora Bora mountains, down a long avenue of trees lined on either side by the green orchards of Jalalabad, along the foaming brown torrent of the river, and up into the rugged hills that have guarded Kabul for centuries. I stare out of the window at the abandoned Russian tanks, the busy teashops, the Central Asian faces. I feel glad the road is so bad that the journey takes twice as long as it did in the sixties.

In Kabul, I camp in a cold house with no hot water inhabited by ten French journalists. That night they take me to an ex-pat party in a smart part of town where there is beer, electricity and dancing. None of them want to come to Ghazni. '*Mais la route, elle est bonne,*' they tell me.

Ghazni lies on the Kabul–Kandahar road, which was built with great fanfare by the US Army and is still practically the only monument in the country to their great democratic project. It gleams black and confident. We speed through quiet villages, past herds of goats moving across the brown hillside like shoals of fish. It takes two hours to reach Ghazni, a little faster than Emperor Babur's estimation that 'those leaving Ghazni at dawn may reach Kabul between the Two Prayers'.

Sultan Mahmud's illustrious capital is a small town now – even in Babur's day it was merely 'humble' – but its twin twelfth-century towers, sultan's tomb and crumbling citadel (sacked by the British in the nineteenth century; today littered with rusting green rocket-launchers) reverberate plaintively with its fraught history. Even the Taliban have made their mark: they smashed up the town's Buddhist statues in 2001.

It is raining when we arrive. I sit in our four-by-four, with its cracked windscreen, transfixed by the Ghaznavid victory towers in the distance. 'It is too dangerous,' says Zebi, my driver, as I point out the sights. He points to the red spots of paint along the roadside: landmines. 'Let's go and see the police and get an escort.' But the police chief isn't in: they send us to see the Minister for Culture. The Minister is in Kandahar: try the Governor. And the Governor is in a meeting. His deputy, an overworked Tajik with ruddy cheeks, gives me a glass of green tea, a plate of sweets, and regrets that I need written permission from Kabul to visit Afghan antiquities. I am walking back down the Governor's regal staircase, through a crowd of soldiers, turbanned petitioners and small tea-boys, when someone comes running after me. 'I have facilitated your visit,' says the deputy.

He shows me into an enormous room, past a conference table

around which fifteen veiled Afghan women are sitting in silence, to a sofa by the window. I sit down opposite six turbanned bearded men and a clean-shaven man in a beige two-piece suit. The one in beige must be the translator. But which is the Governor?

I address the bearded men collectively in reverent Urdu. I explain my love for their great hero, Sultan Mahmud of Ghazni. I beg permission to visit the town's '*dilchaspe puranewale cheez*' (heart-pleasing old things; the word 'antique', I find out later, would have done just as well – it exists in Arabic). The man in beige bursts out laughing. 'Where are you from?' he asks in English. 'London,' I say. 'I have been to London many times,' he tells me. But it is only when he gets to his feet, walks languidly towards the door – and the men in beards scurry after him – that I realize: *he* is the Governor, the youngest in Afghanistan at 'thirty-six', he says ('thirty-eight,' the Americans tell me later). 'And,' says one of the French journalists on the phone from Kabul, 'an obligatory date for every foreign female aid-worker.' 'Sultan Casanova of Ghazni?' I ask. The Frenchman is not impressed. '*Prends soin de toi*,' he says.

Weeks later I look through my photos from the trip to Ghazni. Photos of the Governor smiling flirtatiously at the Americans, at his maulvi advisers, at my camera, and even – in a clipping from a Paris news-weekly – at the French Defence Minister. 'You are Sultan Mahmud come again,' jokes the US Colonel to the Governor that afternoon during a meeting which I attend. 'He seized slaves from India – you will swoop down and abduct ladies of the Bollywood-type.' The Governor laughs coyly. 'Most hated governor in Afghanistan,' the Colonel tells me afterwards in private. 'Well-connected dangerous guy. Will probably be President.' The next day, when I follow the Governor during his tour of Ghazni province, the Colonel rings every now and then to give him (as he puts it) 'very nice advices'. 'An American stooge,' says a Pashtun friend in Kabul. 'The people don't like him. But if the Americans want to make him King . . .' He shrugs.

Sultan Mahmud was famous for having a romance with a man: Ayaz, his slave. Pashtuns – Afghan and Pakistani – are notorious for preferring male to female lovers. But the Governor of Ghazni, like most Pashtun men, denies that homosexuality is widespread. 'You do revere Sultan Mahmud though, don't you?' I ask him that evening, and the Governor rises to the soundbite. 'The Pakistanis and the Afghans love him for different reasons,' he says. 'We love him because he made our city great. They love him because he fought the Indians. Goodnight.'

I spend three days in the Governor's guesthouse. We are twenty at breakfast – the Governor and I the only beardless ones – round a table of goat in various stages of dismemberment. Ghazni is gearing up for its Independence Day celebrations and the Governor spends his days attending endearingly disorganized practice marches. I join the Americans in their heavily fortified but shambolic progress through the province, or pick my way round the town's mined antiquities. I also meet several of the women who have publicly taken off their burqas – the aspiring politician, the TV presenter, the Education Department official – and are now, for the first time in years, politely asking men to treat them as equals.

Still, when all twenty of the Governor's guests go to the Police Stadium in the evening for *atans*, the first public concerts since the fall of the Taliban, there are, as usual in Pashtun society, no Afghan women. An adolescent singer is up on stage. Three hundred men are sitting in the dust. Ten men are dancing in a circle. The Governor's bearded henchman, a former Taliban collaborator, lumbers on to the dance floor. Everyone cheers. Then a teenage boy joins the group. He stamps his feet. He twirls his hands. He flicks his hair. The crowd goes wild. 'Time to leave,' says the Governor.

And time for me to leave Ghazni, I decide the next morning. I get a lift with one of the Governor's friends to Gardez, capital of the neighbouring province. There, I am sitting having lunch alone in the women's section of a roadside restaurant – a delicious meal of mutton and mint which I eat reclining like a king on a red velour bolster – when I am joined by 'Intelligence', in the form of an affable Colonel who interrogates me about the purpose of my visit. Like many Pashtun Afghans who have spent some time as either refugees or trainee Mujahideen in Pakistan, the Colonel speaks Urdu. 'Take care of yourself, Bibi,' he says as he leaves.

The Afghan town of Khost stands on the border, a few miles from Pakistan. The Taliban are 'active' in Paktia province so I share a taxi to Khost – the journalists have told me this is safest – with three other Afghans: an old woman in a burqa, her incontinent husband, and a silent young man in a woollen cap, also a lone traveller. At the top of a mountain pass, the old man pees on the seat, and the young man in the hat stops the car to pick herbs from the roadside. He tucks a bunch under the rim of his cap and holds the rest delicately to his nose. Two hours later, as we clatter along a stony river valley, we stop again so that he can pick up a small lump of firewood from the roadside. 'Wood is expensive in Khost,' the driver says, in reply to my quizzical look.

That afternoon, I visit Khost's head of police intelligence in his mud-daubed office. He proclaims Pakistan the centre of world terrorism; then tells me to return tomorrow to meet his 'reformed Taliban' protégés. The government has recently extended amnesty to Taliban commanders and soldiers, and those who turn themselves in, give up their weapons and warring pretensions, have a chance of being employed in Karzai's government.

The next morning, a turncoat Mufti is sitting quietly in the office, wearing a gold watch, spotless shalwar kameez and crisp silk turban. He is a serious man – an alumnus of Sami ul-Huq's infamous madrassah near the Indus – who despises Mullah Omar for his ignorance but admires Bin Laden. Now he just looks smug; he has been tipped to become one of the government's new Islamic judges.

Sitting close to him on the couch is the young man in the woollen cap from the taxi yesterday. We stare at each other in surprise. 'What are you doing here?' I ask, and explain to the policeman: 'We shared a taxi from Gardez.' 'And he is an ex-Taliban who has come from Gardez to turn himself in,' the policeman says. He twiddles a pen from the marble holder on his desk and declares: 'The Americans had a bounty of thousands of dollars on his head but I arranged his amnesty.'

The young man was the Mufti's bodyguard during the Taliban years, and a Pakistan-based jihadist once the Americans landed. He has spent the last four years across the border in Waziristan; he has a smattering of Islamic education picked up in Pakistani madrassahs; and he is fully trained to shoot the American soldiers who have invaded his country. 'It was good money,' he says a little regretfully.

'Far better than what I could have earned in this country. My wife thought I was working in Kabul.' 'My jihadi name,' he says later, 'was Flowing Locks.' Outside in the sunshine he fluffs out his hair when I take his photo.

It is midday when I say goodbye to Flowing Locks, the Policeman and the Mufti. The Mufti gives me his mobile number; Flowing Locks offers to escort me back to Kabul; and the Policeman tells me to look up his son if I ever go to Moscow. I don't tell them that I am driving south-east from Khost, over the border to Pakistan that very afternoon.

My companions on this trip are two anxious young Afghan men, Najib and Hamid, whom I met the previous evening. As we sat on the roof of the house where I was staying, discussing my plan of crossing the porous border, they had shocked me only by their response to my polite, routine question to Najib: 'What is your wife's name?' But he replied: 'I can't tell you.' Why not? And Hamid explained: 'You might tell some other man, and then he will call out the name of Najib's wife as she is passing in the street, and then all the neighbours will think she is . . .' He gestured helplessly. A fallen woman? (How the other man would know it was Najib's wife, given her likely burqa, I didn't know.)

Perhaps because of the seriousness with which they tried to explain their culture to me, they struck me as sincere, and I trusted them. Our strategy, then, on the afternoon I leave the Policeman's office, is this: Najib will drive us as far as the Durand Line – the de facto border between Afghanistan and British India, drawn on the map in 1893. There, at the Pakistani checkpoint, Najib will turn back, and Hamid and I will cross the border together, following Sultan Mahmud's route (and without, it so happens, the need for passports). Hamid's mother and siblings live as refugees near Bannu, the conservative Pakistani cantonment town just beyond Waziristan in the 'settled areas'. This is where we will spend the night.

South of Khost, habitation quickly falls away. The river valley is dry: I can see why Flowing Locks stopped to pick up wood; nothing grows here. In the 1980s and 90s, Khost was the headquarters of Bin Laden's training camps, and the ancient orchards and irrigation systems were decimated by Soviet tanks. Now there isn't even a shrub for a goat to chew on. We drive up into the hills for an hour, two hours, three, through a desert landscape of yellow rock, striated, layered, crumbling like halwa.

At last we pass three soldiers, standing in the shade of a cliff and smoking: the Afghan checkpoint, I realize afterwards. The car rounds the corner of a hillside and there it is. 'Pakistan,' says Hamid. There is a tent in the distance. One truck. Four soldiers. We draw up at the so-called border. I smile, greet the soldiers in Urdu, hand them my passport. They look surprised, but I explain: I am writing about Sultan Mahmud of Ghazni, he came this way in 1001. 'The one who fought the Indians,' I hear a soldier tell his partner. 'All right,' announces the man in charge. 'You can go.' 'But I need a stamp,' I say, 'an entry stamp.' (I was warned by a suspicious guard at Torkham that an entry stamp is 'essential'; 'didn't you notice our new electronic checking system?') But the ethereality of this border crossing still hasn't dawned on me. 'A stamp?' the soldiers say. 'We don't have a stamp.' 'Can't you write something in my passport?' The soldier walks over to the tent to ring up the Colonel in Miram Shah. He doesn't come back for half an hour.

When he returns, he is looking stern. He calls me over. 'The Colonel says you must return the way you came. This crossing is dangerous and not permitted for foreigners. But – ' he cuts through my objections, 'as this would be very hard for you' (he glances distastefully towards Afghanistan) 'I am going to let you go.' He leans towards me and whispers, 'Put on your burqa. Don't say a word. Don't laugh. Don't cry. Not a sound until you get to Bannu.' He shakes my hand. 'Good luck. May God be with you.'

I bought my burqa in Pakistan – after I discovered that there were all sorts of places in the Frontier that it was impossible to get into without one. I tried on three – a black Arab-style gown with more ties than a bondage suit; a twee embroidered beige costume; and finally a white shuttlecock, with its grid of tiny eyeholes. 'Too old-fashioned,' said my Pashtun companion, but what did he know. I fitted it on to my head in the back of the tiny store and swished the folds around me: its potential was immediately apparent. It was roomy, sun-reflecting, and forbiddingly austere. I could have worn nothing but my knickers beneath its folds and nobody would have known. Visibility was twenty per cent; but diplomatic immunity was instantaneous and total. I pull on this garment now, over my gaudy pink shalwar kameez — and it carries me safely through the most dangerous district of Pakistan, the badlands of Waziristan.

Imagine wearing a mesh of white. I peer out at the desert landscape through four blurred bars. As the teenage Waziri driver (he looks about fourteen) screeches round the hairpin bends of the Tochi river valley, I grip the edges of the eyepiece, press my nose against the burqa and stare out at the world. I see a young man with a pink rose tucked behind his ear sitting on a boulder, his AK47 lovingly upholstered in blue and pink stickers. I see sand-coloured fortresses, the sky cloudless blue behind them. I see graveyard after graveyard fluttering with the flags of jihadi martyrs. I see a gun on every male shoulder. And I see no women at all — not grannies in burqas, not even a little girl.

The taxi drops us in the small capital of north Warizistan, Miram Shah, where we have to take public transport to Bannu. At the bus station I sit, immobile in the empty minibus, as Hamid goes into the bazaar to buy us cold drinks. I clasp my hands together under my burqa, hoping that Hamid will come back soon, that my instincts about him were right, that the van will not start without him, that I will not have to choose between travelling on alone to Bannu or drawing attention to myself, the only woman out in public between Khost and Bannu. Twenty minutes later Hamid returns, the minibus fills up with male passengers, and as the afternoon begins to cast long shadows along the town's sandy streets, we travel on.

I spend that night with Hamid's family in a village just outside Bannu. There is a pink bougainvillea in the courtyard, and I strip off my sweat-drenched clothes and wash under the stars in the open-air bathroom. The next morning I leave as I came, under my burqa.

It is difficult for single women to meet single men in Bannu. When I first arrived in NWFP, friends in Peshawar tried to dissuade me from visiting the town. 'It is the most conservative place in Pakistan,' said one, 'and a bastion of terrorist activity.' 'Women never leave the house. The men do all the shopping,' said another. 'Men don't like women there,' said a third, a little ominously; 'the place has been totally hijacked by the mullahs.'

The rise of the mullah – ignorant, corrupt, socially inferior – is a constant complaint in the Frontier. Since the time of Khushal Khan Khattak's poetic attacks on the pious Emperor Aurangzeb, Pashtuns have scorned the minister of religion. The twentieth-century poet, Ghani Khan, combined both religious irreverence and sensual expression in a verse that every Pashtun knows how to sing: 'The azan sounds and I think of my Beloved.' (Or, as an acquaintance in Peshawar puts it somewhat bluntly: 'When I hear the call to prayer, I want to fuck girls.') And so the mullah was kept in his place – until the creation of Pakistan.

The Pakistan movement inadvertently gave mullahs a voice by pushing religion to the centre stage of politics. The military dictator, General Zia, who ruled from 1977 till his death in 1988, gave them money, weapons and a heroic cause: the anti-Soviet jihad. President-General Musharraf gave them political power in order that he could tinker with the Constitution – and so remain dictator. Thanks to Pakistani state support, covert CIA funds during the Mujahideen days and Arab money today, the former underclass is now the elite. With foreign bank accounts, children at university in America, and votes in the polling box, mullahs have outfoxed the traditional ruling class; their triumph is nothing less than a social revolution.

While I was in Peshawar, the religious parties launched a purification drive by banning music in public places, and ordered a blackout of images of women – thus on a huge billboard of a young boy and girl eating Kentucky Fried Chicken in central Peshawar, the girl's prepubescent face had been obscured with black tape. Then they proposed a return of the *Hisba*, or Islamic Morality Police. The last time that *muhtasib* (ombudsmen) roamed the streets of Peshawar was in the seventeenth century, when Aurangzeb empowered them to banish dancing girls and destroy temples. Now, as then, the muhtasib's proposed duties include the discouragement of 'unIslamic customs' and the 'regulation of weights and measures'. Aurangzeb would have been delighted.

It is one of history's neat ironies that the base camp of mullahdom itself is Akora Khattak, a village near Attock – once better known as the birthplace of mullah-hating, woman-loving Khushal Khan Khattak. Maulana Sami ul-Huq, a small man with a badly dyed brown beard, spent the end of the last century with a Kalashnikov in one hand and the Holy Qur'an in the other (I see a photograph to prove this, hanging in his guesthouse). The madrassah that Sami runs in Akora Khattak produced, according to its own estimate, 95 per cent of the Taliban leadership; when Mullah Omar needed soldiers, Maulana Sami would close down the school and send the boys across the border. After September 2001 – after the Taliban were defeated and Sami went into politics – the rhetoric had to change, along with the curriculum. 'The foreign students have been sent home,' he tells me in his almost incomprehensible, heavily Arabicized Urdu (his jean-clad grandsons have to translate back into the bazaar Urdu I speak), 'the militant training camp was closed, and the AK47s have been taken out of the classrooms.' 'But there was nothing wrong with the Taliban,' he adds. Politicians from Sami ul-Huq's religious coalition repeatedly voice the same sentiment. 'The only bad thing was that they didn't go far enough,' a shaven-lipped Senator tells me. 'First the Arab and Uzbek fighters interfered, then the Americans.' (As in Babur's day, immigrant Uzbeks and local Pashtuns have an uneasy relationship in this Frontier region.)

But to assume that these public decrees of religious conformity are the only face of Pashtun society is to ignore the Frontier's wholly unIslamic private customs. '*Bey pardeh ma shey,*' Pashtuns say to each other: May you never be uncovered. *Sharam,* shame, applies only to the public exposure of a sin; whatever takes place in private carries no stigma. And thus, as the saying also goes, 'A Pashtun has one foot in heaven and one in hell.' Heaven is the mosque; hell the hujra, the communal guesthouse.

Hujras are places where men receive their male guests. They are situated outside the main compound of the house – and wives and daughters never enter them. In the closed, gender-segregated world of the Frontier, older men have always taken younger boyfriends. Homosexuality, like other aspects of Arab culture, was condemned by the Prophet (perhaps inspired by Leviticus), and is still illegal in modern Pakistan (and indeed in India), both of which inherited the colonial British Penal Code. But while women in Pakistan are enthusiastically and mistakenly punished every year for adultery under General Zia's 1979 Zina Ordinance, there has never been a prosecution in Pakistan for sodomy under Section 377. Male-male sex is simply accepted as a necessity and a norm.

Of course, one can distinguish between legitimate close male friendships, even love, and physical relationships between men, which are illegal. Emperor Babur – who had to be pushed into bed with his wife by his mother – fell passionately in love with 'a boy in the camp bazaar'. It was a courtly, homoerotic, poetry-mediated obsession, and it remained, so Babur implied, strictly non-physical. Babur wrote in censorious terms of his relatives who took young boys as 'catamites'. Such 'vice and debauchery', he implied, made very poor kings of those who practised it.

But many did, and still do. For numerous British imperialists, the whole of the Frontier (and to an extent the whole of the Muslim world) was a homosexual wet dream. In the army, 'Up the Khyber (pass)' was rhyming slang for 'up the arse'. After the British conquered Sindh, Richard Burton, then a soldier, was commissioned by Napier to investigate Karachi's numerous boy brothels, and his exhaustive report landed him in trouble after Napier retired, for it was assumed by the new administrators that he must have sampled the wares. Later still, Burton argued with lurid exaggeration that the Afghans only rose up against the British in 1841 because they were affronted by the 'frantic debauchery' of their women – who, overjoyed at meeting men 'who were not pederasts', threw themselves at the British invaders.

Whatever the truth of this, Afghans certainly like their parties camp. In Kabul's Medina Bazaar, I am shown a DVD of teenage boys in sequinned dresses dancing for Afghan warlords. (In Ghazni, the baby-faced US Intelligence officer was wearing a gold wedding ring in a dismal attempt to dissuade male Afghan suitors.) In Pakistan, too, as Burton found, opportunities for gay sex are abundant, cheap to come by – and far less hazardous than heterosexual adultery. Transvestite prostitutes charge barely more than the price of a cup of chai for their services and thus, as Ayesha, the hijra in Karachi, pointed out, 'Many of my clients are sexually frustrated male students.' Mullahs, meanwhile, despite the power they now wield under the army dispensation, have not shed their reputation for preying on their male students. (Naturally, Maulana Sami vigorously condemned homosexuality, when I asked him.)

Bannu's own reputation as a town of sodomites crystallized in the past decade. There was the case of a policeman who raped a young boy; there was the man from Bannu who claimed that John Walker Lindh (the 'American Taliban') was his lover; and there was the poor beleaguered researcher who wrote a report for UNICEF describing how, for Pashtuns, 'the real sex is hot and dry' and 'keeping boys is an absolute addiction.' 'When I visited Bannu after that, they put me in jail,' the researcher tells me when we meet for tea in Peshawar. He gives me the number of some colleagues in Bannu. 'But you should proceed with intensive care,' he says as I leave. 'The first thing you must do is buy a burqa.'

Later, the friend I stay with in Bannu argues indignantly that 'It is all propaganda. Maybe a generation ago warlords were *baccha khush* [fond of young boys], but now all that has changed. It is the foreign NGOs – the ones from Peshawar – who are making a fuss about nothing. Why Bannu rather than any other town in Pakistan?'

He has a point. I think about his words as I wait in Bannu for my Waziri acquaintance Abdullah. Our rendezvous is a tiny, dirty room opposite a cinema where they are advertising a film starring a busty blonde actress in lacy black lingerie (scenes from *Basic Instinct*, it is rumoured, interspliced with naked Pashtun dancing). Sitting on the ground, hunched under my now grubby white burqa, I remember what a friend in Kabul told me. 'The only unaccompanied women wearing burqas in this town,' he said, 'are prostitutes.'

Abdullah, when he arrives, has a paranoid air and overexcited manner. 'Al-Qaeda travel at night through Waziristan, in cars with blacked out windows,' he says. 'They pay ten times the going rate for a room. They move to a new location every night.' He is trying to persuade me to stay in his village in Waziristan, otherwise known as Taliban Central. Last month, he says, a letter from Al-Qaeda was dropped into his courtyard. The note, typed in Pashto, read 'Death to NGO workers'; enclosed in the paper was 700 rupees, to buy his coffin. The army is in north Waziristan for the first time since Pakistan's creation, and I have found it difficult to persuade Waziris to meet me. Noor Khan, the cousin of a Waziri friend in Kabul, whispers down the phone that his neighbour has just been killed by the Arabs for being an army informer. But Abdullah says, 'I'll drive you as far as Razmak. We'll go to Wana.' 'Are you mad?' I say. 'They will kill us.' 'Nobody speaks to Pashtun women,' he says, 'it will be perfectly safe. You can pretend to be my wife.' I think for a moment: 'But then we will have to share a room.' Abdullah smiles. 'I am applying for asylum in Norway,' he explains, 'but I would rather go to England.' 'You are *pagal* [mad],' I say.

But by now I am the one feeling crazy: I have no entry stamp in my passport; I have passed illegally through Al-Qaeda's hideout; I have to decide whether to return the way I came, explain myself at Torkham, or travel back to Afghanistan clandestinely, across a safer stretch of this porous border (through Chitral maybe, or Wakhan). I am still underneath my burqa – I feel it is addling my brain – I have lost all sense of proportion. 'Come to Miram Shah with me,' says Abdullah again, 'I'll introduce you to the old Taliban fighters. I'll show you the latest Al-Qaeda recruitment video. We'll return to Afghanistan the day after tomorrow.'

I am on the verge of agreeing to this plan that will surely get us sent to jail, abducted by Al-Qaeda or blown to pieces by a rogue Waziristani rocket-launcher, when my mobile rings.

In Peshawar there are three brothers: Amir, Suleman and Nizamullah. Amir has the biggest house; Suleman has the fieriest temper; but the youngest and wisest is Nizamullah. 'Where are you?' asks Nizamullah now. 'In Bannu,' I say. 'I have a problem.' 'Bannu?' he says, 'I'm not surprised you have a problem. Come to Peshawar at once.'

So it is with great relief that I say goodbye to Abdullah, take a 'flying coach' over the Kohat pass, around the gun factories of Dara Adam Khel (from which the army's intelligence wing, the ISI – Inter-Services Intelligence – reportedly sourced hundreds of cheap Kalashnikovs to present to the Americans, and convince them that the Taliban were giving up their weapons), and three hours later reach the Frontier capital.

Nizamullah is sitting on his terrace in the sun, sipping lime juice when I arrive. I climb out from under my burqa and tell him the story of my border crossing. He listens in silence. 'Should I return to Khost?' I finish. 'Am I in big trouble?' Nizamullah puts down the glass, and stares into the distance. Finally he speaks. 'Alice, you should know better by now,' he says; and my heart sinks. 'Why are you worrying?' he continues. 'This is *Pakistan.*'

Suleman of the fiery temper is delegated to look after me. I spend the next morning in his office as he rings three tribal Maliks, two Assistant Political Agents, and a Passport Officer. 'Have you got your burqa?' he asks at eleven-thirty. It is the day after the Jalalabad riots: foreigners have been banned from crossing via Torkham; even on a good day they need an armed escort.

Only now do I find out that the day I crossed over the border at Khost, riots broke out in Afghanistan. The country is protesting over *Newsweek*'s story, which it later retracted, that an American interrogator at Guantánamo Bay flushed a Qur'an down the toilet. In Ghazni, rioters attacked the Governor's house, and four people were killed. The *Newsweek* incident also coincides with – or encourages – the resurrection of the Taliban. Today, the road I glibly took to Ghazni has become impassable for foreigners: Taliban checkpoints have sprung up along it like poisonous mushrooms. The Taliban pull out Afghans at gunpoint and flick through their bags. If there are business cards in their wallets, or numbers on their phone, which show they are working with foreigners, they are shot. And the women I met – the ones who dared to show their faces – are once again living as they did under the Taliban. So much for all the 'democracy' bombs dropped on the country.

'You are crazy,' says Suleman to me now, as I slip into my trusty shuttlecock burqa, climb into his car, and we set off up the Khyber. 'Even we Pashtuns avoid Afghanistan.' We sail through the checkpoint at Jamrud, then Suleman turns to me and asks: 'How did you like Bannu?' He flicks opens his phone and shows me a picture message. The graphic is a black and red road-sign: two men fucking. The text reads: 'Bannu 5 km.'

We are now in drug-baron country, and Suleman becomes my tour guide, pointing out the forts of the heroin smugglers as we drive. 'Inside that one,' he says, 'there is a private zoo.' At one o'clock, he draws up in front of another large fort and beeps his horn. Out comes a man in thick glasses: the Afridi tribal Malik. They joke together in Pashto as we drive into Landi Kotal bazaar to collect the Malik's cousin, and are in hysterics by the time we reach the tidy hilltop complex owned by the army. (I can pick out enough names from the Pashto to piece together the route of my journey.) They drop in to see the Assistant Political Agent; then we accelerate down into the lively chaos of Torkham.

The Passport Officer is entertaining a roomful of men with green tea when we arrive. He takes my passport and flicks through the pages. His finger stabs my expired Indian journalist visa. '*Hamaray liey bohut khatarnak,*' he says with a frown: Very dangerous for us. My heart sinks again; I see myself being carted off to the high security jail at Attock. But the Passport Officer laughs. 'Off you go,' he says. 'Tell the Afghans you just came from Kabul.'

So I am led across the border into Afghanistan, where I collect my little stamp of legality, then troop back into Pakistan to receive my entry stamp; and at last the tribal Malik, his cousin, Suleman and I sit down to a huge kebab lunch, courtesy of the Passport Officer. '*This* is Pakistan,' I sigh, as I rip apart a goat's thigh with my fingers. The men laugh: 'Best country in the world. What did we tell you?'

7

Buddha on the Silk Road

3rd century BCE – *8th century* CE

'The River Sin-tu [Indus] is pure and clear as a mirror . . .
Poisonous dragons and dangerous spirits live beneath its waters.
If a man tries to cross the river carrying valuable gems, rare
flowers and fruits, or above all, relics of Buddha, the boat is
engulfed by waves.'

Xuanzang, *c.* 645 CE

IN 1021, WHEN Sultan Mahmud of Ghazni marched north from
Peshawar into Swat and Bajaur – tributary valleys of the River
Indus – Buddhism had been on the wane for two hundred years.
Swat, in particular, had an abundance of Buddhist monasteries in
varying states of dilapidation, and Mahmud took the opportunity to
convert a few idol-worshippers, break a few statues, and lay siege to
the imposing black stone hilltop fortress of Udegram. Then, on a
terrace below the castle, he built a mosque big enough to contain
his army. The mosque floor is still there, and on the hot April day
when I climb the hill towards the castle, Tariq, my Swat host, kneels
down to offer his *zhuhr* – noonday – prayers.

While neither Sultan Mahmud nor his ministers and historians
tended to distinguish one idol-worshipper from another, in fact
many of the 'infidels' of north-west India were Buddhists. The 'lion-
worshippers' that he 'subdued and converted' in Swat and Bajaur,
for example, were not Hindus, but devotees of the Sakya-Sinha
Buddha in his lion form.

As it happened, the Ghaznavids had long campaigned in Buddhist
lands. Ghazni itself had been a Buddhist settlement, and in 994,
Mahmud's father, Sebuktigin, became governor of Buddhist Bamiyan

in central Afghanistan. The lovely river valley of green almond trees and gigantic stone Buddhas entered Ghaznavid folklore almost immediately in a poem by Mahmud's court poet Unsuri.

Sultan Mahmud's foray into Swat coincided with the very end of Buddhism west of the Indus, a decline begun by the falling off of patronage from central India, where there had been a vigorous Brahmin renaissance. The river itself dealt a fatal blow when catastrophic flooding in the seventh century destroyed many of the monasteries. The men who built the mosque at Udegram thus bore witness to the final decay of the religion that had ruled this region for over one thousand years – from the time of Emperor Ashoka of India in the third century BCE, throughout the long, opulent reign of the Indo-Greek kings, and up until the departure of the Tantric wizard, Padmasambhava, to Tibet in the mid-eighth century CE, where he converted the country to Buddhism.

Like layers of silt from the inundations of its river, Swat preserves its Buddhist past in compact seams. An outlandish array of Buddhist kings ruled here, and the historical roll-call of their varying provenance, ambitions and achievements is dizzying. Still more difficult to comprehend, is how that past gave way to this present. Of all the places in the Indus valley, it is modern Swat that seems most removed from its ancient history.

The Swat river runs parallel with the Indus from the moment it flows out of Kashmir in northern Pakistan, through the secluded valleys of Indus Kohistan, to the point where it enters the Punjab. Swat, too, is a secluded, idiosyncratic place. Protected by the Hindu Kush mountains to the north, the Indus to the east, and the scorched straw-gold hills to the south and west, Swat lies between them all like a mirage in the drought. The brash perfection of its indigo-blue river and intensely coloured wooded landscape breeds in its inhabitants a distinct insouciance – they pay no tax, smuggle cars over the mountains from Kabul, and regard the law of the land with casual disregard. Life in Swat clusters around the deep, wide river, which runs from the ice floes of Kalam in the north, through steep hill towns, to the plains east of Peshawar – and thus encapsulates in miniature the three-thousand-kilometre journey of the Indus itself.

Swat is known wistfully today – by government officials and optimistic hoteliers – as the 'Switzerland of Pakistan' and until 2001, its
kitsch mountain landscape was popular with foreign tourists. After
September 11th, tourism fell away, and the only visitors now are
frontier smugglers and rich Punjabis. Tariq, who used to own a hotel
in Mingora, Swat's capital, had to start a school instead.

Swat may be pastoral and pretty – *Ao sanam, Swat chale* (Come
lover, let's go to Swat) reads the tailboard of a truck I follow up the
valley – but it is also bursting with madrassahs. In 2001, after the
Americans landed in Afghanistan, a radical cleric called Sufi
Muhammad led a band of 10,000 angry Muslims (it is reputed) from
Swat, west through Bajaur and over the Nawa pass into Afghanistan.
Sufi Muhammad is rumoured to have helped Bin Laden escape into
Pakistan, before surrendering himself to the authorities.

Near a small madrassah on the outskirts of Mingora, I have an
enlightening conversation with a twenty-one-year-old student whose
own father joined Sufi Muhammad's jihad, having being trained 'for
five years in Khost before that'. This man has never spoken to a
woman from outside his family before – and he does not intend to
look at, or be looked at, by an unveiled woman now. Having left
Bannu behind me, I have gladly shed my burqa and am now dressed
top to toe in a billowing shalwar kameez and headscarf, but even
this is not modest enough. 'You should be doing purdah,' he says.
Instead it is he who sits turned away throughout the interview,
wrapped in a shawl so that I cannot see his face.

In his madrassah it is *haram*, forbidden, to watch television, or
listen to the radio: 'The media is with the government, and the
government is with America.' Nor does he listen to music. But he
enjoys novels about early Islam. 'I am reading one about the Islamic
conquest of Spain,' he says. 'This was Islam's strongest time, when
Muslims first spread out from Mecca and Medina.' What he and his
teachers want above all is to re-create the Islamic Golden Age in
Pakistan with a Sharia-ruled, Taliban-style government – even the
religious party of Sami ul-Huq is not pious enough. 'There is no
good Islamic society anywhere in the world, now that the Taliban
have gone,' he says. 'That was a time of justice.' Comments such as
these do not necessarily indicate a world-dominating desire in

Pakistan's Muslims; but they do illustrate the extent to which ordinary citizens have been let down by the malfeasance of the state and feel disillusioned, often to the point of desperation, by their leaders' perverse dalliance with apparently anti-Islamic foreign powers.

Today, Islam and Buddhism appear to be at opposite ends of the religious spectrum: no two religions, perhaps, have such different modern reputations. Yet in north-western India, along the banks of the Indus, the two came into prolonged contact with each other, and it is undeniable that certain features of the older philosophy influenced the way the younger developed locally. In Bamiyan, after Islam came to the region, the monumental Buddhas were absorbed into 'Shiite popular religious folklore'. Shia devotion may explain the Sunni Taliban's fervour for destroying the statues – which they did, I am told when I go to Bamiyan, by cruelly forcing local Shias to winch themselves over the side of the towering cliff, in order to fix the dynamite in place. Today the locals still refer affectionately and regretfully to the empty holes in the cliff-face as the 'male and female deities'.

Even the much-maligned Muslim institution of the madrassah may have its roots in the Buddhist monastery. Both are institutions of intense religious learning, sustained by charity; for centuries now in Swat, small cliques of religious-minded men and women have sequestered themselves from the world to devote themselves to prayer, the learning of sacred texts and the accumulation of merit in the next life. As I enter the cool underground meditation cells in the second century CE Takt-i-Bahi monastery, south of Mingora, I try to visualize groups of sutra-learning nuns – but it is the study-rooms in Swat's female madrassahs that come most vividly to mind, with their distinct, acrid odour of rhythmically swaying bodies.

The rapid Islamicization of the eastern and western peripheries of India has furrowed many a scholarly brow, for although the Muslim rulers of India made few attempts to mass-convert their 'pagan' subjects, in the two frontier lands along the Indus and Brahmaputra rivers, Islam proliferated unaided, ultimately resulting in Pakistan and Bangladesh. Perhaps Islam, far from annihilating Buddhism with its jihadi scimitars (as colonial historians suggested), merely co-opted its rival by absorbing its rituals. Maybe the similarity of forms – trans-ethnic, proselytizing, attached to merchant networks – made it easier for the Indus people to accept the one, and then the other. Or possibly it was the lie of the land – on the periphery of the Indian scene – that mutated any religion which entered its winding valleys.

For the long, rich millennium prior to the advent of Islam to India, Buddhism had profited – as caste-bound Vedic Hinduism, confined as it was to India, could not – from the cosmopolitan Silk Road caravans. This mobile banking system, or brotherhood of travelling salesmen, stretched from the Mediterranean to China, carrying silk, spice and gold from one end of the world to the other. On the remoter roads where commercial hoteliers would not venture, merchants needed succour and shelter, and local kings relied on the routes staying open. Both kings and merchants were happy to patronize Buddhism's presence in distant valleys, and especially at difficult river-crossings, and so monasteries doubled as Silk Road taverns. In return, the monks received support and made converts. The Swat valley, on the crossroads of the Silk Route between China and South Asia, thrived on this reciprocal arrangement. And thus while it was in eastern India that the Buddha was born, preached and reached Nirvana in the fifth century BCE, it was in the middle Indus valley, three hundred years after his death, that a second Buddhist holy land was established.

Hinduism had strict concepts of ritual pollution, and a rigid notion of geographical impurity. Crossing the *kalapani* (black water) resulted in loss of caste. Kalapani usually meant the ocean – but it was also applied, at times, to the Indus. The river demarcated mainland India from the far north-west, a region known to the ancient Sanskrit texts as *Uttarapatha*. This included part of northern Punjab and the city of Taxila, and the unregulated lands beyond the river. As a frontier region, Uttarapatha's reputation was ambiguous. It was famed for the beauty of its spoken Sanskrit; it was also, for Hindu India, a peripheral, pariah state. Strange, perverted things were rumoured to take place in its isolated valleys.

For an inclusive, non-racist religion such as Buddhism, Uttarapatha was fertile ground for evangelizing. From the third century BCE onwards, Buddhism became the major religion of two large provinces in Uttarapatha: Gandhara, the well-watered plain running eastwards from modern-day Peshawar to the Indus; and perpendicular to it, Uddiyana, or Swat.

Uddiyana is a Sanskrit word, usually assumed to mean 'garden' or 'fair dwelling'. But Karl Jettmar, the German professor of northern Pakistani history, suggested an alternative etymology more in line with the region's reputed character as a place of sorcerers and debauchery: 'Uddiyana may be traced back to the root "*di*", to float in the air,' Jettmar wrote, adding that 'the witches of Swat prefer to ride on hyenas. The rough hair on the spine of the animal is said to give them extreme sexual pleasure.'

Because of its wide river, Uddiyana was self-sufficient in water, fish and timber; and because of its geographical importance as a thoroughfare on the trans-Asian Silk Road, it was never short of patrons or visitors. Kings came and went in central India, but for over a thousand years in Uddiyana, Buddhism remained a constant.

The valley accepted and incorporated each major change in Buddhist doctrine: from Theravada (the practice that the Buddha himself followed, with its emphasis on meditation as the route to enlightenment) to Mahayana (the worship of the Buddha in all his past lives and future incarnations) and, finally, Tantric Vajrayana, which developed in Swat itself. The most esoteric form of Buddhism, Vajrayana showed initiates the secret but rapid route to enlightenment through the union of opposites – pure and impure, high and low caste, and above all, male and female during sexual intercourse. Practitioners were taught to flout sexual taboos, caste laws and social norms, eating forbidden foods and living like outcasts, before attaining enlightenment through sexual union.

Padmasambhava, the man who in the eighth century popularized Vajrayana, was an exorcist and wizard, known to his followers as Guru Rimpoche, the 'Great Master of Uddiyana', 'the Second Buddha' and 'the Precious Guru'. He had two wives, and once lived in a charnel ground. But by the eighth century CE, Buddhism was on the wane in Swat, so Padmasambhava travelled to Tibet, where he subdued the local demons, converted the King with his rituals and incantations, and passed on the knowledge that had been transmitted secretly through generations of Swati gurus. For centuries thereafter, Swat became a major pilgrimage site for Tibetans. Padmasambhava is still honoured throughout Tibet, and all along the upper Indus in Buddhist Ladakh (the northernmost province of India). After his death, secret books written by him in the language of Uddiyana on 'rolled-up yellow leaves' were discovered by his Tibetan disciples; and in Ladakh's monasteries, which honour the road that he travelled and the caves where he slept by the upper Indus river, there are paintings of him sporting a fashionable Pakistani-style moustache. But in his Pakistani homeland, the Great Master has been forgotten.

Tibetan pilgrims continued visiting Swat for at least five hundred years after Padmasambhava's death, and Buddhist tourists from Japan are not an uncommon sight today. But from the fifth to the seventh centuries CE, it was Chinese monks who were the leading chroniclers of Swat's great Buddhist flourishing – and of its steady deterioration.

These epic pilgrimages began because Chinese Buddhists, originally converted by monks from India, soon yearned for first-hand experience of their faith's sacred geography. The journey from China to India was long and dangerous: north through the Icy Mountains, across the Taklamakan desert, and down the perilous northern gorges of the Indus; or via the hazardous southern sea route. But caravans had been taking silk slowly across the world for centuries, and where silk went, Buddhism could follow.

Xuanzang is probably the best known of the pilgrim chroniclers who set out from China and travelled 10,000 miles to witness Swat's living Buddhism – and being one of the last, he was also the most disillusioned. In 629 CE, with 'a character of unequalled virtue', he 'took his staff, dusted his clothes, and set off for distant regions'. With a bamboo-frame rucksack on his back, Xuanzang crossed the 'Great Unknown', visited the Kings of the Silk Road, and paid homage to the Bamiyan Buddhas (fifty-three metres high, and coated with gold). At Bamiyan he turned east, passing by the Buddhist towns near modern-day Kabul and Jalalabad, and trekking through the Khyber pass to Peshawar. Finally, he forded the 'dark and gloomy' Indus.

Unfortunately, what Xuanzang saw as he criss-crossed the Indus between India and Uttarapatha, made him despair. In Gandhara the monasteries were 'filled with wild shrubs and solitary to the last degree'. In Swat the monasteries were 'waste and desolate'. Along the banks of the river in Sindh the monks were 'indolent and given to indulgence and debauchery'. Elsewhere, they ate meat – despite being able to hear the squeals of the pigs being killed for them. They were forever squabbling, and 'their contending utterances,' Xuanzang found, 'rise like the angry waves of the sea.' The serious monks lived 'alone in desert places'.

But Xuanzang travelled far and wide, and during his long journey met many monks who received him hospitably. At last, with their help, he 'penetrated to the very source of the stream' (of religion). What this evocative riverine metaphor meant in practice, was that sixteen years after he set out, Xuanzang returned to China followed by twenty-two horses all laden with booty: 400 'grains of relics', statues of the Buddha in gold, silver and sandalwood, and 520 sutras (holy texts).

It was only when crossing the Indus on his way back to China that Xuanzang met with calamity – his boat overturned and he lost all his botanical collections and sutras. 'It has been so from days of old till now,' the local king explained to the bedraggled monk; 'whoever attempts to cross the river with seeds of flowers is subject to similar misfortunes.' Such was the power of the Indus in antiquity. Xuanzang patiently had the sutras recopied, and went on without the seeds.

Back in China, Xuanzang's trip was a huge success. He was called 'the jewel of the empire' and became a pet hero of the Tang dynasty. Both the detailed account of his visit which he wrote up for the Tang emperor on his return, and his contemporaneous authorized biography, became – for the Chinese at the time, and scholars subsequently – a gold mine of information about Indian Buddhism.

But for a religious man, it had been a journey of bitterness. India was no longer a Buddhist heartland. Xuanzang had read the pilgrim account written by Fa Hsien, the best known of the Chinese monks to have preceded him to that fabled realm, and he could see that the number of Buddhist lay people had declined, the religious places and buildings were crumbling, the support extended by local Indian kings had waned, and even the moral purity of the monks themselves was under question.

Just two centuries earlier, when Fa Hsien made the same pilgrimage in 420 CE, 'everything was flourishing' in Indian Buddhism. Fa Hsien, who hailed from eastern China, reached India just as Swat was experiencing a Buddhist resurgence. He, too, followed a difficult route into India, along the notoriously dangerous upper course of the Indus. There were venomous dragons which spat 'gravel', the valleys 'were difficult to walk in' and the gorges so high, it made one's 'head swim'. But once in the easy green valley of Swat, Fa Hsien was able to relax. He had set out from China with one mission: to collect 'the Books of Discipline' (such was the 'mutilated and imperfect state of the collection' in China). Luckily for him, Buddhism was then at its pinnacle of strength in northwest India.

The Buddha almost certainly never visited Swat, but the Silk Road drew him to it posthumously. Three hundred years after his death, Buddhism invented for itself a whole new field of worship in Uttarapatha. Along the upper course of the Indus, near Skardu, Fa Hsien was shown such unlikely relics as the Buddha's spittoon and his tooth. Near the source of the Swat river, above Kalam, he saw the Buddha's footprint in a rock. Further south on the banks of the 'Su-po-sa-tu' (the Swat river was called the *Suvastu* in Sanskrit), he worshipped at the place where the Buddha had dried his clothes, and again at the scene of his conversion of a wicked dragon. That was about as far as ancient tour guides could stretch the Buddha's historical existence.

Nothing, however, could stop them embellishing his past lives. The Buddha was omniscient – he could remember the past, going back billions of infinite aeons – and his previous incarnations obligingly furnished endless new pilgrimage sites in Swat. There were the places where he had gorged out his eyes, decapitated himself, or offered up his body to feed birds, animals or humans, such was his doctrine of selfless renunciation ('no-self'). At each site, a *stupa* (reliquary) was erected, bearing witness to these exemplary acts. Around the stupas grew monasteries; around the monasteries, communities of monks; and Gandhara and Swat grew too, ever more in importance.

Buddhism liked hills – ideally monks should live at one remove from lay people, yet near enough to beg their midday meal from villages – and archaeologists have found some form of Buddhist settlement on almost every Swati high place. The monks chose wisely: in the paralysing heat of April it is the archaeological sites, alone in all Swat, which are cool and breezy.

Butkara, the main monastery in the region, was unearthed in Mingora, Swat's small hillside capital, in 1956. When the archaeologists began work on it, the site was a mound of mud – a last trace of the flood which buried the monastery and town in the seventh century CE. But beneath the silt, the archaeologists found seven distinct periods of Buddhist history, each one superimposed upon the other.

Butkara is a short walk from the centre of Mingora, and when I arrive there one quiet afternoon, strolling down through the wheat fields and under an avenue of trees, there are only two other people sitting beside the stupa. They jump up as I approach, surprised to see visitors. One is the old watchman, who makes me a cup of tea, and the other is Sanaullah, a history student from Peshawar University, who spends his free time in the shadow of these exotic old stones, dreaming of black schist, blue lapis lazuli and gold relic caskets.

It is Sanaullah who makes me appreciate how the stupa expanded like a gilded balloon during the millennium of its use, 'as each new Buddhist king introduced his own art'. He draws a diagram in the dust, of seven concentric circles. The seventh and top layer, he says, corresponds to the time of the flood. The sixth layer represents the state of the monastery as Xuanzang saw it – by which time the buildings were in a state of near collapse, and the original stone floors had been overlaid with beaten earth.

To understand the previous five periods, Sanaullah and I enter the cool stone stupa courtyard. The stupa itself would have been a large, domed structure – not dissimilar in outline, as Sanaullah points out, to a mosque. Carved into the very top of the stupa's dome were umbrellas – the Buddhist symbol of royalty. All around the main stupa were many smaller votive stupas filled with the bones of monks and patrons, all jostling to be sacred by association. Most of the statues have been removed to Swat's museum because of thieves, but there is enough still carved into the stone here – lotus flowers from India, Corinthian pillars from Greece, Persepolitan columns from

Persia, Roman cupids – to illustrate the miscellany of motifs used in Swati Buddhism. Butkara thus incarnated in stone, gold and paint one thousand years of Swat's continuous Buddhist history, its changing rulers, schools and fortunes.

Each king, Sanaullah explains, added new sculptures and stonework to the dome itself. The fifth layer, decorated with scenes from the life of the Buddha, was embellished by a succession of Indo-Greek and Saka kings and it was this that Song Yun, another Chinese pilgrim, saw when he visited Butkara in 518, and wrote of the six thousand dazzling gold statues there (the gold wash that archaeologists detected on many of the stone images corroborates this). The fourth layer, with its dramatic stucco statues of the Buddha, was commissioned by King Kanishka in the fourth century. Below this was a stupa faced with green and white soapstone, made during the reign of Azes II, king of the Scythian or Saka nomads from Central Asia, in the first century. The second layer, of schist and pink plaster, was the work of the first-century BCE King Menander, an Indo-Greek. And the first and deepest layer of all – the original stupa, built simply and coarsely from pebbles and plaster enclosing the sacred relic casket – was erected in the third century BCE by the Indian emperor Ashoka. Here archaeologists also found a fourth-century potsherd painted with Greek characters – probably brought to Swat by the soldiers of Alexander the Great.

Sanuallah points out the sixteen niches around the walls which once contained stone and stucco statues of the Buddha; the chipped stone floor that was inlaid with lapis lazuli ('the Japanese tourists steal it,' he says); and the stone carvings of humans and animals still visible in the walls of the stupa or, in the case of the lions which once surmounted pillars at the stupa's gates, newly cemented to the ground. 'These lions symbolize both Emperor Ashoka and the Buddha,' says Sanaullah.

Swat, as Fa Hsien saw it, was the legacy of King Kanishka: an energetic patron of Buddhism from the Kushan dynasty. The Kushans arrived in Uddiyana two hundred years before Fa Hsien, probably from north-western China. King Kanishka made Peshawar his capital, organized the Fourth Buddhist Council in Kashmir (during which Buddhist doctrines were codified), and despatched missionaries and texts to China. Kanishka had eclectic tastes: his coins were embossed with Greek, Iranian and Indian deities, and – for the first time in history – with an image of the Buddha.

During Kushan rule, the production of Buddha images became a cottage industry in north-western India. Carved into bare rock, blocks of stone and, later, soft stucco, these icons became so important that, in China, immigrant Buddhism became known as the 'religion of the images'.

It was over the role of images, of course, that Islam distinguished itself most flamboyantly from Buddhism. Sultan Mahmud had prized his reputation as a *but-shikan* – image-destroyer – the word '*but*' (idol) referring to Buddhist statues that the Muslims encountered in Bamiyan and Ghazni, and to Hindu images they saw in India later. Ironically, as Sanaullah points out, 'just as modern Muslims forbid the worship of images of our leader', so did early Buddhists.

Image worship was a new and contentious development for second-century Buddhists and, for some, it went against the previous seven centuries of their faith's history. The emergence of image worship just before, or during, Kanishka's reign was a result of the huge changes in Buddhism that took place four hundred years after its founder's death. Early Buddhism, with its focus on meditation as the route to enlightenment, was centred around the monastic life. But lay people wanted to be enlightened too. 'Mahayana', a movement away from Buddhism as its founder envisaged it, stressed instead the intercessionary role played by the pantheon of bodhisattvas (future Buddhas, awaiting final reincarnation), and the importance of texts, images and artefacts. Images of the Buddha were the natural corollary. But many Indian monks viewed these handsome stone statues as vulgar and debased, and the Buddhist community was split irreparably.

In north-western India, at a significant distance from the main Buddhist community in eastern India, the Buddha came to be seen not just as a wise human, but as immortal and godlike, under the patronage of three consecutive dynasties – the Kushans, and before them the Parthians and Sakas (all western immigrants to Uttarapatha). Buddhist art up to this point had represented the Buddha by his absence – by the horse he rode, the royal umbrella he once carried, or the footprints he left. But in first- and second-century Uttarapatha, an entirely new school of art arose, depicting him in his complete human form. Some masons carved the Buddha standing, one arm raised in protection; others showed him sitting with his eyes closed in meditation; still others, as an emaciated skeleton (from the time before his enlightenment). Sometimes, reflecting Indian ideas, his ears were elongated and the crown of his head raised to show the *usina* or sacred bump; at other times he wore a thickly draped toga with a halo glowing around his head (this was the sun disc, adopted from Persia). Smaller, intimate friezes described his early life in east India – his birth, schooling and departure from his kingdom – and significant moments from his past lives. Along the edges of all these religious scenes hovered vibrant glimpses of secular life: voluptuous, gauzily clad dancing-girls; rich devotees in mountain caps, carrying relic boxes; peepul trees, palm fronds and elephants.

Along with the Buddha and the bodhisattvas, as objects of worship, were added the local gods of India. Mahayana accepted all the erstwhile Vedic deities, who were now shown bowing in subservience to the Buddha; the god of wealth was included (to please the mercantile middle classes); and for the peasants there was a rich abundance of ancient animal spirits, water gods and *nagas* – serpent deities or dragons, guardians of lakes, springs and rivers.

Just as the appearance of the Buddha image divided the Buddhist community during the first century CE, so eighteen hundred years later, when European historians began examining Buddhist history, the issue of the image again caused controversy in India. Many of the early Buddha statues were unearthed by British colonial officers, who, as one historian writes, felt 'a sense of relief' on beholding in those classical lines 'something that was familiar to them'. Unlike the 'strange and exuberant' multi-armed goddesses that filled the temples of India, Gandharan Buddhas – with their togas and wreaths, severe noses and straight-backed poses – appeared to have been lifted from Athens or Rome. To the horror of Indian scholars, some Europeans viewed them not as Indian at all, but as copies of something Greek or Roman. Hellenistic art had entered India in the trail left by Alexander the Great; Buddhism arrived from the east at exactly the same moment; the Buddha statues, Europeans argued, were surely influenced by Greek prototypes. Once again, the scholarship of ancient India divided along familiar lines. Was it invented in India, or imported from outside?

Standing in Mingora's museum face to face with toga-clad Buddhas, in front of stone friezes framed by vine leaves, or before coins punched with images of laurel-crested kings and club-wielding Hercules, the Western influences on the stonemasons and craftspeople of Uddiyana is manifest. So too is the influence of work from China, India and Persia. Today, the best-preserved illustration of the richness and depth of influences on which Buddhist artists drew, can be seen in the treasures unearthed at Begram, the site of King Kanishka's summer capital near Kabul. There, archaeologists found glasses painted with the battle of Achilles and Hector; blue blown-glass fish; Chinese lacquerwork; Indian ivories showing scenes from the Buddha's life; Graeco-Roman bronzes of Alexander the Great, Hercules and Athena; a bronze plate of fish with fins and tails that wave in the wind; a plaster sculpture of Aphrodite; ivory wasp-waisted river goddesses standing on the *makara*, an aquatic beast; and my favourite of all, sculpted into clay during the first century CE, the buxom *Kinnari*, a mythical bird-woman who is still painted on the back of Pakistani trucks today.

The quibble over whether Gandharan art is the child of Greece or India has merely obscured a much more magnificent phenomenon – the mutual interest that these two cultures found in each other. In Swat and Gandhara, Greek and Indian art forms, languages and social structures commingled like rivers for a brief and mutually sympathetic moment.

King Menander, who built the penultimate layer of the Butkara stupa in the first century BCE, was an Indo-Greek. He was also a Buddhist. The archaeologist John Marshall portrayed Menander's Buddhism as wholly pragmatic:

> in Menander's case it was obviously a matter of policy to espouse the Buddhist cause and thus secure the support of what was obviously at that time probably the strongest religious body in the Punjab and the North-West.

But Menander's passion for Buddhism appears to have gone beyond mere rhetoric. He absorbed Uddiyana within his kingdom, and built upon Ashoka's stupas, including that at Butkara. He expanded the ancient town of Taxila, on the left bank of the Indus, which had long housed a Hindu university. According to the Kushan-era Buddhist text, *Milindapanha* (Milinda's Questions), which purports to be a philosophical dialogue between King Menander and his Buddhist teacher, Nagasena, the King was a deeply committed Buddhist. The Buddhist tradition, at least, enthusiastically embraced the notion of its foreign Greek convert.

The *Milindapanha* also related the striking – though apparently apocryphal – story of how Nagasena gave an image of the Buddha to Menander. In fact, despite being an Indo-Greek (and thus familiar with the worship of anthropomorphic gods and goddesses) Menander did not encourage the manufacture of Buddha images: the Theravada form of Buddhism that he followed, forbade it. Nor did he imprint the Buddha's face on his coins. Instead, he used the Buddhist symbol of the *dharmachakra*, the 'wheel of transformation', to signal his religious affiliation.

Menander, Azes and Kanishka were kings who patronized Buddhism and promoted its dissemination. All of them were aware of the fact that they were treading in the shadow of a far greater king – one who had united not just Uttarapatha with Buddhist doctrines, but the whole of India. No Buddhist visitor to Swat – Chinese, Kushan or Indian – ever forgot the influence of Emperor Ashoka. The Chinese pilgrims described how Ashoka's stupas, said to number 84,000, were found all over India. They demarcated the contours of his pan-Indian empire.

The Buddha's ashes were still warm, in the fifth century BCE, when his disciples divided him up – cremated corpse, urn and coals – into ten neat parcels. One parcel was allocated to each of the ten nascent Buddhist states, whose kings had them entombed in stupas. Two hundred years later, Ashoka broke these stupas open, and had the relics redivided into tiny portions which were distributed all over India. Where before there were ten stupas, now there were thousands. With this action Ashoka achieved two things. He made a public declaration of how far his writ as king could stretch. And he single-handedly turned Buddhism from one of many competing sects into a national, exportable religion.

Had Ashoka not taken up Buddhism with the zeal of a convert, Buddhism would probably have faded away – just as its founder predicted. Instead, Ashoka – who became the overlord of the biggest-ever Indian empire, and was probably weaned on stories of the great Greek Sikunder (Alexander), and who could have remained just another bloodthirsty ruler – did something unusual.

In the tenth year of his reign (254 BCE), having defeated all his enemies, Ashoka toured India, preaching non-violence to his people. Then, after his 256-day round trip was over, he began putting up monumental stone slabs all over his empire, inscribed with a message to his people. Part sermon, part confession, part self-promoting advert, Ashoka's fourteen edicts make startling reading, with their hard-headed combination of humility, patriotism, imperial violence. Ashoka urges his subjects to take up the law of *dhamma* (the Buddhist version of the Sanskrit word *dharma*, meaning 'good works') and give up frivolous festivals (women, in particular, are prone to performing 'vulgar and time-wasting ceremonies'). He asks them to stop eating meat – then confesses to his own household's consumption of 'two peacocks and a deer, though the deer not always'. He expresses 'deep remorse' for conquering the eastern province of Kalinga, but warns the forest people that 'the Beloved of the Gods has the power to punish them if necessary.' And he reveals his omniscience:

> At all times, whether I am eating, or am in the women's apartments, or in my inner apartments, or at the cattle-shed, or in my carriage, or in my gardens – wherever I may be – my informants keep me in touch with public business. Thus everywhere I transact public business.

It was a form of control, a way of letting them know that Ashoka was watching them.

Ashoka's semi-Buddhist, semi-authoritarian edicts were a legislative work of art. But they have puzzled historians, who have identified in them some archetypal Buddhist positions (such as the criticism of Vedic sacrifice and superstitious habits) and simultaneously an absence of standard Buddhist doctrines (most notably, the concept of Nirvana). Was Ashoka adapting Buddhism to his own non-sectarian purposes?

Or did his edicts reflect the form that Buddhism took before it was systematically codified?

Like the stupas with which he liberally adorned India, Ashoka's inscriptions staked out his empire. In the core provinces, the message was inscribed on pale pink sandstone pillars. On the periphery – in the lands ruled by regents or princes – the edicts were scratched on any handy rock, sometimes on three adjacent boulders, at crossroads or near large settlements. The message was abbreviated in some places, lengthened in others, but the theme was the same: Ashoka's subjects were as one within 'my vast domain'. Standing at Shahbazgarhi on the road from Taxila to Swat beside one of the northernmost carvings, running my hand over the faded lettering, it is extraordinary to think that this same, personal, pious, generous and intimidating message resounded here on this grassy hillside, as it did in the jungles of Bihar, the deserts of Rajasthan and along the Coromandel coast.

Before Ashoka, no Indian king had thought of carving public messages to their people 'in stone', as Ashoka himself pointed out, 'so that it might endure long and that my descendants might act in conformity with it'. Prior to Ashoka, language in India was barely even a written affair – the entire corpus of the Vedic religion was predicated on memorizing, not writing down, holy Sanskrit verses. Indeed, it was Ashoka's colossal carving project that introduced writing across the Indian subcontinent. 'All modern Indic scripts' – bar that as yet undeciphered script used five millennia ago in the Indus valley – descend from Ashoka's Brahmi.

Subsequent Buddhist tradition has vaunted Ashoka's quasi-sacred status: his humble ancestry has been assimilated to that of the Buddha's own family; Sinhalese tradition has his consecration falling exactly a hundred years after the Buddha's Nirvana; and a legend was even formulated showing the Buddha meeting (and endorsing) Emperor Ashoka in a previous incarnation. In fact, Ashoka's family appears to have hailed from Gandhara, and during his life he spent much time there – serving as viceroy in Taxila when he was a prince, and paying the town particular attention as emperor; he may even have died there.

For Ashoka, whose own capital was in east India, the 'peoples on the western borders' – with their dangerous proximity to the still-threatening Greek and Persian empires – required careful management and frequent admonition. Ashoka mentions the Greeks at several points in his edicts, and his behaviour suggests that he was hyper-sensitive to goings-on in the Indus valley, where these foreigners had infiltrated. His grandfather had won back the lands along the Indus from Seleucus, Alexander's viceroy, and the treaty they signed included the exchange of women and envoys. Ashoka would thus have grown up with first-hand experience of Greeks (the ladies in the harem included Seleucus's daughter). In the edicts, he empha-sized his special friendship with five foreign kings in the West: Ptolemy, Magas, Alexander, Antigonus and Antiochus. The Greek connection was a source of prestige and power. Even so, he did not want another Seleucus harrying his empire. Guarding the fron-tier along the Indus river was essential to the integrity of his India.

The edicts, therefore, went up in strategic places in the north-west: two in Ashoka's frontier lands, at Jalalabad and Kandahar, and three in Uttarapatha, at Taxila, Mansehra (on the Kashmir road) and Shahbazgarhi. In the rest of India, the language of the edicts was Ashoka's home dialect of Magadi, and the script was Brahmi (prob-ably inspired by Greek, and invented specifically for the edicts). But at Jalalabad they were written in Aramaic; at Kandahar (the oldest known inscription) in Aramaic and Greek; and at Mansehra and Shahbazgarhi, in Kharoshti script, a local version of Aramaic.

Even the key concepts of Ashoka's religious propaganda were explained in Hellenistic and Zoroastrian philosophical terminology. The Buddhist word *dhamma* became *eusebeia* in Greek (meaning 'piety, loyalty, reverence for the gods and for parents'). In Aramaic it transmogrified into 'Truth' or 'the conduct of the good', reflecting ideas in Zoroastrianism.

Both trade and religion needed writing in order to spread beyond the borders of India, and it was Ashoka who brought these three elements together. The purest form of Sanskrit was spoken in Uttarapatha, and now Ashoka employed masons from the area to inscribe the edicts all over his kingdom (scribes from the north-west signed their names in Kharoshti on the edicts in southern India).

Unsurprisingly, in the years following Ashoka's death, it was the literacy of the north-west in general (as compared to the rest of India) that was one of the most significant factors in Buddhism's spread outside India. Indeed, it was monks from Uddiyana and Gandhara who first carried Buddhism to Afghanistan and China, in the form of sacred texts written in the languages of the region.

As a result of the attention which Ashoka paid to the Indus lands, the world west of the river re-entered the political and religious sphere of mainland India and the Buddhism which had begun there. As at Butkara, it was Ashoka's religious, administrative and architectural structure that other kings built on, and his reputation that they vied with. Above all, it was Ashoka who recognized how important Uttarapatha and the frontier regions were, both for the strategic defence of his kingdom and for the spread of his imperial and religious dogma.

Ashoka's legacy endured for centuries after the emperor's death but it could not last for ever, and if there were any Buddhists left by the time Sultan Mahmud reached Swat, there are none here today. Standing amidst these ruined and abandoned stupas, the past seems forlornly distant.

There is, though, one facet of the Buddhist empire that is still in robust existence. Late one evening, driving through Mingora bazaar, I notice a teashop full of young men, crowded around a television, watching *Laila Majnun*, the Indian musical film of an old Arabic love-story. Just as Uddiyana's masons copied vine leaves from Roman terracotta jars, so it was Buddhist animal tales that travelled west along the Silk Road and into *The Arabian Nights*, and now it is Indian actors singing Indian songs, who are acting out an Arabic tale of forbidden love for men in Pakistan. That night, those transfixed Swati faces seem to attest to the enduring eclecticism of the Silk Road.

And so the next morning, it is the modern denizens of the Silk Road whom I set out to meet. Today the looms of Swat weave polyester instead of raw Chinese silk, but vibrant merchant networks still endure here – albeit in a nebulous and illicit way.

For twenty years following Partition, Swat remained a semi-autonomous princely state, ruled by the Wali, a hereditary leader. Then in 1969, Pakistan's first military dictator, General Ayub Khan, absorbed Swat into his Republic. In order to soften the blow, the Dictator and the Wali cut a deal: tax-free status for thirty-five years.

That time has now run out, but every time Pakistan's Finance Minister tries to reimpose taxation, Swat takes no notice. It is not just for its mountain peaks that Swat is called the Switzerland of Pakistan. The region has become a scenic factory for luxury goods – anything on which the down-country duty is exorbitant. Lubna's Wonder Wax for Ladies is made in Swat, as is lipstick, and Fair & Lovely skin-lightening cream. That's the legitimate stuff. Then there's the black market goods, the smuggling.

In Mingora's main bazaar I have tea with Salman, a man with fair hair and green eyes from north Waziristan. Salman keeps his wife in gold chokers and silken burqas by driving untaxed cars very fast from Afghanistan, through the Tochi pass to Bannu, and across the Frontier's patchwork of taxed and tax-free states. Smugglers, the police chief in Jalalabad told me (but Afghans are forever badmouthing Pakistanis), will pay thousands of rupees to rent a 'diplomatic gate-pass' from members of the Pakistan embassy in Kabul. With this precious documentation, vehicles can cross the border between Afghanistan and Pakistan unchecked, into Waziristan, or any of the seven other tribal agencies along the border. 'I have a network of drivers in each agency,' Salman explains to me, and gestures to his phone, lying on the tea-stained table: 'With mobiles we are in constant contact to avoid the police posts.' He sips his tea thoughtfully for a moment, and then looks up: 'Are you free next week? If you were sitting in the front seat, nobody would stop me.'

Although there are rigorous checkpoints on the roads out of Swat, the police cannot staff the rivers. And while it would be hard to float a car upwards, there is little to stop goods being transported downstream. Timber, in particular, has been a lucrative export out of Swat since at least the second millennium BCE. Early in the morning, in a small riverside town famed for 'the beauty of its ladies', I meet an old man with a white cap, shaved upper lip and religious air. The sweet-smelling wood in the timberyard Aziz runs is smuggled. It is brought down by river, at night, from the thick forests of upper Swat. The wood is strapped together in twenty-foot batches. To the top are attached four inflated tractor inner tubes: lifebelts for the pilots, who steer the wood along the fast-flowing river. The ice-cold journey takes three or four hours; and every year some of

Aziz's men drown on the job. 'Very dangerous work,' he says. 'You understand?'

Pirating, too, is big business in Pakistan. In Swat it is not just lookalike Kalashnikovs and fake Indian DVDs that are magicked through the mountains. The latest luxury items to take to the Silk Road are passports. Scans and electronic systems have made things difficult, but not impossible, for passport pirates; and Afghan identity papers are easy to recreate. Aziz has a cousin who recently reached London by uncertain means – and with all the wrong papers. Threatened with deportation, he rang Aziz and asked him to arrange an Afghan identity certificate and driving licence. Neither Aziz nor his cousin had ever set foot in Afghanistan – but 'in Pakistan,' says Aziz, 'everything is possible.' Four days and five hundred rupees later, Aziz picked up the papers 'from my contact' and sent them to London. The Swati dropout became a refugee from the Taliban.

Pakistan as a whole has such a laissez-faire attitude to taxation that none of the smugglers I meet are the least abashed when discussing their trade. To my surprise, they open up their illegal operations to my queries with a blasé calm – only afterwards do they display their anxiety. By the time I leave Swat, smugglers are inundating my phone with fretful messages asking me to change their names and details.

One of the most lucrative and damaging forms of smuggling is in art history. British and French explorers removed plenty of Gandharan art from the Frontier Province during the colonial era, to museums or private collections (via smart art shops in Piccadilly). But there is still much left to pilfer. The Archaeology Department does its best to preserve the plethora of Buddhist statues and relics that remain in this valley – but such is the fear of illegal antiques trafficking in Pakistan that most of the statues excavated after Partition have been locked up in museums. Inside the stupas are empty niches where the Buddhas used to stand; outside, a flock of young boys sell fake Gandharan coins or pocket-sized statues. Those images that remain – on immovable rocks – bear the marks of the Taliban's Sultan Mahmud-style vandalism: the faces bashed away, the bodies dismembered. Clustered along the river – and thus the modern highway – Buddhist carvings in Swat make easy prey for angry Muslims.

During the first few weeks I spend in Swat, every Buddhist carving I see appears to have been hideously, recklessly disfigured. It is only towards the end of my time here that I come across the one Buddha in this entire valley that is still untouched. It stands in a narrow gorge north of Butkara, high above the river, its back against the hillside, accessible only through groves of fruit trees, along the edges of wheat fields, past straw-roofed houses which smell of wood smoke. Carved fluidly into pinkish-yellow sandstone, it is a seven-metre-high Maitreya Buddha – the Messiah-like Buddha of the future, whose cult probably began here in Uddiyana. The Buddha's legs are crossed, his hands folded in his lap, his eyes closed in tranquil meditation. Visited only by shepherds, the statue thus endures as a rare memorial; a glimpse of what the valley must have looked like in the days when the kings were Buddhist, when caravans of silk passed through the valley, and when Chinese monks braved the dragons and sorcerers of the Indus river to visit Uddiyana's holy places.

In 2007, local Taliban groups finally took control of Swat, under the direction of Maulana Fazlullah, son-in-law of the radical preacher, Sufi Muhammad. One object of puritanical attack was the last intact Maitreya Buddha: it was dynamited, and its head and shoulders drilled away. The fanatics, then, have largely succeeded in obliterating Swat's pre-Islamic, Buddhist past.

8

Alexander at the Outer Ocean

327 BCE

'The Indus is bigger than any river in Europe . . . This was the river which Alexander crossed with his army, and so entered India.'

Arrian, *Anabasis Alexandri, c.* 145 CE

ALMOST TWO THOUSAND years ago, Plutarch described the meeting between Alexander the Great of Macedon and an Indian boy, 'Sandracottus'. This child, Plutarch attested, never forgot that the foreign king came 'within a step' of conquering India. In fact, Plutarch's story was a wilful exaggeration of Alexander's prowess. In 327 BCE, Alexander had barely subdued the Indus valley, India's namesake. Two years after he returned from India to Babylon he was dead. The string of cities called Alexandria which he had founded in eastern Persia and western India were washed away in the region's many rivers or repossessed by the locals; the soldiers he had stationed there marched home in long foot-columns; and his empire was divided up between his companions. So imperceptible was Alexander's impression upon India that none of the residents thought his visit worth recording in such literature as survives. Instead it was young 'Sandracottus' – Chandragupta Maurya, Ashoka's grandfather – who by 305 BCE had won back all the land along the Indus that Alexander had taken. It was Chandragupta Maurya who accomplished what Alexander had failed to do, and united India as one empire.

But in Greece, nothing could eclipse the exploits of the 'world conqueror'. Alexander was too adept at manufacturing his own myth. And India was too marvellous. The tales his companions told on their return – of the country's gold, elephants and rivers – were the gloss and burnish of the Alexander legend.

When Alexander set out from Greece to conquer the world, his most urgent priority was to better the exploits of his rival, Emperor Darius the Great of Persia, who had invaded 'India' two centuries earlier. None of the campaign historians Alexander took with him to India mention Darius, but they were certainly aware of him. A century before, the Greek historian Herodotus had called Darius the discoverer of 'the greater part of Asia'. He had become so, Herodotus explained, by despatching a sailor called Scylax to navigate the Indus from Attock (where the Kabul river joins the Indus) downstream to the sea. Scylax, who thus mapped 1,400 kilometres of the Indus, became the first Westerner to describe 'India', and gained a reputation as 'the bravest man in early Greek history'. And Darius, meanwhile, annexed the Indus to his empire.

For Darius, conquering the Indus valley was a lucrative venture. As Herodotus attested in his *Histories*, the Indus valley was engorged with gold; the natives wore clothes made of 'tree-wool', and they paid 'a tribute exceeding that of every other people, to wit, three hundred and sixty talents of gold dust'. This was enough to spur on any army. It was from Herodotus that Alexander would have heard of the Nile-like crocodiles in the Indus, and it was Herodotus who first compared the Indians and the Ethiopians: both have black skin, he wrote, and black semen. The Alexander historians appear to have written Darius and Scylax out of their accounts in order to disguise how closely Alexander was following in the Persian king's footsteps.

But for an army trying to conquer a country, Herodotus was part of the problem; he had conceptualized India as the Indus valley: a river-shaped country that ran east to the Ocean on the edge of the world. This is what Alexander the Great was expecting during the eight years and 18,000 kilometres it took to reach India from Greece. He had no maps, his men spoke no local languages. He relied entirely on luck, local guides – and the gods.

After reaching Jalalabad (in eastern Afghanistan), Alexander split his army. Hephaestion, his lover, marched due east through the Khyber or Michni pass towards the Indus. But Alexander went north up the Kunar river valley – ostensibly to subdue the already famously intransigent northern hill tribes – and across what is now the Nawa pass into Pakistan. I want to follow Alexander's journey from Kunar – until recently the home of goat-revering pagans – into northern Pakistan; but I have also had my fill of illegal border-crossings. For a change, I decide to apply for permission.

On a hot day in May, I dress in my most floriferous shalwar kameez, buy a copy of Aurel Stein's book on Alexander's northern-most Indus battle, and make an appointment to see the Dictator's army spokesman. Sitting in an austere air-conditioned room at army headquarters in Rawalpindi, the cantonment town adjacent to the Pakistani capital, I explain to the moustachioed General before me that I am travelling up the Indus from its mouth to the source, and telling the history of the land that is today Pakistan: 'I now want to follow, on foot, the route of Alexander the Great from Afghanistan, along the Indus to Pirsar,' I say. 'Pirsar?' he asks. 'The huge rock above the Indus where Alexander fought the hill tribes,' I say, smiling at the absurdity of what I am about to ask: 'To get there I need to cross the Pakistani border at the Nawa pass.'

Disconcertingly, the General smiles back. He compliments me on my 'excellent' Urdu and 'gorgeous' dress sense, and then he rings the secretary of the Federally Administered Tribal Areas [FATA] in Peshawar. We both know that the Nawa pass is not an official crossing-point – but never mind that: 'A tribal escort will be waiting.' We don't discuss how I am going to get through Kunar, or what the Afghans will say when I turn up unannounced at the border. 'Alexander came here two thousand years ago,' he jokes as I leave. 'Today it is Alice.' 'We have different objectives,' I reply, disconcerted by the parallel with Alexander Burnes, who hubristic-ally compared himself with Alexander the Great (and accurately, for both were on imperialist missions). 'But how old are you?' the General asks; and I am forced to confess: 'Twenty-nine.' 'The age that Alexander was when he came here,' the General says, and laughs.

My second trip to Afghanistan is the quintessence of bad timing. It is early summer, and the annual cross-border terrorism is just beginning. The day I enter Afghanistan via the Khyber pass, there is a huge suicide bomb in a mosque in Kandahar. The significance of this event is immediately apparent, for it marks the return of the Taliban, with a movement more violent than the first.

In Jalalabad, I stay with Hafizullah, a man my age whose house was a weapons' depot during the war. That night, we drink white wine together in his hujra with the local chief of police, and the smell of tobacco flowers rises from the garden. 'My guards will take you to Kunar tomorrow,' says the policeman. 'You'll be at the Nawa pass by sundown.' I ring the Secretary of FATA. He says the escort will be waiting.

But the next day the policeman has changed his mind. 'Early this morning there was an attack at the Nawa pass,' explains Hafizullah. 'Al-Qaeda tried to take the border post, and our men shot an Afghan and an Arab. The attackers carried sophisticated weapons. I'll speak to the Foreign Ministry in Kabul.'

The people in the Foreign Ministry find my journey distasteful; they decide that it is part of a conspiracy by the Pakistan Army. 'We have no clearance for a foreigner to cross at Nawa,' they say. 'Who authorized it?' 'We Afghans don't trust the Pakistanis,' says Hafizullah to me patiently. 'Maybe the Pakistan Army wants to make trouble. We Afghans will look bad if you are killed in Kunar. You told them that you were going to be there today. Don't you think it is a co-incidence that the attack happened on the same day?' Nevertheless, Hafizullah rings a friend from the province, a religious-looking man with a big red beard. 'You will go with him in a local taxi,' he says. 'Al-Qaeda only blow up four-by-fours in Kunar. How do you look in a burqa?'

The third day dawns. I wait in Hafizullah's house for the man with the beard. I pace up and down in my burqa. Eventually, in the afternoon, a car draws up outside the house. It is Hafizullah's cousin. 'Hafizullah is in a meeting with the US Army,' the cousin says. 'The Americans say Kunar is a war zone. They say you are crazy to even try and go there. They want you to go back to Pakistan.' The cousin drives me to the border. The next news I hear from the region is that Al-Qaeda have shot down a Chinook helicopter, killing sixteen US soldiers.

It is Hephaestion, then, whom I follow into Pakistan.

Back in Peshawar, the Secretary of FATA sits in his office surrounded by turbanned petitioners looking pleased by reports that Al-Qaeda has attacked the border post – so pleased that he packs me off to the Pakistani side of the Nawa pass that day, with a contingent of fifteen *khassadar* (guards) in their distinctive black uniforms. We drive north through the tribal agencies, areas that foreigners need permission to enter, parallel with the Durand Line, past abandoned Afghan refugee villages and the former training camps of the Afghan warlord Hekmatyar. It is barren country but the hills that Alexander marched through loom blue and tempting in the distance. The tribal escort stop for lunch and prayers in a small village; and at the Malakand border, they hand me over to the guards from Bajaur. '*Sikunder-e-Azam-wali*,' they say to each other on the radio: the Alexander the Great girl.

'How is Queen Elizabeth Taylor?' the boys from Bajaur ask me as we wind up into the hills. When we get to the pass, I leave the guards on the road and climb up along the barbed-wire fence to the top of the ridge that divides Pakistan from its neighbour, from where I can look down into Afghanistan at the snaking Kunar river. But the fifteen-man escort becomes collectively nervous. The youngest recruit is sent up to bring me down. Ten years ago the Nawa pass wasn't even manned. In today's political climate, they are all very jumpy.

They lead me to a building where lunch is waiting, and there we sit together on the floor, feasting hungrily on mutton rice, yoghurt and apricots, before driving in convoy down the unpaved road on the route that Alexander took through Bajaur. It is harvest time, and men and women are in the fields, tying wheat into piles. The fields are boxed in by pink and grey drystone walls, which lead to mud-smeared houses. Beside each house is a tall stone tower. 'What is that for?' I ask the guard sitting next to me. 'Shooting enemies from,' he says.

I spend that night in Bajaur's small capital, in a generic colonial rest-house, where I am visited by the local historian over dinner. He tells me that it was here that Alexander was hit in the leg by an arrow, and a little further on is a village, Sikundro, now a paramilitary base, the name of which means 'Alexander Stopped' in Pashto. 'We Pashtuns admire Sikunder-e-Azam very much,' he says. 'You do know that Alexander is our ancestor?' I nod politely.

Between here and the Indus, Alexander campaigned more viciously than anywhere else in Persia or India. The kings of the Punjabi plains were models of royal courtesy; but the hill tribes chose not to abide by the invaders' rules. They fought bitterly, ran away through the hills if defeated, and refused to be held to the terms of Macedonian treaties. During the six months that he spent marching from Jalalabad to Pirsar, Alexander massacred as many locals as he could get his hands on. During my journey to Pirsar – a 7,000-foot-high hill on the banks of the Indus, inhabited only in the summer months by shepherds – I will traverse a landscape that in the fourth century BCE bore witness to the Greek army's systematic brutality.

In the morning I am taken – on the instructions of the FATA Secretary in Peshawar – to visit Hakim Ayub. 'His forefathers have been making *majoon* since the time of Emperor Babur,' the Secretary had said. 'The knowledge came from Greece originally. Men use it for . . .' he cleared his throat, 'that *thing*, if you don't mind.' I blushed, and checked later with a knowledgeable friend: 'Local Viagra,' he said.

Powerful aphrodisiacs – along with wine, figs and demands for sophists – were chief among the things exchanged by Chandragupta Maurya and Seleucus Nicator, Alexander's successor. For the ancient Greeks and Indians, an effective aphrodisiac was gold dust, literally. Unani medicine – practised by hakims, Muslim doctors – was developed in Baghdad during the eighth century 'from the ashes of the Alexandrian library' where, thanks to the patronage of the Caliph Harun ar-Rashid, the medical knowledge of ancient Greece was fused with that of Arabia and probably also India. The medical system is still in use today. Hakims are respected members of the community all over the Islamic world, and in Pakistan they do what madrassahs do for education – provide an alternative to the feeble state system.

The fifteen tribal escorts and I arrive at Hakim Ayub's house and crowd noisily into the room where he is mixing up his potions. Out on the table is a pestle and mortar, a set of scales and a bunsen burner; the wall behind is lined with wooden cabinets filled with packets, pots and bottles. Hakim Ayub, a courteous man with a bruise on his forehead from years of vigorous namaz, sits the entire tribal escort down on his workshop benches and gives everybody a crystallized *amla* to eat. This small green fruit has been liberally rolled in silver leaf, and our lips shimmer with the luxury of it. His grandson Aurangzeb allows me to taste the odoriferous arak that they brew in the yard outside. Then the Hakim gives me the recipe for his sex potion.

He unwraps packets, unscrews pots and announces ingredients for my benefit in his resonant Pashto. Aurangzeb, who speaks Urdu, is my enthusiastic translator. 'Testicles of the water hog,' he says, 'deer's navel, intestines of the baby camel, sparrow's brain, lapis lazuli, silver leaf, ground seed pearls, sandfish, pomegranate oil, honey and . . .' 'Is it not haram?' I ask, and Hakim Ayub looks truly shocked. 'Halal, it is all halal,' he says, and mixes in a liberal dollop of hashish butter. I stare at the testicles of the water hog in disbelief; turn over the deer's navel (musk?) in my fingers. Hakim Ayub adds a pinch of gold dust and the potion is replete: a brown, shimmery lump in the bottom of the pestle. He divides it neatly into two plastic pots. 'One for you,' he says, 'and one for the Governor of NWFP.'

'Only eat a little and you will be laughing and happy,' he says as I leave with the district police (we are going back into the 'settled' areas). 'Too much and you will become intoxicated.' 'Unani means Greek,' he calls as I wave goodbye from the police van. 'Alexander would have eaten majoon on his journey. Emperor Babur loved to eat majoon from Bajaur.'

It is true. During his early incursions across the Indus, Babur only drank wine – it was brought down to Bajaur from the hills by 'Kafirs' (non-Muslims) in a goatskin; but a few days later his corruption was complete when he tasted some 'well-flavoured and quite intoxicating confections'. This majoon had such a remarkable effect on the future Emperor of India that he was unable to attend the evening prayers. Over the next few weeks, as he crossed the Indus for the first time and explored the Punjab by boat, Babur ate majoon made by Hakim Ayub's forefathers almost every night.

Bundled into the police van like a parcel, I see the district of Dir pass by in a blur. 'I'd like to walk, please,' I say to the police. 'Walk?' they echo. 'Nobody walks. We have instructions to deliver you to Swat.' 'But I want to follow Sikunder-e-Azam's route on foot,' I explain, 'by walking, like his soldiers.' I ring Aslam, friend of the friends I stayed with in Mingora, who has agreed to walk the four hundred or so kilometres with me from Bajaur to Pirsar. 'Please ask them to let me go,' I say. 'We will leave you in Barikot,' the police retort, 'after you have signed the register. In Pakistan you must sign the register every day. You must always inform us faithfully of your whereabouts.'

Before reaching Swat, Alexander had first to traverse its river (called the Guraeus by the Greeks). According to Arrian, a Roman senator who wrote a history of Alexander's conquests in the second century CE based on accounts compiled by Alexander's friends Ptolemy and Aristobulus, 'He crossed it with difficulty, both because of its depth, and because its current was rapid, and the rounded stones in the river proved very slippery to anyone stepping on them.' On the other side, he defeated an army of seven thousand Indian mercenaries, built two wooden forts, and then marched south to besiege the hill-top fort of Barikot (where, it is said, the chieftain's wife visited him that night, keen to conceive a replacement for the son killed by a Greek catapult).

By now, the local tribesmen had grown weary of fighting Alexander, and so they slipped away in the middle of the night, fleeing east over the Karakar pass and across the 'rough and mountainous country' to Pirsar. Alexander went after them, and that is the way Aslam and I are going today, whatever the policemen say.

Aslam, a lean, reserved man from a village in the far north of Swat, speaker of Urdu, English, Farsi as well as the hill dialect of his village, father of eleven children and repository of knowledge botanical, historical and social, is waiting for me in the Barikot bazaar. I sign the police register, promise not to leave town without due notice, and then Aslam and I sit down in a teashop and study the misinformation of our Pakistani maps, furnished by army headquarters in Rawalpindi (and almost worse than having no maps at all, as Alexander did – large stretches of our journey along the Indus are through apparently blank patches). I also have a map of Alexander's route prepared by the British governor of NWFP, Olaf Caroe; and the charts of Pirsar drawn up by Aurel Stein in 1926 following his trip there (with one hundred porters, thirty bodyguards, four army revolvers, an Afridi surveyor, the blessing of the Wali of Swat and the financial backing of the colonial Government of India). It was

Stein who proposed that Unasar and Pirsar, small mountains on the banks of the Indus, might be the 'Aornos' of the Greeks – the site of Alexander's last major siege, and the symbolic climax of his campaign for world domination.

Before we set off down the country road to the Karakar pass, Aslam pulls a white sheet-like *chador* out of his bag for me to wear. I tie it over my head and tightly around my hair, nose and mouth so that only my eyes are showing. 'You should walk behind me,' Aslam says. 'And don't walk too fast. It would be best if you could pass as a Pashtun lady.'

The path to Karakar is stony, unmetalled and quiet, and during the three-hour walk we see only a shepherd with his flock, one teashop, and some stranded truckers in oil-smeared pyjamas. It is getting dark when we reach Karakar village. None of the houses have electricity – but the mosque is brightly lit. 'What piety,' I say, and Aslam looks proud. We leave the road and climb the hill above the village. 'How far to the pass?' Aslam asks a villager who is collecting firewood. Only an hour, he tells us, but the problem is the other side; it will take three hours to reach another settlement. He gestures back down the valley to a long low house bordered by green terraces. 'You can stay there with my in-laws,' he says.

I had assumed we would be camping, but Aslam explains that this would be too outlandish. 'Pashtun hospitality and protection is everything,' he says. 'You can stay in the house with the women. I will sleep with the men in the hujra.' And so it is. For the next fifteen days we walk through places that neither of us has seen before; and every night a stranger gives us food and shelter.

The house we are taken to that night is large, with a wooden verandah flanked by blackened pillars made from tree trunks, on which hub-caps have been hung as trophies. The eldest brother devotes his retirement to renovating the local mosque, the middle brother works in Saudi Arabia, the youngest at the port in Karachi. The economy of this family is typical of the hill villages – part remittance from abroad, a little local farming, and some work in Karachi if you can get it. Aslam is sent upstairs to the hujra, and I sit down below with the women, who cook our dinner outside, over a pine-cone fire. But they speak no Urdu, and I no Pashto. It is their husbands and brothers, serious bearded men in white Sunni caps, who quiz me on my status. 'Who is this man you are with?' 'If you are married, where is your husband?' 'How many children do you have?' There is some confusion about the object of my journey. 'Sikunder who?' they ask me.

We go to bed at nine, in wooden string beds under the stars. The house takes a long time to get to sleep: there is a second sitting of dinner at ten for the men who have come in from the mosque, and an aged aunt who moans in her sleep. Lanterns move to and fro across the terrace. Eventually everything is quiet. When I wake at dawn, mine is the only bed left in the courtyard.

After paratha and tea – a deliciously greasy and filling fried-bread breakfast – two shepherds lead us over the Karakar pass by a short cut that avoids the police post. 'That is the Malandrai pass,' says Aslam, pointing through the trees, and across the wide valley below, to the faraway hills. It is the Malandrai pass that Alexander is said to have galloped over with his elite Companion Cavalry.

We climb down through the pine forest, and out on to a tarmac road. We are now in Buner district, a place considered by Swatis to be wild and uncouth. The morning light and shadow falls sharply on the hills, and we turn off the main road, into a maze of quiet hedgerows. At ten, we are walking past a village teashop, when Aslam is recognized by a lorry-driver friend from Swat. He stands us tea and biscuits. I am sent inside to the filthy curtained women's section; outside, the lorry driver says to Aslam, 'Do you need a lift? Why are you walking? Do you want me to lend you some money?' He hasn't heard of Sikunder-e-Azam either.

On we go, treading marijuana underfoot as the road becomes narrower and less travelled. For two hours the only vehicle that passes is a tractor blaring sermons ('Do the work of God, be good to your neighbours'). Finally we turn off the jeep road, and by midday are walking on a grassy track around the village of Kohay, when Aslam notices that we are being followed. Two young men – with that under-occupied village air which I will learn means trouble – announce that they have something to tell us. We follow them to their hujra, and here the horror stories start.

The next village is very, very dangerous: 'More dangerous than

Al-Qaeda.' Sons assassinate fathers, uncles murder nephews. They will sell you for fifty rupees, or kill you for the contents of your handbag. I am sceptical, but now we are stuck: it is too hot to walk on till three or four o'clock. I resign myself to being taken into the house, and introduced to the women. From there I am led down to the village well, and exhibited like an exotic creature.

Back at the hujra, I wait for Aslam, who has gone down to the mosque for prayers. He comes in looking grim: 'The people in the bazaar are saying there is 100 per cent risk,' he tells me. 'And there is another village, Yaghistan, near the Indus where we are going, which is just as dangerous.' My scepticism wavers. At five o'clock, somebody locates the school caretaker, who is from the dangerous village: maybe he can take us? But not today, tomorrow. And so the village boys have got their way. We will have to stay the night in Kohay.

Kohay means 'well' or 'spring' but here, as in most Pakistani villages, there are water issues. The villagers farm the land for subsistence not trade, and such is the distance from the road that local employment is difficult to come by. The man who owns the house in which I stay is away in Malaysia; and his son, who has no job, rarely leaves the village – hence his fear of the neighbours.

In the morning, there is more drama in the hujra. The school care-taker has been warned by his father not to help us. Instead, our absent host's brother, Abdul Ghaffar, who *has* heard of Alexander, comes over and tries to reason with me: 'Sikunder rode on a horse?' he asks. 'Yes, Bucephalus,' I say. 'Well, not even a goat could get over Malandrai,' he replies. But by now I don't believe anything they say – and it is already six in the morning. 'Let's go,' I say to Aslam, and the hujra leaps collectively to its feet. 'I am coming with you,' says Abdul Ghaffar.

We walk jubilantly away from the village, and for an hour follow an old riverbed east, past a well where women in flowing, coloured headscarves crouch down beside their water pots, their faces turned away when they see us coming. By seven we have reached the foot of the pass. It is an easy half-hour climb; I eat tiny strawberries all the way up. 'That is Chorbandah,' says Abdul Ghaffar, pointing to a small village in the valley below us. Chorbandah means 'thieves'; was that innocent-looking village what all the fuss was about?

We sit at the top of the pass, looking down across the plain, with its wavy marks of rivers, and the straight, man-made lines of fields, as Abdul Ghaffar tells us the true (but brief) story of the most dangerous village in the district. Last year one of the Chorbandah youths took to hiding in the Malandrai pass and robbing travellers. Eventually, says Abdul Ghaffar, his exasperated uncle shot him dead; but now everything is *saf* (clean).

We begin our descent, and I find that Abdul Ghaffar is right, Buchephalus would never have got over this pass. Even I barely make it. I am wearing the stupidest pair of shoes, my football-playing trainers, which, between the last time I kicked a ball on London Fields, and the moment when I slip down the marble-smooth cliff face and almost fall to my death, have lost all their grip. I pick my way cautiously along the grey rock, marvelling at the shoes that Aslam is wearing – a pair of second-hand brogues he bought in the Barikot bazaar for fifty rupees. 'I don't like your shoes,' says Abdul Ghaffar to me. It takes two hours to climb down the slippery rock and on to the solid mud path. 'Alexander must have crossed the Ali Peza pass,' Abdul Ghaffar says. 'It's just over there. You could take a car over that one.'

Abdul Ghaffar has relatives in the village at the base of the pass, who live in a mud-walled house, with a stream running through the middle of the garden. They sit us down in their small stuffy hujra, with a big glass display cabinet on one wall (containing golden high-heeled ladies' shoes, a gun and an enamel teapot). The tea and biscuits come – and with them the horror stories, all over again. We want to walk to Rustom, a town perhaps an hour away; but 'Nobody walks to Rustom,' say the men, in shocked voices, 'it is too dangerous.' I catch Aslam's eye. 'What is the danger?' 'In this heat,' they say, 'the animals in the fields go mad. There are mad dogs. Mad donkeys.' And then a word I don't understand. I look at Aslam. He translates with a deadpan face, from Pashto into English: 'Mad foxes.' And I burst out laughing.

Our hosts, however, are on the verge of tears and nervous exhaustion: they want to be rid of the responsibility we present. The truth is also that Abdul Ghaffar has trudged a long way with us this morning; now that we have reached a motorable road he would understandably rather ride than walk to Rustom. So we are escorted to a truck that is taking a load of wood into town. I lean out of the window looking for crazy foxes, and barely twenty minutes later we arrive in Rustom.

Abdul Ghaffar leads us down the quiet back streets of the town, to the shade of his cousin's hujra. As the women cook lunch, we examine the map. From here, we will walk south-east to Hund, the ancient river-crossing where Hephaestion set up camp while the rest of the army campaigned in Swat, and where Alexander came before turning north to Pirsar.

Again, Abdul Ghaffar's cousin pleads with us to accept a lift; and again, Aslam explains that we prefer to walk. The cousin gives us the name of a man in Hund with whom we can stay, and in the afternoon, after I have thanked the women, we leave the house.

An hour passes, and then the ridge of Shahbazgarhi, where Ashoka put his inscriptions, emerges from the landscape to our left. This once-busy Buddhist trade route is now deep in the heart of Pashtun country. The women wear all-enveloping spotted chadors, the roads are good, and there is constant traffic between the villages. But here in the plains it is hot. Aslam's village in Swat is snowed in for several months a year, and he hates the heat. 'I can't believe I am doing this,' he says as we walk. I love it – the constant, un-English sweat, the simple need for shade, water and self-control. The road is absolutely flat, and I think gratefully of whoever it was who planted avenues of trees. (Ashoka's boasts about the mango groves he planted suddenly seem justified.)

Every hour or so Aslam asks directions, and every time the response is the same: 'A bus is just coming'; 'It will only cost you three rupees.' 'Tell them I get car sick,' I say eventually. But that doesn't work: 'Give her an injection and put her in an open car,' shout three men from a horse and cart. 'I bet no one said that to Alexander,' says Aslam, and I stand with my back to them, my shoulders shaking with laughter. At five o'clock a man goes past on a motorcycle. 'Are you mad? It will take three days to reach the Indus,' he says. At six, two NGO workers from Peshawar stop and give us a lecture on the instability of the area. At seven, three 'undercover' policemen follow us to the outskirts of a small village called Chota Lahore, a royal capital in Alexander's time. 'We knew you from your *chaal* [gait],' they say smugly. 'You walk too fast. People here don't like the English and Americans. Be very careful.'

In the fields around Chota Lahore it is tobacco-harvesting season. The tobacco leaves are huge, like elephant ears. Hayricks stand in rows like families. We reach Hund, on the banks of the Indus, late at night.

Hund, so significant a place when Alexander came here, lost its importance during Mughal times after the fort was constructed at Attock. Today it has only a concrete Corinthian column as testament to its former glory. The government has just built a dam above Hund taking water out of the Indus for three months of the year and diverting it through a power-generating station. Last time I was here you could walk across the river. But now, to my pleasure and surprise, it is full again, and though we reach Hund when it is dark, the air cools as we approach the riverbank, and I can feel the river, a dark mass of water, just below the house where we will be staying.

Abdul Ghaffar gave us the name of a Syed (one of the descendants of the Prophet, and thus presumably the owner of a big house). Brazenly, we turn up on his doorstep and announce ourselves. Nobody has called ahead to warn them of our arrival, but I hear the servant call indoors to the Syed, 'Your guests have come' – and we are taken in without a second glance.

Our host is a busy man. He has land along the river, a cloth shop in Peshawar, and the fish business when there is water – his hujra stinks of the fish which he sends in ice all over the country. At night he comes into the house carrying a gun. '*Shikar* [hunting]?' I ask, but the women laugh: 'No, just a blood feud.'

The next day at noon, I swim in the Indus. It is wide, blue, cold – and very fast; I have to swim near the bank for fear of being swept away. The huddle of women washing their clothes on the banks of the river are gold-panners – 'low-caste,' say the Syed's women, who never leave the house. In the afternoon, some neighbouring women come to visit, taking me up on to the roof to look at the river and tell me how constricted their lives are. 'Even if my heart says no,' says one, 'other people decide things for me.' 'You have been married for five years and have no children?' another asks me. 'No children,'

I agree, and feel the usual, dislocating sense of not fitting into their notion of gender. 'What do you use?' they ask next – and suddenly, I realize the reason for their secrecy. These women aren't disapproving, they wish to ask me about contraception. There is a lady doctor in the nearby town who says condoms are best, but their husbands refuse to wear them. The 'medicines', they have heard, will do odd things to their 'menses'.

Downstairs in the courtyard, the Syed's young and beautiful sister-in-law, who was married three months ago, is quite clear about what she wants. 'Sons,' she says. 'What is the point of being a woman? Even if the whole world moves on, this place will always stay the same. Nothing will change in a hundred years.'

The next morning at dawn, I have a last cup of tea with the women, and then Aslam and I set off north again. If this was the Ganges or Yamuna, the riverbank would be crowded with Hindus offering prayers to the goddess and taking a *snan* (holy bath) in its waters. In Hund, one of the great pleasures for men is sleeping next to the river, but in the morning the bank is almost deserted. I watch as the Syed's fisherman paddles out into the freezing water, floating on a tractor's inner-tube – the modern version of the ancient practice of crossing the Indus on inflated animal skins. There is one other man having a wash, silhouetted against the sunrise.

All morning, we walk up the path that runs parallel with the Indus, following Alexander's route northward along the river to Pirsar. We are now a third of the way through our journey and Aslam is pleased, for we are walking well, eight hours a day, thirty to forty kilometres. Every day we drink litres and litres of water – from springs where possible, from wells and taps mostly – and hourly cups of tea, or cold bottled sugary drinks.

It is lunchtime when we arrive in the small town of Topi, on the south side of the massive Tarbela dam, which, after its completion in 1974, cursorily displaced thousands of farming families from the river's banks. We are sitting in the purdah section of a roadside restaurant, when a man slips under the curtain – thus outraging my newly-acquired modesty – and introduces himself as a member of Pakistan's 'CIA Police'. He, too, knew me by my *chaal*, my walk. It seems that I walk too fast. He doesn't ask my name but he tells me to be careful. Three female suicide bombers have just been arrested in Swat. 'Did you think I was one?' I ask. He laughs.

After lunch we walk for an hour across the Gudoon district industrial estate. It is, as Aslam says wearily, a *sunsaan jagah* (deserted place). There are no villages, just factories in the distance. Suddenly, Aslam comes to a halt. 'It is too dangerous,' he says. 'We are taking a big risk. We know nobody ahead.' Pakistanis, by virtue of living under a succession of military dictatorships, can be a paranoid people; but it is also true that hitherto we have been passed on from one friend to another, and now the chain of acquaintance has been exhausted. I stand there, thinking: we can turn back, go forward by car, or . . . 'Let's go to the police station,' I say. Normally we avoid the police, but under the present circumstances my suggestion is inspired.

We reach a small town, and walk slowly through it, looking out for the familiar blue and red stripes of Pakistan's police stations. When we finally see it, I pull off my headscarf, and step up to the door, hoping that the complications of the police register will not detain us. The policemen – all three of them – look pleased by the visit. They usher us into the head office, look at my Alexander route map, and come up with the solution to our problem. They have a friend in a village some fifteen kilometres ahead. He is a retired Police Inspector, and an upstanding member of the village Islamic Morals Committee. Everyone smiles in relief. A junior policeman is directed to show us the short cut to the hill road.

Soon we have left the town behind us, and Aslam, who can see the hills now, is happy. We pass a madrassah, are overtaken by a bus and a tractor, and climb slowly into the hills. But as usual there is confusion about how far ahead our destination lies: few Pakistanis know walking distances any more. 'A day's walk,' says the farmer on the tractor. 'You won't get there till Wednesday,' says the motorist. An hour later, we turn a corner in the road and see the village, with its white flat-roofed houses, spread out along the hillside.

The retired Police Inspector's family are tidy, studious people. Two of his sons are teachers, one is a shopkeeper. They speak Urdu with the twangy hill accent which over the next ten days I will grow to love. Months later, when the shopkeeper rings me in London, I am transported back immediately by the sound of his voice, its shallows and depths, to that peaceful, secluded place. That night, I sleep next to his wife and children in the courtyard of their house. I am woken at dawn by a light rain but it evaporates almost as quickly as it falls on our beds.

The next day, the gradient of our journey rises steeply, as we walk up into the hills along the only road. 'Keep walking on it till it runs out,' says the Police Inspector, 'then you will be in the tribal area.' 'What tribal area?' Aslam asks – and then remembers: 'The place called Yaghistan that the men from Kohay warned us about'; and simultaneously I recall Yaghistan from colonial British texts – that wild 'unadministered' area along the Indus which all of Victorian imperialism was unable to tame – a 'sealed book to European travellers' throughout the nineteenth century, marked on maps as 'Unexplored Country'. It is Yaghistan which appears as a blank patch on our modern Pakistani maps.

All day, we walk through small terraced fields ploughed by spotted oxen – perhaps the same highland breed that Alexander so admired (he ordered his troops to steal 230,000 of them, and sent the best home to Macedonia). The farm holdings around us are sturdy buildings made from local materials – stone, wood and mud. Unlike in Sindh and the Punjab, the only fertilizer is manure; big agri-business has not yet arrived to multiply production, increase costs and reduce peasants' self-sufficiency. But 'water is a problem', farmers complain; it is too high for the canals from Tarbela to reach these fields. Central government does not help; people here depend on nature.

Normally Aslam and I rest at noon, but today we keep walking up through the hill villages, along the winding road that curves ever upwards, under trees, past springs, small shops, and the occasional police station. Only one bus passes us during the whole day, and it stops so frequently that we soon overtake it again. By the afternoon, we have left Gudoon district behind us, and are now in Amazai, where we will spend the night. We have been given the name of a friend of a friend of the Police Inspector – he is a Malik, an important man it was stressed, the leader of his tribe.

We are following the narrow grassy path through a village, when Aslam sees something in the field ahead. 'Look,' he says. I have told him how excited Alexander and his men were to see ivy growing in this region – proof to them that the god Dionysus or Bacchus had come here centuries before, bringing his ceremonial plant and revelling followers with him. I follow Aslam's pointing finger. For the first time on our walk there is ivy spiralling up a tree. I climb over the fence and run towards it. *Hedera himalaica*, the Himalayan ivy.

It was during this very journey, from Hund to Pirsar, that Alexander's army saw ivy growing in the hills around 'Nysa', the Indian city which, following Greek mythology, they thought Dionysus had founded here. The Greeks, emotional at the best of times, wept on beholding this botanical souvenir of their homeland. They 'eagerly made wreaths' and 'crowned themselves', Arrian writes, and raising 'the Dionysiac cry', 'were transported with Bacchic frenzy'.

In Arrian's history, the people of Nysa beg for clemency from Alexander by claiming to be the descendants of Dionysus' soldiers. But other historians were divided on the veracity of the Dionysus story. Eratosthenes, whose account is lost, thought it was a cunning fiction. Others credited it, and repeated the key events: that Dionysus had taught the Indians how to cook, plough, play the cymbal and drum; that between Dionysus and Alexander the Indians counted 153 kings, a duration of 6,042 years. Arrian was undecided about the story's truth but he recognized it as propaganda of the highest order. Now that the Greek army knew it was treading on hallowed ground, nobody could refuse to march on into India.

One clue to the actual whereabouts of Nysa might be the cedar-wood coffins which, according to the Roman writer Quintus Curtius, the Macedonians found on a hillside one cold night, chopped up and burnt as firewood. Even today the Kalash in far north-western Pakistan still place their dead in exposed wooden coffins, and modern historians have tended to assume that Nysa must be located in this region. But in the fourth century BCE, this Kalash (or 'Kafir') culture stretched over the entire area between Jalalabad and the Indus. Babur himself drank wine brewed by the Kafirs of Bajaur, in the sixteenth century CE. Instead, Arrian makes it clear that Alexander found his Nysa near the River Indus, between Hund and Pirsar – somewhere along the route that Aslam and I are now walking.

Dionysus was an apt patron for Alexander's Indian journey. His cult had important devotees – not least Olympias, Alexander's mother – and an ancient eastern association. Euripides' play *The Bacchae* opens with Dionysus newly returned from 'Bactria', the ancient Persian province that stretched from Afghanistan to the Indus:

> Overland I went,
> across the steppes of Persia where the sun strikes hotly
> down, through Bactrian fastness and the grim waste
> of Media.

To the Greeks, the ivy must have seemed like final corroboration of what many had already suspected – that the religious cults of north-west India, with their orgiastic practices, proclivity for vines, goats and serpents, were quintessentially Dionysiac. When Megasthenes, Greek ambassador to the court of Chandragupta Maurya, visited India a quarter of a century later, he divided the Indians into two religions: those who worshipped Hercules, and those who followed Dionysus. Centuries after that, when Philostratus (born in 172 CE) came to compose his biography of the Pythagorean sage Apollonius of Tyana, he explained that Indians who lived near the Indus believed there were two Dionysuses, one the son of the River Indus, and the second a Theban Dionysus who became the Indian's disciple. In this story, the Dionysiac cult came from, rather than being brought to, India: such was the ancient influence of India on Western culture.

When they saw ivy, Alexander's men drank lots of wine and danced around the hillside singing '*Ite Bacchai, ite*' (On, Bacchai, on) as if they had escaped from Euripides' Chorus. I have no wine. But I pull out the 'intoxicating confection' given to me by Hakim Ayub, and Aslam and I sit down under the ivy-wreathed tree and eat a glistening lump of majoon each. It is sweet at first (that must be the honey), then sour. 'What is that strange taste?' I ask Aslam, 'the camel intestines?' 'Opium,' Aslam says. 'It's ninety per cent poppy.' Poppy. The one ingredient Hakim Ayub forgot to mention.

By the time we reach the Malik's hujra my head is spinning and I am seeing things. 'I feel strange,' I tell Aslam, 'the majoon has made me ill . . .' 'We ate it on an empty stomach,' he says; 'we were walking uphill, so the blood is moving fast around your body. It will soon pass.' Against all the rules I lie down in the hujra (I should as usual have joined the women in the house). This worries the Malik, and later that evening he gives me a lecture on tribal mores and the bad reputation I will get if . . . But I don't care. Right now I think I am dying. As men from the village queue up at the door to stare, I lie covered in my chador, imagining how my organs will fail, one by one, in this miserable village without even an aspirin, let alone a doctor. Was Hakim Ayub trying to kill me? I remember what Hafizullah had said in Jalalabad: is it an elaborate plot by the Pakistani Army? They failed to get me at the Nawa pass – now they are doing me in on a Bacchic hillside days' and days' walk from a functioning hospital.

Eventually the paranoia passes. I live. By evening I am well enough to go into the house.

A man can invest in his hujra and produce an aura of wealth. Thus the Malik's hujra is a cosily decorated room with specimens of local weaving on the walls. But in the house itself there are only two rooms for twenty people, the toilet is a hole and there isn't a bathroom. The Malik is very young to be the leader of his tribe, and the responsibility weighs heavily upon him. This area was prosperous once – when the villagers grew rich from poppy – before the Tarbela dam submerged fertile land in the valley below, pushing the farmers into the desiccated upland. The villagers, who have exhausted their life savings in failed harvests, say that 'the government never comes here.' The Malik's family look miserable and unkempt. His wife, who has 'gynaecological impediments', has given him just one daughter, and it is not enough: the Malik is getting married again next week. 'They are so poor,' I say to Aslam later. 'What is the point?' But Aslam, who has eleven children, understands. 'The Malik needs an heir,' he says.

All night, the women of the Malik's household toss and turn. One of them tries to massage my legs before I go to sleep. Another (the Malik's wife) goes outside to be sick. They leave on a green bulb and watch Urdu films on a tiny black and white television. I have strange dreams and fitful sleep.

In the morning, the by-now familiar horror stories start in the hujra. Ahead, in the tribal area, the Malik says, we will need to seek permission – that is, protection – from the local jirga to cross it safely. 'It is a ferocious place,' he says. 'Be careful not to stray too far west as you walk. Avoid the hill of Mahaban.' He shudders. 'Over the Indus to the east, there is snow on the hills. In the Kaladaka [Black Mountains] people are still living in caves.' A typical jirga punishment, say his friends, involves putting the offender into a hollowed-out tree trunk head first and leaving him there for three days. 'We are Mughals,' says the Malik. 'We came here five hundred years ago from Abbottabad. Where you are going we cannot help you.'

I stare at a poster of a sunset on the wall and wonder if it was in those strange, remote hills where the Malik fears to go, that Alexander found Nysa. Maybe the dreaded hill of Mahaban was the mountain where Dionysus held his rituals, which Alexander called 'Mount Meros' (possibly confusing it with Meru: in Hindu cosmology the mountain from where the Indus rises).

The Malik lends Aslam a white Sunni cap. 'And you,' he points to me, 'wear your burqa.'

That morning, we climb with the Malik through village after village, along the edges of fields, around small mud-daubed houses, higher and higher into the hills. We stop to drink tea with an embittered farmer, who shows me the names of the traitorous American charity workers who in the 1980s promised him compensation for eradicating his entire poppy crop, and also the business card of his local politician, son of Pakistan's first military dictator, who 'only comes here during electioneering'.

The Malik walks with us for an hour, until he meets a headmaster on the path who can take us onwards to his school. There, after tea with the teachers, two senior boys are pulled out of lessons to show us the path to Kallilard where the Malik has a friend, another leader of a local tribe. 'Tribal people are very nice, good, clean,' say the teachers in the school, contradicting their neighbours. 'Have no fear.'

We climb for an hour along the winding hill path to Kallilard. There, young girls out herding goats point to the house of the Malik's friend, Muhammad Khan, and we have to tip our heads backwards to see it, perched right at the top of this steep hill village.

With his large beard, two wives, many offspring and large amounts of land, Muhammad Khan is a powerful and cheerful man. 'I convene the local jirgas,' he tells me, and points down the hill, across the green terraces to a smudge of brown in the valley below. 'My house will have easy access to the new jeep road the government is building.'

After lunch, he places a row of chairs in the elegant mud court-yard and calls his wives and children for the photoshoot that I am directed to conduct. Then he walks us down to the road. 'Follow this track round the hill,' he says. 'Where the road stops you will see a bulldozer. Go downhill from there until you get to the village of Chanjelo. Ask for Muhammad Rasool Haji. Chanjelo is the last village before the tribal region.'

As we trudge along the dirt track through the pine trees, I find that Aslam has grown worried again. 'This is the most dangerous walk I have ever gone on,' he says. 'But Aslam, that's not true,' I tell him. He once walked across the Pakistan-Afghan border into Nangahar where the Taliban chased him over a glacier. 'You've forgotten how dangerous it was because you survived,' I say. But Aslam says: 'Then I knew the area. Here we are guessing.'

We have trouble finding Chanjelo village. The bulldozer has moved, and the road runs out sooner than expected. It is getting dark as we scramble down the hillside, me slipping and sliding as usual. We skirt a mud field above the village school where some boys are playing cricket, and follow the terraces to the edge of the hill where a villager points out the house of Muhammad Rasool. It sits on a cliff, facing the Black Mountains. Somewhere below us is the Indus, hidden from view by layer upon layer of crevassed blue hillside.

The owner is out. He went to the bazaar by the Indus three days ago, but he may return tonight. His adolescent sons – heavy eyeliner-users – crouch in a row on the edge of the roof where we are sitting, and stare. There is no electricity; the light fades, and moths circle around the paraffin lamp.

Night comes, and a plate of local vegetables is sent up from the house below. Then the boys show us to our beds and I am shocked: for the first time, Aslam and I have been put to sleep in the same room, the male-only hujra. 'Why have they done this?' I ask in English through the dark. Aslam is the voice of reason: 'It may be difficult to accommodate you in the house. They are poor. They probably all sleep together. Don't make a fuss.'

But in the morning, we discover the true reason. Five village elders assemble in the hujra to tell Aslam that they suspect me of being a missionary. Does the government know what I am doing? I make a polite speech in Urdu about the purpose of my book and the great Alexander, their venerable ancestor. They explain their worries about charities and foreign-funded NGOs. A few years ago, they say, NGO officers came from Islamabad, took the women of the village to meetings and tried to *emancipate* them. Emancipation, they say, is against both Islam and Pashtun culture. Muhammad Rasool's father combs his white beard; the younger boys, growing restless, rearrange themselves around the room in languorous poses. The elders grow more heated; angry Pashto words are exchanged. 'I'll explain later,' Aslam says to me quietly.

After much discussion, Aslam and the elders come to an agreement. Two of the men, Noor Muhammad and Noor Gul, will escort us out of the village, through the tribal area and down to the Indus.

Noor Gul (Flower Light) is debonair with his slicked back hair and emphatic make-up; Noor Muhammad is a blunter man, who dispenses theological lectures. As we walk out of the village, over the stream and into the tribal area, he tells me about Allah the creator. He speaks about Adam and Hawa (Eve) – 'we have that story in our book,' I am pleased to inform him. 'Your mullahs have added sweet things for your own enjoyment,' he replies, unfairly. He explains about God's laws for human beings (the most important of all Allah's creations), laws that lay down one work for men and another for women. 'Women's most important work is to do what men cannot,' he says. 'And what is that?' I ask. 'To have babies and look after them till they are two,' he says. He tells me about heaven and hell: even if I commit the worst sins (theft, adultery, alcohol) I just have to get one of my children to learn the Qur'an and they can take me to heaven with them. An *alim* (theologically learned person) takes along one hundred sinners. 'So that's why there are so many madrassahs,' I say to Aslam.

'You should convert,' Noor Muhammad tells me. 'The Qur'an is total revelation, your Bible fifty per cent only.'

As I am being lectured, we crunch over field after field of felled blond poppy stalks. Discarded poppy heads still lie in the parched furrows, three razor slits marking where the sap was bled out. 'Here in the tribal areas,' says Noor Gul, 'opium was harvested a few weeks ago.'

We reach the village where Noor Muhammad's sister lives. And now at last we see the river just as Alexander saw it – the mighty Indus below us in its natural form, a wide blue-grey lake between the hills, undammed, unmolested.

Noor Muhammad's sister lives in a one-storey hut with a buffalo in the yard and four chickens in a basket. She sits us in the cool of her bedroom and cooks us a delicious breakfast of eggs scrambled in animal fat. After tea, the Noors say goodbye to us on a poppy field below the house. Noor Gul poses for my camera, mobile phone pressed to his ear (there is no reception), the Indus in the background. We look down at our destination, Darbund. It is there that the Nazim (Mayor) of the Black Mountains lives. Darbund is in the settled areas, but we must ask for permission from him to cross tribal Kaladaka as far as Pirsar.

On the way downhill, Aslam tells me the full story of female emancipation and the elders of Chanjelo. A few years ago some NGO workers came from Islamabad, called the women of Chanjelo into a room and said to them: 'Are you happy in the house?' 'Yes,' said the women. 'Are you happy with your husband?' 'Yes.' 'Does your husband love you?' 'Yes.' 'Does he do sex with you?' '. . . Yes.' 'What kind of sex?' At this point, Aslam says, the men lost their tempers: all of them had seen naughty sex films in the bazaar; they knew what kind of dirty things the foreign-trained NGO workers were meaning. And sure enough, the NGO workers showed the innocent women of Chanjelo how they should suck this thing, lick that, go on top of their husbands. 'But Pashtuns don't do sex like that,' says Aslam. So the elders confiscated 10,000 rupees from the NGO women and sent them packing. 'That's why the elders of Chanjelo wouldn't let you meet their women,' Aslam says. 'In case you tried to teach them naughty tricks.'

The path down is steep and hot, through a jungle of stunted trees in which monkeys sit, screeching. We cross over a stream – back, says Aslam, into the 'settled' areas – and walk downhill to the river. The sun is beating down on our heads as we hire a small, painted wooden boat to take us across the Indus.

Darbund is actually 'New Darbund': the old one was submerged beneath the waters of the Tarbela reservoir. New Darbund is a makeshift, sandy place, with clouds of flies in the bazaar. We walk slowly up from the banks of the Indus to the Nazim's house but the servant woman who comes to answer the door refuses to admit me. So we go next door, to his hujra, where any petitioner however humble is permitted to sit and wait. There is a water fountain and a clay tumbler. I sit down in the shade and fall asleep.

I am woken when the Nazim returns, and relocated immediately to the main house. The women who refused me entry earlier now give me tea and wash my filthy clothes. The Nazim takes me upstairs to the large panelled room where they hold jirgas. His cousin gives me a photocopy of a British-era map of Kaladaka, and one he has drawn himself, with the names of the tribes along the Indus. Later, in the hujra, the Nazim says: 'You will go by boat to Pirsar.' Aslam looks at me concernedly: he knows I would rather walk. But the Nazim's cousin says: 'Alexander went by boat, didn't he?' – and of course, he is right. According to Arrian, after the siege of Pirsar, Alexander found 'a wood, good for felling, near the river' which he had 'cut down by his troops, and ships built. These sailed down the Indus.'

The next morning we buy places on a local taxi-boat which is taking passengers the five or so hours upstream to Kotlay, where Khaliq, the Nazim's servant, and now our escort, lives. Our boat, each board of which has been painted a different colour, is the brightest in the harbour. Here, where the Indus is hemmed in by high hills and the villagers are forced to live according to the river's changing moods, it is not hard to imagine those oar-powered long-boats which Alexander constructed from Kaladaka wood for the ride downriver. We make regular stops, to drop villagers, with their bazaar-bought packets of sugar, tea and mangoes, on the rocks below their homes. After an hour and a half Khaliq calls to the boatman to stop again so that he can show me the rock where, high on an empty hillside, Alexander left his two-metre-tall handprint. Later, we pass women washing clothes in the river – they turn away their faces – and boys noisily bathing. The Nazim's family come from a village near here, high up in the tribal areas. 'We go back to our village in

summer by boat, when the water is high,' the Nazim's wife told me
last night. 'It cuts three hours off the journey.'

By noon, all the other passengers have been offloaded, and the
taxi is far beyond its usual run; but we are still two hours' walk from
Kotlay. The boatman now claims that the water is too low for his
craft to go any further, and though it is midday, the time Aslam and
I usually avoid, we have no choice but to get out and walk. We walk
for an hour along the riverbank, the sand of the Indus grey beneath
our feet. At a wooden madrassah we stop and rest; and the students
bring us murky, ice-cold river water to drink.

At last we reach the Kotlay crossing-point, just as some smugglers
are rescuing a load of wood that has been floated down the Indus.
Three boys take us across in their boat, and on the other side, in a
bankside hujra belonging to Khaliq's friend, we stop and sleep. You
can tell that we are in the tribal areas again, I think as I drown in
tiredness: the houses have shooting towers.

I wake in the afternoon to an argument between Khaliq and
Aslam. Aslam wishes to walk on towards Pirsar today. This is tribal
land outside the writ of Pakistani law; further upstream and we will
reach the 'settled' areas again. But Khaliq is insistent: it will be a
dishonour to his tribe if we leave today, we will never reach Kabulgram
before nightfall (he is making this up), the Nazim will be angry . . .
We relent. After all, I am intrigued to see how these infamous tribes-
people really live.

Khaliq's friend brings in a huge opium cake with tea: an oozing
melon-sized lump wrapped in poppy leaves. It was a good crop this
year. They make 5,000 rupees per kilo for opium; better than onions
and tomatoes. The villagers are rich, but nobody in Khaliq's family
reads or writes. A few years ago the government built a school on
the banks of the Indus. 'Who wants to have their children educated?'
Khaliq asks me. I see the school the next morning – now first-class
accommodation for the village buffaloes. (In a grim irony, it is the
emptiness of the schools in Kaladaka that later saves children during
the Kashmir earthquake; many died in less education-averse areas.)

That evening I am led round the village by Khaliq, followed Pied
Piper-style by fifty children. Khaliq takes me to the gun shop. He
tells me how he dynamites fish out of the Indus. He shows me his

hand-grenade collection and his rocket-launcher. The houses in this village are several storeys high, with arches and pillars and paintwork in at least three clashing colours. I sleep that night next to Khaliq's auntie, on the roof of her green-painted, beige-windowed, pink-arched, poppy-funded mansion, to the sound of the Indus rushing past.

Early the next morning we walk upstream for an hour, looking for a suitable crossing-place. I walk warily behind Khaliq, who has insisted on carrying his AK47. We find a boatman to take us across the water; and the boat tosses and turns fretfully on the blue-grey waves.

It is an uphill walk from Kabulgram, on the other side, to Martung, at the top of the hill. Khaliq bids us goodbye regretfully. 'You'll be there in half an hour,' he guesses.

But he has no idea. It is a long hard walk, up along a stream bed for two hours, through a tangle of forest, and then the worst part: climbing steeply along another dusty, half-built jeep road. At last we reach the ridge at the top, eat some stale biscuits from a tiny shop, and drink greedily from a spring on the ridge above Martung.

Now that we have left the tribal areas, there is no more poppy in the fields, no more decrepit wedding-cake houses. Water has been carefully channelled into glistening rice paddies, there are modest dwellings solidly built from stone. There are also holm oaks along the road – another reason why Alexander felt at home here, perhaps. Every slope is green, well watered and conscientiously terraced.

We turn a corner in the road, and suddenly we can see the Chakesar valley spread out below us. 'There it is,' says Aslam, pointing to the hills that rise above the village. 'That must be Pirsar.' We walk down through the fields, past a village cricket game, into town. An old woman leans over her hedge as we pass, and hands us some apricots from her garden.

In Chakesar town a shopkeeper points out the rose-decorated hujra belonging to a friend of Khaliq. I experience that inevitable moment of apprehension – will they let us stay? The owners, summoned from their houses, arrive looking wary. Aslam explains about our journey; and as always, the frowns of incomprehension give way to warm Pashtun smiles and the offer of hospitality.

The family in Chakesar have four large houses. I am sent to the one containing Uzma, who grew up in Karachi and did an MA in English. She recently made a love marriage with the son of the house, and has just given birth. She is holding court in her bedroom, enthroned on a red-velvet-covered bed, surrounded by at least thirty female cousins. Her husband sits meekly by, holding the baby.

At dinnertime Uzma takes me next door, where the women sit around a huge plastic sheet on the floor. It is an exuberant, noisy meal. Children hover on the edges, pulling naan and chicken legs off our plates. There are several sets of co-wives: 'But generally no more than two wives at once,' says Uzma.

The next morning it is raining as we leave Chakesar. 'Do you have a raincoat?' I ask Aslam, and he shakes his head. 'Do you?' I have often thought, while walking through the hills, of the naked Brahmin philosophers who mocked the Greek soldiers for their leather boots, cloaks and hats. Now I feel that a Greek toga, or cheap London anorak, would have been useful. But Aslam has a solution: 'We can buy some plastic sheeting from the grocer's store,' he says. Swathed in green plastic, we walk out of town, following the local children up to the school just below the 'girls' maidaan', which the men in Chakesar have told us marks the upper limit of the per-manent settlements.

From here, through the pine trees, we can now see the snow-topped mountains of Swat to the north-west. 'I live over there,' says Aslam, pointing. He tells me about his family as we walk, about the diffi-culty of educating his six daughters: 'In Pakistan girls can only walk to school if they are accompanied by their brothers,' he says. Up here, the Gujars, nomadic shepherds, are only just returning to their summer pastures, and many of the houses still stand empty. We sit on a bank beside a house where some Gujars are repairing the roof and pick thyme to eat with the roti we have packed. A shepherd walks past carrying a gun. 'Just follow that path to Pirsar,' he says confidently.

But there is no obvious path. The wood changes complexion, grows more dappled, and as the settlements dwindle, it metamor-phoses from a lush Asian marijuana and pine forest, into a temperate deciduous wood. There are stinging nettles and dock leaves under-foot now, and the air is cold and moist. We stumble on, up hills and down ravines. Suddenly, I realize that infallible Aslam is lost. I walk along behind him, tripping on roots, and thinking dreamily, hungrily, of English forests. In *Comus*, Milton's masque, did they get out of the tangled wood alive? Wasn't Comus like Dionysus? Wasn't the lost lady called Alice?

We climb another hill, and Aslam hears voices. There in the ravine below, with their goats beside a stream, are two shepherd boys. We run down towards them, and as I fill our water bottles, Aslam approaches the children. But though he tries the five or six languages in which he is proficient, they refuse to talk to him, and run away through the wood without saying a word.

Now that we are down by the stream, however, we can see up through the trees to a clearing on a hill, where there are two houses and a recently ploughed field. As we climb towards the settlement, we see two women crouching in the field, weeding. But they refuse to sell us anything to eat: 'We just came up for the day,' they say, 'we don't live here.' We walk on up to the second house, where there is a dog tied to the verandah. Aslam teaches me the words for bread and tea in Pashto.

I walk round to the door of the house. Inside, everything is black. The bed, the pots, the chairs, are thick with dust and soot. I call out, and a woman emerges from a room at the back with her two shy daughters. She stares at me without understanding. From the yard outside, Aslam, who cannot appear before an unknown woman, shouts down something. She comes to the door to listen, and then she smiles at me, crouches down in front of her stove, and puts on her black kettle. Her name is Bibi Ayesha.

Aslam and I are sitting on the wall above the house, drinking Bibi Ayesha's tea, when a man comes by with a Sunni cap on his head and a load upon his back. 'Pirsar is this way,' he says. 'Follow me.' He is a student at the Binori Town madrassah in Karachi – infamous in the West as the nursery of the Taliban – where he is studying to be an alim (and get one hundred friends into heaven). We follow him for an hour through the wood. Before he leaves us, he shows us a stream where all wayfarers stop for water. 'Just go straight,' he says.

But the path disappears again as the undergrowth grows thicker. By now we have been walking for almost ten hours without eating.

We sit down against a tree and share out the last packet of salty biscuits. Above our heads, a storm is gathering – and we have no tent. Aslam, though, has a hill person's sense of direction. We climb up another hill, emerge on to its crest, and then we see it: Pirsar.

'The Rock' as Arrian called it – Aornos, 'birdless place', as it was known to Alexander's army – juts out over the Indus, seven thousand feet above that agitated mass of water. Between it and the hill we are standing on, is the ravine that Alexander spent three days filling with brushwood in order to avoid the strategic disadvantage of descending into the ravine between Unasar and Pirsar (in fact he probably bribed, or forced, local tribesmen to show him the best way up to the Rock). The rain is just beginning to fall as we climb down Unasar towards some shepherds' huts. We meet a man who is bringing his cow back home for the night, and follow him along the path towards a wooden mosque where we shelter while Aslam assesses the practicality of climbing up to Pirsar tonight.

Clouds are darkening the sky as we leave the mosque and walk down into the ravine, and up around the south side of Pirsar. It is a slippery goat path; the hill is littered with blistered trees felled by lightning, and had the storm hit us then we would have been washed into the valley below. But we are lucky. The rain clouds pass over our heads and fall on the valley's eastern side.

At last, we emerge above the trees and on to the top of the ridge, where my elation at finally being here is tempered by the fact that the sky is still dark with rain and we have nowhere to stay. Down a path comes an old Gujar woman, who is taking her grandsons into the forest to gather some kindling. Curiosity gets the better of her, and she turns round and leads us along the ridge to her house, a three-bedroom hut where her daughter-in-law has a fire going.

I sit inside by the hearth, removing my wet clothes bit by bit and drying them as the children crowd round and assess me. They cannot understand why I have walked for ten days to reach their house, so I tell them the story of the foreign king called Sikunder who marched up the Indus valley, of how he built altars to his gods in this very place, and of how, three months after he sailed back down the Indus to the sea, the tribesmen of Pirsar returned and exacted revenge on the remaining Greek contingent. The children listen with polite, wide-eyed interest as I expound the idea of their home being recorded in a two-thousand-year-old history book in ancient Greece – but it is my rendition of an old Indian film song that they really enjoy. They dance around the fire, joining in with the chorus, and Bazarini, their mother, who has been watching me silently as she snips wild spinach, suddenly smiles.

Just as suddenly, the sun comes out, and I go to the door of the hut. To the east, over the Indus, emerging from an eddy of rain clouds, is a rainbow, and the trees and tiny fields of Pirsar are iridescent in the sunshine. There are thirty Gujar huts up here, small structures made of just one cooking room, a bedroom, and a place for the animals. Around every house is a fence and beyond the fence is a patchwork of fields, where maize is already coming up. I walk with Bazarini's children to the eastern edge of Pirsar, and look down at the great silver crescent of the Indus, which curls around us on three sides, 'washing at the base of the Rock', as Strabo, Diodorus and Quintus Curtius put it. Encircling us to the north, east and west, like the gods on Olympus, are the snow-capped mountains, for it is here that the Hindu Kush, Karakorams and Himalayas meet.

The hill tribes of Pirsar had been relying on the steepness of their mountain retreat as defence from the Greeks. But when they saw Alexander and his men filling up the ravine, they pushed some boulders on to the advancing army, beat their drums, and ran away down the north face. When Alexander and his men reached the top of the Rock, they met with little resistance. Naturally, they killed everybody they could find.

Alexander, triumphant, ordered his men to build altars to Athena, the patron of war. This was more than just homage to a martial goddess – it was an epic gesture. Athena was Achilles' special protector in the *Iliad*; and Alexander, who slept with a copy of the *Iliad* under his pillow, thought of himself both as Achilles' physical descendant (through his mother's family) and his spiritual heir as a warrior.

Throughout his journey, Alexander used Greek myth as a stimulant to ever-greater martial conquests. Since the start of his world-conquering journey he had taken to calling himself the son of Zeus. In India, his compliant generals found cattle branded with the shape of a club: proof of the Indian wanderings of Hercules (Alexander's other legendary ancestor). It was this very Rock, said Alexander's campaign historians, that Hercules had tried and failed to besiege during his Labours. And if Alexander was Hercules' equal on earth, so too on Olympus. Alexander began to encourage the rumour that he was immortal.

From Pirsar, Alexander sailed down the Indus to Hund, where he 'sacrificed to the gods to whom it was his custom'. This list did not yet include the rivers of the Indus valley, though it soon would. The Greeks worshipped rivers in various ways – by consecrating hair to them at puberty, for example (a villager at Hund told me that the clumps of hair I saw on the pebbly riverbed there, were left for a similar purpose). But for now, Alexander did not need to worry about the anger of India's rivers. Thanks to Hephaestion's bridge of boats – a stratagem that Sultan Mahmud, the Mughals and the British would all use after him – he crossed the Indus with comparative ease, triumphantly reflecting that he had gone further than Hercules, further even than Dionysus.

Alexander was adept at playing local kings off against each other, and he did this to perfection at Taxila, capital of the local king Ambhi (or Taxiles), one hundred kilometres downstream from Pirsar. Taxila was already an ancient site of Hindu learning; centuries later it would become a Buddhist university; after that, a Greek-style city, and two millennia later still a World Heritage site ringed by orange groves. The Taxila which Alexander saw was populated by 'tall, slim' Indian noblemen carrying parasols, wearing 'white leather shoes' and with indigo, red, green or white-dyed beards. The men in this area, Arrian emphasized, were the finest fighters in all Asia. Yet King Ambhi turned traitor, welcoming Alexander into his country, allowing him to fell wood for boats and bridges, and sending him a present of 10,000 sheep, 3,000 cattle, 200 silver talents and 30 elephants. Perhaps this lavish generosity was a portent: in every Greek tragedy there is a *peripeteia*, a turning point. For Alexander, his peripeteia happened – literally and metaphorically – in the Indus valley.

Alexander believed, when marching from Taxila across the Punjab towards the River Hydaspes (as the Greeks knew the Jhelum), that he was coming face to face with his greatest enemy: King Puru – or Porus, as the Greeks knew him – the Indian king with his huge army and elephants like towers. But Alexander's downfall was caused by something harder to grapple with than military opponents – rivers in spate.

Alexander, Arrian writes, reached the Punjab just after the summer solstice, 'when heavy rains came down on the land of India' and 'all the rivers of India were running deep and turbulent with a swift current'. For a man who read the *Iliad* on his travels, and thought of himself as Achilles' progeny, the flooding waters of the Punjab would have been disturbingly reminiscent of Achilles' battle with the river god, Xanthus or Scamander – a warring Hellene, in Asia, pitting his wits against the primordial force of an angry river. In Homer's story, Patroclus has just been killed, and Achilles is in a homicidal frenzy, cutting down Trojan after Trojan, and throwing them into the river. 'Lie there among the fish where they can lick the blood from your wound,' he screams at his victims, as he watches the water turning red. But Scamander – 'Xanthus of the silver pools' – soon tires of Achilles filling 'my lovely channels' with 'dead men's bodies'. He unleashes the full force of his waters upon the warrior and only the intervention of Zeus saves Achilles from being drowned in the 'heaven-fed' river.

Perhaps Alexander thought that just as he had proved himself superior to Hercules, so he could outdo Achilles too. He stood with his Companion Cavalry on the banks of the Jhelum, looking east across the water to where Puru's army was waiting. It would be foolhardy to try and ford the river during the rainy season. Puru knew that too. But Alexander was an Achilles with the cunning of Odysseus. Night after night, his cavalry charged along the bank, making as much noise as possible. At first the Indian king 'moved parallel with the shouts, bringing up his elephants', but eventually he grew tired, realized it was a false alarm, and stirred no more from camp. So Alexander lulled Puru into complacency.

Alexander's scouts, meanwhile, had located an island near a bend in the river. One night, during a summer thunderstorm, Alexander and a band of cavalry waded over on horseback to the island, and even though the rain was still falling and 'had swollen the river', they were halfway to the other side before the Indians saw them. Puru, who was far away in camp, began marching towards them, but as he did, Alexander's reserve force crossed the river to the south, and attacked him from behind.

As always, everything turned on the elephants. Usually these enormous Indian beasts petrified the Greek horses. But Alexander's tactical victory was to press the Indian army from the left and right, forcing their infantry up against their elephant phalanx, and shooting down their drivers until the wounded mounts, 'maddened with suffering, attacked friends and foes alike and . . . kept pushing, trampling and destroying'.

Unlike Alexander's other formidable opponent, the Persian emperor Darius III, who fled the battlefield, the Indian king fought on until his soldiers were too weary to continue. Alexander, always one for a magnanimous gesture to bequeath to his biographers (and perhaps keen to make up for the indiscriminate slaughter of the Indus valley highlanders), sent Puru a royal pardon and asked him how he wished to be treated. 'Treat me, Alexander, like a king,' Puru replied proudly, and thus was their alliance sealed in high-flown rhetoric.

So Alexander and Puru became allies – not only because the Macedonian king admired the Indian's beauty and pride; or because Alexander made Puru his regent and put him in charge of more land than he had owned in the first place; but also because it was simply not practical to do otherwise. As Puru himself pointed out, there were many other powerful Indian kingdoms to the east, with more elephants, wide rivers and large armies. Alexander needed all the help he could get if he was to succeed in reaching the Ocean on the edge of the world.

Alexander now began his fateful march on through the Punjab. He had probably been apprised by Puru of the fact that the Herodotean view of India was faulty; but if so, he kept it secret from his men. The army had crossed two Indian rivers already. By the time it reached the Chenab, the river had overflown its banks and water was racing across the surrounding fields, inundating the Greek camp, and clogging the hooves of every weary horse. The soldiers waded across the Chenab; then they forded the Ravi; and at last they arrived at the banks of the Beas. A fifth, angry Indian river was breaking point for Alexander's homesick army.

In Greece, where the streams dry up in summer, the sea is the patriotic motif of mythology. The monsoon-fed rivers of India were alien objects; even the rivers of Europe – those 'navigable water-courses', such 'limpid', 'delicious' waters – were wonders of nature for Strabo and Herodotus. Every Greek had a passion for the Nile, which they had recently colonized. When Alexander saw crocodiles in the Indus, and bean plants on its banks – similar to those he had seen in Egypt – he jumped to the pleasing conclusion that the Indus was the source of the Nile, and hence that the Mediterranean must be nearby (which gives some indication of his geographical confusion).

Today the Punjab is a semi-arid irrigated landscape of monocultural crops; but in the fourth century BCE it was thick with forests populated by rhinoceros, tigers and snakes. Hanging from the trees like a curse was a 'tree-pod', 'as sweet as honey' – the banana? – which gave the soldiers such bad dysentery that Alexander forbade his troops to eat them. Maybe morale would have held in the dry uplands of Afghanistan or Persia. But here in the boggy Punjab – where every forward march brought on foot-rot and every night the fear of snakebite, where fevers spread under a cloud of malarial mosquitoes – the endurance demanded was too great. Rumours began spreading through the camp about the true, vast nature of the land that Alexander was attempting to subdue. Sensing the mutinous feeling, Alexander called a meeting of the regimental commanders.

The Greek king was young and impetuous, and in the past his men had loved him for it. Alexander knew the strength of that feeling, and with huge confidence, he rose to his rhetorical best. 'It is sweet for men to live bravely,' he told them, 'and die leaving behind them immortal renown . . . it is through territory now our own that the Indus flows . . . the land is yours; it is you who are its satraps; the greater part of the treasure is now coming to you, and, when we overrun all Asia, then by heaven I will not merely satisfy you, but will surpass the utmost hope of good things each man has.'

Unfortunately, Alexander's army failed to appreciate the historical importance of this moment. There was silence. Eventually, a veteran called Coenus stood up to speak for them.

Alexander was renowned for his irrational longings – for his desire, as Arrian put it so well, to do 'something unusual and strange' – a desire which had carried him through Persia to the edge of India.

The word Arrian used for this feeling was *pothos*. For Homer in the *Odyssey*, this nebulous word conveyed the sense of homesickness; for Plato, of erotic desire; but Arrian's Alexander experienced *pothos* as a bid for heroic status. *Pothos* afflicted Alexander at critical moments in his journey – the most important, spectacular and disastrous of these being in India. He was 'seized with a longing [*pothos*] to capture' Pirsar; he was 'seized with a yearning [*pothos*] to see the place where the Nyseans honoured Dionysus'; he had a 'longing [*pothos*]' in Taxila that one of these 'Indian sophists who go naked . . . should live with him'. Finally, when he reached the Arabian Sea he 'had a longing [*pothos*] to sail out and round from India to Persia'.

It was this powerful word that Coenus now threw back at Alexander. In the Greek the word is repeated three times: the soldiers, said Coenus, longed to see their parents (if they were still alive); they longed to see their wives and children; and they longed to see their homeland. Coenus stopped speaking, and the audience erupted with emotion – some weeping with nostalgia, others raging against their cruel commander. The army had had enough of the *Iliad*. Like Odysseus' men, all they wanted was to go back home.

Alexander angrily dismissed his officers. The next day, he called them back to tell them that he was going on into India alone; and then he retired to his tent to sulk like Achilles. He sulked for one day, for two, for three: until he saw that the army would not be shamed into doing what he wanted, and so, like Achilles, he was forced to compromise. The gods came to his aid. When he offered sacrifices on the banks of the river, the omens for continuing the march into India were unfavourable – and his men shouted for joy.

Before the army turned for home, they performed one last task for their leader's reputation. Alexander had twelve huge altars built to the Olympian gods – 'as broad and high as the greatest towers' – and also some outsized mangers, horse bridles and huts containing eight-foot beds. According to Arrian these were 'thank-offerings to the gods'; but Quintus Curtius gave a more cynical interpretation: Alexander's 'intention', he observed, was 'to make everything appear greater than it was, for he was preparing to leave to posterity a fraudulent wonder'. Perhaps the Greeks' tower-like altars were a riposte to this land of 'tower-like' elephants. The Indus valley had defeated Alexander; but he wanted to give the impression that his retreat was a triumph.

Alexander's adventures in the Indus valley were not over, however. Refusing to march back home the way he had come – through Afghanistan – he announced instead that he wished to sail down the Indus to the sea (as Scylax had done). But this time, he would take no chances with the Indian river deities: and so, on the banks of the Jhelum, at dawn, he made sacrifices to the usual Greek gods. Then, going on board ship, he poured a libation into the river from a golden bowl, and 'called upon the Acesines [the Chenab] as well as the Hydaspes . . . he also called upon the Indus.' Only now, once Alexander had appeased the river gods of India, and the Indus had joined the Greek pantheon, was the fleet ready to depart.

Unfortunately, Alexander's soldiers – not being great navigators of rivers – were 'struck dumb with amazement' when they saw the rough and roaring confluence of the Jhelum and Chenab rivers. At least two longboats, with all on board, were lost, and Alexander himself was almost drowned. After that, the army had to fight the fierce Malloi tribe at the point where the Punjab rivers join the Indus – a reminder if any were needed that India was full of strong kings and unfriendly armies. It took the army nine months to half-sail, half-fight its way down the river. Some soldiers drowned, some were killed, and Alexander received a near-fatal wound in the chest. His men, believing him dead, despaired at being left without a leader in 'the midst of impassable rivers' with 'warlike nations hemming them in'. Despite his grave condition, Alexander forced himself to appear before them on deck, and to raise his hand to show he was alive. Once again, the emotional army 'wept involuntarily in surprise' and sprinkled him with a confetti of ribbons and flowers.

At last the army reached the sea – leaving in its wake a trail of cities named after the king, his horse or his victories, each with its own dockyard. At the river's mouth, Alexander spent some time exploring the twisty river channels of the Delta, and made more lavish sacrifices. He knew that the salt water he could taste on his lips was not that of the world-encircling Outer Ocean – that he had not, in fact, reached the edge of the earth – but it was better than nothing. Alexander sailed out into the sea, and like Nestor in the

Odyssey, sacrificed bulls to Poseidon. Then he threw the bulls, and the golden libation bowls, into the water. It was a typically ebullient climax to a campaign that had almost ended in disaster.

Alexander died two years later in Babylon – some said of poison, others of fever (malaria, contracted in the Indus valley?). He died, it is said, just as he was preparing a campaign to Arabia, because the Arabs, despite being worshippers of Dionysus, refused to recognize Alexander as a god.

Throughout his life, Alexander looked to his posthumous reputation. He took historians with him to India, and when they refused to eulogize him properly, he put them to death (this was the fate of Callisthenes). After his death, his obedient campaign historians wrote authorized versions of his Indian conquest, and this gave rise to a series of contradictory accounts, eulogistic or condemnatory, by subsequent Greek and Roman writers. These, in turn, fed the popular medieval Romances. And it was here, centuries after his death, that Alexander really came into his own – as an East-West pop-hero.

During the Middle Ages, the *Alexander Romance* – a Greek prose story of his life that merged history, epic and fable – spread all over Europe, from Athens to Iceland, acquiring embellishments as it went. In some versions, Alexander went up to heaven in a basket and down to the bottom of the sea in a glass barrel. In others, he received prophecies from Indian talking-trees, lost soldiers to the Indus crocodiles, and was reprimanded for his ambition by naked Brahmin philosophers. The ballad-singers of medieval Europe loved Alexander's foolhardy courage. In an age when the countries east of Constantinople had once again become a mystery, his peregrinations beyond the bounds of the known world tantalized all of Christendom. Even theologians read the *Alexander Romance* – and wondered if the 'tree-pods' described therein could possibly be the fruit that Eve gave to Adam in Paradise. Didn't it say in Genesis, 'the Lord God planted a garden eastward in Eden'? Was the Indus one of the rivers of paradise? The legend of Prester John, a fictional Christian ruler of a lost kingdom somewhere in the Orient, was inspired by this conflation of the *Alexander Romance* and biblical exegesis. In the letter he wrote to the medieval monarchs of Christendom, Prester John boasted of the River Indus: 'Encircling

Paradise, it spreads its arms in manifold windings through the entire province.'

Startlingly, at the very time that Alexander's conquest of the east provided a heroic model for medieval Christian kings and knights – intent on reclaiming the Christian lands from the Muslim infidel – Muslims also began to eulogize Alexander as a hero. In the Middle East, Alexander metamorphosed from a daredevil conqueror into a monotheistic preacher. Passing through Hebrew and Christian-Syriac translations into Arabic, a version of Alexander's story apparently entered the Qur'an, where he appears as the mysterious character Dhul-Qarnayn, the 'two-horned one' (an epithet derived perhaps from the legend that Alexander was the son of the Egyptian ram-headed god Amon). The Prophet Muhammad was told in a revelation of Dhul-Qarnayn's journey from the West to the East, where he 'saw the sun rising upon a people . . . exposed to all its flaming rays'. As Allah's 'mighty' agent on earth, Dhul-Qarnayn was readily accepted by early Muslims as a minor prophet – though some modern Muslim scholars now repudiate any link to the pagan Alexander.

This Muslim version of the Alexander story was carried south to Ethiopia, and north to Mongolia. Horsemen in the Pamir mountains of Central Asia told Marco Polo how their steeds were descended from Alexander's Bucephalus. The Persians whom he had conquered, made him the hero of the *Iskandarnamah*, their national epic – the son not of Philip now, but of Darius; no longer a worshipper of rivers but a *ghazi*, a holy Islamic warrior who led the way for Sultan Mahmud, Emperor Babur and countless others:

> Alexander . . . spurred by religious ardour, shouted, 'Charge! For these are infidels, and if we kill them we will be *ghazis*.'

And thus even now in northern Pakistan – in the very place where Alexander forded the Indus, worshipped it as a god, and killed the hill tribes – modern-day Pashtuns still claim him as their forebear.

9

Indra's Beverage

c. 1200 BCE

'Unconquered *Sindhu*, most efficacious of the efficacious, speckled like a mare, beautiful as a handsome woman.'

Rig Veda, *c.* 1200 BCE

T HE PEOPLE WHOSE coffins Alexander the Great burnt, once ruled the whole of north-west Pakistan, but their likely descendants today live in just three hill villages, 150 kilometres north of Pirsar. With their pantheon of gods, night-time harvest-dances and cowrie-shell headdresses, the Kalash have so far held out against history's homogenizing tendencies. Instead, their distinctiveness has roused a chorus of noisy speculation. During the past century the Kalash have been hailed as Slavs by Russians, Alpine shepherds by Italians, Alexander's children by Athenians, and Englishmen by maverick colonials (albeit in a story by Rudyard Kipling). Now the Pakistanis, following boldly where European anthropologists went before, have proclaimed them the key to India's Aryan mystery.

The search for the Aryans has unsavoury forebears. The Rig Veda, India's most ancient Sanskrit text, enshrined the notion of the Arya: 'noble' Sanskrit-speakers pitted against their uncouth enemies, the Dasas. Subsequent Sanskrit law books and epics testify to the perpetual struggle to define who were Arya, and who were not. Traditionally, Indians have assumed that the descendants of the Arya can be found among the caste-Hindus, with Brahmins at the top of the hierarchy.

In the late eighteenth century, East India Company officials began learning Sanskrit. A Company judge, William Jones, quickly discerned that Sanskrit was closely related to Latin and Greek, and by 1786, he was confident enough to declare that all three languages had sprung from one source. The logical corollary of this was that Indian and European peoples must be cousins. Europe had not yet borne the brunt of Darwin's challenge to the biblical theory of Creation, and Jones clung to the belief that both Europeans and Indians were descended from the sons of Noah, and that Hebrew was older than Sanskrit.

While the Creation theory was soon undermined, the scrupulous linguistic analyses of nineteenth-century Sanskritists gave credence to Jones's theory of an Indo-European language group. But as the German Indologist F. Max Müller explained in 1883, many Europeans 'would not believe that there could be any community of origin between the people of Athens and Rome, and the so-called Niggers of India'. Instead, around the slender historical thread of Sanskrit's origin was woven an entire mythology – of an ancient, fair-skinned, martial race of Aryans who invaded India on horseback and defeated the uncivilized natives. European reactionaries such as the Scottish philosopher Dugald Stewart, in an essay of 1826, had explained away the similarity between Indian and European languages by arguing that the Brahmins learned their language from Alexander the Great: the Sanskrit of the holiest Hindu books was 'a sort of slang, or *Gypsey jargon,* (a sort of *kitchen*-Greek)'. As Max Müller himself commented, Stewart's reaction showed 'better than anything else, how violent a shock was given by the discovery of Sanskrit to prejudices most deeply engrained in the mind of every educated man'.

During the twentieth century, Aryan theories took their ugliest turn, as Hitler's Nazi Party appropriated the vocabulary of Sanskrit studies – the 'Aryans', caste purity, the Swastika (an ancient Indian symbol of well-being) – to endorse racism and genocide based on the myth of an Aryan master race of blond-haired Teutons.

In India, anti-imperialist freedom-fighters struck back, asserting that the Aryans were indigenous to India. Hindus had always believed that their inherent nobleness was home-grown, and the British theory of their mutual Aryan ancestor entering India from the West – precursor of numerous subsequent invasions – was an insult to Indian nationalism. Some argued that Sanskrit was the world's oldest language, and that mankind had originated from a homeland in the Himalayas. Hindu fundamentalists, almost as blinkered as their right-wing

European brethren, began to assert that the Aryans had sallied west from the Ganges and colonized the world with their linguistic dexterity, even teaching the Aztecs their art. At the end of the twentieth century, during the rule of the right-wing Hindu Bharatiya Janata Party (BJP) – who, as the 'party of India', use the ancient Hindu name for the country, 'Bharat', rather than the invaders' neologism, 'India' – archaeological material was concocted to prove that the Aryans were Made in India.

There have been equally ingenious attempts to rewrite history over the border, where the vestiges of Sanskrit contained in Urdu, Pakistan's national language, are routinely denied. A patriotic Pakistani has even shown 'mathematically' that Sanskrit was derived from Arabic. In the post-colonial, partitioned subcontinent, ancient history is capricious.

Every Aryan-origin hypothesis contains a grain of truth and a veritable Himalaya of speculation. Inevitably, every theory runs up against the same problem – the chasm that yawns between the material evidence of people in the second millennium BCE, and the inscrutable text which gave the world 'Aryanism' in the first place.

The most ancient Sanskrit text in India, revered by all Hindus, nothing could be stranger or more obscure than the hymns of the Rig Veda. 'Dark and helpless utterances', Max Müller called them. They implore the gods for favour; they beg the deities of fire and water to listen to their cries. Modern Sanskrit scholars, struggling to interpret their obliquities, have understood them as descriptions of the ritual required to please the gods, as verbal connections between the earth and heaven, or as contests of eloquence between rival tribal poets: 'Striving for the victory prize, I have set free my eloquence; let the god of rivers gladly accept my songs.' But the Rig Veda is particularly resistant to scholarly penetration. It engenders two types of scholarship: politicized polemic and extreme academic caution.

The Rig Veda was composed over many years, from approximately 1200 BCE onwards, and once completed, it was not written down. Rather, it was committed to memory – the sacred mode of transmission. Schools of priests were formed to learn the Rig Veda by heart, and the system appears to have been flawless. The Rig Veda as we read it today is a record of the passions and obsessions of Sanskrit priests three thousand years ago.

The 1,028 hymns, arranged in ten books or *mandalas*, are a paean to the mystifying power of Nature. The gods of later Hinduism are consolingly anthropomorphic; but those in the Rig Veda are natural phenomena: Agni (fire), Aditi (dawn), Indra (thunder) and Sindhu (simultaneously the Indus, water, floods, sea and rain).

What in the Rig Veda is fact? What, in this 'rich and secret book', is metaphor? Amidst the swirl of perplexing symbols, one thing stands out clearly: geography. Like a poem-map, the hymns delineate the Indus and its tributaries, from the Yamuna in the east, through the Punjab, to Afghanistan in the west. The river to which all these rivers 'hasten' – 'like mothers crying to their sons' – is the Sindhu. Sung on the banks of the Indus, the hymns echo with imprecations to the river.

> Sindhu exceeds all the other wandering rivers by her strength . . .
> Sparkling, bright, with mighty splendour she carries the waters across
> the plain – the unconquered Sindhu, the quickest of the quick, like
> a beautiful mare – a delight to see.

Max Müller believed that it was the very experience of beholding the river's creative-destructive power which had engendered humanity's concept of the divine.

Sanskrit has many words which are similar to European equivalents: the fire god Agni becomes *ignis* in Latin, for example. But scholars found the etymology of the rain god Indra perplexing. Some wondered if it had a non-Sanskrit root, others whether it meant 'giant', 'quick', 'conqueror' or 'man'. Only for Max Müller was its meaning incontrovertible:

> The derivation of the name Indra, a god who is constantly repre-
> sented as bringing rain, from the same root which yielded *ind-u*,
> rain-drop, is beyond the reach of reasonable criticism . . . there can
> be no doubt that in the mind of the Vedic poets *ind-u* and *ind-ra*
> were inseparably connected.

If Indra shares a linguistic root with *ind-u*, rain, it also shares one with the Indus. The river is the physical manifestation of the storm god's power. Indra controls the waters, 'setting them free' in spring and taming the floods so that humans can cross them. The waters are 'Indra's special beverage'.

Indra's waters fill the Indus to the brim, fertilizing the land for the Vedic flocks. 'Ye goddess floods,' the poets sing, 'ye mothers, animating all, promise us water rich in fatness and in balm.' The wealth of the Indus – 'Sindhu with his path of gold' – is a recurring theme. 'The Sindhu is rich in horses, rich in chariots, rich in clothes, rich in gold ornaments, well-made, rich in food, rich in wool . . . the auspicious river wears honey-growing flowers.'

As bemused Sanskrit scholars have long pointed out, the Rig Veda is about the Punjab, principally; its vision also encompasses what is now eastern Afghanistan and north-west Pakistan. Sindh and peninsular India are unknown. There are rare mentions of rivers to the east. The Yamuna (which today runs through Delhi) is invoked a handful of times; the Ganges no more than twice at the most; and the Saraswati, a fabled eastern river that dried up around 1000 BCE, is only praised in later layers of the text. Disconcerting as it is to pious Hindus, the Rig Veda has its heartland in Pakistan.

From subsequent Sanskrit literature, it is clear that the Rigvedic people gradually migrated east towards the Gangetic plains, where the rivers they worshipped were perhaps less fickle and erratic, less subject to sudden, life-threatening changes of course. Ancient Vedic commentaries such as the *Satapatha Brahmana*, and the epic, the Mahabharata, esteem north-central India. The medieval Sanskrit plays and poems shift the centre of Sanskrit culture south; and the Ramayana appears to describe the conquest of Sri Lanka. In classical Sanskrit literature, the Ganges – an insignificant river in the Rig Veda – is promoted as the ultimate sin-cleansing goddess, the holiest of holies.

As Sanskrit moved east and south into India, the Hindu sacred landscape (*aryavarta*) was reoriented. The old homeland became the new periphery: and an Oedipal hatred of the land they had come from developed. Western India's mountains and deserts, even the lush Punjab, were thrust beyond the pale, fit only for *mlecchas*: Sanskrit-illiterate barbarians. In the Mahabharata there are faint memories of a time when the land of the five rivers was sacred. But more often, the Punjab is roundly vilified. 'How indeed would . . . the Sindhu-Sauviras know anything of duty,' one of the characters comments, 'being born, as they are, in a sinful country, being mlecchas in their practices, and being regardless of duties.' Where 'those five rivers flow . . . which have the Sindhu for their sixth . . . those regions are without virtue and religion. No one should go hither.' The men of the five rivers drink alcohol and eat beef with garlic; their women dance naked.

As the reputation of the Indus valley grew ever more dire, many Hindus seized instead on the vanished Saraswati. It was mythologized as the mother of all Rigvedic rivers, and its location was shifted eastwards into the Gangetic heartland: Hindus now believed that it flowed invisibly to the junction of the Ganges and Yamuna (at Allahabad near Varanasi). The Indus, by contrast, became so neglected that in 1922 a Brahmin priest from Sindh had to write a book reminding Hindus of the river's holiness. Partition, in 1947, sealed centuries of Hindu feeling about the Indus. Now that the river was lost almost completely to Pakistan, the Saraswati acquired a cult following.

The eastward-shifting geography of ancient Indian literature had encouraged men like Jones to see Sanskrit as an immigrant language to India. This gave rise to the theory of the 'Aryan invasion' – to which many Indians reacted with understandable fury. Most academics in India now agree that there was indeed some kind of population migration into north-western India during the second millennium BCE. But during the rule of the BJP, right-wing Hindu politicians denied the Aryan invasion in Parliament, and ordered that authoritative accounts by the country's leading historians – whom they denounced as 'unpatriotic leftists' – should be excised from classroom textbooks.

In Pakistan, however, it is different. Here, the idea of an 'Aryan invasion' carries no unpatriotic stigma; indeed it is considered natural, in a country where any Muslim with social aspirations can trace their descent from Arab or Persian émigrés, that the 'noble' Aryans were immigrants too. Since 2003, a team of Pakistani archaeologists has been excavating ancient graves along the banks of the northern Indus tributaries. According to the results of their most recent researches, the graves are tantalizing traces of what they call 'the ancient Aryans' journey' from Central Asia, south-east into Pakistan.

In a sweeping sabre-swipe that cuts India off from its Aryan past, these archaeologists tell me that while the immigrant Aryans colonized the Indus valley, 'this culture ends here. The Aryans did not cross the river into India.'

Hitherto, archaeologists have been frustrated by the fact that while the authors of the Rig Veda created a complex world of verbal images, it has been difficult to locate their material remains. Unlike Ashoka, who wrote his name on rocks all over the country, the Aryans were probably pastoralists who shunned the usual recourse of archaeologists – urban settlements and writing. As far as physical artefacts go, like Macavity the Mystery Cat, *the Aryans are never there.*

Sanskrit scholars have had to scour the Rig Veda for clues, arguing over the meaning of almost every word. From the mass of entwined metaphors it has been established more or less conclusively that the Aryans' two most important status symbols were cows and horses. On ceremonial occasions they drank the sacred *soma*, a mysterious juice pressed from a mountain mushroom, or maybe a leafless pulpy plant like rhubarb. They liked to live near rivers; they used copper; they practised herding and hunting.

In the 1960s, artefacts were recovered from graves in Dir and Swat (known in the Rig Veda as *Suvastu*, 'good dwelling place') that were carbon-dated to the second millennium BCE, around the time of the Rig Veda's composition. The grave-people's main source of meat was cattle; and they had contacts with far-off northern places. There was lapis lazuli from northern Afghanistan, earrings made of gold (probably from the upper Indus) and pottery gracefully painted with horse shapes. There were various forms of burial on the banks of the river, including bodies buried in a foetal position (as in Central Asia) and cremation (as happened later in India). There were many things, wrote the Italian archaeologist Giorgio Stacul, which suggested 'a connection with the Vedic literature'.

The most contentious finds, though, were the bones of *Equus caballus*. Horses are the quintessence of Rigvedic culture: 'Surely the child of the waters, urging on his swift horses, will adorn my songs, for he enjoys them.' There are whole hymns about horses in the Rig Veda; gods are called horses; as in Homer, the horse-drawn chariot is the Rigvedic people's most important weapon. The significance of the horse in the Rig Veda reflects the dramatic changes it brought to human life after its domestication during the fourth to second millennium BCE in the Ukraine. Horses allowed the people who rode them to cover huge distances, and to rout their enemies.

To the annoyance of those who allege that the Aryans were indigenous to India, traces of the horse have not yet been found there in the pre-Rigvedic archaeological record. The presence of horse bones in the Dir and Swat graves signalled to excited archaeologists that horse-riding Proto-Sanskrit speakers entered north-west Pakistan during the second millennium BCE. The use to which the horses had been put even suggested Rigvedic ritual. Images of horses were buried as grave-goods with humans; there were horse burials, and some of the horse bones had 'marks of butchery' upon them. This is reminiscent of the Rig Veda's royal horse sacrifice, the *asvamedha*, which culminated in a horse being butchered, parboiled and roasted – a mouth-watering feast that would warm the heart of any Gaul:

> The racehorse has come to the slaughter, with his heart turned to the gods . . . Those who see that the racehorse is cooked, say, 'It smells good!'

In 2003, the oldest graves in the region were discovered in Chitral and Gilgit, the two far north-western provinces of Pakistan, which border Afghanistan and are within spitting distance of Tajikistan. For the Pakistani archaeologists, this discovery vindicated their Aryan invasion hypothesis: the oldest graves are furthest north, they say, because these people entered the area from the north-west. Although no horse graves have yet been excavated, archaeologists have so far unearthed a 'heavily rusted' iron stirrup, and a long iron mace or spearhead – carried, they speculate, by a people who fought battles on horseback. 'They came through the Baroghil and Darkot passes directly into Chitral and Gilgit,' I am told by Muhammad Zahir, a young archaeologist from Peshawar, who led the excavations. Could this be the journey that the Rig Veda appears to hint at? Indra, it is written, has carried the tribes across 'many rivers' and 'through narrow passages'.

The Chitral graves have also reopened the debate over the origins of the Kalash people – one ancient graveyard was found in the Kalash village of Rumbur, and another on the site of a medieval Kalash fort. This, the archaeologists say, suggests that the Kalash are the long-lost Aryans, still living where their ancestors had three millennia before. There is a tempting neatness to this theory. But it is with some trepidation that I pack a copy of the Rig Veda, and set off into northern Pakistan to meet – as one nineteenth-century colonial commentator dubbed the Kalash – these 'pure Aryans of the high type.'

By the time I reach the Kalash villages, I have read enough archaeological reports and amateur nineteenth-century ethnography, seen enough pictures and heard enough rumours, to know that north-west Pakistan is a tapestry of prehistoric remains. But nothing has prepared me for the beauty I encounter in those lonely valleys – for the carvings of hunters; for the megalithic stone circles; above all for the extravagant landscape of these ancient people's lost peregrinations. Standing amidst walnut trees, rushing streams and jagged cliffs, it is easy to see how this land could have inspired poetic devotion:

> By his great power he turned the *Sindhu* towards the north: with his thunderbolt he ground to pieces the wagon of the dawn, scattering the tardy enemy with his swift forces: in the exhilaration of the *Soma*, Indra has done these deeds.

For the people who still live on the banks of the raging Indus tributaries, the river has lost none of its fearful power since Rigvedic priests first tried to assuage it with their hymns. On my first day in the Kalash mountain village of Bumboret, a boy is swept to his death. That afternoon, I walk out to the graveyard under the holly-oaks on the edge of the village. The ground is littered with wooden boxes carved with solar discs – Kalash coffins, just as Alexander saw them two thousand years ago. Few Kalash are entombed above ground like this any more, partly because of the fear of grave-robbers. All over Chitral and Gilgit, the illegal trade in antiques encourages the pillaging of everything from Kalash coffins, to stone circles, to three-thousand-year-old 'Aryan' graves.

Kalash burial practices are also dying out as a result of proselytization by Muslim missionaries, whose alluring promise of five-star accommodation in heaven (*jannat*) maintains a steady conversion rate. Neither the Kalash themselves (nor the Christians nor the Hindus) can offer such an unqualified assurance of paradise as the Muslims do. (Later, during a bus ride along the Indus to Skardu, I discover just how marvellous this heaven is when two gaunt madrassah students insist on replacing the Bollywood music on the stereo with a religious sermon in Urdu: 'There will be one hundred million different kinds of fruit in heaven,' says the preacher, before getting on to the houris. The other passengers listen, silent and observant.)

Tradition is a fragile thing in a culture built entirely on the memories of the elders. Neither Muslim, Hindu nor Buddhist, the Kalash religion is syncretic, involving a pantheon of gods, sacred goats, and a reverence for river sources and mountaintops. The Kalash have no holy book, and hence absorb influences idiosyncratically and seemingly at random. In the nineteenth century, the neighbouring Afghan Kafirs, who had a similar culture to the Kalash, boasted that they had killed the sons of Ali (the grandsons of the Prophet). In the twenty-first century the Kalash are more diplomatic: they have begun calling their creator god 'Khodai', after the Persian word *Khuda* used for God by Muslims and some Hindus all over the subcontinent.

Such is the pressure from Islam in Bumboret, few young Kalash seem proud of their pantheon, or even to know of its existence. There is incredulity when I say that I have read about a Kalash female household deity. Gul, one of the first Kalash girls to have gone to college in Chitral, looks confused. 'Yes, we have more than one god,' she says; but protests break out from her mother and brother; and two young Muslim men, her former schoolmates, raise their voices: 'If it is true that the Kalash have a female god in their houses then there will be fighting between us.'

Every Kalash family has a vineyard from which they ferment wine – the sacred Aryan *soma*, say enthusiasts of the Aryan-Kalash hypothesis – a Dionysiac cocktail, said ancient, and latterly modern, Greeks. On my first day in Bumboret, an old Kalash lady invites me in to sample her home brew: sour white wine fermented in a goatskin, followed by mulberry *tara*, all before ten in the morning. As we knock back shots of tara, my sense of our kinship expands in step with my inebriation, for all women are by definition unclean according to Kalash tradition. In the hour before the tara headache strikes, I savour the miscellaneous company we women keep – cows, chickens, and the mouths of rivers are also deemed dirty – and wonder if it is in spite of, or because of, their quintessential impurity that Kalash women enjoy a freedom which should be the envy of their Muslim compatriots. Villagers hold night-time dance parties, everybody drinks, and the unveiled women – who on an ordinary day wear a clutch of plaits in their hair, beaded-headdress hats, and hundreds of saffron-coloured necklaces – choose their own husbands.

But the 'free and easy' Kalash ladies have gained notoriety elsewhere in Pakistan, and in the summer, the villages are beset by sex-starved Punjabi tourists keen to ogle ladies without headscarves. This is the second major reason for Kalash conversions. 'It was the sight of her dancing with other men that made me do it,' a recent convert called Fazlur tells me as we sit under a mulberry tree eating the slender white fruit: 'I took a course in Islam in Karachi, and when I came back, I made my wife say the kalma by the river. Now she never leaves the bottom of the garden.' 'Have you given up sharab [alcohol]?' I ask. Fazlur's Kalash friends snigger. Drinking is part of Chitrali culture – no Muslim in this land can live without their mulberry tara. 'But I have a place in heaven guaranteed,' Fazlur says.

In Rumbur village on the other side of the hill, the Kalash appear more at ease with their unusual way of life. The land is communally owned; there is no class or caste. There is a small hydroelectric dam, and everywhere I walk in the hills around the village, I step across small, carefully constructed canals bringing water to every villager's fields. Compared with the situation in other parts of Pakistan, it is an ecological paradise.

Lying here and there on the ground in the Rumbur graveyard, are wooden *gandao* – effigies of dead horsemen, mounted on one, sometimes two, large steeds. If gandao were still made today, they would presumably show the Kalash astride motorbikes, jumping on buses, or turning the ignition of a jeep. Horses are no longer an important part of Kalash daily life, and the same is true all over Chitral, where jeeps and highways have rendered equine transport redundant. It is the end of a long tradition, for in ancient India, this part of the country was always famous for its horses. Kalash mythology maintains that the 'horse was created first of all animals'; the Kalash sun god Balimain rides a mount, and wooden sculptures of Balimain's horse still guard the sacred worship-place on a hillside high above the village. Until the nineteenth century, horse reverence stretched at least as far east as Chilas on the banks of the Indus, where the local people kept a 'rude sculpture' of their god Taiban's horse. In 1895, when George Robertson visited the neighbouring Kafirs in Afghanistan, he was told that thunder was the noise of their god Indr playing polo, and that horse sacrifices took place next to the river.

For Robertson, this could mean only one thing. As he saw it, all the 'essential components' of the Afghan Kafir religion tallied with the Rig Veda – their Indr to the Vedic Indra, their Imra to the Vedic Yama. This led him to speculate that the Kafir religion represented an early 'protest movement among tribal Aryans'.

Linguistics was on Robertson's side. The Kafirs in Afghanistan spoke an archaic form of Indo-Iranian, and the Kalash language, like that spoken in the rest of Chitral, is one of the most ancient in the Indo-European linguistic group – older even than Rigvedic Sanskrit. From this, linguists have guessed that the Kalash were living in Chitral at least from the second millennium BCE – perhaps before the Rig Veda was codified. Maybe the priests with their sacred hymns moved on towards the Indus, leaving the Kalash behind to become, as the linguist Georg Morgenstierne put it in 1932, 'the only existing remnants of ancient Aryan religion not affected by literary traditions'.

As I sit watching three Kalash women hoeing a maize field, like exotic crested birds in their orange and black headdresses, I find that I am already being seduced by the easy parallels that can be drawn between Kalash and Rigvedic culture. But there are, unsurprisingly, serious gaps in the theory. The Kalash today have no special reverence for *agni* (fire), and they consider the cow, sacred to the Rig Veda, unclean.

But there are constant reminders of how central the river has been to both societies. During the spring festival, held after the snow has begun to melt and the rivers to swell, Kalash women are allowed into the upper valleys, and then a young girl is made to invoke: 'O

Khodai, Supreme God, lead the stream to flow in its normal course. Don't let it jump here and there and bring floods.' The word for God is borrowed from the Muslims, yet the prayer itself is more reminiscent than anything else in modern Pakistan of the incessant Rigvedic plea: 'Thou . . . didst stay the great stream . . . at their prayer didst check the rushing river . . . make the floods easy to cross, O Indra.'

A century ago, the Kalash were still performing sacrifices to the river god Bagej: animals were burnt on the banks of the river and their heads were thrown into the water. Even in the drabber twenty-first century, it was the river that Fazlur chose as the place for his wife's conversion to Islam. It may never be possible to prove a direct cultural or genetic inheritance between the Kalash and the Aryans; but the effect of these people's shared riverside habitat has not changed with the centuries. Water still exerts its power on the imaginations of the people who live here, just as it did on the minds of the Rig Veda's authors. This legacy is witnessed all over Chitral and Gilgit.

From the Kalash villages I wind north on a tour of Chitral's ancient grave-sites, with Mir Hayat, curator of the local museum. A bustling young man with kohl-etched eyes, the curator sees Aryanism all around us. As we drive, he counts off Chitral's plethora of 'Aryan artefacts' on his fingers. His colleagues in Peshawar, he tells me, have even sent bones dug up from the 'Aryan' graves to America for DNA testing – they hope to prove a genetic link between the dead Aryans and living Kalash.

We reach the village of Ayun, a Muslim settlement that neighbours the Kalash villages but is outside the shadow cast by the mountains and thus weeks ahead in the agricultural cycle. (In Rumbur and Bumboret the wheat was green; in the flood plain of the Kunar river, the terraced fields are a ripe sun-gold.) 'As soon as we begin excavating,' the curator says, 'the local people start looking for treasure.' Clay pots were discovered in the 1920s, which were later linked by a Cambridge archaeologist to the arrival of 'Indo-European-speaking' people in the second millennium BCE. Ever since then, every farmer in Ayun has dug up his fields in search of pots to sell to antique dealers.

We have come to see a villager who has just unearthed five such

'Aryan' ceramics. Usually he keeps them locked away beneath his bed, but at Mir Hayat's insistence, he brings them outside and lays them in the sun. 'There was an even bigger one,' he says, 'but I gave it to an American man last summer.' He picks out a small greyish pot from the pile. 'This is for you,' he says, as he places it in my hands. 'I can't take this,' I say – alarmed at yet more of their archaeological heritage being casually misplaced. But the curator whispers to me in English: 'Give it to the museum. This man never lets us take his pots. Say thank-you nicely.' And so, for about twenty minutes, I am the owner of a supposedly three-millennia-old piece of pottery; such is the perilous state of archaeology in Pakistan. 'I'll put your name on the acquisition card,' says Mir Hayat, and grins.

There are more signs of archaeological depredation at the site of the old Kalash fort a few miles away upriver, where Mir Hayat's school-friend lives. A combination of professional and private excavations, Mir Hayat tells me, has revealed that this site has been continuously inhabited for thousands of years, 'at least since the time of the –' '. . . Aryans,' I finish for him. Mir Hayat rewards me with a gracious smile. 'You are a very fast learner, Ellis.'

While Mir Hayat waits for us outside, his friend leads me inside his traditional Chitrali home of mud-smeared walls, heavily carved black wooden beams, three young wives, and many more young children. In the main living area, fetchingly illuminated by the sunlight which streams through the large hole in the roof, is a big round pot that looks as if it was fired last week. In a grain store there is another pot buried beneath the mud floor and filled – I put my hand down and feel around – with decaying pomegranates.

The Archaeological Department does its best to preserve the exca-vation sites, but it is already involved in one court case and litiga-tion is lengthy and expensive. Ten years ago, I am told, villagers would never dishonour graves by stealing from them. But where archaeolo-gists lead, international antique smugglers, Pashtuns from down-country, and the astronomical prices they pay, follow.

The next day, serenaded by plaintive local love-songs, we drive north along the deep red and brown gorges of the Mastuj river. Parwak is a small village in the mountains wedged between the Afghan border and the high mountain pass leading to Gilgit. It is said to be on the heroin-smuggling route and is thus considered by the archaeologists – even those from Peshawar, where everything is contraband – to be 'dangerous'. It is a dramatic place, one of those sudden plains that open up like an unfurling fist in a landscape rendered claustrophobic by mountains. To the west is Tirich Mir, the highest peak in Chitral, which the linguist Morgenstierne considered a candidate for Meru, the sacred mountain of the Hindu scriptures.

The graves, dated to 1600 BCE, were found just beyond the junction of the rivers and they prove, says Mir Hayat, that the people who lived here were goat- and stone-worshippers. One group of bodies was buried in a circle around a large boulder; a skeleton was found with the skull of a goat next to its head. Across the river, high on a hill facing the mountain of Tirich Mir, is an ancient stone circle. Since Mir Hayat was last here, however, the boulders have been dynamited into pieces by villagers looking for gold.

From here, Mir Hayat points out the plateau of Parwaklasht, where the archaeologists found another stone circle-lined grave. To reach it, we cross the river again, and climb up a goat path to the plateau, which now rises above us like the mud wall of a medieval Muslim fort. When the people who built these stone circles lived here, the river ran across the plateau; since then it has eroded a ravine hundreds of feet below and nobody can subsist here any more.

Because of the absence of modern settlements, Parwaklasht is the first place I have been where my Rigvedic imagination can run wild. As we stand on the plateau, looking around us at the villages which crouch like fecund animals at the point where mountain streams join the valley, the songs of the Rigvedic poets suddenly make sense. For nine months of the year, the rivers here are frozen solid, but now the streams cascade downwards in energetic white spurts. The 'waters are set free', the poets sang, like cattle released from their pens, like the milk of cattle, like sperm.

> The rivers having pierced the air with a rush of water, went forth like milk-cows . . . exuberant with their full udders . . . their water mixed with butter and honey.

We solicit from you, Waters, that pure, faultless, rain-shedding, sweet essence of the earth, which the devout have called the beverage of Indra.

The Rig Veda, like the Bible, evokes a land flowing with milk and honey.

Thanks to the floods, I have a chance to think about Indra's special beverage all week. When Mir Hayat and I reach Mastuj, the village just north of Parwak, we find that the road ahead up to the Shandur pass has been washed away. 'You cannot go onwards to Gilgit,' announces the curator over lunch. 'You will have to come back with me to Chitral.' 'What about going north to the Baroghil pass?' I suggest, thinking of the grave-site at Brep, but he shivers, plainly thinking of the heroin smugglers. As we are sipping tea and considering this dilemma, a man appears. He is Yusuf, the local Engineer Inspector. He has a wife in purdah, a house here in the village, five sons of varying ages who can 'protect me', and a cherry orchard.

Engineer Yusuf and I arrive at his house to find his sons on the roof, picking the red fruit and loudly counting the days (approximately seven) until the annual Shandur pass polo match between Chitral and Gilgit. Five thousand Pakistanis and VIP guests and foreign dignitaries are expected (says the eldest), ten thousand (corrects the Engineer), twenty thousand (confirms the youngest) – and the road still isn't open. For fifty-one weeks of the year, Mastuj exists in the dark amnesiac part of Pakistan's national consciousness; for seven glorious days the VIPs and Pashtun tourists will make it feel like the centre of the world as they trundle past in jeeps on their way up through the mountains.

Everywhere I go that week, the Engineer's sons come with me: north to the graves at Brep, or south again to Parwak. One evening, we get back to the house to find Engineer Yusuf squatting by the fire in the kitchen and looking – for him – quietly excited. His men have built a temporary bridge over the flooded road, and now at last the Pashtun tourists can drive up to the Shandur pass with their wads of rupees and illicit bottles of gin and packets of marijuana; the VIPs, of course, will be coming by helicopter. That night the boys roll up their sleeping carpets, pack some roti, and the next morning we set off up the mountain with a kiss from mother.

At the top of the mountain road, we overtake a long line of men and cows: 'Shepherds from the village of Laspur,' says the Engineer. 'During the summer they live by the lake with their cow and goat herds.' Lake? Migratory shepherds? My Rigvedic ears prick up. Lakes, according to the Vedist Harry Falk, are key to Rigvedic topography – especially lakes that sedentary pastoralists live beside; above all lakes where temporarily resident shepherds tend cows for a living. Moreover, the hillside is luminous with strokes of colour, there is snow on the ground still, and the streams are running like milk. We round the last bend in the road, and then the lake comes into sight. What an incongruous pastoral scene it is. Cows are grazing on the reeds at its edges. Clouds drift incandescent across the lapis-blue sky.

The Shandur pass is 3,734 metres high, so the air is thin, and I am breathless and dizzy by the time I make the short journey up from the shores of the lake towards the cluster of stone huts on the green and purple hillside. Four shepherd boys are hitting a ball with a miniature wooden polo stick when I arrive; an old woman in a yellow shawl and Chitrali cap is sitting on the steps of her house in the sun. One of the boys, a twelve-year-old in a Royal Mail sweater, shows me around his home. Identical to all the others on the hillside, it rises like a little heap of brown sugar from the square lines of the stone boundary walls. The two main rooms (a kitchen and a storeroom) are circular, and roofed with wooden branches filled in with a cone of gorse and heather. A one-gallon ghee tin is the chimney. In front of each hut is a verandah made from grey and black stones, as speckled as the goats. And adjacent to each verandah is a Rigvedic cow-pen. ('They have stepped over all barriers like a thief into the cow-pen.')

As I am wondering whether it is the lack of oxygen that is encouraging these allusions, the shepherd children gather round and quiz me. 'Where is your husband?' they ask as I ask them about their religion. They tilt back their heads and demand: 'Where have you left your children?' as I speculate about the 'Shamanism' reportedly practised here as late as the 1950s. 'Did your husband,' they say, 'give you permission to come here?'

They tell me that their cousins are playing for the Laspur team. 'Have you always lived here in the summer?' I ask. 'We used to live down there' – a boy with a green Pakistan cap points towards the lake, 'but we moved up after the *maindak* jumped into the milk.' *Maindak?* They mime for me. A frog. I sit down on the wall of the cow-pen, pull out my copy of the Rig Veda, and as the boys go through the contents of my bag, I read:

> When the heavenly waters came upon him dried out like a leather bag, lying in the pool, then the cries of the frogs joined in chorus like the lowing of cows with calves.

The thin air is making me obsessive. Soon I'll be brewing soma and conducting asvamedhas with the polo ponies.

Soma is probably local to these parts – it is said to be made from a mountain plant – but the polo ponies at Shandur, being large Punjabi imports, do not resemble those given in sacrifice by Vedic-era humans in northern Pakistan. Chitrali ponies, on the other hand, though too small for polo, might have made good votive offerings: the horse skeletons at Dir were barely '135cm up to the withers', small and just right for pulling chariots, like the tough ancient breed from Siberia.

For three days I watch from the hill as the lakeside fills up with men: local villagers, Pashtun touts, Punjabi holidaymakers and even a handful of foreign tourists. Engineer Yusuf surveys the fresh white helicopter circles his men have painted on the grass, the newly trimmed seating and the long line of free-standing toilets, with obvious satisfaction. At night there is Chitrali dancing. By day the rumour goes round: the President is coming. I bump into friends of mine from Swat, seven men who have driven up with a box of plucked chickens, a luxury tent and ten bottles of Peshawar's finest smuggled vodka.

But I soon tire of polo, even if it is a local sport, played on the most archaic form of transport. Once the first match is over, and I have witnessed the dancing on the pitch and happy male cheering, I say goodbye to the Engineer and his sons, fold up my tent, and buy a seat in a jeep taking villagers down into Gilgit.

Ever since I crossed the Lowari pass into Chitral, the landscape has been growing by turns lusher and starker. We alarm a herd of feral cows with huge horns as we accelerate down through a meadow of flowers. The turquoise lake at the head of the Gilgit valley breached its banks this summer, and the glinting waters are still lapping at the houses in the flood plain ('the wide dispersed waters that shine with many colours, the honeyed waters'). At the crest of the hill above the lake, the jeep stops and we climb out to appreciate the beauty and destruction that the river has wrought. The jeep driver stoops down to pick wild flowers from the verge to tuck beneath his white woollen cap. From here to Gilgit, the road along the river is perilously balanced between the water on one side and the rock face on the other.

Gilgit is part of the disputed Northern Areas, a mountainous land that was marked on Soviet maps as part of India. Like Pakistan's tribal districts, it has tax-free status, and the usual combination of timber smuggling and car running – but without the clannish Pashtun code. Many of the people are Ismailis, devotees of the Aga Khan, who tells them that purdah is unnecessary, 'two children are enough', and that they must 'think in English, speak in English, dream in English'. Here you feel a different sphere of influence: less Afghanistan and Iran than China and Central Asia.

The jeep drops me in the village of Goopis. From here I hitch a lift in a small battered car – smugglers again; I pity the buyer they are scamming with this one – up into the narrow, sombre valley of Yasin.

According to the Peshawar archaeologists, this valley was one of the migration routes of the Aryans. There have been no excavations here, but I have come across a reference to ancient stone circles in a book by John Biddulph, who was Britain's Political Officer at Gilgit in the late nineteenth century, at a time when this whole area was an unknown and therefore disconcerting place for the colonial authorities. In 1880, Biddulph wrote a brief paragraph on Yasin's 'remarkable stone tables of great antiquity'. He drew no pictures or maps of their location; and since then there has been no archaeological study of their meaning and history. As we drive towards Yasin village, my only fear is that, as at Parwak, they will already have been destroyed.

In Yasin, I am told to report to the Magistrate. But the Magistrate strokes his beard and says, 'We just blew up the stone circle to find the gold inside.' 'No!' I say, distressed, though hardly surprised. Happily, he is joking. Or partly joking. He takes me that evening to an orchard on the banks of the river where there is a stone circle – larger than the one at Parwak – with a tree growing in the middle. The stones sit deep in the earth, shoulder to shoulder as Biddulph described. I count. Seven stones are missing – removed to build the new Sunni mosque, so I am told when we locate the landowner.

The next day I hire a jeep and drive up the valley almost to the border with Afghanistan, asking comically in every village we come to for *pattar ka chowk* ('stone roundabout': the best I can do in Urdu). Just north of Yasin village, where the River Tui meets the Yasin, there is a Muslim shrine with ibex horns above the door (a practice dating from Neanderthal times 40,000 years ago, when graves were decorated with ibex horns). Nearby, there are three distinct, though diminished stone circles, an ancient cemetery perhaps. The river in this valley flows southeast, which according to the *Satapatha Brahmana* is the very best location for a Vedic burial ground.

I climb the hill that rises steeply above the river. On the plateau at the top, stone circles spring out from the craggy terrain and disappear again when I draw near, like teasing children. Twice the 'circles' turn out to be three or four large boulders, where the gaps in between have been filled with smaller stones. I see several huge flat table-stones; boulders that have been split in two; stones that have been upended; and on one rock, a carving of an ibex with a curly tail and horns almost as long as its body. Most distinctive of all is a standing stone, cut roughly on the top and both sides, a small flat boulder at its foot like a table or sundial, with the shadow sharp upon it. Twenty years ago, when the German archaeologist Karl Jettmar visited Gilgit, he found that people still had memories of a time when such stones were sacred. Once the entire village, men and women, would come to the hillside to drink and dance beside these stones 'in complete sexual abandon'. The standing stone was the seat of the protecting spirit of the ancestors, and the smaller stone at its foot was used for carving up the sacrificial goat. There used to be many such stories about the worship of stones in these remote and independent valleys.

Now I hear nothing but the wind. There is a shout: I turn, and see the jeep driver. I have been away for an hour, if not two. He has grown worried, and climbed up to find me.

We drive up to the next village, which is spread out gently along a slope on the further side of the river. From here, Afghanistan and the Oxus river are barely two days' walk. The river has breached its banks and we have to leave the jeep and walk up under the walnut trees, along the village path to a meadow of blue wild flowers. From the path, through the trees, we can see the circle of large boulders, four foot high, standing shoulder to shoulder like people in a ring. The orchard belongs to a farmer, Akhil, whose aged father puts on his sunglasses, takes up his lyre and, in between songs, tells me the local legend of the circle's construction. 'People round here,' he says, 'might report that the circle was built by giants, but my family were rajas in this place a century back, and our fathers knew that the circle was made one, two thousand years ago by a *Russi* warrior.' 'Russian?' I ask. He nods: 'People have always come to these parts from outside. The Russi built it to mourn the death of his best friend. They are very sentimental people.'

We walk inside the circle through the entrance at the eastern side. Some stones are square, some V-shaped, and this gives each one a personal, individual air. The lichen has grown slowly across those that point north, and stones on the southern side have carvings of ibex upon them. There used to be flat table stones on top, Akhil says, but they were easy to remove, and every time he went to Skardu one of his neighbours would steal them. A standing stone is missing too: it was taken during Akhil's childhood to use as a grindstone. 'There was another circle like this one just over there,' Akhil says, pointing to a field of waving maize near the river. 'But the owner got fed up with it and pulled it down last year.' 'People might pay money to see this circle,' I say to Akhil, 'but only if you protect it.' I try to describe Stonehenge. He looks at me, unconvinced.

That evening, back in Yasin, I explore the village with the help of Sayed Junaid, a burly young member of the border militia, who drives me up and down the stony paths on a borrowed motorcycle. In another orchard near the river we find the remains of a stone circle which the owner has dismantled and chopped up, in order to build an extension on his house. He has also dug out the centre of the circle, where he found some clay pots, which his children have planted with basil, and four graves (thus confirming Biddulph's speculation that the circles were 'in all probability funeral mounds'). The bodies, encased in green schist coffins, were in varying states of putrefaction. One was quite '*taza*' (fresh: perhaps an ancient grave reused in historic times). The other three were just a pile of bones, and they turned to dust as soon as the graves were opened. He scooped up the bone dust and scattered it on his fields.

The Magistrate, for whatever reason, warns me not to listen to Sayed Junaid, who says that there is one of these *pattar ka chowk*s on his own land at the southern end of the valley near Goopis. 'These men know nothing,' he says. So I arrange to meet Sayed Junaid at his house the following afternoon, and tell the Magistrate I am leaving for Gilgit. It is a bright, cold day when the jeep driver drops me outside a green door in a wall just short of Goopis.

Sayed Junaid and his brother are waiting for me under a white mulberry tree on the bank of the river. The river is too wide and fast to cross by boat at this time of year, so the family have strung up a cable car, made from a crate, between the mulberry tree and a rock on the other side. I stand on the riverbank and watch Sayed Junaid clamber on to the crate, slide down to the middle of the river, and up towards the cliff, as his brother sits in the mulberry tree and tugs. Then it is my turn. I perch in the crate, clutch on to its sides, and watch the river rushing past far below me. In the middle, the crate comes to a halt, and I look up towards the rocky slice of land on the other side. Where the rivers meet, the tongue of land narrows, and it is here that the stone circle is supposed to stand.

I tip myself out of the crate, and Sayed Junaid leads me over to the mound. 'There it is,' he says.

I hear myself gasping out loud. The circle is resplendent, majestic, isolated – a solid ring of stones in this silent, empty place. On our left is a sheer brown wall of rock, and the blue slither of the river; to our right, a wider, greener river, and a dark mass of mountains in the distance. In the east, beyond the point where the rivers meet, snow-topped mountains shine fiercely in the afternoon light. I can almost hear, like a whisper, the footsteps of the people who created this circle. For the first time in my life I want to get down on my knees and worship at this altar to human endeavour, to the power of Nature.

We walk slowly towards the circle, then around it. The standing stones are huge – almost as tall as me, and wider than my arm span. The circle's isolation has saved it from thieves: without a bridge nobody could tow away these stones, and even the flat table-stones on top have been left intact. Somebody, though, has tried to dig out the graves in the middle – green schist slabs stick out from the earth like broken arms. Two drystone walls have been built leading from the circle's eastern and western point towards each of the rivers. There are carvings on the circle stones themselves, though they appear to vary in age: ibexes, mostly, but also a warrior on horse-back with a pennant in his hand.

Since Biddulph's day, nobody has done a thorough study of Yasin's circles. Professor Dani guessed that they were built for chieftains, monumental versions of the stone circle-topped graves in Chitral. German archaeologists dispute this, but until permission to excavate has been granted by the Pakistan Government, everybody's guess is valid. They could be Iron Age, Bronze Age, or even relics of that three-thousand-year-old Vedic-era grave culture. Or examples of how, till recently, age-old traditions and customs persisted to modern times in these remote mountain valleys.

I stay that night in Ishkomen valley, parallel with Yasin, where more 'Aryan-era' graves were found in 1996. There is no hotel, but the woman I sit next to on the bus, the wife of a stonemason, offers to have me to stay. Gilgiti women have a charming kissing habit. They take each of your hands in each of theirs, kiss both, extend their hands to your lips to be kissed, then exchange cheek kisses. (The Kalash kiss like this too, though there the embrace is not confined to separate genders.) The physical contact is unusual in Pakistan. It creates a feeling of intimacy that lasts throughout the evening, as the women show me round their house – down to the stream where their fridge, a little wooden house, sits over the water – in and out of their orchard, and back into the room with posters of Saddam Hussein and the Aga Khan on the walls, where I will sleep. That night they tell me that there are many martyrs in this village from the 1999 Kargil War – Musharraf's brief failed invasion of that part of Kashmir occupied by India, which triggered his dismissal as army chief, and in turn resulted in his coup.

Above: This is all that remains of the Bamiyan Buddhas in Afghanistan after the statues were destroyed by the Taliban in 2001. When the monk Xuanzang visited Bamiyan in the seventh century CE, en route to Gandhara (in what is now Pakistan), the Buddha statues glistened with gold. Xuanzang also described a 1,000-foot-long 'sleeping Buddha' – which archaeologists believe may be buried somewhere at the feet of the standing Buddhas.

Right: A seventh-century CE Maitreya Buddha in Swat, Pakistan. In autumn 2007, this statue – the last intact Buddha in the Swat valley, which has stood here untouched since the time of the Prophet Muhammad – was attacked by extremists who dynamited the rock and drilled away the Buddha's face and shoulders.

Alexander the Great watching as his men are eaten by river beasts in India. It was after seeing crocodiles in the Indus that Alexander came to the conclusion that this river must be the source of the Nile. A Flemish illumination for a French version of the *Romance of Alexander* (1338–44).

Alexander calling across the river to naked Brahmins he encountered in the Indus Valley. An illumination of an English version of the *Romance of Alexander* (c. 1400).

My host in Kaladaka, the Black Mountains, a 'tribal' area which straddles the Indus in Northern Pakistan.

Mansoor and Ferooza, Gujar shepherds, on Pirsar, the mountaintop in Pakistan encircled on three sides by the Indus. This place, known as 'Aornos' to the ancient Greeks, was where Alexander the Great finally defeated the hill tribes.

Kalash girls just back from school in the village of Bumboret, Chitral, Pakistan. The Kalash are non-Muslim and follow an ancient religion that pre-dates Hinduism.

A Kalash graveyard of wooden coffins in Bumboret village; it was apparently boxes like these that Alexander the Great's army found on a hillside and burnt as firewood.

A stone circle near Yasin, Gilgit valley, northern Pakistan: probably an ancient burial mound.

A prehistoric carving of archers in the hills near Gakuch, Gilgit valley, northern Pakistan.

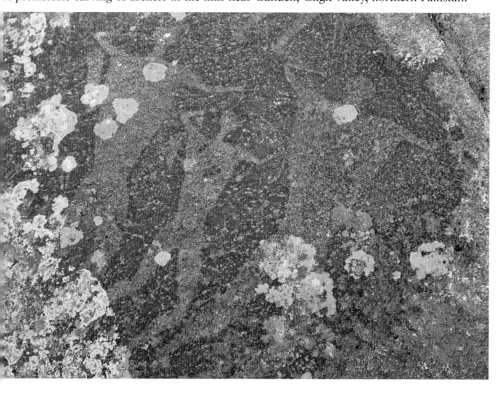

Pakistani men in the Punjabi village of Harappa making clay pots in much the same way that potters here did, five thousand years ago. The nearby brick city of Harappa, the archaeological remains of which are still being excavated, dates to 2600 BCE.

Menhirs at Burzahom near Srinagar, Kashmir, India. The people who lived here in the third millennium BCE traded cedarwood with merchants from cities further south in the Indus valley, such as Harappa.

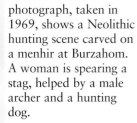

Above left: Girls returning home with baskets full of foliage gathered from the hills around Bomoi village, near Sopore, Kashmir, India.

Above right: A recently discovered upper Palaeolithic rock carving above Bomoi village. The carving seems to show a hunt, and possibly a map of nearby lakes and rivers.

Middle: This photograph, taken in 1969, shows a Neolithic hunting scene carved on a menhir at Burzahom. A woman is spearing a stag, helped by a male archer and a hunting dog.

Bottom: A rock carving of a 'shroud' on the banks of the Indus near the Dard village of Dha, Ladakh, India.

Drokpa (nomads) at their encampment two days' walk from the source of the Indus, Tibet.

Senge Khabab: the 'Lion's Mouth', a mossy spring traditionally held to be the source of the Indus in Tibet. Both my cameras broke in Tibet, so these photographs were taken on a cheap camera I bought in the Chinese shop in Darchen.

Early the next morning, I climb up to the excavation site where circle graves were discovered. A formal report has never been written, and estimates of its connection to other graves vary. Grave-goods included cowrie-like shells – clear evidence of long-distance trade, and also of a possible connection with the Kalash. The same green schist has been used to make the graves here as was used in the stone circles at Goopis and Yasin.

Every other field in this valley has yielded some ancient grave or other. In the village of Hatun, further downriver, where a large black rock is carved with Ashoka's Brahmi, amateur excavations have yielded many lucrative objects. In a field where women are cutting up apricots and laying them out in the sun to dry, a farmer this year found a small metal horse which he reputedly sold to a Pashtun dealer for 52,000 rupees.

I reach the main Gilgit road, hungry and exhausted, and am drinking my fifth cup of tea in a small shop, when an old shepherd comes in to see his son, who is the waiter. We get chatting, and it soon turns out that the shepherd knows every rock this side of Chilas. 'There are many carvings in these hills,' he says, 'but the best one is high up on the mountain, a picture of men fighting.' He pulls his arm back as if drawing a bow taut. 'Like the war between Pakistan and India. Follow the stream to the top. Keep walking upwards. It's on a big flat rock.'

The mountainside is bare of settlements. We walk for hours – Mohsin, the shepherd's son, and I – up along the stream, and into the barren brown face of the mountain. As we walk, Mohsin teaches me his mother tongue of Shina – the word for horse, *aspa*, is similar to the Sanskrit, *asva*, for Shina is an archaic mountain tongue. There is a lake at the top, he says, where the cowherders live in summer. South of us, eighty kilometres away as the crow flies, is the Indus. We are in Rigvedic territory again, I think.

Panting for breath, I stop and see the river, a pale thread encrusted with green far below us; to the right are gorges still scattered with the last snows of winter. It is early afternoon now. 'Where is it?' I call down to Mohsin. 'I can't find it either,' I hear him shout back. We climb up rock faces and over boulders; and are on the point of returning, despondent, when Mohsin gives a shout. I scramble down quickly to where he is standing, anticipating a crude line drawing: stick men on horseback, the usual ibex and dogs. But when I kneel down on the edge of the large, pale-grey rock, what I see etched there is far more lithe and vivid than that. Bodies falling through the sky, I think at first, or struggling upwards from the depths. Once again, I am left entranced and wordless by northern Pakistan's ancient beauty.

The carving is of six hunters. They are tall, muscular and naked, as strong and energetic as Matisse's dancers. They have all been carved in the same pose: running after their prey, arms drawn back, legs slightly bent, bow poised to shoot. All are of different sizes, perhaps implying a sense of perspective, and each version is exact and evocative and complete. In contrast to the line drawings that are common to most prehistoric art along the Indus, the hunters have been etched in three-quarter profile, the shape of their bodies filled in by a technique known to petroglyph academics as 'bruising'. Unlike the awkward carvings of warriors in caps and cloaks that appear in this region from the first millennium BCE, these hunters are naked: you can see the outline of their thighs and calves, their huge upper bodies, their small, alert heads. They could be men or women: only one of the seven figures has a penis.

'Look,' says Mohsin. In the top left-hand corner of the rock, there is a stark white mark: something has been carved, a name, Jalil, graffitied in Urdu. One of the only ways of guessing the age of a carving, aside from stylistic details, is the extent to which the lines scratched into the rock have recoloured over time. The original rock face is layered by a patina known to geologists as 'desert varnish', which builds up over thousands of years. The very oldest carvings, like this one of the hunters, are almost the same colour as the background rock, repolished to a brown lustre which is visible only in direct sunlight. The newest ones are the colour of Jalil's name.

I crouch on the rock and wonder. The old shepherd described the carving as a scene of war; and remembering the skeleton found in a grave at Dir with a copper arrowhead in his chest, I wonder if he is right. But in the top right corner of the carving are two animals – one a domesticated dog with a curly tail; the other an ibex. The herders here still hunt; only a few weeks ago, Mohsin and his friends went on an ibex hunt up to the lakes at the top of the mountain. Maybe, as in north-western China, this is the art of Mesolithic hunters who subsisted even into historic times. Possibly, it is a drawing by one of the Kalash, who were still using bows and arrows in the nineteenth century. Or is it, as the colour of the stone, the primitive weaponry and lack of clothes suggest, much older than that? 'I fled like a buffalo before the bowstring of a hunter'; 'Our words flow together like rivers . . . like gazelles fleeing before a hunter.' A proto-Sanskrit-speaking herder, summering at the lake? A Rigvedic warrior, chanting praises to the dark and dangerous Sindhu? Or a non-Sanskrit-speaking hunter, fleeing to the highlands from invaders on horseback?

Most of the rock carvings in northern Pakistan have been found at Chilas, on the banks of the Indus. For several hundred kilometres, the Indus cuts its way deeply and inhospitably through the mountains – and so humans have long preferred to live in its more fertile side-valleys. But if the deep-brown gleaming rocks along this hot dry stretch of riverbank make a desolate habitat, they are excellent canvases. From Stone Age times up to the incursions of Islam, humans have come down to the river's banks to worship it and other deities with carvings and rituals, or to leave indelible images of their culture and themselves. But of all the many thousands of carvings that I see, pecked or hammered with stone tools – pictures of giants and demons, hand and foot shapes, river gods or river scenes – nothing compares with the sophistication of the hunter engraving.

Nevertheless, one morning when I am standing in the sun over-looking the narrow blue cleft of the Indus, in front of an ancient carving that time has almost completely recoloured, the shapes etched into the rock make me think. The drawing is a stiff but confident outline of a person with spiky hair, long arms and fingers, whose feet come together in a boat-shape – a river god, one Pakistani archaeologist has argued. The spikes on its head are like the rays of the sun – perhaps this is how a child might draw a god it has heard about in song or prayer. That afternoon, during a rainstorm, I shelter under an overhanging rock and read of Agni, described in the Rig Veda as having flames protruding from his head: 'Seven bay mares carry you in the chariot, O sun god with hair of flame, gazing from afar' – Agni who is an integral part of the Vedic rain cycle – 'O Agni full of moisture' – drawing the water out of the rivers and letting it fall as rain.

It is not impossible that the Rigvedic people, who created such complex verbal images, also drew images on rock. What is probable, is that the prehistoric grave-builders, horse-eating horse riders, rock carvers, stone-circle makers, and Rig Veda singers meandered through the same dramatic landscape of northern Pakistan; and for a moment in history all were bound together, by their deep, primeval regard for this river and its landscape.

Travelling north along the Indus from Chilas to Gilgit on the Karakoram Highway, there is a point on the road where bus drivers always stop. It is here that the great Indus river, which for a thousand kilometres has been flowing west, is suddenly forced south by the geological mass of the mountains. The vista on the road opens up, and suddenly it is possible to see down along the river and across the hills to Nanga Parbat, the 'Naked Mountain'. Today the pride of people from the Northern Areas, Nanga Parbat is also another candidate for the Vedic people's sacred Mount Meru – and here, for me, the circle is complete. This is the easternmost point in the sphere of culture described by Pakistan's prehistoric grave complex, its valley of stone circles, its riverside carvings.

In the centuries after the Rig Veda was first sung, a whole culture went east into the easy world of the monsoon-fed Ganges. And in the centuries that followed, the landscape they left behind, with its precipitous streams and enigmatic valleys, became nothing more than a memory, part shameful, part wistful.

IO

Alluvial Cities

c. 2600 BCE

'I stood on a mound of Mohenjo-daro . . . all around me lay
the houses and streets of this ancient city . . . What was the
secret of this strength? Where did it come from?'

Jawaharlal Nehru, 1946

SUNLIGHT GLINTS OFF acres of salt-encrusted brick. The streets
are wide, the houses solid, the wells deep. There are public dust-
bins, indoor toilets and covered drains. To the west is a citadel, containing
grain stores, pillared assembly halls and a public bath; to the east a
residential area housing up to 75,000 people. Compared with the
chaotic nature of many modern Pakistani cities, this metropolis is tidy
and neat. But nobody lives here. Residents have not walked these
streets for the past four thousand years. Called Mohenjodaro ('Mound
of the Dead'), this planned, grid-like city is an archaeological relic.

Scraped free of the overlying layers of earth in 1922, the discovery
of the Indus Valley Civilization transformed the understanding of
Indian history. Colonial Victorians had portrayed the history of the
Indus as backward and unedifying, enlightened only by Alexander's
peregrinations. Historians had assumed that India's oldest civilization
was that of the legendary Aryans. But long before the authors of the
Rig Veda camped on the banks of the Indus, an entire empire had
been built here from the river's alluvium. Archaeologists now believe
that the people of the Indus cities moulded bricks from mud, baked
them in kilns, and constructed what were probably the world's first
planned cities. Each of the hundreds of towns and cities along the
banks of the river were identical, as if the Indus Valley Civilization
was conceptualized, planned and constructed according to one model.

It was a linear empire which exploited the power of the river to produce enough grain to feed cities, organize urban society, and trade with foreign lands. Among the cities' debris, archaeologists found small seals depicting wooden ships, a miniature sculpture of a dancing girl, and scented coffins made of cedar and rosewood. The Indus cities were semi-industrialized, manufacturing mass-produced clay pots, stone weights and copper beads. They were trading with Mesopotamia, using the river to irrigate vast cotton-growing projects, and importing semi-precious stones from Afghanistan, conch shells from the Arabian Sea, fish from Lake Manchar and cedarwood from the Himalayas.

Unlike Egypt with its pyramids, or Mesopotamia with its temples, their biggest structures were not symbols of monarchical tyranny or priestly power, but civic buildings such as public baths and grain stores. Discovered at a time when Europe was reeling from the impact of the First World War, this utilitarian city, 'devoid of any semblance of ornament', was hailed as a Fabian utopia.

The significance of finding a pre-Aryan Indian civilization was not lost on the chief archaeologist, John Marshall: 'before ever the Aryans were heard of,' he wrote in 1931, 'the Panjab and Sind . . . were enjoying an advanced and singularly uniform civilization of their own.' Nor was it lost on Indian freedom-fighters, who seized on the discovery as a rallying point for national pride. This was no immigrant invaders' culture; it was of the soil. At a time when the forebears of their colonial masters were still using stone tools, the citizens of the Indus valley were enjoying a life of high urban sophistication. The future Prime Minister of India, Jawaharlal Nehru, made a pilgrimage to the cities, and years later, as he was penning his memoirs in a British colonial jail, he described the impact their discovery had on him: 'that vision of five thousand years gave me a new perspective, and the burden of the present seemed to grow lighter.' (It was thus an acute disappointment to many Indians when the Indus valley cities were lost to Pakistan at Partition, and the search for equally ancient cities on the banks of the 'Saraswati' in India began almost immediately.)

Looking back across the river from the militarized northern border between Pakistan and India, towards the apparently peaceful civilization nurtured in the plains, the scale of that achievement seems fraught with irony. This homogenous culture covered an area larger than the contemporaneous civilizations in Egypt and Mesopotamia, stretching from the high Himalayas, to the hills of Afghanistan, right down along the river to the sea. The regularity of the town planning in all of the one thousand settlements, the uniform objects, the identical size of each of the millions of bricks, suggest a river empire with an aesthetic imprint more exacting than Victorian England's, an ambition as grand as Ashoka's, and a standardizing urge as dominant as that of modern corporate globalization. Lasting more than five hundred years it survived longer than most major empires. But it is not clear who controlled it. According to some historians, it was a socialist system, ruled neither by one dynastic despot nor, as in Pakistan, by the tyranny of an army, but by a democracy of civic bodies.

Whoever was in charge, it was the economic relationship between the interlinked cities of the river's plains and the villages in the mountains which facilitated the cities' huge construction projects and boat-building. Wood was floated downriver from isolated hill communities – still in the Stone Age – and with this, the cities in the plains built granaries, houses and boats. The transport of wood down the Indus and its tributaries, between the Himalayas and the plains, is the oldest trade that we know of in the region. It anticipated the Silk Road, pre-dated the ships of King Solomon, and facilitated the creation, in the Indus valley, of cultural artefacts which still endure in modern Pakistan.

But while it was once possible to travel this ancient highway from Kashmir to Karachi, sixty years of fighting have put an end to that. Where once merchants in the upper Indus valley exchanged cedarwood for carnelian beads, gold for cotton cloth, or – as in the case of the villagers on the banks of the Indus in Baltistan – vegetables for Tibetan salt, now the only things exchanged are shells. Not cowries but explosives.

The Line of Control is a temporary ceasefire line that was drawn across the Indus valley in 1949 and redrawn in 1972. All along it to the west, into this place of glaciers and lakes, the Pakistan Army has brought battalions and guns; from here, it sends militants across the mountains to wreak havoc in the emerald wedge of land known in Pakistan as 'India–Occupied Kashmir'. The fighting in the valley of Kashmir has come to be regarded as a battle between India's secularism and Pakistan's Islam; but Kashmir is also the source of an important Indus tributary, the Jhelum – and this, perhaps, is the real reason for the never-ending warfare.

With the cessation of this millennia-old traffic, the citizens of India and Pakistan have suffered the stifling of their mutual history, and the loss of access to lands, languages and faces that were once part of their shared vocabulary. But it is the villagers on the rim of the Indus as it enters Baltistan from India who have fared worst of all, who have indeed barely survived the cleaving of their river in two. Cut off from families and culture over the border, fired upon by Indian shells, unable to tend their fields or travel to nearby towns for supplies, the villagers in north-eastern Pakistan compete with those of the Delta as the saddest in the whole Indus valley.

Baltistan was once known as 'apricot Tibet' or 'Little Tibet'. As in the adjacent Indian provinces of Kargil and Ladakh, the people here speak a dialect of Tibetan; and though they are Shia Muslims, not Buddhists, their culture, like their language, is affiliated with the lands to the east. In a dry upland like Baltistan, the fields yield only one annual crop, and before 1947, farmers would spend three or four months of the year on trading trips east along the river to Leh, north to Kashgar in China, or down through the Deosai plains to the valley of Kashmir. Even after 1947, villagers could still move with their herds discreetly across the de facto border. Only after the 1971 war, when the army occupied Baltistan, did walking the ancient pathways become more difficult.

I want to visit the very place where the river – which for hundreds of kilometres and thousands of years has been Indian – becomes Pakistani; but it is now a transit zone beyond civilization. The capital of Baltistan is Skardu, a riverside town whose sand-swept fort juts grandly into the Indus. From Skardu to the border with India, Baltistan is off-limits to foreigners and local civilians. To go there, I will have to ask permission from the army.

Normally such a mission fills me with misgiving, but by the time I reach Skardu, I am ill, and thus I lose all inhibitions. From a small public call office on Skardu's main street, I ring Army Headquarters in Rawalpindi and ask to be taken to the border. The army, at least, does not suspect me of being a spy: I am told to report to Brigade Headquarters next morning at nine o'clock.

The Brigade Major looks me up and down. I am wearing another florid shalwar kameez and am almost sick when he offers me one of the greasy snacks disguised with mayonnaise that come regularly from the canteen in place of a proper lunch. 'This is most unusual,' he says. 'We never take civilians, or women, to the Line of Control.' He allows this information to sink in, and then he says: 'Can you wear something muted, something . . . green?' It takes me a moment to realize what he is talking about. Will the Indians mistake me for a rare bird and shoot me? 'You will be under enemy surveillance,' he says in a reprimanding tone; and I remember this remark when, weeks later in India, I drive from Srinagar to Kargil and see a sign by the road: CAUTION: YOU ARE UNDER ENEMY SURVEIL-LANCE. Like the water in the Indus, even the military language is the same on both sides of the border.

The Major, however, is exaggerating: not about the lack of women in military messes, but about the danger of being hit by Indian rockets. The ceasefire was declared in November 2003, and the farmers have almost all returned to their shell-shocked villages.

Our departure is delayed by four, five, then six days because of floods upstream. The Indus has risen and destroyed a bridge near the border, and the roads are impassable. On the seventh day we are delayed by our jeep, which breaks down outside Skardu. I stand on the banks of the Indus, looking up at the mountains all around us. The river from here to the border is grey-brown, thick with silt, and it draws the mountains right to its very edge. The cliffs are by turns sharp with serrations, or smooth with heaped sand, as if some gigantic burrowing creature has kicked up the landscape during the night. Around every stream, villages cling to the rock, fields painstakingly terraced, the greenery a tiny fringe of lace between the dull grey rock and glinting river. As we drive eastwards, a smudge of apricot trees denotes settlements in the distance, the only relief in a valley grey and brown with water and light.

During the day that it takes to reach the border, the chubby junior officer with innocent shiny cheeks who has been delegated to look after me, talks about his life. Engaged to be married, he is being sent to Siachen once he has returned me to Skardu. The tone in which he utters that name betrays his dread. All the soldiers hate it: the glacier where nothing else lives, the high altitude, the inhuman living conditions. They shave their heads before they go, then slam on their caps and do not remove them until they get back to Skardu, such is the danger of frostbite. In Baltistan, Siachen is known cynically as the army's Kuwait: 'the soldiers are paid double, they get very rich,' a jealous resident of Skardu tells me. But the shiny-cheeked officer protests at the unfairness of this statement: 'We spend all our extra pay just on rations to make life bearable,' he says.

'What is the point?' I ask. 'Why are you doing it?' He looks shaken, and hesitates before answering: 'To serve my country.'

As we drive, I am surprised to discover that many of the village names are different from those on the map I was carrying (a CIA survey from 1953, itself based on the 1945 Survey of India, and long since declassified). Over in India, the Ladakhi settlements along the Indus are still called by the names they were known by one hundred years ago. But here in Pakistan, almost every name has been superseded. Parkootta has become Mehdiabad; Gidiaksdo is now Gidiakhad. Where is Bothicho, Phulbrok or Kazburthang? Which sonorous Tibetan titles have the new Urdu names Madhupur and Mayadur replaced? There is still more confusion on the border itself. There, a village which the army calls by three different names – Vadsha, Vachra, Vadhra – is Chathatang on my map. The army says it is deserted, but the villagers who live just across the Indus from it, disagree: they tell me that thirty families live there, cut off from the world by a military cordon. I suggest to my shiny-cheeked escort that we pay it a visit. 'Impossible,' he says.

We are to stay that night at Hamzigon, the last military mess before India. The smart officers are watching an Indian film about Ashoka when we arrive, and as they have waited for us before eating, we sit awkwardly in their reception room as bikinied Indians dance distractingly on the huge TV screen and I cast about for subjects that it is safe to mention. Normally in such situations I would talk about Alexander the Great but perhaps because we are so near the border, I tell them instead that I used to live in India. 'I worked in Delhi,' I say, and then point to the television, where a dhoti-clad Kareena Kapoor is singing her love for Ashoka from a boat at Marble Rocks, a famous tourist spot in Madhya Pradesh: 'I went there once,' I say nostalgically, and enthuse about Calcutta (Kolkata), Rajasthan and Kerala: 'But I haven't yet visited Kashmir,' I say into the sudden silence, and add, 'There was the threat of terrorism and . . .' The only movement in the room is that of Kareena Kapoor's bosom on television. At last Colonel Adil, who has staring eyes and shiny boots, speaks from the line of khaki-clad soldiers on the sofa. 'Terrorism is an incorrect propaganda term,' he says, and his voice grows shrill as he adds, 'What is happening in India-Occupied Kashmir is a freedom fight.'

Something about the sight of all that khaki loosens my tongue, and having blundered once, I blunder on, and broach the subject of Kargil. This small 'war-like situation' occurred in 1999, after Pakistan invaded Indian territory unprovoked. Surprisingly, the officers in the mess are frank. 'It was badly planned,' they say, 'General Pervez was ill-advised.' But what did Musharraf hope to gain from his invasion? Indian officers argued that Musharraf aimed to cut off India's access to Ladakh, its distant northern border, as a bargaining tool to claim land from India elsewhere in India-Occupied Kashmir, and with it the Jhelum and Chenab tributaries. 'Positions are easy to defend once you have the high ground,' a Sikh officer in Kargil tells me later. 'Pakistan was very nearly successful. The hills here are treacherous.'

At first, in May 1999, after India belatedly discovered that its neighbour had crossed the Line of Control, Pakistan denied that the infiltrators were military. (Ever since their first foray into the valley of Kashmir in 1947, the army has been labelling the incursions of its own soldiers 'militant activity'.) In 1999, the army once again called the soldiers 'Mujahideen', but in Skardu, I meet a man who was employed during the war to cross the border and collect these dead 'martyrs'. 'That's when we Baltis knew there was a war going on,' he says: 'when we saw the bodies of our relatives.' Even after India captured some of the 'Mujahideen', and proved that they were army soldiers, Pakistan continued to insist that the men were not 'regular army recruits'. This was semi-true: most of those sent to die in Kargil were soldiers local to the disputed Northern Areas, and thus not part of a standard regiment. Forbidden to wear uniforms, disguised instead in tracksuits as militants, the soldiers were ill-equipped for war.

Then there was the ordeal of fighting their co-religionists. The Northern Areas is predominantly Shia – as is Kargil in India. '*Wo bhi kafir hain* [They too are unbelievers],' a Sunni officer was rumoured to have shouted at a reluctant Shia soldier. 'Shoot.'

Killing Muslims has become a big identity problem for an army whose whole ethos is religious. Sikhs and Hindus are a far more comfortable target than the Muslims it was sent to fight in Kargil. So the Punjabi officers treat Shias as Kafirs, and lies are peddled to the young recruits, to make killing fellow Muslims bearable. During the journey from Skardu to Hamzigon, my shiny-cheeked escort draws a parallel with army operations in Waziristan: 'Ninety-nine per cent of the militants killed there by the Pakistan Army were non-Muslim,' he says. 'So?' I ask, amazed. 'They were Russian, Spanish, Italian,' he says; 'internal army reports have confirmed this.'

'How many soldiers are deployed along the Line of Control?' I ask Colonel Adil now, but he flushes angrily: 'I'm afraid I can't tell you.' 'How much of the border do you patrol?' 'We are still in an enemy situation with India,' he says. 'It is not good to discuss. Indian Intelligence probably knows everything, but nevertheless.'

In fact, Kargil was an embarrassment for the Indian Army, because it had not acted on its own intelligence: that Pakistan was preparing to cross the Line of Control. It was embarrassing for Pakistan's Prime Minister, too, who claims not to have been forewarned of the operation by the Chief of Army Staff – one General Pervez. Afterwards, when the Prime Minister tried to sack Musharraf, he instead staged a coup. By October 1999, the Prime Minister was in prison, and Musharraf was installed as President.

Sitting in the mess, I tell Colonel Adil that I moved to Delhi soon after the Kargil War had ended. In 1999, India had its own fundamentalist politicians in power, and the rhetoric about Pakistan was morbid and belligerent. During my first week working for an Indian environmental organization, colleagues took me to see a play about Kargil, and I remember, in my innocence, being shocked by the jingoism. Then, on 12 October 1999, I arrived to find the office in commotion: 'Pakistan has a new military dictator.' I sat in the high brick building, watching green parrots swooping through the trees below me, and wondered what it must be like to live in the Pakistan of the Indian media: a grimly religious, violently black-hearted nation, apparently the opposite of everything that pluralist India stood for. 'Nobody liked Pakistan in those days,' I say to the soldiers on the sofa. 'I think that's one of the reasons I wanted to come here.'

After a dinner of lamb cutlets and 'pudding' – a set custard: relic of the Raj – I am shown to my room adjacent to the little-frequented mess mosque. Judging by the name on the breast pocket of the jacket which hangs like a reproach from a peg in the dressing-room, I am occupying Colonel Adil's quarters. There is a pirated copy of Clinton's autobiography on the shelf, and a book entitled *Strategic Military Surprise: Incentives and Opportunities* on his bedside table. I fall asleep thinking about warfare – about the Indus valley cities, which seem to have been undefended, without major fortifications or stores of weapons. What a civilization that must have been.

The next morning, standing on a hill barely a kilometre from the Line of Control, I look down along the vertiginous river valley into India. In 1984, the French explorer Michel Peissel claimed that this place, Dansar, solved the mystery of the legend that Herodotus had recounted, of giant ants which dig up gold along the Indus, for the villagers who live here used to forage for gold-bearing sand from the burrows of marmots. Below me are artillery lines, curved stone walls built in overlapping crescents along the hillside. I wonder what scholars of the future will make of them, the stone circles of our war-torn generation.

At Marol, a bullet-pocked hamlet used as a staging post for the Kargil War, the villagers point out the marks of Indian shells. For two years, while India bombarded the border with artillery, the villagers of Marol, Ganoks and Dansar (as Gambat Ganoks is now known) lived in a camp in Skardu. An hour's walk away in India, the villagers of Darchiks and Dha live in sunny hamlets – the warmest in Ladakh – surrounded by fields that yield two crops a year and a superfluity of flowers of every colour. But in Pakistan, the border villagers are impoverished in every way by the new political situation. The ibex they used to hunt have fled because of the firing; they live in fear of the army;

their crops frequently fail; there is no electricity (the contractor brought the pylons but not the wire); and they are forced to find work in Skardu as daily-wage labourers. They subsist at the outer edge of Pakistan, 100 kilometres from Skardu, a kilometre from India, without any rights as Pakistanis. (Baltistan is part of the disputed Northern Areas, and thus outside the Constitution: a limbo status useful to the authorities who can build dams and extract resources from the province without allowing Baltis to elect their own politicians to the National Assembly.)

'How far is it to Leh?' I ask the villagers, for the notion of travelling to India from here seems simultaneously natural and tragic. 'Riding or walking it takes nine stages, four or five days,' they say, and then add hastily: 'That is what our elders have told us, anyway. We have heard the name "Ladakh" but we have never seen it.' Until 1947, the villagers would load their fruit and vegetables into boats made of wood and animal skins (known as *zakh* in Balti) and take them along the river to Olthingthang (or Olding, as the army calls it). There they bartered apricots for supplies brought from Kargil, Leh or Srinagar. Ganoks itself was a 'halting-place' on the caravan route between Ladakh and Baltistan, where tax was levied. But now that Olthingthang is on the border, the local trade has vanished. Instead it is a long trek west to Skardu.

The inhabitants of Ganoks once shared an unusual, Kalash-like culture with the villages on the Indian side of the border. These 'Dard', 'Minaro' or 'proto-Aryans' worshipped mountain fairies, and set themselves apart from their Balti and Ladakhi neighbours with flowery headdresses. As long ago as the seventeenth century, Ali Sher Khan, who ruled Baltistan, forced his people, including those at Ganoks, to convert to Islam. But the gorge along the Indus is so narrow that armies on the march bypassed the villages altogether, and this, more than anything else, kept old customs intact. Until 1947, women from Ganoks married into the Buddhist Dard villages now in India. With Independence, and the Kashmir dispute, came army-built roads. Concomitantly with that, the Buddhism of the Indian villages and the Islam of Ganoks – for centuries thin veneers over the stronger undercurrent of collective memory – hardened into habit. In India the villages have become a tourist industry, but in Pakistan they have faded from view.

The fighting in Kashmir has severed the river road, and my journey onwards along the Indus is impossible. The only open border to India is in the Punjab, a three-day journey south. It is thus a long loop round: down to Lahore and up through Jammu to Srinagar. But this route does have advantages, for it allows me to trace the connection between the Indus valley cities of Harappa and Manda, and their Neolithic outpost in the Kashmir valley. It was an affiliation which made the ancient cities great; for in their ability to extract resources from a distance, and use the Indus as a vehicle of trade, lay their power.

Harappa stands on the banks of the same defunct river as Lahore, the Ravi. In the early nineteenth century it was here that Charles Masson found mysterious seals, imprinted with the figures of animals and the symbols of an unknown language. In 1922, these found their match in those being dredged up at Mohenjodaro, and when Harappa was finally excavated, it became apparent that the cities were models of each other. Unfortunately, much of the brick at Harappa had been removed by colonial railway builders during the laying of the line from Multan to Lahore (they saw a pile of old bricks and used them as ballast). A similar thing happened three centuries earlier, when Muslims used the bricks to build a mosque, and a thousand years before that at Mohenjodaro, when Buddhists constructed a brick stupa. Layers of history dissolve into each other around the ruins of these ancient cities.

Harappa, like Mohenjodaro, was inhabited by 'hydropathic' citizens who revelled in 'water luxury'. Built on giant platforms to elevate them above the flood plain, their raised height made it difficult to channel water from the river, and thus numerous deep wells were sunk. At the centre of the city was an enormous public bath lined with red-painted bricks. Almost every household also had an indoor bathroom, with chutes made from terracotta pipes or channels built into the wall to carry the dirty water away. Every street was properly drained and sewage pits were regularly cleaned. (I wonder from which class the sewer cleaners of the Indus Valley Civilization were drawn: the modern-day 'Bhangis', or the ancestors of today's Pirs and Syeds?) Neither Mesopotamia nor Egypt came close to the technical mastery achieved over water by the people of the Indus

valley. Not until the Romans developed their spa towns two thousand years later, would any other people rival it.

If the provenance and politics of the Indus valley people remain
a mystery, much can be learned about them from their art, if art it
was. There are small terracotta figurines of animals such as bulls, ibex
and rhinoceros, and models of men and women. Pictures were
engraved on tiny square and cylindrical clay and stone seals. These
suggest a culture that valued, even worshipped, powerful women.
One seal shows a naked woman fending off attack by two wild
beasts. Another depicts a horned female huntress with a tail, attack-
ing a tiger with her hands. Numerous clay figurines of full-breasted
women in black fan-shaped headdresses and very short skirts were
discovered – icon of a mother goddess, or perhaps a child's doll. The
most pleasing representation of womanhood, though, is the eleven-
centimetre-high bronze sculpture of a dancing girl. She is naked but
for some arm bangles and a cowrie-shell necklace; her hand sits
lightly on her hip, her feet seem to beat time, and her face is an
inscrutable study in self-assured poise.

The dancing girl's facial features are similar to those of the small
bust of a bearded man found at Mohenjodaro. Both have full lips
and a rounded nose – evidence, say some, that the Indus people were
direct descendants of migrants out of Africa 80,000 years ago. Perhaps,
as some historians have long argued, the Indus people were subsequently displaced from the valley by immigrant Aryans, thus becoming
the non-Sanskrit-speaking 'Dravidians' of south India. '*Meluhha*', the
word that Mesopotamians used for people from the Indus valley,
may be related to *mleccha*, the term that the Sanskrit-speakers used
for anybody who could not speak their language – such as those in
south India. But until the Indus valley script is deciphered, this theory
remains just that – tempting but unsubstantiated.

If only we knew what the Indus valley seals meant, they might
provide a clue to the city-dwellers' anonymity. But of all the provoca-
tive relics retrieved from the ruins, the script has remained a mystery.
A century later, there have been some ingenious but unconvincing
attempts to decode them. A scholar from Tamil Nadu in south India
has argued that the script is related to his own Dravidian mother
tongue. North Indian Hindu 'historians', wishing to prove that the

horse-riding Aryans were indigenous to India, gratuitously adapted a seal of a bull to make it look like a horse (there is no evidence of horses in the Indus Valley Civilization). In Pakistan, one historian has compared the symbols with marks made by Muslim masons and even modern washer-people. In Hyderabad, I meet a translator who claims that the language is related to Sindhi – and to my delight, he writes my name in Indus valley script.

Given the lack of clear evidence, many theories have sprung up about the Indus people's provenance, beliefs and social organization. But if it is true that the Indus cities are a lost paradise, where even the workers lived in tidy, well-planned houses with good drainage and free access to sweet-water wells, then the contrast with modernity is shameful. In the countryside around Harappa, feudal lords live in whitewashed mansions, a constant rebuke to the straw huts of their workers. I stay in a village where the landowner has one well for his garden, and another for all three hundred sharecroppers. Then again, who fired all the bricks, and channelled the water, five thousand years ago? Did the Indus cities keep slaves, whose presence in the archaeological record has simply disappeared? At the kiln next to the archaeological site at Harappa I watch labourers loading raw grey bricks into the kilns and hauling pink ones from the ashes. Today, this is one of the worst-paid jobs in Pakistan; a quick route to indentured labour. I wonder if it was any different then.

From the excavation site at Harappa it is a short walk down across a field of green spring maize, to the village of Harappa Basti where the modern potters live. There are mounds of broken pots here, walls of them, hills of them. The cities of the Indus valley used waste from kilns as damp-proof layers in most of their buildings. Centuries later, the Vedic texts describe 'ruined places where one might collect potsherds for ritual purposes'. Perhaps it was the ruins of Harappa that the priests were describing.

Harappa Basti is a poor village: everything from wheel-turned pots to blacksmithery to joinery, is done by hand, for there is no electricity. In a street particularly notable for the mass production of clay jars to be sold for a pittance in Lahore, is a man who makes a living reproducing artefacts from the Indus Valley Civilization. Muhammad Nawaz has little clay replicas of female figurines with their breasts stuck on like currants. There are striped clay tigers, elephants, and birds that whistle when you blow across them. Using his everyday wheel and kiln he can reproduce exact copies of Harappan pots – suggesting that the technology has not changed for five thousand years. Here in Harappa Basti, one could almost imagine that Harappa and Mohenjodaro never died; they just submerged themselves beneath the tides of oncoming cultures.

If it is still impossible to say whether or not the Indus valley language has continuities with those in south Asia today, it is easy to observe non-linguistic parallels: in the wreck of these cities, the antiquity of Pakistani life is visible. The sculpture of the bearded man found at Mohenjodaro wears a shawl engraved with a trefoil pattern and encrusted with traces of red pigment – a garment similar to the red and indigo *ajrak*, a hand-printed cotton scarf worn by every Sindhi peasant. The boats plied by the Mohana boat-people of Sukkur, and the bullock carts driven by Pakistani villagers, are almost identical to those carved on Indus valley seals or moulded into terracotta toys. A version of the Sindhi *borrindo*, a hollow clay ball with holes that the musician blows across, was found at Harappa. Even Islamabad, Pakistan's planned capital, echoes Mohenjodaro's ordered grid formation.

When I first went to Mohenjodaro – where the saline soil is destroying the bricks and threatening the ancient remains – I was prepared to see this non-Islamic culture as an anomaly in Pakistan. Replicas of the famous dancing girl statue are rarely to be found in the houses of the elite (the dancing girl, dressed only in bangles, does not do purdah). The lack of interest in the ancient history of this land seemed symptomatic of a larger malaise: a disregard for the simple pleasures of the *desi*, the local – cloth, pottery, art – that cuts across the classes in Pakistan.

But when I reached Mohenjodaro, I changed my mind. My guide was a muezzin, the man who called the prayer in the local mosque. 'Double-storey,' he kept saying proudly as we walked round the excavated city. 'Look. Double-storey house.' He lived in a one-storey hut behind the museum. Walking through those wide streets, past houses, wells and baths, it was impossible not to feel the puzzlement and awe that archaeologists must have felt when these cities were suddenly uncovered in the 1920s, and that the muezzin was expressing now. The afternoon was casting long shadows over the third millennium BCE brickwork as he led me finally to the front of the complex where there was a line of modern clay water pots and a small brick mosque. I watched as he took off his shoes, performed his ablutions, and walked inside to call the prayer. It seemed a harmonious juxtaposition: the simple twentieth-century brick mosque (without even a loudspeaker) and the ruins of the cosmopolitan brick city that once traded cotton across the seas.

Like all subsequent civilizations on the river, the people of Mohenjodaro and Harappa became rich by developing the technology of flood defence — burnt brick — which allowed them to exploit the alluvium that the river brought down from the mountains. By 7000 BCE farmers in the Indus valley had adapted the technology of agriculture, which arrived from the Middle East in the form of wheat and barley, to domesticate their own wild plants, sesame and aubergine. In Sindh, there is a legend that the date trees which grow here germinated from the seeds that Muhammad Bin Qasim's soldiers spat out as they marched upriver in 711 CE. In fact, the date, *Phoenix dactylifera*, is one of the earliest Indus valley crops, cultivated here since before 5000 BCE. Acacia and neem trees are depicted on Indus valley seals, as is the peepul tree (*Ficus religiosa*), an object of worship today in India.

The Indus people also domesticated the cotton plant, and it is this that made them prosperous: the export of cloth downriver and across the Arabian Sea to Mesopotamia and possibly to Egypt. The Egyptian pharaohs, Sindhis say, wore Indus cotton. Centuries later, the Babylonian word for cloth was *sindhu*, and in Greek it was *sindo-n* — as today, cotton was the Indus valley's most important export.

A crucial adjunct to Mohenjodaro's prosperity was boat-building. The cities of Mohenjodaro and Harappa were built in the wake of a 'transport revolution'. Once they had mastered the technology, and learned how to use the river to export surplus goods, everything else followed. Maybe, as some in Pakistan maintain, Mohenjodaro ought to be known as *Mohana*-daro — the city of the boat-people. From the time of the Indus cities, until the advent of trains in the nineteenth century, the river was the spinal cord of all local trade, connecting towns and villages, resources and people that otherwise would never have met.

The extraordinary reach of the Indus valley cotton trade has been proved beyond doubt by the seals found in contemporary Mesopotamian sites. Villages inhabited by the 'Meluhha' were located near Mesopotamian cities. What the Meluhha took home to the Indus valley in exchange is less clear. Bitumen, perhaps, to line the great bath; possibly copper. Another theory is that they imported wheat.

To build large houses and solid granaries, the Indus cities needed strong, tall timber from trees which did not grow in the moist jungles of the plains. Cedar was as important to the Indus valley cities as it was to King Gilgamesh on the banks of the Euphrates (who made an epic pilgrimage up into the mountains to kill the demon of the cedar forest). The best and nearest cedar was grown in the Himalayas – hence the importance of the Indus and its tributaries. In order to manage this vital trade, a Harappan satellite settlement was established in the north on the banks of the Chenab, a river that flows from the wooded highlands down to the Punjab and into the Indus. This was Manda, the midpoint on my journey from Harappa to Srinagar in Indian Kashmir.

Manda now stands in the hills above Jammu in India, only a few kilometres from the border with Pakistan. It too is an army town. Perhaps because of its strategic location in a sensitive border area, tourism is not encouraged, and today this dramatic site is difficult to locate beneath the overgrown weeds. During the eighteenth century, a fort was built over the third millennium BCE city; and since then the whole area has been encroached upon by the police and by the state government. The office of the local archaeological department, inside the fort, is a sedate mess of decomposing files.

I step into the battlements of the fort and look down through the castellations at the fast-flowing river. A wooden boat is bringing twelve passengers over the water to the Kali temple below the fort, and as it reaches the landing stage, the small craft spins in the current. Unlike at Mohenjodaro and Harappa, where the river has shifted away, the Chenab still flows in its original channel and, for the first time, I am able to stand in the middle of an Indus valley city and witness with my own eyes the convenience afforded to these ancient cities by a riverbank location.

Archaeologists believe that Manda's own trading post was Burzahom, over one hundred kilometres away to the north, in the valley of Kashmir. The journey from Jammu to Srinagar takes ten hours in a small bumpy jeep. After a day of climbing through steep conifer forest, the jeep reaches the lip of the valley, and there Kashmir opens up like the wings of a green and yellow butterfly on a dull brown rock. It only takes this journey and this vista to understand the devotion Kashmir has inspired in emperors and poets throughout India's history. Haunted by Islamic militants, policed by the Indian Army – whose soldiers stand like tense scarecrows in every mustard field and orchard – Kashmir has not yet been destroyed by the clashing martial power of Pakistan and India. But it has come very close.

In 2600 BCE, Burzahom and Manda were separated by a cultural void. Unlike the sophisticated urban settlement at Manda, Burzahom was a Neolithic community, lifted out of its Stone Age context only by the luxury goods which it received from the people downstream – agate beads, black-painted pots, copper pins, bangles and arrow-heads. While the merchants from Manda, who bought Burzahom's wood, built brick houses in the plains, the people of Burzahom continued to live in square, rectangular, circular or oval pits. Their tools were made of stone or polished bone, they fired pottery, and smeared the skeletons of their dead with red ochre. On the land adjacent to their wattle and daub pit-houses they erected menhirs in a semicircle. It was an impulse they shared with prehistoric people from northern Pakistan to England, from Ireland to Tibet. At Burzahom, as at other places, the huge stone menhirs may have been a form of solar worship. (The name of Srinagar, nearby, means City of the Sun.)

Like today's tall, rosy-cheeked Kashmiris, Burzahom's Neolithic community was unusually healthy. Skeletal remains show that the people were tall – if not nine foot, as the modern villagers tell me, six foot at least – and well nourished. They ate venison and goat; pigs and rice were introduced from China around 2000 BCE; and wheat and barley, winter crops, grew easily, needing no irrigation.

Burzahom was occupied by Neolithic humans until at least 1000 BCE, some nine hundred years after the decline of Mohenjodaro and Harappa. Whatever calamity suddenly rendered the cities of the plains uninhabitable, it appears not to have affected the Stone Age humans. Enclosed by the mountains, on the edge of the lake, circled by tall cedars, they had everything they needed. The site was never completely abandoned and today there is a small village nearby. A Muslim graveyard abuts the menhirs.

Down in the plains it was different. There, around 2000 BCE, the Indus cities were suddenly deserted. Archaeologists still disagree over the causes of this abrupt exodus. Perhaps resources dried up in the mountains; maybe deforestation caused disaster in the plains. Some blame the Aryans (presumably the lightly fortified Indus cities would have been unable to defend themselves from attack by horse-riding invaders – a fate militarized Pakistan hopes never to repeat). Others suggest that it was the river, with its flooding and meanderings, which caused their destruction.

If the Indus cities' dependence on water ruined them, then the story today may be mimicking that ancient plotline. Water shortage has reached critical levels in both India and Pakistan. The Pakistani states of Punjab and Sindh are on the brink of war over access to the Indus waters; in India, the neighbouring states of Punjab and Haryana dispute how the waters of the Ravi and Beas should be shared. Both countries need the waters of the Jhelum and Chenab, and many people agree that it is a thirst for water that has caused them to vie for control of Kashmir. Just as Manda and Harappa extracted resources from the distant mountains, so the ongoing war repeats that archaic refrain.

At Burzahom where the menhirs stand, it is easy to see Kashmir as paradise on earth, as Indians long have. One can only hope that when Pakistan, India and China dam the life out of their rivers – when the brick cities in the plains perish once again – the paradise will survive, as it has done till now.

I I

Huntress of the Lithic

Stone Age

'How was the world of humans formed?
In the beginning there was water and some ice froze
Some dust settled upon the ice
Some grass grew upon it
Then arose three mountains.'

Mi-Yul Dangpo (Dard song)

B URZAHOM, WITH ITS semicircle of Neolithic menhirs, has been studied since at least the 1930s. But when Indian archaeologists began to excavate there in 1964, they discovered that its history ran deeper than a mere five thousand years. A large stone menhir had been used as the outside wall of a building occupied in the third millennium BCE. On its underside, in a part buried deep in the mud, was a carving that had been made several thousand years before that.

The carving, a hunting scene, tells a rare and redolent story. In the middle of the picture is a stag. On the left is a man crouching, taking aim with a bow. In the sky are two rayed discs, possibly the sun and moon or the rising sun, and near them is a dog. The archer, stag and dog all have prominent penises, but there is a second hunter in the carving who does not. Standing to the right, holding a long spear that pierces the stag right through, is a buxom woman dressed in a skirt. This carving was a wonderful find. Were I an Indian feminist, this stone would be my icon.

The very far north of India, from Kashmir to Ladakh, has been renowned since antiquity for the freedom of its women. The ancient Sanskrit-speakers called this area '*Strirajya*': Government by Women. The Mahabharata, India's defining Sanskrit epic, speaks half-nostalgically of the ancient liberty of women, who once 'roved about at their pleasure, independent'. 'Such was the rule in early times'; 'it is still practised among the northern Kurus.'

Uttarakuru, the land of the Northern Kurus, was known in ancient Sanskrit texts as a paradise. In the Ramayana, the Northern Kurus are described as 'liberal, prosperous, perpetually happy, and undecaying. In their country there is neither cold nor heat, nor decrepitude, nor disease, nor grief, nor fear, nor rain, nor sun.' Uttarakuru's boundary was the River Sila, which turned to stone anything that touched it. It was a land ruled by women, where no man could dwell for more than half a year.

Foreign visitors to India repeated stories they had heard of Uttarakuru's legendary women. It is probably Uttarakuru that became Megasthenes' 'Hyperborea', the Indian land to the north whose inhabitants lived for a thousand years. In the seventh century CE, the *Sui Shu* (History of the Sui Dynasty) described Ladakh as the 'Empire of the Eastern Women'. The backpacking monk Xuanzang, who journeyed through the Buddhist lands of India in the seventh century, repeated this lore, noting that Uttarakuru is the '*kingdom of the women*' where for 'ages a woman has been the ruler'. The husband of the queen 'knows nothing about the affairs of the state', he wrote. 'The men manage the wars and sow the land, and that is all.'

According to the twelfth-century Sanskrit history, Kalhana's *Rajatarangini*, Uttarakuru was north-east of Kashmir, equating to present-day Ladakh. The Kashmiris feared and respected the beautiful mountain Amazons. King Lalitaditya, who ruled Kashmir in the eighth century, only managed to defeat Strirajya by making its queen fall in love with him. The women of Strirajya, meanwhile, seduced Lalitaditya's warriors by exposing their 'high breasts'.

The Sanskrit texts described Uttarakuru as a land where for both men and women, promiscuity was the norm. This was probably a reference to polyandry – when a woman takes more than one husband – which is still practised in Ladakh and Tibet. Polyandry was possibly more widespread throughout India in ancient times than it is today: the five brother-heroes of the Mahabharata share one wife, Draupadi. But in the Mahabharata this arrangement was strange and shocking enough by the time the epic was compiled to need explanation, and was thus probably a last, faint memory of an era when matriarchs still controlled families and polities. North-west of India, however, in what is now northern Pakistan, Kashmir, Afghanistan and Central Asia, polyandry endured. Alberuni, the eleventh-century Muslim historian of India, observed that polyandry was practised from eastern Afghanistan to Kashmir. An eighteenth-century Chinese text noted that it was prevalent not only in Ladakh and Tibet but also in Baltistan, the Hindu Kush and Central Asia.

That the freedom of women was integral to the utopia in the Indian texts, says as much about the attitude of the Sanskrit-speakers of the epics, as it does about the Northern Kurus themselves. Other male visitors to Ladakh and Tibet, however, found polyandry disturbing. Alberuni called it an 'unnatural kind of marriage'. The eighteenth-century Jesuit priest Desideri, one of the first Europeans to visit Tibet, condemned it as an 'odious custom'. Alexander Cunningham, writing in 1854, speculated that polyandry was responsible for the short stature of the women in Ladakh. In his novel *Kim*, published in 1901, Rudyard Kipling characterized this area as the 'lands where women make the love' and told a cautionary tale of a polyandrous Buddhist woman from Kinnaur (just south of Ladakh). This Woman of Shamlegh, adorned with 'turquoise-studded headgear', propositions Kipling's handsome young hero and disparages her many husbands as 'cattle'. Kipling's contemporary, an easily shocked Moravian missionary, the Reverend A. H. Francke, noted that there was a strong strain of archaic mother-worship in the Buddhism practised in Ladakh, and that during British censuses, the children of Tibetan Buddhist families were unable to state who their father was, there were so many possible candidates. Polyandry, he concluded, was 'one of the ugliest customs'. Chinese scholars writing on Tibet in the 1950s echoed centuries of male consensus, calling polyandry an 'abnormal form of marriage' in which women are 'physically ruined by primitive and barbarous habits'.

If any of these men had asked the women at the centre of the polyandrous marriages their opinion, they might have been surprised by the response. Adelphic or fraternal polyandry, as the practice of brothers sharing a wife is known, was eventually outlawed in Ladakh by the Maharaja of Kashmir in 1941, and in Tibet by the Chinese in

1959. Nevertheless, some families in Ladakh are still polyandrous, and in Tibet it is once again on the increase. The reason is partly cultural, and partly to do with economic prudence: polyandry keeps the birth rate down, avoids inheritance issues and lessens the pressure on scarce resources. In contrast to the situation among Hindu and Muslim families in India and Pakistan, where properties are subdivided among the new children of each generation, in polyandrous families brothers share a wife, so population does not increase and landholdings remain entire. With multiple fathers contributing to the well-being of their joint children, women also benefit. In marked contrast to other places in the Indus valley, the women of Ladakh are said to be 'powerful' and 'uninhibited' with a 'strong position' in society.

The pre-Buddhist religion of both Ladakh and western Tibet was Bon, an amalgam of animistic hunting beliefs with a more formalized set of demons, spirits and especially female goddesses and fairies. The Dards, also known as Brokpa ('hill person') or Minaro, were living in Ladakh before the arrival in the eighth century of the Tibetans, who today make up the ethnic majority of Ladakh, and they still worship female deities in the form of stones and ibex horns. Today the Dards exist only in that military zone where the Indus flows from India into Pakistan; but once they dominated most of Ladakh, at least as far east as Leh, and possibly as far west as Gilgit and Chitral in Pakistan; the Kalash may be part of the same cultural group. With their diverse marital arrangements – polyandry and polygyny were practised in their villages until recently – the Dards, like the Kalash, have a more relaxed attitude to sexuality than any of their Christian, Muslim or Hindu visitors and neighbours. With their mountain fairies, goddesses of water and hunting, and witches, they still celebrate powerful women. Perhaps it was Dard culture, then, which first earned for northern India its feminist designation.

The carving at Burzahom thus stands chronologically in the vanguard of an ancient tradition. But if this is the case, it is a theory which has received no attention from Indian archaeologists. Partly this is because the stone has been misinterpreted by later scholars. For forty years now – ever since the original stone carving was taken out of Kashmir by the Archaeological Survey of India and sequestered away from public view – academics have relied for their analyses on photographs, or drawings taken from bad photocopies. And so this carving, after lying unaltered for eight thousand years, has undergone a sex change. The first photographs, taken in 1964, clearly showed the spear-holding figure to be a bosomy woman, wearing (unlike the man) a dress. B. M. Pande – who examined the carving – affirmed in 1971 that the 'small chip between the legs of the female figure is a natural break and does not represent the genitalia'. A decade later, this chip had become a penis; and in more recent drawings, the woman's bosom – voluptuous in the original photographs – grew flatter and eventually disappeared altogether. Frustratingly, I am unable to study the stone because the Archaeological Survey of India won't show the original to the public (I asked them). Are they afraid of the revolution this ancient example of cooperation between the sexes might foment? Or have they forgotten where they put it? I spend a week arranging an interview with the man in charge of the Burzahom carving, and then, thirty seconds after explaining my request, I am ushered out of his office.

Most archaeologists have been more preoccupied with determining the carving's age than the social order it represents. The latest Indian interpretation, from 'archo-astronomers' in Mumbai, is that the carving is a 'sky chart' from the sixth millennium BCE. The discs in the sky are the full moon and a supernova (an imploding star at the end of its life). The stag, dog and human figures (both of which they take to be men) are constellations; and the four penises they see in the carving are plotted as stars in the sky over Kashmir. The archo-astronomers have decided that the Burzahom people carved a picture of Supernova HB9 on the rock, a star which died in a burst of white light in 5700 BCE. If they are right – and this estimate matches earlier guesses as to the antiquity of the settlement, based on the discovery of stone tools – then the carving was drawn by people who lived in Kashmir a full three thousand years before Harappa.

As I am standing beside the menhirs at Burzahom, the caretaker wanders over. I ask him why there is no museum, even though according to archaeological reports from the time of the excavations, one was due to be built in the 1970s. I have already visited the State Archaeology Department in one of Srinagar's heavily guarded government buildings, where clerks sit drinking tea all day long in darkened rooms stacked high with unread files. The people there explained that 'Funds for a museum were not forthcoming' and that 'There is too much tension in the valley.' But the caretaker has an idea: 'There is a man who has been working here,' he says, 'a man from the University. A good, sincere man.' 'Is it Dr Bandy?' I ask, for I have heard about him from the State Archaeology Department. 'Exactly,' says the caretaker. He walks with me down into the village and bangs on the door of his cousin, who drives an auto-rickshaw. 'Take her to the University,' he says.

The University is in northern Srinagar, beyond the Nageen lake and opposite the mosque distinguished by its possession of a hair from the Prophet Muhammad's head. At the gate I make enquiries and am directed down a long avenue of rose bushes towards the Central Asian Museum where, despite the 'tension' of living in a war zone, Dr Bandy and his staff have assembled an absorbing collection of artefacts representing Kashmir's history over the past ten millennia. Dr Bandy shows me the reconstruction of one of the dwelling pits at Burzahom, and points out a large print of the absentee carving. We sit in his office as he elucidates the different theories about the people who carved the Burzahom hunting scene. 'You must meet my student, Mumtaz Yatoo,' Dr Bandy says, picking up the phone. 'He has just discovered a rock carving even more ancient than the Burzahom one, in the hills near Sopore, his home town.'

Mumtaz arrives ten minutes later, carrying copies of the articles he has written on the carving and smiling at the spectacle of my excitement. 'It is probably Palaeolithic, up to twenty thousand years old,' he says, spreading a drawing of the carving on the office desk. 'Stone tools were found in the woods nearby which show that the area was occupied by humans even before that.'

The son of a local apple farmer, Mumtaz was shown the carving after months of methodical searching by a shepherd. It is, he says, located high up on a wooded hill in northern Kashmir, incised into a rock face, and thus immoveable, even for India's Archaeological Department. Pleased by my enthusiasm for his discovery, he offers to take me there himself: 'You can stay in Sopore with my family,' he says. 'When shall we set off?'

We leave Srinagar the next morning, taking the bus north through carefully tended apple orchards to Sopore, where Mumtaz persuades a friend to drive us on to the village of Bomoi. The friend drops us where the road ends at the edge of the village, and we walk the rest of the way along a dirt track and up into the hills.

It has rained hard this summer and the earth is heavy and dark. The afternoon light trickles through the leaves of the thin Kashmiri trees, illuminating the wooded slope where women in headscarves are gathering herbs. Moving slowly through the luminescent sheen cast by the trees, it is as if we have swum down below the surface of a light-dappled pond into another, more serene world, far away from jihadis and men with guns. But this is an illusion. 'This area was a hotbed of Mujahideen,' one of the villagers says later.

The women of Bomoi village ignore us but the menfolk appear to have the afternoon off; as we climb, all able-bodied males between the ages of seven and twenty-seven drop what they are doing and follow us steeply up through the trees to the rock face. There must be a crowd of fifty men and boys by the time we get to the stone, all of them wearing the Kashmiri *pheren*, a full-length woollen shirt-cloak. The boys speak little English, but it is the cricket season now, and from the babble of Kashmiri that surrounds me, entire phrases of BBC commentary emerge fully-formed: 'Flintoff is coming in to bowl,' says one twelve-year-old. 'It's a bouncer,' says another. 'Next time,' says Mumtaz, 'we will come during a cricket game, and then nobody will take any notice.'

The pale-brown rock face looms above our heads and even today is distinct from the rocks around it by being clear of lichen and moss. The carving itself is deeply cut but faded, and the best view is had from the glade of trees below, which leads Mumtaz to speculate that the carving might have been the seat of a priest or priestess. Nothing I have seen in northern Pakistan, or will see along the Indus in Ladakh, is quite like this surreal, dreamlike tableau. It is a busy, even frenzied drawing, a hallucinatory hunting scene. There are human stick-figures wearing masks or armour, running to and fro. Towards the middle are two splayed animals or animal skins. On the left, and down the right-hand side, are circles of varying sizes, each made up of concentric rings. Connecting all these elements are long carved lines.

Little is known about the lives of Palaeolithic humans, less still about the meaning of their art. Archaeologists and art historians have argued about the cave pictures found in Spain and France – the lithe paintings of bison and deer that inspired Picasso and which have been carbon-dated from 15,000 to 32,000 years old. Masked human figures have been interpreted as shamans or oracles, and broad correlations have been drawn with the hunting rites of tribes elsewhere in the world, in which the skin and bones of the dead animal are laid out on the ground as a means of symbolically regenerating the hunted beast. Both these elements – the masked hunters and the skinned beast – appear to be represented in the Bomoi carving, and advocates of the school of Palaeolithic history which has it that human society all over the world at this time was dominated by magic-led hunting rituals, would undoubtedly read this carving as a depiction of shamanistic rites. But Mumtaz, the villagers and I all have other, competing theories.

With its rayed discs and human hunting scene, the carving at Bomoi is clearly related to that at Burzahom, and this suggests a local continuity of culture over a period of 20,000 years. Standing under the trees, trying to make out the faded carved lines, I wonder if there is any connection between the Palaeolithic stone-carvers and the Dards, who still hunt ibex and are the earliest known inhabitants of the north-eastern Indus valley – or whether it is absurd to draw correlations between Palaeolithic and modern humans, who, even if they do have a common genetic inheritance and inhabit the same landscape, might not necessarily share the same culture. If there is an answer, it lies in Ladakh. Dard groups still exist north of Sopore along the Kishanganga river, but the most distinctive Dard villagers are those next to the Indus on the Baltistan–Ladakh border, and in the Zanskar valley, a remote Indus tributary in central Ladakh.

As Mumtaz and I are examining the stone, the children crowd round us. Bemused by the strange woman who has marched straight through their village to look at some ancient scratches on a rock, one of them says drolly in English: 'Very big rock. Very solid rock.' 'Very important rock,' says Mumtaz; and he asks the boys in Kashmiri: 'Well, what do you think it shows?' There is some conferring. 'They are saying,' translates Mumtaz, 'that it was carved by an Englishman one hundred years ago.' Mumtaz points to the top circle: 'That is the sun [*aftab*]. That is the moon [*zoon*]. And that,' he indicates the circle on the left with rays sticking out like legs, 'that is a samovar. A teapot.'

I laugh, but with my usual bias to things aquatic I have developed a different theory. Through the trees, the landscape below glints with water, reflecting the colours of the valley's fecundity. 'What is the lake in the distance?' I ask Mumtaz. 'Wular lake,' he says. 'So,' I say, 'the concentric circles are pools of rippling water. The rays coming out of them are their tributaries. The three large circles represent lakes, and the smaller circles are ponds. This is Wular,' I point to the top circle, 'and that is the Dal lake,' my finger moves to the middle circle. 'No, that would be Manasabal,' says Mumtaz; 'the bottom one is Dal perhaps.' 'And this' – my finger traces the long curved line that bisects the picture horizontally from side to side – 'is the Jhelum river.' 'Ingenious,' Mumtaz says, 'but I think it is more likely that these three circles are the rising sun.' 'Last ball of the over,' says a boy behind me.

Months later, when I am back in England, Mumtaz writes to tell me that soon after I passed through Sopore, the archo-astronomy team from Mumbai visited the carving with him and proposed an even more ambitious theory. 'The circles are a comet moving through the sky,' Mumtaz writes, 'and simultaneously the lakes that were formed in Kashmir after the comets crashed into the earth.' The research is still at an early stage but the archo-astronomers are trying to establish whether the Wular, Manasabal and Dal lakes were indeed formed by meteor impact; and they are searching the astronomical record for meteor showers from Palaeolithic times. They are sure that the carving was drawn by humans who hunted and foraged their food from the surrounding hillsides, much as the women are doing now.

On the other side of the rock face from the carving is a small cave where it is thought that Palaeolithic humans may have camped. From there, Mumtaz, his three village friends and I walk down through the trees and along the spine of the hill. Only the children are following us now. We jump over an almost invisible stream and walk up towards a Neolithic burial mound where the villagers have found stone mace-heads, axes and sling balls – and where Mumtaz once looked up from excavating to see five wolves staring at him with big yellow eyes. From the brow of the hill I turn and see the children standing below us, ranged in a forlorn line along the stream we have just crossed. 'Why have they stopped?' I ask. 'They won't follow us beyond the village boundary,' Mumtaz says.

At dusk we reach the adjacent village. There, houses are being rebuilt following the Kashmir earthquake – using old-style timber rather than concrete, for modern building techniques have proved fickle in this tectonically unstable land. As we move along the edges of the flooded fields, the village men talk of Kashmir, unburdening themselves of their disappointed life histories. They speak bitterly of the Pakistani Mujahideen: 'Nowadays we are not so deceived by their false promises of freedom,' one man says. Nor does the Indian state offer much hope; nobody in India, they say, wants to employ a Kashmiri Muslim. The only advantage that Kashmiris have is the law which forbids Indians from buying land in the valley: 'So even poor people here have a house and farmland.'

They press us to stay the night in the village but Mumtaz refuses. Back in Sopore, his mother is cooking our supper.

That night, I discuss the rest of my journey with Mumtaz. From here I will travel east, following traces of Palaeolithic culture into Ladakh, the high altitude desert bisected horizontally by the Indus. Mumtaz, who knows so much about Kashmiri history, has never been to neighbouring Ladakh. The Indo-Pakistani dispute has its own internal reverberations within India, and Ladakhis, who are predominantly Buddhist, no longer trust their Muslim neighbours. So the next morning I bid Mumtaz farewell, and with my pockets full of apples from his orchard, travel on into Ladakh alone.

Cut off from India for six to eight months of the year, Ladakh was opened up comparatively recently to the army (1962), and to tourism (1974), only after it acquired strategic importance for India on account of two international border disputes: one with China to the north and the other with Pakistan to the west. How completely it exists at one remove from the Indian mainstream was illustrated clearly when L. K. Advani, India's right-wing Hindu Home Minister, visited Ladakh in the late 1990s. 'What is the river here?' he asked his hosts, who told him that it was the Senge Tsampo – using the local Tibetan name for the river; the Sindhu, they added, using the Sanskrit appellation. 'The what?' Advani asked; then somebody explained: the Indus. Back in Delhi, perhaps to compensate for his poor geography, Advani founded the 'Sindhu Darshan', an annual Hindu pilgrimage to Buddhist Ladakh in order to purify the river with the waters of the Brahmaputra and Ganga before it flows into Muslim Pakistan. It is a mission of the extremist Hindu groups with which Advani is affiliated to reclaim 'western India' from Pakistan; and so, in the Home Minister's hands, the Indus – which the rest of India had largely forgotten – became 'a symbol of nationalism and national integration', evocative of the sacrifices made by Indian soldiers during the Kargil War and the loss of life and land at Partition.

If Ladakh's prehistory has been bowdlerized by politicians, it has also been neglected by historians. Numerous scholars have written about Kashmir since Kalhana first put his thoughts down on paper; but the ancient history of Ladakh has been very little studied. During the past sixty years since Independence, the Archaeological Survey of India has made only cursory examinations of Ladakh's Neolithic and Palaeolithic settlements, and there has never been a comprehensive survey by a trained archaeologist of the thousands of prehistoric rock carvings all along the river. Thus historians are still unsure when humans first arrived in Ladakh, where they came from, and how they relate to the two distinct groups that survive here – the Dards and the Tibetans.

Twenty years ago, one isolated clue was published in an academic journal: a rock carving of a giant made on the banks of a small Indus tributary near Kargil, that district of western Ladakh inhabited by Shias. The new giant was similar to the fifty or so carvings found on the banks of the Indus at Chilas in Pakistan – a large human figure with outstretched arms and a small round head. But intriguingly, it also had both a long penis and a child upside down in the womb – not an easy topic to discuss with polite, purdah-observing Muslims. However, the article did not specify the carving's location, so I draw an edited version of it in my notebook and set off for Kargil.

The route traverses the Zoji-La pass, and here the landscape changes just as dramatically as it did at the other end of the Kashmir valley, from verdant fields and trees to dry twisting valleys of folded rock. I remember the folk tale about the fury of a spurned goddess that is told by the people of Ladakh to explain their country's dryness.

The Tibetan goddess Du-zhi Lhamo discovered that her husband was planning to leave her behind in Kashmir while he travelled to Ladakh, because, he complained, she smelt Kashmiri. Angered at this insult she turned her back on Ladakh, causing it to 'dry up, and Kashmir to become fertile'. Perhaps because of its aridity, the people of this land have always been thrifty, self-sufficient (and polyandrous). Given the limited possibilities of agriculture at such a high altitude, every household in Ladakh spends the summer drying the one annual crop of vegetable leaves and roots to last through the long hard winter.

The bus drops me on the empty Leh road and I walk down the path into the river valley, where, in the small village at the bottom, I show the men sitting outside the teashop the drawing I have made. But they shake their heads. Never seen anything like it, they say, and we have roamed the hills here all our lives. They call the shopkeeper, then a village elder. They too shake their heads. Somebody hands me a cup of tea in compensation.

At two o'clock the school closes, and the Headmaster, a male secondary school teacher and Fatima, a primary school teacher, come over and join me. The Headmaster is a broad-minded man who tells me that his family only converted to Islam from Buddhism 'a generation ago.' 'Much of our culture is Buddhist still,' he says. He is intrigued by the carving, though he too has never seen it.

With every cup of tea my conviction has deepened that the carving must have been destroyed by anti-nudists. But just then a labourer comes by from the neighbouring village. 'Yes,' he says, 'there's something like that just over the stream. I remember it from my childhood.'

The teachers and I climb into the Headmaster's car and we drive the short distance to the neighbouring village. When we get to the rock face we find to our relief that nobody knows about the carving simply because a screen of willow trees was planted in the past ten years, and this has obscured it from sight. In the time since it was first cut into the rock thousands of years ago, the earth has given way below, and the carving now stands on a cliff face twenty feet high. From the ground I can see only parts of the carving through the fluttering willow leaves.

The three teachers stand at the bottom of the cliff as I climb up the screed and out along the narrow ledge. If I fall I will break both legs. Already I can see the giant's outstretched arms and long thin fingers. As I edge closer, I can see the penis and the upside-down baby in the womb. Level with my legs are cruder carvings of hunters and ibex; and where my navel touches rock are elaborately drawn animals and a bird probably added many centuries later. But I cannot see the giant's face through the branches: and my knees are shaking with fear. The Headmaster shouts that somebody has brought a ladder, and so I climb slowly down.

There are two ladders. One is put up against the cliff. It reaches to the base of the carving and the Headmaster climbs up it and pulls back the branches. The other is propped against the tree, and as Fatima shrieks at me to be careful I clamber up and crawl out along a branch from which I can bounce up and down and examine the carving bit by bit through the leaves. The rock face is a warm pink, and as at Bomoi, the engraved lines have coloured more darkly than the uncarved areas. I had guessed from the drawing that the genitalia and womb were added later; but up close there is no discernible difference in the texture of the lines hammered into the rock. Perhaps this giant really was intended from the beginning as a deity of both sexes.

Dancing up and down in the willow tree, trying to glimpse the giant's penis-womb, I think of the much more recent giant carving at Mulbekh, twenty kilometres up the valley from here. This nine-metre-high Maitreya Buddha, the cord of whose tunic dangles between his legs like a massive member, was carved into a 'phallus-shaped rock' (as the Kargil Government literature puts it) in the eighth century. Standing face to face with the male-female giant I wonder if it was this that inspired the Mulbekh stonemason. Moreover there is something feminine about the tilt of the Mulbekh Buddha's hips – the union of male and female is a Tantric notion – and I can understand how, when British archaeologists began exploring Ladakh, they mistook some of the more sensuous Buddha statues for depictions of women.

When the first Buddhist missionaries came into this land in the first century CE, they often appropriated the worship-places and deities of the local people. Both megalithic standing stones and ancient rock carvings were inscribed with images of stupas to make them

Buddhist. Giants, clearly a central part of the cosmology of the indigenous people of this land, also informed Buddhist legends. The Tibetan theory of the Origin of the World is that the earth was cut out of the dismembered body of a giant; and the Ladakhi national epic, drawn from pre-Buddhist stories, describes the slaying of a giant. Not all these giants, it seems, were male.

Today, the Dards who live beside the Indus in Ladakh still worship goddesses and tell stories of a blissful antiquity when humans and deities lived together – until men tried to rape the goddesses, after which the humans were banished. Michel Peissel, a French explorer interested in the continuity of Stone Age beliefs into the modern age, noted in 1984 that although the original Dard deities were women – goddesses of springs and water, of hunting, fertility and fortune – they had recently been superseded by Babalachen (Father Big God), presumably under the influence of Buddhist, Christian or Muslim missionaries. Peissel's theory, however, was that the original matriarchal religion had gradually been superseded by a 'men's liberation movement in rebellion against the rule of women in Neolithic times'. Dard culture, he suggested, far from being a last remnant of the vanished feminist paradise that the ancient Sanskrit-speakers, Chinese travellers and Kashmiris had heard tell of, was for some men nothing more than a dystopia. Dard women are important members of society but Peissel caricatured them as 'ferocious . . . loud-mouthed and aggressive' husband-beaters; 'true witches, in fact'. The freedom of women in Uttarakuru often shocked male commentators and it seems that Peissel was no exception.

The Indian authorities forbade Peissel from visiting the Dard villages on the banks of the Indus, which were closed to foreigners at the time, and thus he was unable to test some of his more extravagant theories. After he left Ladakh, two villages were opened to outsiders in the late 1980s, and while I am in India permits are issued for the first time in sixty years to the last two, right on the border with Pakistan. The army also opens up an access road from Kargil, so it is with a sense of déjà vu that I find myself driving on another military supply road right up to the border. As the jeep turns down the steep mountain road I see the Dard villages clustered along the slender sheen of water where the Indus flows, and I remember standing beside a soldier on the other side of the Line of Control, straining my eyes to see through the silence of that sad place and into India.

The Dard settlements in Ladakh, with their fecund fields of barley fringed with marigolds and foxgloves, could not be more different. Like the Kalash, the Dard women wear *peraks* – long headdresses covered with coins, flowers and beads. Francke likened the fashion to the hoods of cobras: 'Perhaps,' he wrote, 'the Ladakhi women wished to look like Nagis' – the female snake deities of ancient India, Buddhist guardians of lakes and rivers – 'because these water fairies were famous for their beauty.'

Hunter-gatherer societies apparently lived without social hierarchy; and it is the same with the Dards today. The neighbouring Buddhist villages on the banks of the Indus still practise a caste system, with blacksmiths and musicians treated as outcasts and banished to the settlement's periphery. The Dards, who are considered unclean by other Ladakhis, live as equals. Even women, whom the Kalash believe to be fundamentally impure, in Dard villages have the same power and status as men.

Perhaps in retaliation for being treated as morally suspect by Buddhists, it is outsiders whom the Dards till recently considered unclean. Before the villages were opened to the public, juniper branches were burnt to cleanse those who had returned from trading trips to Leh or Skardu. The Dards are not so insistent any more and nobody waves a burning juniper branch in my wake as I climb up along the steep paths towards the new Buddhist monastery at the top of the village of Darchiks. The Dard houses are built very close together, so that their second storeys meet above the path, and in the winter when the villages are snowed in, neighbours visit each other by jumping from roof to roof.

It is raining hard by the time I reach Dha further east along the Indus, and I have the leaky guestroom in a house called Bangbang to myself. At the top of a hill in the middle of the village, with a fine view right down along the Indus, the family who live here hold the longest local record of polyandrous marriages, according to Rohit Vohra, who studied Dard culture in the late 1980s. The Dards still marry only between themselves, and Vohra observed polyandry, monogamy, polygyny and group marriages 'where all partners have

275

access to each other' (two sisters marrying two brothers; a wife shared between father and son). Given how effectively these arrangements obscure biological descent, it is the continuity of the household name rather than genetics which is important – and this is the same all over Ladakh. When a couple have no son they adopt a son-in-law into the house rather than lose the household name by marrying their daughters outside the family.

Until anthropologists – and tourists – arrived to watch their fertility dances, the Dards were not prudish about celebrating sex. During their song festivals men and women traded insults ('Your penis is like a dog's penis / Your vagina is like a bitch's vagina') and bargained over the price of sex. But Francke, who first translated these songs into English one hundred years ago, employed the services of a Dard whom he personally converted to Christianity and together they obscured the songs' orgiastic nature. They called them 'hymns', and ambiguous and misleading phrases such as 'Is this not a pleasure ground' and 'Oh Show (love!)' camouflaged the true meaning of songs which actually meant 'Did we have sex?' A song which Francke had rendered Christian with the title 'Love One Another' was in truth so sexually explicit that, eighty years later, the Dards refused to explain to Rohit Vohra what it meant.

If Francke was misleading, Vohra's efforts to keep his anthropological analysis within the bounds of academic politeness engendered a language of perplexing vagueness. He went as far as hinting that the bawdy dancing culminated in an 'act' the 'extreme degrading nature' of which 'reveals to the participants the true nature of things'. Ever since then, Indian and foreign visitors have come here in the hope of witnessing Dard 'degradation', and the villagers now refuse to perform their dances in public.

In addition to the songs about sex, the Dards also sing odes to hunting and ancient pastoralism, songs describing the migration from the west, and cosmological descriptions of the creation of the world from water. When I ask the owner of Bangbang house about these songs he leads me up through the stone streets of the village, past the Buddhist monastery to the old fort, where apple trees now grow wild and darkly together. We climb over the tumbledown walls, picking the tart white and pink fruit as we go, until suddenly the ground gives way and I find myself looking down at the Indus in the ravine far below us. An old couple are sitting together in the shade of an apple tree, he clad in a long sheepskin coat, she in a heavily flowered headdress that nods as she talks. I am pleased when it is the wife who offers to sing, piping up sweetly in a wavering, nonagenarian voice. 'It is a song in our Brogskad language,' her husband says afterwards, 'about flowers.'

I ask the three old people about the oddly shaped standing stones I have seen in the arid hills above the village, wondering if they are Dard equivalents of the bloody altars and spirit-places in Baltistan. But the old people shrug. I am also curious to know about the many carvings of ibex and humans I have seen on the rocks near the river. Those, says Mr Bangbang, are carved by the Iliproo: 'Fairies which, if you meet them on the road at night, will give you your heart's desire, money if you need money, children if you need children.' He eyes me and raises one eyebrow.

When Michel Peissel visited Dard villages at Zanskar, a remote river valley that runs north into the Indus, the villagers there told him that their ancestors once followed huge flocks of ibex up to the high pastures in the summer and hunted enough to last them through the winter, which they spent in caves by the frozen river. They also told him that they hunted the ibex by chasing them over cliffs – one of the oldest forms of hunting in the world, from a time before bows and arrows were invented. Even now, they said, after every hunt, the goddess who owned the ibex had to be assuaged with an offering of the animal's entrails, horns and a carving of the animal on a rock. Thus each hunted animal was commemorated by being drawn into the landscape – a neat explanation for the abundance of ibex carvings all along the northern Indus.

Most of Ladakh's Dards have became Buddhists, but ibex reverence, like giant worship, has continued in this land, albeit in a modified form. Ladakhi Buddhists believe that the Buddha was an ibex in one of his past lives, and at a monastery near the Tibetan border there is a sacred ibex-horn bow. On the riverbank below Alchi, the most exuberantly painted of Ladakh's monasteries, there are graceful ibex carvings overlaid with Buddhist designs. Palaeolithic stone tools were also found here, showing that this place was always an important settlement and river-crossing.

Of all the thousands of carvings in Ladakh, only a handful have been mentioned in academic publications, and were it not for one Ladakhi, I might never have seen the country's rich collection of prehistoric petroglyphs. During the past twelve years, in the absence of any interest from the Archaeological Survey of India, the most thorough and dedicated exploration has been undertaken by an amateur pair: Tashi Ldawa Tsangspa, a local man, and S. D. Jamwal, an enthusiastic policeman posted here from Jammu. The policeman has since been transferred. That leaves Tashi, and it is he who shows me the rock carvings he has found all along the Indus from Kargil to Leh and east to the border with Tibet.

I meet Tashi in Kargil, where he works as a lecturer, and he takes me to see a new rock-art site that he has just located on the outskirts of this austere and nervous Shia town: a huge polished brown rock covered with prehistoric carvings of ibex and hunters, and the modern graffiti of Urdu-speakers. Tashi points right to the middle of the boulder, and there, as darkly patinated as the surrounding rock, almost invisible, is a handprint.

I spend much time thinking about handprints over the next month, for we come across them at almost every major rock-art site. On the dark rocks along the banks of the Indus it is always the handprints that are the most richly coloured, and therefore the most ancient, of the carvings we see. The hands are carved in one style – small, narrowing at the wrist, with fingers close together – which bears a strong resemblance to the hands 'spit-painted' with ochre pigment by Palaeolithic cave painters in Spain and France. But while I can see that in a cave, blowing paint out of your mouth and around an outstretched hand is easy and practical, it is difficult carving on to rock, and a hand in particular requires patience and skill. The hand was special in many ancient cultures. It was a pagan symbol in pre-Islamic Arabia, and this became the 'Hand of Fatima' erected above every Shia shrine and worship-place. Aristotle called the hand the 'universal organ'; it is our hands, he wrote, which distinguish us from beasts: 'the hand of all instruments the most variously service-able, has been given by nature to man, the animal of all animals the most capable of acquiring the most varied handicrafts.' Perhaps a handprint was a prehistoric signature: a way by which humans signalled their presence to one another in a time before anybody learned to write. Hands are also sexless; they could be male or female.

Paintings and drawings of humans from the modern era tend to focus on facial features. But to Stone Age humans in Ladakh, it seems that the eyes, nose and mouth were not important subjects. Legs, too, dwindle into insignificance; and there is only occasional emphasis on genitalia. Instead, there are many small, intricate carvings of humans in lines – dancing perhaps – with their outsize hands, like massive boxing gloves, raised in the air. There are no portraits of couples, and the few pictures of individuals are of solitary hunters or giants – also with prominent fingers.

One afternoon, Tashi and I come across a rocky beach on the banks of the Indus that is so full of carvings it must once have been a meeting-place – sacred, festive or commercial. Near the river is a huge rock overladen with drawings of ibex and dancing humans, and I am crouching on the ground, transcribing them into my note-book, when suddenly Tashi gives a shout: 'A giant.' Half buried, and extremely faded, is a figure with spiky hair, arms outstretched to a span of seven feet, an exact replica of many of those found on the banks of the Indus in Pakistan.

Then, on a table-rock nearby, we find another human outline, six foot long. But this figure does not have the usual spiky hair or outstretched arms and sturdy legs: the arms are tight beside the body and the feet together. 'It is a dead person,' I say to Tashi instinctively, 'the outline of a shroud.' Some three feet above the head, and blacker than the shroud-line, is a handprint, the fingers pointing towards the river. 'Do you think this was a funeral site? A cremation ground? A place of execution?' Buddhists in this region sometimes disposed of dead bodies by throwing them into the river – but perhaps the practice was much older. In the stillness of this place the solitary outline on the rock is eerie, and standing looking down at it, I shiver. For the rest of my time in Ladakh I dream of this image at night, and I am still unsure whether I read or dreamt that in an ancient form of capital punishment transgressors were bound with rope and tipped, alive, into the Indus.

At Domkhar further east, where the river narrows, there are many ancient carvings including another smaller spiky-haired giant, reinforcing the notion that the ancient Ladakhis were giant-worshippers. Tashi and I sit on the rocks by the river with the village Lambardar (headman) eating roasted barley flour – *ngampe*, Ladakhis call it; *tsampa* is how it is known in Tibet – the staple food for people from this mountain land for thousands of years. Barley is the oldest crop known in Kashmir, and was eaten at Burzahom before rice arrived from China. But while there are continuities of diet from Palaeolithic times, both Tashi and the Lambardar agree that they feel no connection to the ancient pictures. 'The Dards believe the carvings are made by fairies,' I say. Tashi shakes his head: 'Most Ladakhis, like me, are descended from invaders who came here from Tibet hundreds of years ago. These carvings were made by the original inhabitants of this land.'

From the moment we leave Domkhar and head towards Khalatse, the Indus valley metamorphoses: the narrow gorge opens up, the river has the run of the desert plain, and the valley is guarded by the parallel mountain ranges which are Ladakh's southern and northern borders. The Indus, progressing between these twin stone ridges, is so heavy with silt that it is the same colour as the rock. Human and botanical life gather around the glacial streams that run down into the river but the monasteries stand apart. Perched high on sheer cliff faces or on rocky islands in the river, these severe, whitewashed buildings with their flat roofs and heavy brown lintels cling to the arid stone like the stubborn accretions of nature.

Though the monasteries trumpet Ladakh's Buddhism, even at these holiest of sites the culture which it supplanted has not vanished entirely. At a monastery west of Leh, Tashi points to a red-painted building on the edge of the stark white monastery complex. 'Do you see that?' he asks. 'It is in honour of Paldan Lhamo, our protective goddess.' Paldan Lhamo was one of the ancient native deities of Tibet and Ladakh, a fierce Bon demon only absorbed into the Buddhist pantheon in the eighth century. In Ladakh, she is depicted wearing the flayed skin of her son, carrying a bag of diseases, her waist girdled with decapitated human heads, her mule bridled with snakes. Later, when we visit Matho – passing a field where men and women are singing 'Good work, kind work' as they scythe – and climb up to a cave once inhabited by Neolithic humans, Tashi points to a mark in the rock at the cave's entrance. 'The villagers say this is the shape of Paldan Lhamo,' he says, 'and that the landscape itself has drawn a picture of the goddess into the rock.'

All along the river where ancient settlements have been found, the practice of respecting powerful women still prevails. There are many living *lhamos* – female oracles or healers – in Ladakh. In a small village near Leh, a lhamo has become famous locally for sucking disease out of the ailing. The taxi driver who takes me to meet her recently converted to Islam and believes her to be a fraud: 'Even though she is my cousin I know that these people are commercially minded,' he says, and adds: 'She teases Muslims.' The Lhamo prescribes Muslim patients the supposedly retrograde therapy of hanging a prayer flag on their local mosque. 'All mosques in Ladakh were decorated like this once,' the taxi driver explains, 'until our educated Muslims told us not to.'

On Sunday morning there is a long line of patients waiting in the oracle's garden for her healing session to start – children with flu, a man with a back problem, a lovelorn girl. After an hour, when enough customers have assembled, we are ushered into the Lhamo's kitchen. She enters the room wearing a Chinese brocade silk poncho and a tall gilt hat, and kneels in front of a small fire. As her pink-tracksuit-clad granddaughter hands her the tools of her trance, she wails, mutters and shrieks in quick succession. One by one, her patients are made to lift up their shirts and expose their bellies to the Lhamo, who swoops upon them, tongue stuck out, and presses her lips to the skin near their navel. She sucks, and if the patients are well behaved they fling back their bodies in horror or shock. Then the Lhamo lifts her head and spits on to a plate of ash. The granddaughter leans against the kitchen stove, filing her nails in boredom.

'Why are there so many female oracles?' I ask when it is my turn to sit before her, hoping for a reference to Strirajya, or some other age-old northern lore about female power. But the Lhamo looks dismissive. 'It is all down to chance,' she explains in the Lhamo Tibetan dialect that has to be translated through the room in a relay of Ladakhi, Hindi and English. 'Sometimes men become oracles, sometimes women. My spirit,' she boasts, 'comes from Amdo in Tibet, where the fourteenth Dalai Lama was born.'

Later, a Buddhist tells me that the number of oracles in Ladakh increased after the Chinese invaded Tibet because the spirits fled west along the river to escape oppression. And indeed, although at the time the Lhamo's trance seems unconvincing, later when I reach colonized Tibet I think back wistfully on Ladakh with its oracles and monks, monasteries and mosques, local politicians and societies, magazines and debates. From that vantage point, the Lhamo seems to symbolize freedom.

The tranquillity of Ladakh dissipates again near the Tibetan border. Here, where the river froths and twists once more through sombre gorges, and it is easy to imagine how the belief in fierce water spirits came about, soldiers have ensconced themselves. Boulder-painting has superseded rock-carving: 'Paradise Lies in the Shadow of Swords,' the army has written in pious white letters by the road; 'Darling I Like You But Not So Fast,' retorts the Border Roads Authority in lurid yellow. The paint will fade, but there are hundreds of ancient rock carvings also heading for oblivion. Construction is big business and the villagers chop up rocks like cake to sell to builders. Just beyond Gaik − a Palaeolithic site carbon-dated to the fifth millennium BCE − there is a large geometric carving on a rock, a giant oracle's mask, perhaps. Nearby are many other smaller but equally mysterious mask-shapes. An entire school of history has been forged around similar carvings in Siberia; and if this area was properly studied it might change historians' view of the past. Instead, the valley echoes to the tap-tap-tap of men with hammers. Soon these unique petroglyphs will be sold to builders as rubble. Where, I wonder, is the Archaeological Survey of India?

If ancient evidence of the Empire of the Eastern Women is gradually being destroyed, nature offers geological legends in their place. The overhanging rocks along this part of the river almost touch each other across the roaring water, and at each turn the valley reveals a different scene − the shape of a woman, a slope of pebbles compacted together by some unimaginable geological force, the marks where a stream once passed over rock like the wrinkles on a face.

Human settlements are ephemeral in this landscape, for this is nomad country. Mahe Bridge, the furthest east along the river that civilians are allowed to go, is also where the Changthang begins: the dry Tibetan plateau north of the Himalayas, which stretches from

Ladakh into Tibet. In Ladakh many of the nomads who live in the Changthang – they are known as *Changpa*, or *Drokpa* in Tibetan – escaped here along the Indus when the Chinese invaded. They thus preserved both the age-old pastoralism which was once practised all over the world by Palaeolithic humans, and the polyandry that was part of the ancient fabric of Strirajya, both of which the invaders attempted systematically to destroy. It is difficult keeping up those old traditions, but the Changpa today make the burghers of Leh jealous with their pashmina businesses ('They cook on gas, drive gypsy vans, and eat imported rice,' somebody tells me). The Drokpa of Tibet, I find later, have not been so lucky.

I stand on the bridge looking at the Indus through the haze of hopefully fluttering Buddhist prayer flags. A young Indian soldier, wary of my camera, picks up his gun and walks out to join me in the middle of the bridge. 'Until the war with China,' I say to him, 'the Changpa migrated along this river between Ladakh and Tibet. Now all that has changed.' 'Everything has changed,' he agrees. 'In the olden days, thirty years ago, it was nothing but plain here, there were no mountains.' I look at him in surprise and laugh, until I realize that with his youthful conception of time he has missed out the word *arab* (million).

This land was flat once, fifty million years ago, before the Indian plate crashed into Asia, displacing the sea, launching the river on its long journey south, sending the mountains up into the sky. In Zanskar, I found three delicate seashell fossils – relics from the Tethys Ocean – embedded in a smooth black rock near the river. Here on the border between the two countries, the geological antiquity of the river begins to assert itself. And the Indus, which is older than the mountains, older than the Ganges, follows the fault line from western Tibet right through Ladakh, tracing the seismic join between the continental plates.

In the face of the tectonic revolutions which have convulsed this land and created this river, the loss of a few human scratches from the surface of the granite batholith through which the Indus passes seems momentarily insignificant.

12

The Disappearing River

Fifty million years ago

'There is a plain in Asia which is shut in on all sides by a
mountain-range . . . The Great King blocked up all the passages
between the hills with dykes and flood-gates, and so prevented
the water from flowing out . . . From that time the five nations
which were wont formerly to have use of the stream . . . have
been in great distress . . . the king never gives the order to open
the gates till the suppliants have paid him a large sum of money
over and above the tribute.'

Herodotus, *Histories*, fifth century BCE

O N THE UPPER reaches of the Indus, in the town of Ali (the
Chinese-built headquarters of far western Tibet), I check into
a hotel, pay the mandatory fine for entering the 'Autonomous Region'
illegally – and rush to the river. The town, which is also called
Shiquanhe (the Chinese name for the Indus) and Senge Khabab (the
Tibetan name for the source), straddles the river two hundred kilometres upstream of where I last stood watching it flowing past me
in eastern Ladakh.

I was prevented from continuing along the river by the militarized border, guarded by the Indian Army on one side and the
Chinese on the other, and so to complete my journey to the source
I had to make a four-thousand-kilometre loop around to the nearest
legal crossing-point. This meant descending again into the Punjabi
plains, travelling west into Pakistan, over the mountainous border
with China, and then east, in a jeep driven by a maniac, through
the high-altitude desert of Aksai Chin (which the Chinese took from
India in the 1960s), and thence into Tibet (stolen property).

Now that I am here, I stand on the river's bank in confusion, wondering whether I am in the wrong place. There is a blue boot and a bicycle tyre where the water should be; Chinese instant-noodle packets are scattered about like flowers – but where is the water? My map clearly shows the Indus running straight through the middle of this town. Have I travelled 1,400 kilometres from Kashgar . . . in the wrong direction? I look through the list of Emergency Chinese in my guidebook and stop a passer-by: 'Shooee?' I say. Water? 'Tsangpo? River? Darya?'

The passer-by, a middle-aged Chinese man with a limp, looks down at the river and up at me. He makes a noise like a cat coughing; a cutting motion with his hand; he swipes the air. Then he flicks through my phrasebook and rifles through my bag. The former does not deal with emergencies of the riparian sort but in the latter he finds my Ladakhi handpress torch. He holds this up to my face, switches it on and off, and I feel strongly, though I am not sure, that he swears at me in Chinese. Before he can assault me for my stupidity, I click: the answer to my question is *electricity*.

Twenty-four hours ago, as I was hurtling through Aksai Chin, vomiting repeatedly because of the high altitude, unable to communicate with anyone around me, I was troubled by a thought, which I wrote like a portent in my notebook. I am reading that note now, scrawled in handwriting distorted by lack of oxygen: 'What will happen if the Chinese dam the Indus?'

The man with a limp ushers me into a taxi and gives a rapid set of instructions to the driver. I have no friends in Tibet, and no common language with this stranger. That I have decided to trust him is not the consequence of judgement; it is instinct born of exhaustion and distress. Besides, I have to discover what has happened to the Indus. I grip the ragged taxi seat and watch as the town rattles slowly past.

Despite its imposing police station, saluting soldiers and plate-glass tower blocks that stand empty, opaque with dust, Senge-Ali is a small town barely five streets broad. There are very few Tibetan inhabitants; Han Chinese run the supermarkets, march up and down in green uniforms outside the government buildings, and apply lipstick inside the neon-lit hair salons that double as soldiers' brothels. I imagine that the towns of the British Raj looked as anomalous as this; there is something morgue-like in the neatness with which the foreign culture superimposes itself on the landscape.

The tarmac soon ends, along with the bureaucratic buildings, and after that we bump along a track. Dark hills encircle the town, removing any grand illusion of modernity. Their forbidding aspect is reassuring: humans have not yet managed to tame this land, they seem to say. I stare out of the window into the stony emptiness as the taxi driver and my impromptu guide confer. After a little while I see, stretched across the road in the distance, a barrier, an army checkpoint. The driver draws up beside it and beeps his horn.

It is only nine o'clock in the morning, and the soldier is still asleep: he comes slowly out of his hut, rubbing his eyes, and indicates that I should crawl under the barrier. But the car is not allowed to advance further. To my consternation it reverses and turns. 'Please stop,' I say, 'please.' It will be a long walk home along this empty road. But my guide leans out of the window and makes it clear that the car won't wait. I hand over the money for the fare; the car disappears in a cloud of dust; and I am left all alone.

Not quite alone: the soldier. He yawns, and waves me on.

I am still unsure whether the stranger and I have understood each other perfectly. But I have no choice now, and so I obey the policeman, and walk on down the track. Beyond the checkpoint is a cluster of small huts and a large fence, enclosing a compound. I hear a dog barking, and pick up a stone to defend myself. The gate of the compound opens and out comes a large dirty truck, with twenty Chinese workers in the back. It rounds the bend in the road ahead of us and disappears.

Ten minutes later I too turn the corner, and then I see it.

The dam is huge, pristine. Its massive concrete curve looms up from the riverbed like a vast wave frozen in mid-air. I stare at it in disbelief, fighting back tears. The structure itself is complete, but the hydroelectric elements on the riverbed are still being installed. There are pools of water this side of the dam, but no flow. The Indus has been stopped.

I walk towards the dam, expecting any minute to be arrested and searched; but nobody even asks me where I am going. The fence along the road is lined with multicoloured flags – State Grid of China, they say in Chinese and English – and I follow them over a bridge across the dry river and up along its banks to where the Chinese workers are encamped. When I arrive at the dam itself, I step tentatively out along it – and still nobody stops me. Instead, when I reach the middle and pause to look down at the hydroelectric plant, the men in hard hats wave. Take our picture, they mime; but in a spirit of precaution, accustomed to the forbidding signs on every bridge in India and Pakistan, I do not remove the camera from my bag.

On the other side of the dam the road ends abruptly, submerged beneath the water. The river lake is huge; opaque and green, it fills the mountain valley and I want to cry out at the unkindness: at the demands imposed by other people's needs, somewhere far away in China. Is the dam just for electricity? Or will the Chinese use it to supplement their falling water tables, as the Pakistanis do, for irrigation or drinking water elsewhere in the great Republic? I stand on the edge of the lake as the water laps at my feet. After a while, the workers call out to me, and so I walk silently back.

From now on, for the rest of my journey to the river's source, I feel stricken: there is no Indus. 'They cut the river,' a kind Tibetan policeman explains later that day, 'two months ago.' So for the past two months, as I have journeyed east through Baltistan, Kashmir and Ladakh, it is not the Indus I have been following upwards, not the Indus's history I have been writing, but the sum of its tributaries: the Gar, Zanskar, Shyok, Shigar. 'Were there any protests?' I ask, and the policeman laughs. In Ladakh, four hundred Buddhists marched against the Basha dam downstream in Pakistan, which will submerge the prehistoric and Buddhist-era rock carvings at Chilas. In Pakistan, Sindhis regularly protest against army dam-building in the Punjab. Here in the Tibetan Autonomous Region, the inhabitants have no forums through which to debate how their landscape, customs and language should be preserved; they no longer have any power over their river or their land.

My own sadness is only slightly tempered by my trepidation at embarking on the final stage of my journey up to the source of this once-immortal river. I return to Senge-Ali with a group of dam-workers and search for transport to Darchen. Three hundred kilometres away to the east, the village of Darchen is the staging-post for pilgrims wishing to circumambulate the sacred mountain of Kailash. From the watershed of this iconic mass of rock, four great rivers of South Asia rise. The Indus flows west towards Pakistan, the Sutlej south-west through Kashmir, the Karnali south-east into the Ganga, and the Brahmaputra east into Bangladesh.

Where the four rivers begin, four faiths – Bon, Buddhism, Jainism and Hinduism – congregate in pilgrimage. The worship of mountains and rivers is intrinsic to the fabric of South Asian tradition, and the mountain where these rivers begin is the epitome of that philosophical intermeshing. Tibetan Buddhists call it Kangri Rinpoche: 'Precious Snow Mountain'. Bon texts have many names: Water's Flower, Mountain of Sea Water, Nine Stacked Swastikas Mountain. For Hindus, it is the home of the wild mountain god Shiva and a symbol of his penis; for Jains it is where their first leader was enlightened; for Buddhists, the navel of the universe; and for adherents of Bon, the abode of the sky goddess Sipaimen. For early European travellers who heard tell of its mythological dimensions, it was both the Garden of Eden and Mount Ararat. For modern Chinese and Western trekkers it is still a zone of exploration that carries cachet on account of the strenuousness of the trek, the difficulty of getting there, and the lack of amenities. This is no place for frivolous Western itineraries. The Hindus' Mount Kailash – so the guidebooks say – is rooted in the seventh hell and bursts through the highest heaven. It certainly lies in what some trekkers call the 'dead zone' – a place of such high altitude, prone to such dramatic variation in weather, that every year pilgrims and trekkers die trying to make the three-day walk around the mountain. The source of the Indus, meanwhile, lies days' and days' walk to the north, in the mountains beyond Kailash.

Until now, my entire plan for reaching the source has been based on the assumption that in Senge-Ali – as elsewhere on my journey – I will be able to glean all the reliable knowledge I need about the lie of the land from local people. Out of curiosity, expedience and an utter lack of mountaineering knowledge I have already decided that I want to see the mountain and its river just as Tibetan pilgrims see it, without the paraphernalia of modern trekkers. Looking in vain through travel guides for directions to the source, I turned to the map of western Tibet, and decided that the people who actually live in the mountains should have everything I need. In Senge-Ali, I imagined, I would be able to find a Tibetan guide, rent a tent and stove, and thus settle my vague fears of walking into the mountains without any local languages or accurate maps.

These illusions prove laughable in reality. The town has a super-market selling tinned pineapple; boutiques hawking underwear from Thailand; even a karaoke bar. But while it caters to the Chinese administration, soldiers and traders, most pilgrimage parties and tour groups to Kailash come from the east, from Lhasa or Nepal; and they come carrying everything they need from elsewhere: equip-ment, provisions, expertise.

Pinning all my romantic notions and slender hopes on the resi-dents of Darchen – at least one of whom must know the way to the source of the Indus – I buy a seat on a jeep. The seven other passengers are Chinese tourists, all strangers to each other, all only-children. Normally the journey to Darchen takes six hours, but the rains have been severe this year, five rivers have flooded, and so we spend two days and a night reaching our destination. We break down every few hours – the jeep's engine is flooded. I have a long time in which to contemplate the landscape.

We are so high here – the Tibetan plateau is twice as thick as the rest of the earth's crust – that never before has the sky been so large, or so full of cloud and light: the sun seems to emanate from six differ-ent parts of the sky, like a Turner blown out of proportion. The land-scape, too, runs the gamut of every form known to the Indus valley: rivers in spate, sandy Sindh-like desert, green Punjabi hills, snow-topped mountains, all in an eye's glance. I feel as if the whole of the Indus valley is laid out before me in one vista. *Senge Khabab*, Tibetans call the source of the Indus: the Lion's Mouth. From the source to the sea, the entire trajectory of the river is contained in this sad place.

We reach a river but the jeep's wheels churn up mud on its edge and we are unable to cross. It has begun to rain. On the far side are two buses full of Tibetans; and stranded in the middle of the roaring waters – I feel sick when I see this – is a bus whose passengers press their noses to the glass in alarm. A Chinese Army bulldozer has moved into the river to rescue it. The bus driver is handed a rope by a soldier, and he climbs with it round to the front, down into the swift black water, and connects the two vehicles together. The bulldozer judders backwards; the bus lurches to one side; the rope snaps; and fifty Tibetan passengers sway in fear.

There is a second bulldozer too. I watch, amazed, as at a signal from a Chinese Army officer, it ignores the two other buses and moves across the river to where our jeep is moored in the mud. My fellow passengers are Chinese: the army is coming to our rescue. A soldier lashes our jeep to the bulldozer with a metal cable and we are towed across the river in a moment. This neat operation, I realize as we arrive on the other side, is being filmed by a young officer. He continues filming as the students cheer, the soldiers salute, and the driver shakes everybody's hand. The Tibetans are still stuck in their swaying bus as we accelerate away into the distance.

The Chinese Government, which opened Kangri Rinpoche up to pilgrim and tourist traffic in the late 1980s, must make plenty of money from visa fees and fines. But it is difficult to see how the Tibetans benefit. Darchen, when we eventually reach it, has all the joy of a Native American reservation; and the analogy extends beyond the coincidence of drunk men with long black plaited hair (wearing cowboy hats, to confuse the issue). The sight of Tibet's heritage for sale in dollars or yuan; the disappearing language and culture; the dominance of Chinese businesses, shops and goods – were it not for the high altitude, I would follow local example and drown my sorrows in a bottle of Lhasa beer.

The man who runs the telephone booth saves me from despondency. I am unlike all his other customers in that I burst into tears every time I use the phone. It is strange to recall now, but I weep almost every day that I spend in Tibet. These are not just tears of sympathy for the people and for a culture disappearing as fast as the river is dying (though I feel this too). Nor tears of anger at the Chinese colonizing project. By now, I weep for myself. I feel myself imperilled – in a way that I had not in proximity to gun-toting tribals, peasant-raping feudals or any of the other stock lower-Indus horror stories – by that unquantifiable, non-reasonable thing: the emptiness of the landscape. In Kashgar, in Senge-Ali, in Darchen: every time I speak to my husband on the phone I shed tears like a river in spate.

I stand there weeping in Tsegar's shop as Tibetans crowd around me, waiting their turn, and for three days Tsegar sits and watches, hunched into his leather jacket, until eventually he moves me into his house next door where there is a phone my husband can ring me back on, and a mother-in-law who thankfully says nothing as she shuffles around the kitchen in her long Tibetan robes sweeping up the droppings of the baby pet goat and pouring me cup after cup of salty buttery Tibetan tea. 'What is wrong with you?' my husband asks, for I weep at the slightest endearment. Later I put it down to the psychosomatic effect of high altitude. Or strange geology: Tibet's 'Magsat crustal negative anomaly field', as geologists put it.

Tsegar is the only person in Darchen who speaks comprehensible English, and he translates for me valiantly, from Tibetan and Chinese, as I struggle with the indifference of the Yakman, the person officially in charge of allotting yaks and guides to pilgrims and tourists. September is the end of the season in Darchen, and the Yakman has already made enough money. He now wishes to be left in peace to spend it on drink and repose, and it takes all Tsegar's efforts to rouse him out of his lethargy and persuade him to summon from a nearby village an old pony man called Chumpay who knows the way to the Indus. Meanwhile, I find eight trekkers from the Mountain Climbing Club of Poland in a noodle shop who have a spare tent which Chumpay and I can share, and who decide, on a whim, to trek with me to the source. They are in a hurry to leave, so we set off immediately. But on the second day the youngest member of the party falls into a glacial mountain river and her boyfriend is drenched in the rain; so they both turn back. On the third day, we walk through a blizzard. And on the morning of the fourth day, the remaining six men, each six foot tall, Goretex-clad, equipped with trekking poles, whirring digital cameras and vitamin-rich powdered meals, announce to me that carrying on through the snow 'would be like suicide'. We are forced to turn back. I am so incandescent with rage that it camouflages me against the heavy snowfall, and childishly I pretend that the Poles are invisible too, and hence speak only to Chumpay during the long march back to Darchen.

In Darchen once more, the Yakman takes my money and explains to Tsegar that Chumpay is going home to his village for an important yak-meat distribution ceremony. He won't be available for another fifteen days, by which time my permit will have expired and winter snowfall will have frozen the passes. His friend, the only other person in Darchen who knows the way to Senge Khabab, refuses to accompany me on account of the cold and the distance. 'There is a monk from Driraphuk Gompa who knows the way,' says Tsegar that afternoon, 'but he has gone to Lhasa'; and when my husband rings that evening I dissolve into tears once more like a globally warmed glacier.

By the next morning, Tsegar has had an idea; but he seems cautious about it, as if it might result in disaster. Leaving his mother-in-law in charge of the phone booth, he walks me over Darchen's river and down its dirtiest street right to the end where there is a pile of rubbish so imposing that the ferocious village dogs that lie beside it appear sedated by its fumes and yelp wearily without moving when we approach. Opposite the rubbish tip is a kind of hut, and inside is the man we have come to meet, a Nepali called Karma Lama whose personal odour – by the end of ten days I know it well – is akin to that of the rubbish tip, putrid and sweet. Karma Lama sits wrapped in five dirty blankets in the middle of a room that looks as if the same rubbish tip has meandered through before settling down outside; but he speaks a bit of Hindi, was born with 'the handprint of a Lama on his stomach', and says that he knows the way to Senge Khabab.

Business is rapidly concluded: Tsegar settles the rate (the same as the government's but without the government's cut), a Tibetan is plucked from the street outside to act as a porter, and Karma Lama summons his neighbours: two skinny twenty-year-old pilgrims from Lhasa with slicked-back hair and pointy shoes, and they sell me their tent. We unroll it on the ground outside. It is large, white, with blue, red and yellow designs on the flaps. But there are no tent pegs and: 'It is not waterproof,' I point out. 'But all Tibetans sleep in tents like this,' says the porter, whose name is Yujaa. Tsegar agrees. He gestures across the river to the Tibetan pilgrim encampment. 'Buy some plastic sheeting from the Chinese shop,' he says.

So this is what we do. I give Karma ten yuan for sheeting; Yujaa volunteers his friend's stove; we agree to spend tomorrow buying supplies and packing; and the day after is fixed for our departure. 'We Tibetans,' Tsegar says to me ominously as we take our leave, 'have too much luggage.'

The next evening I walk through the rain to Yujaa's house for our final pre-departure meeting. There I find him sitting in domestic bliss as his wife wets, combs and plaits his hair, and their infant daughter piddles through her clothing on to the floor. (Tibetans clothe their babies in multiple layers, all of which have slits at the crotch to avoid the necessity of undressing in the cold.) Yujaa's house is also a teashop, and as we wait for Karma to arrive, Yujaa plays cards intently with a Tibetan woman and a Chinese soldier. He and his wife speak no English, and I no Tibetan, so we communicate in shrugs and smiles until it is dark, when at last I trudge back home to Tsegar's house pondering the whereabouts of Karma.

In my morbidly despondent state I had imagined that Tsegar was a widower, with only a mother-in-law to care for his two young babies; but his wife was merely on a shopping trip to Lhasa, and I arrive back to find her, a tall, cheerful woman chewing gum, triumphantly reinstalled, and with her like a royal entourage her six younger sisters. The sisters enjoy watching Chinese films, and everybody is pleased when Tsegar reveals that the new solar panel has generated enough electricity to power the black and white television. So it is that we are sitting happily slurping yak meat noodles, when the door bursts open – and standing in a gust of cold air and rain is Karma Lama, the bad fairy, his hair sticking up from his head and alcohol fumes rolling from him like fog. He has spent the plastic sheeting money on Chinese brandy and now he doesn't want to walk to the Indus after all. The luggage is too heavy and it is raining.

The seven sisters watch open-mouthed, their eyes flicking from one combatant to another, as Tsegar and Karma argue. Karma gestures at the luggage, heaped by the door, at the skies, at me. Tsegar shrugs, lifts the luggage piece by piece, and delivers his verdict quietly in Tibetan. I know that a truce has been effected when Karma, snivelling slightly, sits down on one of the beds and accepts a cup of yak butter tea from Tsegar's wife. When he eventually leaves, he even closes the door quietly behind him. 'What did you say?' I ask. Tsegar grins. 'I understand how his mind works,' he says. 'I told him how happy you are that he speaks Hindi. This pleased him. Now he will not be any trouble.'

The next morning Karma shows up at eight o'clock, apparently chastened, but looking and smelling as if he has been wrapped in all his belongings and rolled around the streets of Darchen. With him is Yujaa the Porter, trim in a hand-knitted hat and polished boots. I am wearing my trousers from Quetta, a yak-wool jacket stitched six years ago by a tailor in Delhi, and a straw sunhat from Kashgar. But something is amiss, for Tsegar's wife rummages in a dragon-painted cupboard, and pulls out a fluorescent-coloured synthetic neck muffler: 'Now you look Tibetan,' she says, and Tsegar, after appraising each of us in turn, buys three pairs of yellow washing-up gloves from the Chinese shop: 'Against the snow.' We don the gloves, heave the bags on to our backs, Karma picks up the stove and Yujaa and I each take up one of our two ten-foot metal tent poles, which I now find bear more than a passing resemblance to jousting spears, and I am glad that we are not riding up to the source on ponies (which is how many rich Indians begin their pilgrimage), and that wind power has not yet reached Tibet: 'quixotic' is an adjective I prefer to forget. Thus accoutred, we set off.

I have never seen Darchen so misty. In a way it is a relief, for the ugly Chinese buildings are barely visible; but nor are the hills to the south, nor anything but the narrow path ahead. White cloud hangs above us and dribbles rain on to our bags. It speeds Yujaa and me up, but gives Karma an excuse to dawdle. Or maybe he is taking long brandy breaks.

Mount Kailash — or Kangri Rinpoche, as Tibetans know it — is only a thousand metres above us. It seems smaller than before but larger in impact: everywhere we turn that day and the next it looms over us, its black and white striations glowing through the mist like a jewel. During the day-long walk from Darchen to Driraphuk Gompa, the monastery which marks the end of the first stage of the Kailash pilgrimage, the red hills seem to lean in towards us, as if they might tumble into the river. We pass many Bon pilgrims coming the other way — that day they outnumber the Buddhists and Hindus by three to one – and only two small tent teashops. In the second we sit and wait for Karma. A polite party of South Koreans is already there: an expensive-looking group, with compact tents, a line of yaks and even oxygen bags to mitigate the dangers of altitude sickness. Karma's eyes light up when he sees the oxygen. Within minutes of his arrival he has contrived to steal a bag.

We walk on, Karma's oxygen pillow fluttering over him like a speech bubble. When we arrive at the monastery, Karma throws a tantrum and demands to stay the night here with his friends, instead of continuing on to the nomads who live an hour's walk ahead. 'If you carry on shouting and being angry,' I say to him, in tears again, 'I will turn around and go back to Darchen.' In fact nothing would induce me to go back, not even Karma's drunken raving. But the tears achieve two things: Karma is astonished into silence; and I am resolved into overcoming my fear, resigning myself to being led through the mountains by an eccentric drunk, and trusting instead in the wisdom of Yujaa, with whom I cannot communicate verbally but have developed a fluent mutual understanding based on the language of gestures. We stay that night at the monastery.

The monks – there are six – are all dressed in dark red Timberland fleeces. Despite abiding by the Chinese prohibition on displaying pictures of the Dalai Lama – only in the remotest places did I meet Tibetans who could afford to disregard this stricture – they seem content, visited by pilgrims from all over Asia. We sit in the monastery kitchen as I munch raw spinach from their garden (I fear I may be getting scurvy) and everybody else drinks yak leg stew. ('Bad food in the gompa,' mourns Yujaa on the morrow.) The monks take it in turns to translate the words on my ring, a Tibetan silver coin that I have been wearing for a decade: one of the many minted by the Tibetan Government between 1911 and the Chinese invasion of 1951. On the obverse are the eight auspicious symbols of Tibetan Buddhism – every monk recognizes those; but the reverse causes more problems. It reads: 'the Ganden Palace, victorious in all directions', and is thus a symbol of Tibetan independence. The monks seem to regard it with a mixture of curiosity, fear and pride.

As I leave the smoky kitchen to go to my bed in the monastery dormitory a monk says to me: 'There was a party of Americans who tried to get to the Indus. They had to turn back: the whole valley was flooded, there was water water everywhere.' He looks at me as Karma translates. 'When was this?' I ask. 'A week ago,' says the monk; and to his surprise, I laugh: that was me and the Poles. Already our misadventures have become part of Kangri Rinpoche folklore.

We wake to thick snow. Karma has found a Shaivic trident under the monastery stairs and he strikes off boldly into the glaring white, using this as a trekking pole; Yujaa and I follow squire-like close behind. We are leaving the Kailash pilgrim track, and thus from now on, we have no map. But I walked through this valley a week ago with Chumpay, and know roughly which way we should go. Karma, however, has other ideas.

By eleven o'clock we see, as I have been anticipating, two tents in the distance with smoke rising blackly up against the snow. They belong to Drokpa, the nomads who have grazing rights over this valley. This family of nomads are much given to tutting, and Karma furnishes a selective translation over tea and curd: they tut at the long way we have to go, at the weight of our bags, at the difficulty of the route, at my distance from home, at my solitary state (this is a theme to which they return with especially vigorous tuts). Presumably they also tut at the fact that thanks to Karma's hopelessness we may get fatally lost, but luckily I know no Tibetan and thus miss the close questioning to which Karma subjects them on the best way to reach the Indus (they don't know). The gravity of the situation seems to have affected the entire family: the tall, bent grandmother who pours us yak curd, her strong young son with his long plait of hair, his shy staring daughter. Only the grandfather seems unconcerned. He lies back on his bed in the tent, sipping tea and trying hard to change the subject.

I refuse the Drokpas' kind offer of a packhorse (remembering how Chumpay's pony detested crossing the glacial streams which lie ahead) and we continue on our way. On our return, seven days later, I will fail to recognize this place until we reach the nomads' tent again. By then bright sunlight will have entirely melted the snow, and the grassy valley strewn with mammoth boulders will seem a different place altogether, a geological quirk. Today, the nomads' valley is a long white undulating expanse of snow.

A few hours later, Yujaa and I stop at the other end of the valley on a small hill for lunch, and wait for Karma. From here the only way onwards is up into the mountains. Yujaa presses snow into the kettle and takes out his matches and pliers. He alone knows how to light his friend's stove – which is really just a blowtorch, and so powerful that even careful Yujaa burns a hole in the lid of the kettle. He is carrying five foodstuffs: tsampa (roasted barley flour), yak butter, a dried yak leg, tea leaves and salt. I have the Chinese instant noodles that I already loathe, some almonds I bought in Rawalpindi, and a sweet instant cereal from Kashgar that I swap with Yujaa for tsampa (he takes it home for his baby). Yujaa makes sure that I eat tsampa, wettened with tea and seasoned with yak butter, at least once a day; he cannot conceive of a day without tsampa; it is the backbone, substance and spice of the Tibetan diet. Karma's attitude to food, which is the Indian one of concealing all blandness with chilli powder, disgusts Yujaa. He winces as Karma adulterates his tsampa with sugar or oats or curd. But Karma's enormous rations are an important part of his self-image; he unwraps them lovingly every evening and spreads them around him like a spell: little twists of spice, cloth bags of grain and flour, instant soup filched from a tourist, foodstuffs that he has acquired hither and thither, all wrapped up in individual parcels and secreted about his person.

Yujaa and I sit grandly in the middle of the snowfield, sipping salty tea and watching Karma's slow approach. But when he reaches us, he offloads his bags and instead of sitting down, veers up the hill. 'Where are you going?' Yujaa shouts, and Karma motions to the top of the ridge, where three Drokpa horsemen are now just visible, black figures outlined against the snow. The horsemen wait for Karma to approach, and then the four men enter a long discussion. There is much gesticulation towards the west; and eventually our Nepali skips down the hill towards us.

It is only three hours, he announces, to the next Drokpa settlement. The horsemen have come from there, so we can follow their tracks and stay at their encampment for the night. All we have to do is climb that hill. He waves nonchalantly towards a distant brown mountain. 'Isn't it that way?' I ask, pointing out the route I took with Chumpay, due north. 'There are many ways to Senge Khabab,'

Karma says philosophically, and then adds: 'Who has been there before, you or me?'

Normally paths through the mountains follow the line of least resistance: a 'pass' is by definition a low crossing-point. But that afternoon, following Karma's instructions, we go right up over the mountain, and I think that my lungs are going to burst. As we climb, leaving Karma further and further behind, we can hear the thunder in the distance growing nearer, and when we reach the lakes at the top we can see black clouds gathering on the other side. For an hour Yujaa and I walk along the top of the mountain, following the horsemen's tracks but without being able to see the Drokpa tents that are surely pitched just round the corner; by now we have been walking for three hours and it is already getting dark. We reach the prayer flags that mark the highest point and stare down into the valley below. It is beginning to rain. If the rain is heavy it will wash away the tracks in the snow; and these tracks at the moment are the only guide we have.

It was, on reflection, the most beautiful point on our journey: the deep gloaming of the valley, the contours and outlines roughly etched like the black and grey strokes of a lithograph. But I was never so frightened as then, descending into nothing: into the hail, the darkness, the cold of an unknown Tibetan mountain valley.

We walk for three hours as hail clatters down on our backs, across a landscape so marshy that we step from one island of soil to another as the melting ice splashes our feet. I look back and see Karma, a tiny blue figure in the distance. Then the tracks run out: we have descended so far that the snow has melted. I wipe rain from my face and force myself not to panic.

The landscape here is unguessable; I thought we had descended into a valley, but in fact we have only reached the valley's lip: now we find ourselves at the top of yet another valley where the grass is showing through the ice in green patches. *Walk faster,* Yujaa indicates, for I am shivering, my feet are wet, and the storm shows no sign of abating: *Leave Karma behind,* he says. But we cannot leave Karma, however slowly he walks; we have no choice but to wait, our backs to the hail, as night falls.

And then, within half an hour, everything changes. The clouds overhead shift, the hail stops, and the sun, which I thought had gone down for the night, comes out, numinous, sacred, illuminating the valley in warm, low evening light. We descend still further, along a stream and on to a tableland. Now the clouds lift, and for the first time I can see across the valley to where the ground is strewn with hundreds of little black dots. Perhaps it is some kind of odd rock formation, part of western Tibet's erratic geology. I call to Yujaa and point. But he utters the word that I have not dared hope for:

'Yak.'

'Drokpa?' I ask.

'Drokpa.'

We smile at each other in relief: we are safe.

As the evening sunshine lights up the entire lower valley, picking out the white dashes of sheep on the farther hillside, the green pasture and the black yak-wool tents, we climb down to a mountain river and splash through the water, and despite our heavy bags, run towards the Drokpa tents, pitched beside the river that cuts through the bottom of the valley. Now we can see the Drokpa themselves, little marks of black on the hill beyond, rounding up their animals for the night. We sit and wait for a Drokpa couple to bring their sheep across the river – they wade through the freezing water in baseball boots – and then we accost them shamelessly and ask for help.

By the time Karma arrives that evening we have a new companion, Sonamtering. He has a wide smile, a long plait, and a fringe of curls over his forehead. Over the next week his air of tranquil authority has such a sobering effect on Karma that he entirely stops drinking (or maybe the drink runs out), walks faster and throws no more fits. 'Alicay,' Sonamtering calls me, and his voice is as soothing and re-assuring as a lullaby.

Sonamtering is the younger brother and the younger husband – for both brothers live in the same tent with one young wife between them. Karma, too, shares a wife with his brother (in his case, it seems, extended religious tours to Tibet are one means of dealing with the clash of conjugal interests). Polyandry was banned in Tibet as part of a general Chinese attack on the Tibetan way of life during the Cultural Revolution. The institution of the family as an economic unit was also abolished and a commune system was enforced upon the Drokpa. This brutal reorganization of the Drokpa's ancient livelihood pushed many of them to starvation, and many nomads died.

The Drokpa who survived the 'winter of genocide' (1967–8) eventually lived to see these experiments reversed. In 1981, all livestock was redistributed once more between every living Drokpa (nine yak, twenty-five sheep and seven goats), and life reverted to partial normality. Even polyandry, though still illegal in the Chinese Constitution, is now tolerated by the authorities and is today on the increase in Tibet. The Drokpa are still not taxed, and while the elders go to town during periods of extreme hardship to ask for basic supplies from the government, Sonamtering says that the police and army never come here, it is too remote.

The next morning Sonamtering is ready before we have even packed up. He is still wearing his cotton baseball boots, and now a sheep-wool overcoat with long sleeves, only one of which he uses. The other he slings around his waist like an extra pocket, and there he keeps a knife, a bag of tsampa and his precious spectacles.

We say goodbye to Sonamtering's wife, brother and children, and leaving behind the serenity of their summer pastures climb up out of the valley towards the pass, Tseti-La. This, explained Sonamtering's brother to me last night, as he drew me a map of our route to the source, is the highest pass on the journey ahead of us.

It begins to rain as we climb, and then it hails, but Sonamtering merely smiles and offers to take the stove from Karma and the tent pole from me. I walk close behind Yujaa, and just as I am beginning to despair – for the hail has got between the crevices of my waterproof clothing (I am wearing the plastic sheeting) – the sun comes out again. Looking around us, we find that we are in the middle of the pass: a huge plain of grass and snow and lakes enclosed by a ring of glaciers and mountains.

Sonamtering leads us across the streams and rivers that criss-cross the plain until we reach a place he likes, beneath the gaze of the northernmost glacier. After eating tsampa we spread out our coats and shoes on the grass, and as they steam dry in the sunshine we drift into sleep with the sea-like roar of the glacier in our ears.

'Look at the *jungli* horse,' says Karma, waking us an hour later; 'it must have lost its child.' It is standing watching us on the other side of the lake. There is something childlike about its spindly legs and huge head, its delicate colouring of pale brown and white. We see many of these *kiang* or *kuang*, the Tibetan wild ass, as we walk towards the Indus. When they see us they canter along the horizon, or stand watching as we walk slowly past.

Ladakh is a desert but in Tibet there is an abundance of water streaming from the land. Most of the energy of our walk is expended in stepping and jumping over streams, negotiating rivers, keeping ourselves warm from the snow, and sheltering from the rain and hail. Indeed, the greater part of the water in the River Indus comes from its upper reaches – from Tibet, Ladakh and Baltistan – rather than from its Himalayan tributaries in the Punjab. All the water that drains from these mountains, I remember, is currently being stopped by the new dam at Senge-Ali.

After crossing Tseti-La we enter a series of mountain valleys. From now on the land around us changes with every step; it changes colour, form, complexion. Sometimes we walk through gorges where green stone merges into black and then into red. There are craggy hills, and next to them smooth rolling hills, and after that hills with swirls of different colours. There are mountains of warty rocky outcrops, with abrasions all over the surface, like the rough skin on an elbow. There are fields of rubble in which every stone is a different colour: orange, red, white, grey, blue, brown; and every one a different consistency: flecks of crystal, brushstrokes of colour on a white or black base, hollowed out like honeycomb, smooth and polished, speckled, ringed like Saturn.

Occasionally, between the stones, are red, yellow or purple wild flowers. And in the fissures we pass between the rocks, in the empty humanless silence of this enormous place, it is easy to imagine the force that created it: the plates slamming together fifty million years ago, India pushing north into Asia, displacing the Tethys Ocean so that the seabed became the mountains, and leaving this river in its trail. In the thin air up near the source there is a whole new vocabulary of peculiar, mouth-filling geological terms: orogenic, flysch, zircon, gneiss.

Kangri Rinpoche itself, say geologists, is debris from the volcanoes that erupted during the tectonic collision of the Indian and Eurasian plates. Here at last geology and myth coincide, for this most sacred mountain, like the river formed from its meltwaters, is older than the Himalayas, one of the oldest and highest of the mountains that tower over the Tibetan plateau.

The Indus, born in the wake of Kangri Rinpoche some thirty to forty-five million years ago, is the 'oldest known river' in the region. Clouds blew in from the sea, snagged on the mountains, and fell forming glaciers. In summer, these glaciers melted and flowed westwards. Thus a river was created, stretching from Tibet to the Arabian Sea, which, with its huge drainage area and unusual degree of erosion, created in turn at its mouth one of the largest deep-sea fans in the world. The Delta is made of sediment brought down from Tibet, Ladakh and the Karakorams.

The immensity of this geological timescale diminishes the human history of the river, rendering it invisible by comparison. Instead, as we walk, I think of the pre-human inhabitants of this river system, of the blind dolphin which is one of its oldest inhabitants – a rumoured relic of the receding Tethys Ocean. So murky is the heavily sedimented Indus that the river dolphin evolved without the use of sight. Instead *Platanista minor* catches its prey by echo-location, and sleeps on the wing like a bird, snatching two- or three-second measures of repose.

Birds, too, have always used the path which the Indus has forged through the mountains. A million migratory birds from East Africa, Asia and Europe fly along the Indus every year; to ornithologists the Indus is 'International Flyway Number 4'. Some birds enter the Indus valley through the Karakoram, Khyber and Kojak passes (like medieval Muslim warriors and twenty-first-century smugglers). Others camp at the freshwater lakes in Sindh for the summer, like fisherfolk or nomads. Still more emigrate west from the Himalayas during the hot weather, and return east for the winter. The Indus is visited by sea birds, river birds, marsh birds, desert birds, hill birds, forest birds and mountain birds. There are petrel from Antarctica in Karachi, storks from Germany at the Sindhi lakes, red turtle-doves from India in the Punjab, and Tibetan black-necked cranes in Ladakh.

In their annual migrations, birds are probably following the routes their pioneering ancestors took after the last Ice Age ended. This phenomenon has entered the earliest recorded culture of the humans who live on the birds' flight path: an ancient motif in Hindu poetry is the soul journeying to God like the goose migrating to Lake Manasarovar. The Kerigars, a tribe who pan gold in the Indus from Chilas to Attock, believe that the gold is brought down from the high mountains on the claws of migrating cranes. But as the river shrinks, so do the numbers of flamingos, pelicans and geese.

The lower Indus was first colonized by *Homo sapiens* following the migration out of Africa around 80,000 years ago. Forty thousand years later it was the Indus that humans crossed to reach India; and the Indus they followed north to populate Tibet and Central Asia. Recently, the lower Indus has nurtured *Homo sapiens* in their millions, and has in turn been transformed. But up in Tibet, the indigenous people have not altered the river at all. Drokpa such as Sonamtering watch the arrival and departure of migratory birds from their ancestral pasture lands but they never kill or eat them. They do not eat fish from the river. Nor do they fence the land, or cut it, or sow it. The contrast with the dam-makers is instructive. If a dam is the supreme symbol of man's attempt to control nature, the nomads of the Tibetan plateau are exemplars of harmony.

In this place Karma is as free as a migrating Manasarovar goose: he walks along slowly, always last, picking up the things that we have missed – sheep's wool up on Tseti-La, prettily coloured stones, mushrooms, nettles near the Indus – and presents them to us demurely, a magpie-like treasure, when we stop at night to pitch camp. The oxygen bag which for three days has been floating above his head like a standard detaches itself from his trident while we are crossing Tseti-La and drifts away into the snow; but it is soon replaced. By the fourth day the thin strands of off-white sheep's wool and black yak wool have become a thick stream entwined in the trident's forks. He is beginning to resemble a mountain Neptune, seaweed strewn, barnacle encrusted.

'Where is Senge Tsampo?' I ask Sonamtering every now and then, using the sonorous Tibetan name for the Indus river; and he points over the hills into the distance. A little bit further. With Sonamtering to guide us I never again feel the pure fear I experienced when it seemed as if Karma had led us recklessly over a mountain and into a hostile, unknown world. But I feel awe as we walk, tiny specks beneath an ever-changing sky, through a landscape empty of humans.

We camp that night in a valley that is a gentle wave of hills and slopes. Sonamtering chooses a place near a mountain stream, sheltered by the brow of a hill, and no sooner is our tent up – this takes time, twisting the poles into place, lugging boulders to pin the ropes in lieu of tent pegs – than the rain comes crashing down. I lie in the tent next to Yujaa, praying that the lightning, which seems to draw nearer with each crack, won't fizzle down our metal tent poles; that the mountain streams will not spread across the plateau and lift the groundsheet from under us.

In the morning, Karma is up at first light, singing his Buddhist prayers. Having got used to dawn at around five o'clock in Ladakh, it seems odd that in Tibet it is still dark at seven – the country is run anachronistically on the time in Beijing, over five thousand kilometres away to the north-east. This morning, as Karma returns with a kettleful of water from a stream and calls to Yujaa to light the stove, Sonamtering makes an announcement. 'Today,' he says, 'we will see Senge Tsampo.'

After a day's walk over a pebbly plain as wide and empty as a beach we finally reach the river. It is deep and fast, even so near the source. Sonamtering points out his winter home on the further side – impossible to reach now, for the gorge is sheer and the water glacial. He lives here for five months in the cold season, for unlike Himalayan pastoralists who descend to the plains in winter, the Drokpa go up to higher elevations where there is sedge for their yak to eat.

The huge landscape is very still. Then something moves: we turn and see a herd of kiang on the horizon. Yujaa whoops and jumps to scare them away. Like me, he has never been on a journey so far into the mountains before, and he finds them frightening.

Two hours later, a bridge looms up out of nowhere. 'What is that?' I say to Karma. 'A bridge,' he says, and laughs at my dull-wittedness. We draw nearer. Robustly made of poured concrete, the bridge reminds me, in its incongruity – remote as it is from cars and trucks – of the one I saw in Sindh, near Johi, a huge road-bridge suspended in the desert but with no road for miles on either side. That was a planning scam, an embezzlement scandal. This is utilitarian, an example of Chinese foresight: for though there is nothing coming over it now, something will, one day – army trucks, perhaps, to put down an insurrection; or prospecting jeeps, after some mineral. Gold was mined near the source of the Indus as late as the early twentieth century; and as Herodotus knew, the Indus has been associated with gold throughout its human history. (The heavily dammed Indus now yields less and less gold, and since the construction of the Tarbela dam, the Kerigars do not work down-stream of Darbund.) Chinese geologists, however, have recently identified six hundred new mineral sites in Tibet, a discovery which, the government says, 'will fundamentally ease China's shortage of mineral resources'. Or maybe the Chinese are simply banking on jeep-loads of tourists.

We cross the bridge which spans the Kla-chu, an Indus tributary, just before the two rivers' junction, and walk along the Indus: now a throng of sinuous silver streams. Within an hour we see another unfamiliar sight: a group of abandoned stone huts, a second Drokpa wintering site; and we pitch our tent in the yard outside, next to a mound of hard sheep-dung pellets, a fuel store. It is instinctive, the false sense of safety one feels at being within sight of these remnants of human culture. The bridge, the empty huts, the road along which no cars ever come – there is loneliness here too, as if we have stum-bled across a lost civilization.

That night, the night before we reach the source, Karma the magpie finds an old kettle outside one of the Drokpa huts. He chops and boils the nettles picked from the riverbank; throws in the mush-rooms that he has collected during the walk, some yak butter and tsampa; and then he crouches over the fire he has made using the yak dung (Yujaa alone has dominion over the blowtorch), pushing his hair out of his eyes and singing his prayers, stirring the pot like a happy witch. The three of them eat the soup that night. I watch them warily, remembering my majoon experience in the Kaladaka and hoping that Karma knows his fungi, that I won't find them dead in the morning. On the morrow, when I am woken by singing,

Karma is vindicated, and I finish the soup off for breakfast. It is thick and luscious, the mushrooms as succulent as Yujaa's yak meat is stringy.

Usually, we are woken every morning by Karma, as he moves around outside the tent, singing his prayers. But today it is Yujaa who breaks into song, and the songs he sings are rich and expressive; love-songs for Darchen and paeans to Kangri Rinpoche. Yujaa is singing because he is happy: we are now an hour's walk from the source, and then we can turn around and go home. He has been counting the days. Sonamtering, who has a deep, modulated speaking voice, joins in shyly, and hearing him is like listening to running water; but when Yujaa sings it is like listening to pleasure.

There are three rivers to cross on the way to the source. Until now, each time we have reached a stream that is too wide, we have simply walked upstream to where it narrows, or thrown in some stones to step across (except for Karma Lama, who wades in without taking off his boots, as the others weep with laughter). Here, however, the rivers are too wide to jump. Sonamtering, Yujaa and I sit on the riverbank, removing our shoes. The water, when we enter it, is so cold it brings tears to my eyes; and the water of the second river reaches my thighs. I look down at my feet moving across the bed, across pebbles the colour of the gorges we have walked through: sky blue, tsampa pink, turmeric yellow.

We dry off our feet in the sunshine and warm up by walking quickly onwards. Suddenly, we come upon the source. 'There it is,' says Karma, pointing to a long low line of chortens (Tibetan stupas) in the distance and a mass of prayer flags, pushed taut in the wind. 'But it can't be,' I say, expecting a steeper walk to the source and thinking: he hasn't been to Senge Khabab after all. But we follow the stream up to the top of this gentle hill and there it ends, in a pale rock face at the foot of which water bubbles up from the mossy earth.

'This is the Lion's Mouth,' says Karma, pointing to the rock face as he translates Sonamtering's words into Hindi. He points to the hill behind. 'That is Senge Uré, the lion's mane.' His finger moves west. 'That is Senge Norboo, its claws. That is Senge Nama, the lion's tail.'

Karma sits down beside the source, lights a dung fire, and begins an hour-long incantation. He says it is by Guru Padmasambhava, the man who came from Swat (in Pakistan) to spread the teachings of the Buddha through Bon-Tibet by subduing or killing the demons: the mountains are their petrified entrails. Sonamtering looks on with interest, as he does at everything we do; but Yujaa just giggles. He has no respect for Karma's self-administered charms and spells.

After Karma's prayers are over we follow the stream downhill again and I check: the river it joins is ten times as large. So this is the Senge Khabab – the stream issuing from the mouth of the lion. But is it really the true source of the Indus? I understand that the main river can be joined by a tributary larger in volume than itself – this is the case in Ladakh, where the Zanskar flows into the Indus. But can a source really be a source if other tributaries rise further from the sea than it?

That night in the tent I ask Sonamtering which of the Indus tributaries that we crossed this morning is the longest. All of them, he says, start at least a day's walk away from here. The Bukhar begins near the village of Yagra. The Lamolasay's source is in a holy place: there is a monastery there. The Dorjungla is a very difficult and long walk, three days perhaps, and there are many sharp rocks; but its water is clear and blue, hence the tributary's other name, Zom-chu, which Karma Lama translates as 'Blue Water'. The Rakmajang rises from a dark lake called the Black Sea.

One of the longest tributaries – and thus a candidate for the river's technical source – is the Kla-chu, the river we crossed yesterday by bridge. Also known as the Lungdep Chu, it flows into the Indus from the south-east, and rises a day's walk from Darchen. But Sonamtering insists that the Dorjungla is the longest of the 'three types of water' that fall into the Senge Tsampo.

I lie in the tent, wondering: the Tibetans must have chosen Senge Khabab for a good reason. These Drokpa know every part of the Changthang that is theirs by grazing right. The early twentieth-century explorer Sven Hedin was told by his Tibetan guides that Senge Khabab emits the same amount of water winter and summer – that it, unlike the other tributaries, was not dependent on seasonal snowmelt. This is visibly true, for this source does not rise from a glacier, but from the ground, and thus is perhaps known as the source on account of its year-round reliability.

Nevertheless, that night in the tent I suggest to the three men that instead of turning back tomorrow, we should continue onwards to where the Dorjungla rises. They look at each other and laugh. Karma translates my Hindi into Tibetan, Yujaa shakes his head in disbelief, and I hear Sonamtering utter my name – Alicay – through his laughter. That night, as our tent is filled with the music of Yujaa's singing, I am resolved to accept, for my companions' sake if nothing else, that I have indeed reached the source of the Indus.

The next day, we turn for home. Yujaa is in buoyant spirits. Sonamtering is looking forward to seeing his *shrimati* (Karma's Nepali word for wife). 'If he stays away any longer,' Karma teases, 'his Shrimati will scold him.' Karma himself is cheerful, and chatters to me all the way back to Tseti-La. But as we walk home through the mountains, I am overcome by sadness, even despair. Even when we climb Tseti-La again, so that the peak of Kangri Rinpoche comes into view, and Yujaa and Sonamtering fall to their knees, prostrating themselves in the snow like Muslims saying namaz; even when Sonamtering, before he turns for home, walks up and down the slope of the mountain, collecting a blue wild flower – the *Pang-kin-u-lu*, he says – and presents one to each of us; even when, two days later, we complete our circumambulation of the mountain, thus obliterating the sins of a lifetime; even when I walk into Tsegar's house in Darchen and see the smile of relief on his face; even then I am filled with sadness.

I feel sad for the river: for this wild and magnificent, modern, historic, prehistoric river; for this river which was flowing for millions of years before humans even saw it; for this river which has nurtured the earth since the land rose from the ocean.

Most creation stories begin with water. Those told by the Dards of Ladakh, by the Kalash in Chitral, by the Aryans of the Rig Veda, all attribute the creation of the world to the fetching forth of land from water. In the Qur'an it is written:

> So let man consider of what he is created:
> He is created of water pouring forth.

But for how long will the waters continue pouring forth? The river is slipping away through our fingers, dammed to disappearance. The Atharva Veda calls the Indus *saraansh*: flowing for ever. One day, when there is nothing but dry riverbeds and dust, when this ancient name has been rendered obsolete, then the songs humans sing will be dirges of bitterness and regret. They will tell of how the Indus – which once 'encircled Paradise', bringing forth civilizations and species, languages and religions – was, through mankind's folly, entirely spent.

Glossary

There are many variations, throughout South Asia and beyond, in the way that words from South Asian languages are transliterated into and used in English. The forms used here follow current local practice: thus 'shalwar' (as in Pakistan) rather than 'salvar' (as in India).

A – Arabic	Pu – Punjabi
C – Chitrali	Skt – Sanskrit
Pali – Pali★	S – Sindhi
Pa – Pashto	T – Tibetan
P – Persian/Farsi	U – Urdu, Hindi

★ Language of the earliest extant Buddhist scriptures in India

agni – fire; fire deity from the Rig Veda (Skt)

ahl-al-kitab – literally, 'people of the book'. That is, those who take the Bible, Jewish scriptures or Qur'an as their religious guide. Under some interpretations, Hindus are also ahl-al-kitab, because they follow the religious teachings in the Vedas (A)

ajrak – richly coloured indigo and red hand-printed cotton shawl worn by Sindhi peasants and politicians; the word is a Sindhi indigenization of the Arabic word *azraq*, blue (S)

alim – theologically learned person (A)

arya – noble, a term from the Rig Veda (Skt)

asthana – the seat of a saint (P)

asvamedha – horse sacrifice, a royal ritual for claiming land in ancient India (Skt)

azan – call to prayer which issues from mosques alerting Muslims to prepare for the five daily prayers (A)

basti – a settlement (U)

begum – lady; a title for married women (U)

bhajan – Hindu devotional songs

bhang – marijuana (U)

Bhangi – the generic name for sewer cleaners in India and Pakistan, generally low-caste Hindus or Christians (U)

bhangra – traditionally a Punjabi harvest dance performed by men (Pu)
brahmi – Indian script coined by Emperor Ashoka for his edicts
burqa – all-enveloping covering used by some Muslim women (A)

chaal – gait, walk (U)
chador – a huge cotton shawl used in place of a burqa in some parts of the North West Frontier Province (U)
chai – tea (U)
charpay – literally, 'four feet'. A wooden bed with a woven rope base, ubiquitous in India and Pakistan (U)
chillah – a meditation session lasting forty days (P)
chorten – Buddhist *stupa* or reliquary in Tibet (T)

dargah – a shrine complex: the tomb itself and attendant outbuildings (U)
Dasa – *das*, as in *Dasa Avatara*, is the Urdu word for the number ten. Dasas were an Indian tribe demonized by the *arya*, the writers of the Rig Veda (Skt)
dhammal – religious dancing to the beat of a drum at Sufi shrines (P)
djinn – a spirit, sometimes benign often malign, believed to inhabit human beings (particularly beautiful ones) and cause distress (A)
dupatta – headscarf (U)

Eid-ul-Azha – the celebration at the end of the *Haj* which commemorates Abraham's pact with God (A)
Eid-ul-fitr – Muslim celebration at the end of Ramzan, the holy month of fasting (A)

faqir – a religious devotee of a saint who puts faith above material cares; from the Arabic *faqr*, poverty (A)

ghazi – holy warrior (A)
giddha – the female equivalent of the *bhangra* dance (Pu)
gompa – Tibetan monastery (T)
gurdwara – Sikh temple (P)
guru – religious leader (Skt)

Hadith – the collected traditions or sayings of the Prophet, and an important reference point for devout Muslims (A)
Haj – the pilgrimage to Mecca and Medina that it is enjoined on every Muslim to perform at least once in their lives. A *hajji* is somebody who has performed Haj (A)
halal – 'permitted'; the Islamic equivalent of the Jewish concept of 'kosher', particularly in reference to meat (A)
haleem – a kind of meat porridge (U)

halwa – a warm cooked sweetmeat (U)

haram – the opposite of *halal*: forbidden (A)

hari – peasant or sharecropper (S)

hijra – transvestite, eunuch, transsexual. In Pakistan hijras earn a living by dancing at weddings, blessing newborn children, or through prostitution: a service they generally provide at lower rates than women (U)

hujra – male guesthouse situated outside the family compound (Pu)

iftari – food with which the fast is broken during Ramzan, the holy month of fasting (A)

jannat – heaven; from the Arabic word for garden: the Arabic for heaven is *jannat-ul-firdaus* (Garden of Paradise) (U)

jheenga – shrimp (S)

jihad – there are two types of jihad: the greater jihad is an internal spiritual battle for self-improvement; the lesser jihad, a defence of the faith which includes holy war (A)

jirga – a meeting, usually of men, convened by a community to arbitrate on a dispute (Pa)

jungli – wild or uncouth; from the Sanskrit *jangala*; hence the English word 'jungle' (U)

kaccha – literally, raw or uncooked; temporary; the opposite of *pukka* or *pakka*, cooked or permanent. Thus a concrete-built house is 'pukka' while a shanty house or hut is 'kaccha'. This word also describes the fertile lands which lie along the banks of a river directly in its floodplain, and for which the land tenure is not fixed (U)

kafir – 'unbeliever', a non-Muslim (A)

kalma – Islamic creed (A)

Khan – a clan name or title implying a leader (Pa)

kiang – wild ass; an alternative spelling is *kuang* (T)

lakh – 100,000; hence *lakhi*: the forest of one hundred thousand trees in the Punjab (Skt)

lama – Tibetan religious male teacher (T)

lhamo – Tibetan religious female teacher (T)

lingam – symbol of Shiva's penis worshipped by Hindus (Skt)

madrassah – Islamic religious school (A)

maidaan – open space in a settlement or town (U)

majoon – a herbal confection mixed by a hakim. Some majoons are made of hashish, opium and other intoxicating substances and are sometimes sold as aphrodisiacs (A) *malik* – a headman or leader of a tribe (A)

mandala – literally 'circle'; a painting, chart or text representing the cosmos and used by Buddhists and Hindus as an aid to meditation (Skt)

masjid – mosque (A)

maulvi, mufti, mullah – Islamic religious teacher (A)

mela – literally 'gathering'; a religious meeting of Hindus, or a fair (Skt)

mitha – sweet (U)

mleccha – a non-Sanskrit-speaking person, an outcast (Skt)

mugarman – a waist-high drum with feet, sacred to the Sheedis; also called *maseendo* (S)

Mujahideen – combatants, soldiers who fight for their faith; in Afghanistan, this was the name given to those who fought Soviet rule during the Communist period, 1979–89 (A)

murid – devotee of a saint (A)

nafrat – enmity, hatred (U)

naga, nagi – snake deities, guardians of rivers, springs and lakes, reverenced by Buddhists and often depicted in Gandharan art (Skt)

nala – a ditch or drain (U)

namaz – Islamic prayer (P, U)

namkeen – salty (U)

nawab – chief (U)

nazim – mayor (U)

paan – a mildly intoxicating confection of betel nut, lime paste and other condiments chewed after dinner as a digestive (U)

paanch – the number five (U)

paisa – one-hundredth of a rupee; plural, *paise* (U)

panchayat – a group of five community leaders (U/Skt)

pandit – a Hindu religious teacher (Skt)

pir – holy person, generally a man (U)

purdah – literally, 'curtain'; the Muslim practice of covering the hair or face of women from view (A)

qalandar – a wandering religious mendicant (U)

Qawwali – religious devotional songs sung at the shrines of Chishti saints in the Indian subcontinent (U)

Quaid-e-Azam – 'Great Leader'; the title given to Muhammad Ali Jinnah by his acolytes (U)

raag – Indian musical form (U)

raja – king (Skt)

Ramzan – the holy Muslim month of fasting (A)

313

risalo – the generic name for a poetry collection, from the Arabic (S/A)
roti – flat bread (U)

sadhu – Hindu holy person (Skt)
Sajjada Nasheen – guardian of saint's shrine; a hereditary position (S)
sarovar – bathing tank; lake (Skt)
sehri – food eaten during Ramzan before sunrise; from the Arabic for 'dawn' (A)
shalwar kameez – baggy trousers and long shirt. The first word is derived from
    Persian; the second probably came into use from the Arabic *qamiz* (the same
    root as the Latin *camisia*) (U)
sharab – alcohol (A)
silsila – literally 'chain' or 'thread'; the school or teaching to which Sufis are affili-
    ated
sindoor – red powder smeared by Hindu wives in the parting of their hair, a symbol
    of their marital status (Skt)
soma – iconic and mysterious Rigvedic juice drunk by the ancient Aryans (Skt)
stupa – Buddhist reliquary, where the bones or remains of the Buddha and other
    holy Buddhists are stored. Stupas vary in size from tiny monuments to struc-
    tures as large as temples (Pali)
sutra – religious text (Skt)
syed, sayed – descendants of the Prophet through his two grandsons Hasan and
    Hussain, the children of his daughter Fatima and cousin Ali; Syed is also an
    honorific, meaning 'Sir' (A)

tara – local moonshine in Chitral (C)
taravih – recitations of the Qur'an held in the mosque during Ramzan after the
    night prayers (A)
tsampa – roasted barley flour, the staple food of Ladakh and Tibet (T)

urs – literally, 'marriage', the word denotes the date when a union finally occurred
    between the seeker and the sought. In practice an urs is the death-anniversary
    celebration of a saint's life held at his tomb (P)

Wali – leader, e.g. of Swat (A)
wallah (masculine), *wali* (feminine) – an associative suffix (P)

yogi – Hindu holy person (Skt)

zabardast – literally, 'upper hand'; wonderful, marvellous (U)

Notes

Preface

xvi 'sliced off and "thrown out"': Collins and Lapierre, p. 70.

1: *Ramzan in Karachi*

4 '"Recite!" it told him': Lawrence, p.24. *Iqra'a* was the first word of the revelation; hence *Qur'an*: recitation.

5 'diminishing length of its 114 *suras* (chapters)': Haleem, p.6. Muslims generally believe that the order of the Qur'an is also sacred and part of the divine revelation.

5 'the arrangement of the Rig Veda': Bryant, p.66.

5 'to pollute it is an abomination': Haleem, p.40.

7 'Lyari Expressway': see http://www.urckarachi.org/Aquila.htm

8 'Indo-Saracenic . . . Anglo-Mughal': Lari and Lari, p.x.

10 'a thousand miles of India': Ziring, p.98.

10 '*ten weeks' time*': In May, Mountbatten devised 'Plan Balkan' which aimed to transfer power to as many separate states as necessary – but after he showed it privately to Nehru, and Nehru 'violently' objected, the June plan was concocted instead. The criminally accelerated timetable was Mountbatten's initiative, almost his obsession. Nehru repeatedly voiced his concern about it; Jinnah was not consulted at all. See Sarkar, p.448; Mansergh, X: pp.714, 771.

10 '"Japan's surrender"': Collins and Lapierre, p.49.

10 'access to Kashmir': Ziring, p.56. All records of the boundary-deciding process were destroyed – from the official notes of the Commission to Radcliffe's rough jottings. Michel, p.169.

10 '"confusion . . . bloodshed"': Jalal, 1985, p.268.

10 'Congress which insisted on it': ibid., p.262.

11 'equally naive sister Fatima': conversation with Hamida Khuhro, Karachi, 17 December 2004.

315

11 'excluded from editions of Jinnah's speeches': for example that edited by M. Rafique Afzal. None of the editions of 1966, 1973 or 1976 includes this speech.

11 'a village not far from . . . Mahatma Gandhi's': Wolpert, p.4.

11 'state-sanctioned biographies': see for example Bolitho, 1954: 'Jinnah's father was a hide merchant', p.6.

12 'Jinnah replied that': conversation with Dr Z. H. Zaidi, Islamabad, 8 December 2003.

12 'Ramzan wasn't yet over': Mountbatten, p.258.

12 'an official body count was never made': Moon (1961) estimated 200,000; Guha (2005) suggests the total was between one and two million; the Pakistan *Defence Journal* (2000) puts the total at over two million. See also Mushirul Hasan (2002) and Gyanendra Pandey (2002).

12 '"two million Indians"': Collins and Lapierre, p.50.

13 '"It was like Karbala"': Zohra Begum is referring to the Battle of Karbala, when the Prophet's grandson Hussain was killed, an event which is mourned every year by Shias during the month of Muharram.

14 'Jinnah's *Times* obituary': *The Times*, 13 September 1948.

14 'Pakistan receiving the smaller share': Mosley, p.201.

14 'Nizam of Hyderabad': a cantankerous man proverbially richer than the Republic of France, who did not want to secede to either country, though in the end Indian soldiers forced his hand.

15 'along the edges of newspapers': conversation with Bhajia, Karachi, 17 December 2004.

15 '"an inevitable period of austerity"': *Dawn*, 1 January 1948.

15 '"Alternative to Partition"': Jalal and Seal, p.419.

16 'doubled in size': *Dawn*, 22 May 1948.

16 '44,000 Muslim government employees': *Dawn*, 21 January 1948.

17 'disgruntled Pakistan Secretariat clerks': M. S. M. Sharma, p.151.

17 '"no Hindu had the courage"': Prakasa, p.68.

18 'passage to India': *Dawn*, 16 January 1948; 6 February 1948. The Indian Government estimated that between 'five to eight thousand' Hindus were leaving Pakistan daily; see Kirpalani, p.358.

18 '"blackened my face"': Khuhro, 1998a, p.327.

18 'Mirza Qalich Beg': Schimmel, 1986, p.181.

18 'much to gain from Hindus leaving': see Cheesman, p.448; Khuhro, p.171.

18 'Jinnah caps into the sea': *Dawn*, 13 January 1948; 18 January 1948.

18 '"only to spite Pakistan"': *Dawn*, 8 October 1948.

19 'to disrupt Pakistan': *Dawn*, 25 September 1948.

19 'four-fifths of Sindh's Hindu population': Kirpalani, p.359.

20 '"latrines of Karachi"': Prakasa, pp.75–6.

21 'the Mohajir tongue': A. Hasan, 1999, p.24.

21 'migrants got very rich, very quick': Feldman, p.219.

22 'the entire Sindhi administration': A. Khan, p.140.

22 'G. M. Syed': On the same day that Syed was placed under house arrest, the government interned Khan Abdul Ghaffar Khan, the popular Pashtun leader who had peacefully opposed the Pakistan movement and campaigned for an independent Pakhtunistan.

22 '"authoritarian methods of government"': Z. H. Zaidi, ed., p.450.

23 '"exotic and exalted" Indian cities': Khuhro, 'Another Kind of Migration', in Shamsie, ed., p.107.

24 'In 1938, he agreed with his colleagues': Khuhro, 1998a, p.315.

24 '"the grand old days before Partition"': Bolitho, p.218.

24 'unscrupulous and opportunistic': Ziring, p.71.

24 '"in a frenzy to consolidate Pakistan"': quoted in Wolpert, p.343.

24 'he lay on the roadside next to a refugee camp': Ziring, p.80.

25 'Kashmir and Junagadh': two princely states contiguous with Pakistan, the former Hindu-run with a Muslim majority population, the latter Muslim-ruled with a Hindu-majority population.

25 'tuberculosis was considered . . .': Dawn, 12 September 1948.

25 '"defending and maintaining Pakistan"': Dawn, 13 September 1948.

2: Conquering the Classic River

26 '"a foul and perplexing river"': Wood, 9 February 1836, in East India Company, 1837, p.6.

26 'the old Indus Delta': The old delta was in what is now Karachi, and certain quarters of the city – Gizri, Korangi – still bear the names of the active tidal creeks they once were. See M. Ahmed, p.13.

27 'over-zealous coastguards': see Sanghur.

31 '"commodious" "River Syndhu"': Foster, 1926, pp.75–6.

31 'the English had beaten the Portuguese': Keay, 1993, p.108.

31 '"they laugh at us for such as wee bring"': Foster, 1926, pp.76–7.

32 '"coullers most requireable"': Foster, 1911, p.191.

32 '"flower of the whole parcel"': Foster, 1912, p.274.

32 'Agra, Ahmedabad and Basra': Duarte, p.34.

32 '"clove, cinnamon, purple"': 'Scindy Diary', p.8.

32 'in 1775 they evicted the Company': M. Ali, 1983, p.13.

33 'Crow was expelled': Duarte, pp.66–8.

33 '"and for the most part unsatisfactory"': J. Burnes, 1831, p.27.

33 The Periplus of the Erythraean Sea: Anon., tr. Schoff, 1912, p.37.

33 'Indus, incolis Sindhus appellatus': quoted in d'Anville, 1759, p.8; 'ad Indum amnem': Wink, p.132.

33 '"classic river"': J. Burnes, 1831, p.11.

34 'woefully imprecise': d'Anville, 1753, p.15.

35 'charted in 1842': Vigne, 1842, p.123.

35 'they thought the Indus rose in Kashmir': Thornton, I, p.264. As late as 1951, David Lilienthal, who brokered the Indus Waters Treaty, wrote that the Indus rises in Kashmir (p.58).

35 '"Wheat, Rice and Legumen"': Hamilton, pp.121, xii–xiii, 125.

36 '"The Indus forms a strong barrier"': Forster, 1798, p.47.

36 '"that Country, *has* been successfully invaded"': East India Company, 1830, f.27v.

36 '"tribe of the French"': East India Company, 1839, p.315.

38 '"Horses of the Gigantic Breed"': A. Burnes, 1831b, Sheet 11.

39 '"navigation into a most fertile country"': A. Burnes, 1831b, p.2.

39 '"the Indus which flows through Sinde"': treaties signed by the rulers of Hyderabad and Khairpur, see East India Company, 1837, 'Appendix 1: Colonel Pottinger's Arrangements for the Navigation of the Indus', p.11.

39 '"The haughty Lords of SINDE"': letter from A. Burnes to John McNeil, 6 June 1837, in A. Burnes, 1837.

40 '"As we ascended the river"': A. Burnes, 1834, I, p.ix; III, pp.136–7, 37–8.

40 'He was feted in every salon': *The Times* commented that 'No book of travels has for some years past presented stronger claims to notice than the narrative published by Lieutenant Alexander Burnes', 20 August 1834, p.2, col.f. See Kaye, 1867, II, p.26.

40 'The French and English Geographical Societies': see Laurie, p.6 n.1.

40 'the *Monthly Review*': 1834 (August, II:4), p.456.

40 'the *Spectator*': 5 July 1834, p.637.

40 'was translated': German (1835), Italian (1842), French (1855) and an abridged Spanish translation under a different title in 1860.

40 'European pioneers in a "virgin" land': A. Burnes, 1834, II, p.395.

41 'Auckland gave his reasons': 'Simlah Manifesto' of 1 October 1838, quoted in Kaye, 1874, I, pp.369–74.

41 '"flowery imagination"': Anon., 1845, p.12. See also Hall, pp.54–9.

42 'the Afghans appeared ungrateful': Anon., 1845, pp.15–16; Holdsworth, p.72; Jackson, p.3. Kaye called the entry of the Shah into Kabul a 'funeral procession': 1874, I, p.479.

42 '"a nation almost unknown in the days of Alexander"': Holdsworth, Preface: pp.v–viii.

42 'Sir John Hobhouse': *Hansard's Parliamentary Debates*, 1840 (LI:col.1169ff, 1321ff).

42 '"stirring like Lions"': quoted in J. Burnes, 1842, f.135.

42 'The Court of Directors': Kaye, 1874, I, pp.380, 177n.

43 'They chose the late lamented Burnes': Kaye expressed his 'abhorrence' of the manner in which officialdom had 'garbled the correspondence of public men': ibid., p.203. James Burnes also protested at his brother's posthumous mistreatment.

43 'Charles Napier, the future conqueror of Sindh': W. F. P. Napier, 1845, p.11.

43 'Ellenborough even ordered that the sandalwood gates': Kaye, 1874, III, pp.380–1.

43 'the gates were not Gujarati at all': Thapar, 2000, p.44.

43 'Sir Charles Napier – a sixty-year-old General': Lambrick, p.149.

44 'The loot from the fort': Hughes, p.43.

44 'As for the army': see Kaye, 1874, I, pp.380ff, for a summary of the main objections. British merchants also condemned the 'wanton demolition of the Grand Bazaar in Cabool' as hindering the progress of Ellenborough's own commercial policy in the region (see 'British Prospectus', in Napier Papers, p.39v).

44 'the reputation of the trans-Indus provinces': British attitudes to the 'barbarous tribes' of the Indus valley changed from hostility and suspicion to one of gratitude and even admiration; see, for example, Greathed, p.x; also Bell, pp.iii, 2; and Aitken, p.142.

45 'a "nation of shopkeepers"': Masson, III, p.453; I, pp.v–xii; III, pp.430–3.

45 'The first sixty miles of river': East India Company, 1837, p.3. Tavernier had pointed to this problem long before: 'The commerce of Tatta, which formerly was considerable, is decreasing rapidly, because the entrance to the river becomes worse from day to day, and the sands, which have accumulated, almost close the passage': p.9.

45 'Merchants had long since "abandoned the Indus"': Heddle, p.442.

45 '"a foul and perplexing river"': Wood, 9 February 1836, in East India Company, 1837, p.6.

45 '"the ever-changing channels of our Indian rivers"': Wood, 1838a, Mf.1068, p.549.

46 '"4 of the War Steamers on the Indus"': C. Napier, 1846, p.26.

46 '"the combined system of railways and steam-boats"': Andrew, 1859, p.1.

46 'By 1861, passengers': Bombay Government.

46 'not to say dangerous': river accidents gave impetus to the construction of the railway line from Karachi to Kotri; see Aitken, p.356.

46 '*Our Paper*': 19 February 1867, p.57.

46 '"inefficient, uncertain, unsafe, costly"': Andrew, 1869, p.3. In 1886, the Scinde-Punjaub Railway eventually became subsumed within the new 'imperial . . . North-Western Railway': Aitken, p.345; also Kerr, pp.44, 76.

48 '60 per cent of the surface water': quoted in Michel, pp.74, 84–8.

48 'The Delta lands': A. Hasan, 2002, p.130.

48 'a barren, unpeopled land': A. Burnes, 1834, III, p.37.

49 'The need to build more dams': Michel, pp.197ff.

49 'a confidential British Foreign Office memo':'Indus Waters Dispute', Government of Britain: Foreign Office, 1 November 1951.

50 'the Delta shrank': A. Hasan, 1999, p.27.

3: Ethiopia's First Fruit

52 'The state of my Sheedi brothers in Sindh': Mussafir, 1952, Preface.

54 '24 March 1843': This is the date given on the plaque by the Young Sheedi

Welfare Organization (Badin). Others say 23 March, some 26 March.

54 'Hosh Muhammad Sheedi': Burton (1848) described him as 'the favourite attendant of Shere Mahomed' (the Talpur ruler from Mirpur Khas) but it seems in fact that he was by birth in the service of the Talpur rulers of Hyderabad, and only joined Sher Muhammad when all the other Talpur rulers had capitulated to the British. See also F. Ahmed, p.25.

55 'Slaves were not objects': Segal, p.5ff.

55 'Freeing a "believing slave"': Qur'an 4.92.

55 'soldiers, advisers or generals': Toru and Philips, p.ix.

55 'From the ninth century onwards': Wink, p.13.

56 '"[A Towne Misse]"': quoted in Aravamudan, p.34.

56 'the revolt by black slaves': Edward Alpers in Pankhurst and Jayasuriya, eds, p.22.

56 'forever the servants of non-blacks': Helene Basu in Pankhurst and Jayasuriya, eds, p.230.

56 'al-Masudi and Avicenna': Segal, pp.47–9.

57 'Ferishta, the Persian historian': Friese.

57 'A Kashmiri Hindu recoiled in horror': see Pollock, p.277.

57 '"The word Mogull in their language"': Coverte, p.39.

57 'Asia, which already had a large agrarian population': Segal, p.4.

58 'Ibn Battuta, a Moroccan trader and writer': quoted in Gibb, tr., p.632.

58 'the Portuguese sailor João de Castro': quoted by Richard Pankhurst in Pankhurst and Jayasuriya, eds, p.200.

58 'African admirals worked for the Mughal empire': Segal, p.72.

59 'the Marathas in western India': Pankhurst, in Pankhurst and Jayasuriya, eds, p.213.

59 'the period of "Shidi rule" in Bombay': Hotchand, pp.94–101.

59 '"Frizled Woolly-pated Blacks"': Fryer, pp.147, 168.

59 '"faithful and even affectionate service"': Grose, p.149.

59 '"the part played by the Habshis"': Ross, II, pp.xxii, xxxviii.

59 '"the greater number of Sidis, or negroes"': Beachey, p.50.

60 '"Zanzibarees, Bombasees, and Hubshees"': Burton, 1848, p.646.

60 '"monstrous muscular arms"': Burton, 1851b, pp.52–3. Burton changed some words of this description in the 1877 updated edition: 'monstrous' became 'mighty', 'uncomely' became 'buffalo-like'.

60 '"sea-Thugs"': Burton, 1877, pp.13–14.

60 'shaydâ, "fool" or "senseless"': During, p.54. An alternative etymology suggests that 'Sheedi' derives from Arabic Syed, the literal meaning of which is Master/Lord/Sir (although it has come to be associated with the Prophet's descendants). In Morocco, for example, this Arabic word is pronounced 'Sidi'.

61 'twenty-five slaves on board': Baillie, p.36.

61 'fighting men from Zanzibar': Hotchand, p.175.

61 'dark skin and tightly curled hair': Pashington Obeng in Catlin-Jairazbhoy and Alpers, eds, pp.143–7.

62 'The Sanskrit law books of classical Hinduism': Jha, p.22.

63 'the authors of the Rig Veda': quoted in Muir, II, pp.391ff.

64 '12 per cent of paternal Y-chromosomes': Qamar et al., pp.1107–24.

69 'A North American musicologist': Edward Alpers in Pankhurst and Jayasuriya, eds, p.35.

70 'Swahili-speaking tribes': Freeman-Grenville.

70 'the *ngoma* drum from Zimbabwe': Catlin-Jairazbhoy, in Catlin-Jairazbhoy and Alpers, eds, pp.189–90.

70 'Mai Mishra': Helene Basu in ibid., p.67.

73 'Bilal's conversion to Islam': Later Bilal's name was changed again, during an illness, to Gulab.

77 'emancipation being "to them a real evil"': Burton, 1851a, p.253.

4: River Saints

80 '"debt bondage"': see Anti-Slavery International, 2002.

81 'Local pirs, who had lost *murids*': There was a local precedent: two centuries earlier, Mian Adam Shah Kalhora found the force of the Mughal army bearing fatally down upon him after his experiment in communal farming angered the local aristocracy.

81 'The nobles wrote letters to each other': Schimmel, 1969, p.160.

82 '"the depravity in this sink of iniquity"': Manrique, II, p.240.

83 'Sarmad's nudity did not': Singer and Gray.

83 '"how can I tell a lie?"': Seth. A similar story is told of the eccentric/ecstatic Baghdadi Sufi Shebli; see Arberry, tr., 1979, p.286.

83 '"Mansoor of India"': ibid., p.5.

83 '"He sacrificed everything"': Syed.

84 'The result was a feudal system': See Sarah Ansari on 'the British practice of distributing patronage based on the preservation of landed interests': 'the relationship between the British and Sind's religious élite came to form part of the "balancing act" which the authorities performed in order to maintain overall control in the Sindhi countryside' (p.36).

88 '"lower-income housewives suffer from anxiety"': Mirza and Jenkins, p.796; and N. Husain et al., p.5.

89 'Water is a blessing': Schimmel, 1986, p.14.

90 '"Pot in hand, trust in God"': This translation is a mixture of that of Elsa Kazi (repr. 1996) and Amena Khamisani (2003).

92 'Latif invented an instrument': Colonel Todd was of the opinion that the Indian scale was invented on the banks of the Indus; see Tirathdas Hotechand in Akhund, ed., p.160.

95 'Hussamuddin Rashdi': quoted by Schimmel, 1976, p.153.

95 'These verses are also interpreted': Advani, p.16.

96 'The early Jesuit missionaries': Stuart, pp.259–63.

96 'the Ismaili Satpanthi community': Khakee.

97 'Lal Shahbaz Qalandar's whim': A. Burnes, 1834, III, p.57.

97 'by Muslims as well as Hindus at two places in Sindh': Arif Hasan writes that in Karachi there was once 'a mosque and a temple dedicated to Daryalal, the water deity' (A. Hasan, 1986, p.76).

101 'the hitherto nameless friend of Moses': Later he assumed an important role in Sufi circles as the mystic initiator of new masterless disciples; see Schimmel, 1976, p.22.

101 '"river godlings or saints"': Temple.

103 '"throne of serpents"': A. Hasan, 2002.

104 '"the entire Hindu social organization"': Ajwani, p.89.

104 'Muslims had stifled its revival': Ajwani, p.3. Claude Markovits notes that this trend was exacerbated by Partition: the beliefs of Sindhi Hindus who left Pakistan to live in India 'underwent a redefinition', he writes, in order to 'fit within "mainstream" Hinduism'. The Sufism was dropped; the cult of Jhule Lal was promoted (Markovits, p.285).

106 '"the special duty of Zinda Pir"': Mariwalla, p.136.

5: The Guru's Army

109 'Panj Piriya': Y. Husain, pp.31–2.

110 '"a sort of Vatican"': quoted in Mosley, pp.211–12.

110 '"Bestow on the Khalsa"': Shiromani Gurdwara Parbandhak Committee, 2004, p.10.

110 'during the 1881 and 1891 censuses': Markovits, p.255.

111 'The people whispered': K. Singh, 2005, p.31.

113 'a pool of water in the south Indian desert': McLeod, pp.49, 47, 57.

113 'the "future confluence of world-cultures"': Shiromani Gurdwara Parbandhak Committee, 2002, p.2.

115 '"Religion lieth not in visiting tombs"': tr. K. Singh, 1978, p.167.

115 'He did not believe in reincarnation, avatars or caste': ibid., p.4.

116 'Lying directly on the route from Kabul to Delhi': The destruction wreaked by the Mongol Taimur (Tamerlane) in 1398 was only the most dramatic in a long succession of such attacks. When the Sultan of Delhi entered Lahore in 1421, he found the city deserted: 'only the owl of ill omen had its abode' (quoted in Ahuja, p.56).

116 '"His hordes are perpetrators of sin"': tr. K. Singh, 1978, p.166.

117 'Padmanabhan': pp.168–71.

118 'Sikhs as "murderous butchers"': See Rubina Saigol: 'The Sikhs appear primarily as knife-wielding and murderous butchers' (2004).

118 '"Hindu–Muslim marriage in Pakistan"': interview with Rukhsana Noor, 17 February 2004.

118 '"from a pietistic Hindu sect into a martial faith"': Cohen, 2004, p.16.

119 'Jahangir, the new emperor': K. Singh, 2005, p.57.

120 'celebrated Hindu festivals, married Muslim wives': That was the broad picture; in the detail, Ranjit Singh ruled much as the Mughals had done – by placing the heaviest burden on the peasantry. See Purewal, p.38.

121 '"their glittering and bespangled faces"': A. Burnes, 1831a.

121 'the gold-embossed letter': Ranjit Singh's letter to Alexander Burnes was kindly translated for me by Dr Yunus Jaffery.

121 'In his army there was a Sikh cavalry': K. Singh, 2005, p.200.

121 '"Muslims and Hindus are completely different"': quoted by Nayyar and Salim, p.80.

123 '"I will not let you drink the water of my Punjab"': quoted by K. Singh, 2005, p.75.

123 'a French-trained standing army': Lafont, p.207.

124 'army recruitment manual': quoted by Cohen, 1990, p.212, footnote 18.

124 'During both World Wars': Cohen, 1999, pp.41–2.

124 'the British tricked Sikhs': Shiromani Gurdwara Parbandhak Committee, 2002, p.20.

124 'In a direct continuation from the colonial era': Imran Ali, pp.237–42.

126 'Dams, they say, are highly wasteful': Kaiser Bengali and Nafisa Shah in Bengali, ed., p.xv.

126 'Pakistan's foreign debt': Khalid Ahmed in Bengali, ed., p.86.

126 'entirely inoperable by 2030': A. R. Memon in Bengali, ed., p.180.

127 'in particular Kalabagh': Kalabagh was even criticized recently by a governmental report commissioned by the President (the Abbasi Report, 2005). Unfortunately, the report advocated two alternative dams in Kalabagh's place. One is Basha, north of Islamabad on the Karakoram Highway, which would submerge a hugely important prehistoric rock art site. The other is the Skardu dam in the far north of the country, which some fear would flood an entire city.

127 '"Worshippers who praise the Lord"': tr. K. Singh, 1978, pp.18, 110.

127 '"lions, tigers, leopards"': K. Singh, 2005, p.9.

128 'drops it on to his tongue like sherbet': It is reminiscent of the story told of Divan Gidumal, the Hindu minister during Kalhora times in Sindh, who offered an Afghan invader the wealth of Sindh in two bags: one contained gold and the other holy dust collected from the tombs of Sindh's saints (Schimmel, 1976, p.21).

6: Up the Khyber

131 '"Give a hundred thanks, Babur"': Babur, tr. Beveridge, pp.484, 526.

132 'a big red sandstone fort at Attock': 'One of the occurrences was the founding of the fort of Atak Benares. It was the secret design of the world-adorner that when the army arrived at this boundary, a lofty fortress should be built. On this occasion the place which far-sighted men had chosen was approved of. On 15 Khurdad (near the end of May 1588) . . . the foundation was laid by the holy hand in accordance with this name, just as in extremity of the eastern provinces there is a fortress named Katak Benares' (Abul-Fazl, 1910, III, p.521). Olaf Caroe, however, says the fort was begun in 1581 and finished by 1586 (pp.208–11). G. T. Vigne wrote that 'The name Attok is derived from Atkana, or Atukna, signifying in Hindustani, *to stop*; no pious Hindoo will venture beyond it of his own accord, for fear of losing caste' (1840, p.30).

132 'a "noble barrier"': Abul-Fazl, 1910, III, pp.520–1.

133 '"I am a drinker of wine"': C. E. Biddulph, p.81. Pashtunwali also forbids drinking, at least in public.

133 '"I am well acquainted with Aurangzeb's justice"': Raverty, 2002, p.188.

133 'Khushal's scorn': Caroe, p.165.

133 'Aurangzeb camped for two years at Attock': C. E. Biddulph, p.xiii.

133 'Khushal died heartbroken': Raverty, 2002, p.146.

133 'He wrote over three hundred and sixty works': Mackenzie, p.12.

134 'Kama Sutra-like, the *Diwan*': interview with Professor Raj Wali Khattak, former head of the Pashto Academy, Peshawar University, April 2005.

134 'his mother was an Afghan from Zabul': Caroe, p.120.

134 'spoke Turkic at home with his slaves': Bosworth, p.130.

136 '"The Establisher of Empires"': The latter two titles were for his sons. Ferishta, tr. Briggs, I, p.81.

136 'In the Hadith . . .': Wink, 1999, p.193.

136 '"The King," wrote the historian Ferishta': Ferishta, tr. Briggs, I, p.62.

136 '"Fanatical bigots representing India as a country of unbelievers"': Abul-Fazl, tr. Blochmann and Jarrett, 1927–49, III, p.377.

137 'a monotheistic system': Alberuni, tr. Sachau, p.xviii.

137 'He drew favourable comparisons': S. Sharma, p.137.

138 'Mahmud is said to have so admired': Elphinstone, pp.554–5.

138 'Having sacked the temple of Somnath': M. Habib, p.57.

138 'He pardoned a Hindu king': from Ferishta, tr. Briggs, I, p.67.

138 'He even had a coin minted': Kazmi, p.23.

138 'In Zarang they sacked the Friday mosque': Bosworth, p.89.

139 'he shouted at the Caliph's ambassador': M. Habib, p.36.

139 'Al Utbi described the end to one campaign': Elliot, II, p.30.

139 'Daud, the "Karmatian heretic"': Nazim, p.97.

142 'Sultan Mahmud was famous for having a romance with a man': ibid., p.153.

148 'Ghani Khan': son of Khan Abdul Ghaffar Khan, the 'Frontier Gandhi'.

148 'The last time that *muhtasib* . . . roamed the streets': Bilgrami, pp.178ff.

148 'the muhtasib's proposed duties': Government of NWFP, 2005.

149 '*Sharam,* shame': M. Ismail, 1997; Muhammad and Zafar.

150 'there has never been a prosecution in Pakistan for sodomy': 'As elsewhere
with unenforced sodomy proscriptions, the existence of the law is a threat – a
threat conducive to blackmail' (Murray and Badruddin Khan, p.120).

150 'Male-male sex is simply accepted': 'You know what he is promised in paradise?' Emma Duncan, the *Economist* journalist, recalls the Nawab of Bugti
remarking disdainfully of his religious nephew, 'Houris, ghilmans and sharab.
Prostitutes, little boys and wine' (Duncan, p.144).

150 'they were affronted by the "frantic debauchery" of their women': The same
thing, Burton claimed, happened during the Mutiny of 1857: 'There was a formal
outburst of the Harems, and even women of princely birth could not be kept
out of the officers' quarters' (Burton, 1919 (X), pp.205, 236).

7: Buddha on the Silk Road

155 'the Sakya-Sinha Buddha in his lion form': M. Habib, p.14.

155 'Ghazni itself had been a Buddhist settlement': Baker and Allchin, p.24.

156 'a poem by Mahmud's court poet Unsuri': ibid., pp.24–5.

158 'In Bamiyan, after Islam came to the region': Kepel, p.234.

159 'It was famed for the beauty of its spoken Sanskrit': Salomon, 1999, p.4.

160 '"the witches of Swat prefer to ride on hyenas"': Jettmar, 1961, p.94.

160 'enlightenment through sexual union': Cammann, p.8.

160 'Padmasambhava travelled to Tibet': Beyer, p.38. Some scholars maintain that
Padmasambhava came from Ghazni: see Waddell, p.26.

160 'Swat became a major pilgrimage site for Tibetans': G. Tucci (Foreword) in
Faccenna, 1964, p.7. See also Makin Khan, 'The Tibetan Pilgrim, Urgyan-Pa,
also passed through Swat valley in 1250 AD' (p.16).

161 'After his death, secret books written by him': Tucci, p.38.

162 'The serious monks lived': Xuanzang, tr. Beal, 2000, pp.98, 120, 272.

162 'a pet hero of the Tang dynasty': Wriggins, p.xv.

163 'Along the upper course of the Indus': Fa Hsien, tr. Legge, p.23.

165 'a fourth-century potsherd painted with Greek characters': Faccenna, 1964, p.17.

166 'Kanishka had eclectic tastes': Foltz, pp.44–5.

166 'immigrant Buddhism became known as the "religion of the images"': Lopez,
p.97.

166 '*but-shikan*': M. Habib, p.56.

167 'the local gods of India': These were shown in subservient positions to the
Buddha but their presence was nevertheless comforting to the people who had

once worshipped them. As with Islam later, it was a means of incorporating local faiths – a means, some have argued, of subordination: see Lopez, p.42.

167 'all the erstwhile Vedic deities': as dazzlingly attired, the scholar Etienne Lamotte noted, as their bejewelled human worshippers (pp.688–90).

167 'lakes, springs and rivers': Many of these sites had once been temples to the Nagas, and were converted by Buddhists into monasteries or stupas. See Coomaraswamy, p.13.

167 'British colonial officers': van Lohuizen de Leeuw, p.377.

168 'influenced by Greek prototypes': Narain, p.10; Tarn, p.408.

168 'Menander's Buddhism as wholly pragmatic': Marshall, 1921, p.21.

169 'the *dharmachakra*': Narain, p.2.

169 'Ashoka's stupas, said to number 84,000': according to the *Ashokavadana*, an early chronicle of the emperor's reign. See Lamotte, p.239; Foucher, 1942, p.272.

169 'The Buddha's ashes were still warm': Lamotte, p.23.

170 '"At all times, whether I am eating"': Sixth Major Rock Edict, quoted in Thapar, 1997, pp.252–3.

171 '"All modern Indic scripts"': Salomon, 1998: 'the history of writing in India is virtually synonymous with the history of Brahmi script and its derivatives' (p.17).

171 'Subsequent Buddhist tradition has vaunted': Lamotte, p.13.

171 'serving as viceroy in Taxila': according to the Tibetan tradition; see Marshall, 1921, p.17.

172 'In Aramaic it transmogrified': Thapar, 1997, pp.276–7.

173 'it was monks from Uddiyana': Salomon, 1999, p.6.

173 'Buddhist animal tales that travelled west along the Silk Road': Alberuni, tr. Sachau, p.xxix.

174 'Timber, in particular, has been a lucrative export': Stacul, p.76.

175 'easy prey for angry Muslims': The rise of vandalism also coincides with the Wali's loss of control over Swat, according to Sardar (p.168).

8: Alexander at the Outer Ocean

178 'a sailor called Scylax': Herodotus, tr. Rawlinson, p.313.

178 '"the bravest man in early Greek history"': Lane Fox, 1973, p.333.

178 '"three hundred and sixty talents of gold dust"': Herodotus, tr. Rawlinson, p.265.

178 'black skin, he wrote, and black semen': Karttunen, 1989, p.73.

182 'Unani medicine – practised by hakims': Balfour, p.13.

183 'Babur ate majoon': The word used for majoon, 'confection', is *kamali*: Babur, tr. A. Beveridge, I, p.373.

184 'called the Guraeus by the Greeks': This was either the Panjkora, or the combined waters of the Panjkora and Swat rivers. See Arrian, tr. Brunt, p.508, and Caroe, p.51.

184   "'He crossed it with difficulty'": Arrian, tr. Robson, I, p.427.

184   'one hundred porters, thirty bodyguards, four army revolvers': Stein, pp.74, 113.

193   'marked on maps as "Unexplored Country"': see the map in Knight.

193   'the same highland breed that Alexander so admired': Lane Fox, 1980, p.319.

194   "'transported with Bacchic frenzy'": Arrian, tr. Brunt, II, p.9.

194   'modern historians have tended to assume that Nysa must be located in this region': Robin Lane Fox deduced that Nysa was in Chitral (1980, p.313); Martha L. Carter argued for Kunar (1968, p.136).

194   'the entire area between Jalalabad and the Indus': see Jettmar, 2001, pp.77–9.

195   "'Overland I went'": Euripides, tr. Arrowsmith, pp.155–6.

195   'Centuries after that, when Philostratus': Philostratus, tr. Conybeare, p.139.

197   "'Where you are going we cannot help you'": The Malik's comment, I find later, encapsulates the attitude of people from the 'settled' areas – who live according to the writ of central government – to those in the 'tribal' areas, who live by their own rules, grow poppy, and shun outsiders.

201   "'These sailed down the Indus'": Arrian, tr. Robson, I, p.447.

207   'Strabo, Diodorus and Quintus Curtius': Bunbury, pp.496–7.

208   'consecrating hair to them at puberty': Hornblower and Spawforth, eds, p.1320.

208   'a *peripeteia*, a turning point': Ehrenberg, p.53.

210   'maddened with suffering': Arrian, V.17.6, tr. Brunt, II, p.53.

210   'where the streams dry up in summer': see P. A. Brunt in his translation of Arrian, II, p.453, Appendix XVII.

211   'such "limpid", "delicious" waters': Strabo, tr. Jones, IV, 2; Herodotus, tr. Rawlinson, IV, 53.

211   "'It is sweet for men to live bravely'": Arrian, V.25–6, tr. Brunt, II, pp.83–7.

212   "'a fraudulent wonder'": Quintus Curtius, IX.3.19, tr. Yardley, p.219.

214   'he was preparing a campaign to Arabia': Arrian, VII.19–20, tr. Robson, II, p.271.

214   'the fate of Callisthenes': Stoneman, p.21; Gunderson, p.4.

215   "'manifold windings through the entire province'": quoted in Allen, p.155.

215   'Muslims also began to eulogize Alexander': Schildgen, p.96.

215   'Horsemen in the Pamir mountains': Stoneman, p.1.

215   'he "saw the sun rising"': Qur'an 18.89, Dawood, p.213.

215   "'Alexander . . . spurred by religious ardour'": Southgate, p.20.

215   'Pashtuns still claim him as their forebear': as did the Gyalpos in Baltistan, along the river's north-eastern course, at least until the nineteenth century (see Cunningham, p.28). Other Pashtun origin myths, meanwhile, suggest they are one of the lost tribes of Israel.

9: Indra's Beverage

217   '"the so-called Niggers of India"': Bryant and Patton, eds, p.472.

217   '"*Gypsey jargon*"': Stewart, IV, p.92. Max Müller commented on Dugald Stewart: 1891a, p.164.

217   'As Max Müller himself commented': Max Müller, 1891a, I, p.229.

218   '"Dark and helpless utterances"': Max Müller, 1891b, p.xxix.

218   '"Striving for the victory prize"': Doniger O'Flaherty, p.105.

218   'resistant to scholarly penetration': As the Sanskrit scholar Harry Falk writes, 'The language of the poets obscures more facts than it clarifies' (p.70).

219   'engendered humanity's concept of the divine': Max Müller, 1907, p.152.

219   '"The derivation of the name Indra"': Max Müller, 1903, pp.395–6.

220   'Indra's waters fill the Indus': Griffith, p.139.

220   '"honey-growing flowers"': Wilson, pp.205–6.

221   'their women dance naked': cited in Karttunen, 1989, p.217.

221   'a Brahmin priest from Sindh': Das.

222   '"The Aryans did not cross the river into India"': interview with Muhammad Zahir, Peshawar Museum, 2005.

222   'In the 1960s, artefacts were recovered': Dani, 1967, p.49.

222   'a connection with the Vedic literature': Stacul, 1987, p.123.

222   '"Surely the child of the waters, urging on his swift horses"': Doniger O' Flaherty, p.105.

223   'Proto-Sanskrit speakers entered north-west Pakistan': Parpola, p.200; Dani, 1967, p.375.

223   'warm the heart of any Gaul': Horses were indeed the main food of Palaeolithic humans in Europe; see Curtis, p.21.

223   'Indra, it is written': Michael Witzel in Erdosy, ed., p.322.

224   'pure Aryans of the high type': J. Biddulph, p.128.

224   'Indra has done these deeds': Wilson, 1854, II, p. 246.

225   'they had killed the sons of Ali': J. Biddulph, p.131; Jettmar, 1986, p.133.

226   'famous for its horses': In the Buddhist text *Majjhima* the land of the Kamboja people was known as the homeland of horses; in the *Arthasastra* horse-dealers are known as Northerners.

226   'Kalash mythology maintains': Jettmar, 1974, p.75.

227   'a "rude sculpture" of their god Taiban's horse': J. Biddulph, p.15.

227   'horse sacrifices took place': Parpola, too, considered that this signified that the 'tribes of Nuristan in Northeastern Afghanistan have, in their isolation, kept their archaic Aryan religion and culture until the present century' (p.245).

227   'an early "protest movement among tribal Aryans"': The similarities of the Rig Veda to the Iranian Avesta suggest a similar, rival relationship.

227   'linguists have guessed': A. and A. Cacopardo, pp.307, 310.

227   '"the only existing remnants of ancient Aryan religion"': Morgenstierne, p.2.

228   '"Don't let it jump here and there and bring floods"': Wada, p.17.

228 '"make the floods easy to cross, O Indra"': Rig Veda 4.19.6, tr. Griffith, p.125.

228 'they hope to prove a genetic link': Genetics may yet prove where the Kalash came from. Preliminary studies have shown that they are a 'distinct' population cluster with 'external contributions' to their gene pool. See Qamar et al.

228 'a Cambridge archaeologist': F. R. Allchin, p.4.

230 'One group of bodies': Ihsan Ali, ed., 2005, p.140.

230 'like the milk of cattle': Doniger O'Flaherty, p.155.

235 'a practice dating from Neanderthal times': B. Allchin, p.153.

235 'according to the *Satapatha Brahmana*': Bryant, 2002, p.202.

235 '"in complete sexual abandon"': Jettmar, 1980a, pp.63–4.

236 'In another orchard near the river': The Pakistani archaeologist Professor A. H. Dani, who visited Yasin valley with Karl Jettmar, mistook this circle, which in those days belonged to a man called Ishaq (the current owner's grandfather), for that described by Biddulph as being the most complete circle in the valley. In fact, Biddulph's 'circle in most perfect preservation' is further south – exactly as he described it, on a tongue of land between two rivers.

240 'repolished to a brown lustre': Martin Bemmann at the Felsbilder und Inschriften am Karakorum Highway (Heidelberg Akademie) was kind enough to examine my photographs of the carving, which he knew about from an article by Haruko Tsuchiya (2000). He estimated that it was carved between the sixth and second millennium BCE.

241 'the art of Mesolithic hunters': Jettmar, 2002, p.91.

241 'a drawing by one of the Kalash': Vigne, 1842, II, p.309.

10: Alluvial Cities

243 'to the east a residential area': B. and R. Allchin, p.175. The population estimate is based on Irfan Habib, pp.22–3.

244 'scented coffins': Stacul, p.117; Chowdhury and Ghosh, pp.12–13.

244 'a Fabian utopia': Marshall, 1931, p.15.

249 'This was semi-true': Cloughley, p.376.

251 'the burrows of marmots': Peissel, p.148.

252 'Ganoks itself was a "halting-place"': Vohra, 1989a, p.39.

252 'in Pakistan they have faded from view': There are stories from the Indian side, relating to Pakistani intrusions into India during the Kargil War, which tell that men from Ganoks in Pakistan still speak Brogskad, the Dard language. See Swami.

253 '"hydropathic" citizens': Marshall, 1931, p.24.

253 '"water luxury"': Ardeleanu-Jansen, p.1.

254 'wishing to prove that the horse-riding Aryans were indigenous to India': see also the German writer Egbert Richter-Ushanas who has claimed both that 'the Indus inscriptions are identical to verses of the early Rig-Veda'

and that the 'Indus writers . . . are identical with the first Vedic seers and priests' (Richter-Ushanas, pp.7–9).

255 '"ruined places"': Michael Witzel in Erdosy, ed., p.98.

256 'the technology has not changed': see Kenoyer, p.151.

257 'the alluvium that the river brought down': B. and R. Allchin, p.167.

257 'sesame and aubergine': Diamond, p.100.

257 'the date, *Phoenix dactylifera*': B. and R. Allchin, p.108.

257 'in Greek it was *sindo-n*': quoted in *Illustrated London News*, 7 January 1928, p.32.

258 'Villages inhabited by the "Meluhha"': Perhaps the Indus valley *Meluhhas* became the *Mlecchas* – non-Sanskrit-speaking barbarians – of the later Rigvedic civilization.

258 'moist jungles of the plains': Marshall, 1931, p.19.

259 'smeared the skeletons of their dead': Pande, p.134.

260 'Others suggest that it was the river . . . which caused their destruction': The story of the flood in the Hindu *Puranas*, it has been argued, was derived from archaic legends of the unstable Indus river, themselves partly inspired by Mesopotamian stories (see Thapar, 1966, p.30).

260 'Punjab and Haryana dispute how the waters . . . should be shared': Waslekar, p.58.

11: *Huntress of the Lithic*

261 'Government by Women': Karttunen, 1989, p.187.

262 '"Such was the rule in early times"': Muir, II, pp.335–6.

262 'Megasthenes' "Hyperborea"': Karttunen, 1989, pp.186–9.

262 '*Sui Shu* (History of the Sui Dynasty)': Francke thought that *Sui Shu* was compiled *c.* 586 CE (1914, p. 74). In fact it was written a century later, from 622 to 656 CE.

262 'Kalhana's *Rajatarangini*': Kalhana, tr. Stein, I, p.137.

262 'exposing their "high breasts"': ibid., p.138.

262 'The Sanskrit texts described Uttarakuru': Karttunen, 1989, p.188.

263 'An eighteenth-century Chinese text': Enoki, p.54.

263 'Alberuni called it': Alberuni, tr. Sachau, I, p.108.

263 'polyandry was responsible for the short stature': Cunningham, p.295. See, for contrast, Arthur Connolly's reaction to a Khan he met on the way to India from Russia: 'He would not be persuaded that our matrimonial law was not reversed in Europe, and that every woman might not take unto herself four husbands; he had read it in a book, and would not be gainsayed. I was able, I hope, to correct some very erroneous impressions that he had formed with regard to the laxity of our moral system' (Connolly, p.207).

263 '"lands where women make the love"': Kipling, Chapter 14.

263 '"one of the ugliest customs"': Francke, 1907a, p.172.

263 'women are "physically ruined"': quoted in Jiao, p.24.

264 'the women of Ladakh': Norberg Hodge, 2000, pp.57–8; also the video based on the book, 1993.

264 'The Dards, also known as Brokpa . . . or Minaro': The Dards may be either the descendants of the Minaro, or an immigrant people who adopted the indigenous Minaro customs.

264 'once they dominated most of Ladakh': Lamayuru, an ancient monastery just south of Mulbekh, is said to have been a Dard colony (or possibly a Bon settlement) before it became Buddhist. In the twentieth century there were still Dards in central Ladakh, and Rohit Vohra, who studied Dard culture in the 1980s, was of the opinion that 'if one scratches beneath the surface one will discover archaic Dard customs' (1989a, p.36).

265 'the "small chip between the legs of the female figure"': Pande, p.135.

265 'a full three thousand years before Harappa': This corroborates earlier guesses: 'the megalith site of Burzahom . . . yielded great numbers of artificially flaked stones, among which were flakes and cores reminiscent of palaeolithic technique' (de Terra and Paterson, p.233).

268 'Dard groups still exist': Vohra, 1982, p.69.

271 'in the Home Minister's hands': www.bjp.org/today/june_0203/june_2_p_25.htm

272 'Angered at this insult she turned her back': Francke, 1914, p.107.

273 'a "phallus-shaped rock"': http://kargil.gov.in/tourism/monastery.htm

273 'they mistook some of the more sensuous Buddha statues for depictions of women': Francke disagreed with Cunningham about the sculptures at Dras. The former thought they were Maitreya Buddhas; the latter, nuns. See Francke, 1914, p.105.

274 'Not all these giants, it seems, were male': Francke, 1905, p.95.

274 'the original matriarchal religion had gradually been superseded': The religion whose traces Peissel observed may have been that of Bon, with its demons, gods and goddesses. They were Bon deities whom Padmasambhava 'subdued' during his tour of Ladakh and Tibet in the eighth century CE.

275 'the longest local record of polyandrous marriages': Vohra, 1989a, p.110.

275 'polyandry, monogamy, polygyny': Vohra, 1989b, p.25.

276 'was in truth so sexually explicit': Vohra, 1989b, p.99.

277 'Palaeolithic stone tools were also found here': There are also small, neat carvings of bent-legged hunters, like drafts of the Matisse-like hunters from Gakuch (which in their Pakistani context seemed so rare).

279 'At Domkhar further east, where the river narrows': Francke described how the Dards used to make bridges: 'They fasten several beams to the bank in such a way that they project into the river. After a short time they are frozen in an encrustation of ice of such solidity that it is possible to walk on them as far as the outer end. Then several more beams are fastened to the first . . . and so on, until the other bank is reached' (1907a, p.157). Laurianne Bruneau, who is writing a PhD on rock carvings in Ladakh, showed me a photograph

of a giant carving even further east, at Stakna in central Ladakh. She believes
it may have been recently destroyed by bridge-building in the area. See
Vernier, p.50.

282 'a Palaeolithic site carbon-dated to the fifth millennium BCE': Fonia.

12: The Disappearing River

284 '"There is a plain in Asia"': Herodotus, tr. Rawlinson, pp.273–4.

287 'their falling water tables': Monbiot.

295 '"the Ganden Palace, victorious in all directions"': Bertsch, p.34.

300 'many nomads died': see *World Tibet Network News*, 28 December 1994.

300 '"winter of genocide"': Allen, p.6.

300 'polyandry . . . is today on the increase in Tibet': Jiao.

301 'orogenic, flysch, zircon, gneiss': 'mountain-forming'; 'a series of tertiary strata . . .
consisting of slates, marls, and fucoidal sandstones'; 'a native silicate of zirconium,
occurring in tetragonal crystals, variously coloured, red, yellow, brown, green,
etc.'; 'a metamorphic rock, composed, like granite, of feldspar or orthoclase, and
mica, but distinguished from it by its foliated or laminated structure' (*OED*).

302 'some thirty to forty-five million years ago': Peter D. Clift speculates that the
proto-Indus river was formed at least forty-five million years ago (p.254);
John R. Shroder Jr and Michael P. Bishop estimate thirty million years (in
Meadows and Meadows, eds, p.243).

302 'the "oldest known river" in the region': Clift, p.237.

302 'International Flyway Number 4': Muhammad Farooq Ahmad in Meadows and
Meadows, eds, p.9.

302 'sea birds, river birds, marsh birds . . .': Mubashir Hasan, p.xvi.

303 'In their annual migrations': Dorst, p.376.

303 'the soul journeying to God': Pauwels, p.34.

303 'claws of migrating cranes': I. Ansari, p.155.

303 'the migration out of Africa': Oppenheimer, map.

308 'saraansh: flowing for ever': Das, p.34; kindly translated for me from the Sindhi
and Sanskrit by Gian Chand. *Sarana*, 'causing to go or flow': Monier-Williams,
p.1109.

Select Bibliography

For a full Bibliography of all works consulted during the writing of this book please go to www.empiresoftheindus.co.uk

Abbas, Shemeem Burney, *The Female Voice in Sufi Ritual: Devotional Practices of Pakistan and India*, Austin, 2002

Abbasi, A. N. G., *Report of Technical Committee on Water Resources* ['Abbasi Report'], Islamabad: http://www.cssforum.com.pk/off-topic-discussions/general-knowledge-quizzes-iq-tests/2173-report-technical-commitee-water-resources.html, 2005

Abul-Fazl, *The Akbarnama of Abu-l-Fazl*, tr. H. Beveridge, Calcutta, 1910 (III)

—— *Ain-i-Akbari by Abu l-Fazl Allami*, tr. H. Blochmann and H. S. Jarrett, Calcutta, 1927–49

Advani, Kalyan B., *Shah Latif*, Delhi, 1970

Afzal, M. Rafique, ed., *Selected Speeches and Statements of the Quaid-i-Azam Mohammad Ali Jinnah [1911–34 and 1947–8]*, Lahore, 1976 [1966]

Ahmad, Aziz, *Studies in Islamic Culture in the Indian Environment*, Oxford, 1964

Ahmed, Feroz, 'Africa on the Coast of Pakistan', in *New Directions: The Howard University Magazine*, Washington, DC (XVI:4, pp.22–31), October 1989

Ahmed, Muzammil, 'Animal and Plant Communities of the Present and Former Indus Delta', in *The Indus River: Biodiversity, Resources, Humankind*, ed. Azra Meadows and Peter S. Meadows, Karachi, 1999, pp.12–30

Ahuja, N. D., *The Great Guru Nanak and the Muslims*, Chandigarh, [1972?]

Aitken, E. A., *Gazetteer of the Province of Sind*, Karachi, 1907

Ajwani, Hazarisingh Gurbuxsingh, *A Short Account of the Rise and Growth of the Shri Sadhbella Tirath, Sukkur*, Sukkur, 1924

Akhund, Abdul Hamid, ed., *Shah Abdul Latif, his Mystical Poetry*, n.p. [Pakistan], n.d. [*c*.1991]

Al Utbi, *The Kitab-i-Yamini, Historical Memoirs of the Amir Sabaktagin and the Sultan Mahmud of Ghazna*, tr. James Reynolds, London, 1858

Alberuni, *Alberuni's India: An Account of the Religion, Philosophy, Literature, Geography, Chronology, Astronomy, Customs, Laws and Astrology of India about A.D. 1030*, tr. Edward C. Sachau, London, 1888

Ali, Ihsan, ed., *Frontier Archaeology: Explorations and Excavations in NWFP, Pakistan*, Peshawar, 2005 (III)

Ali, Imran, *The Punjab Under Imperialism, 1885–1947*, Princeton, 1988

Ali, Mubarak, *The English Factory in Sind: Extracts Regarding Sind from William Foster's 'The English Factories in India'*, Jamshoro, Pakistan, 1983

—— *In the Shadow of History*, Lahore, 1998

Al-Idrisi, *India and the Neighbouring Territories in the Kitab Nuzhat Al-Mushtaq Fi'Khtiraq Al-Afaq of Al-Sharif Al-Idrisi*, tr. S. Maqbul Ahmad, Leiden, 1960

Allchin, B., 'South Asian Rock Art', in *Journal of the Royal Society of Arts*, London, 1988, pp.138–56

Allchin, Bridget and Raymond Allchin, *The Rise of Civilization in India and Pakistan*, Cambridge, 1993 [1982]

Allchin, F. R., 'A Pottery Group from Ayun Chitral', in *Bulletin of the School of Oriental and African Studies*, London, 1970 (XXXIII)

Allen, Charles, *The Search for Shangri-La: a Journey into Tibetan History*, London, 1999

Allwright, Gavin and Atsushi Kanamaru, eds, *Mapping the Tibetan World*, Tokyo, 2004 [2000]

Andrew, W. P., *The Indus and Its Provinces, Their Political and Commercial Importance Considered in Connexion with Improved Means of Communication*, London, 1859

—— *On the completion of the Railway System of the Valley of the Indus*, London, 1869

Anon. [by a Bengal Officer], *Recollections of the First Campaign West of the Indus, and of the Subsequent Operations of the Candahar Force under Major-General Sir W. Nott*, London, 1845

Anon., *The Periplus of the Erythraean Sea*, tr. Wilfred Schoff, New York, 1912

Ansari, Ishtiaq, 'Kerigar: Gold Pickers of the Indus', in *Journal of Pakistan Archaeologists Forum*, ed. Asma Ibrahim and Kaleem Lashari, 1993 (II:1 & 2, pp.155–66)

Ansari, Sarah F. D., *Sufi Saints and State Power: the Pirs of Sind, 1843–1947*, Cambridge, 1992

Anti-Slavery International, www.antislavery.org/archive/submission/submission2002-pakistan.htm, 2002

Aravamudan, Srinivas, *Tropicopolitans: Colonialism and Agency, 1688–1804*, Durham, 1999

Arberry, A. J., tr., *The Doctrine of the Sufis (Kitab al-Ta'arruf li-madhhab ahl al-tasawwuf. Translated from the Arabic of Abu Bakr al-Kalabadhi*, Lahore, 2001 [1935]

—— *Muslim Saints and Mystics: Episodes from the Tadhkirat al-Auliya' ('Memorial of the Saints') by Farid al-Din Attar*, London, 1979 [1966]

Ardeleanu-Jansen, Alexandra, 'Who Fell Into the Well? Digging up a Well in Mohenjo-Daro', in *South Asian Archaeology 1991*, ed. A. J. Gail and G. J. R. Mevissen, Stuttgart, 1993

Arrian, *Anabasis Alexandri*, tr. E. Iliff Robson, London, 1929

—— *Anabasis Alexandri*, tr. P. A. Brunt, Cambridge, Mass., 1976

Ashley, James R., *The Macedonian Empire: The Era of Warfare Under Philip II and Alexander the Great, 359–323 BC*, Jefferson/London, 1998

334

Babur, *The Babur-nama in English (Memoirs of Babur)*, tr. Annette Beveridge, London, 1921

Baillie, Alexander, *Kurrachee: Past, Present and Future,* Calcutta, 1890

Baker, P. H. B. and F. R. Allchin, *Shahr-i Zohak and the History of the Bamiyan Valley Afghanistan*, Oxford, 1991

Balfour, Edward, *Medical Hints to the People of India: The Vydian and the Hakim, What do they know of medicine?*, Madras, 1875

Baloch, N. A., *Musical Instruments of the Lower Indus Valley of Sind*, Hyderabad, 1966

—— *Hosh Muhammad Qanbrani* [booklet in English and Sindhi], Karachi, [1975]

—— *Lands of Pakistan: Perspectives, historical and cultural*, Islamabad, 1416 AH [1995]

Baloch, Shargil, *Ki Jana Mai Kaun* [documentary film produced by Action Aid], Karachi, 2004

Bashir, Elena and Israr-ud-Din, eds, *Proceedings of the Second International Hindukush Cultural Conference*, Karachi, 1996

Beachey, R. W., *The Slave Trade of Eastern Africa*, London, 1976

Bell, Evans, *The Oxus and the Indus*, London, 1874

Bemmann, Martin, 'Rock Carvings and Inscriptions along the Karakorum Highway', in *South Asian Archaeology 1991: Proceedings of the Eleventh International Conference of the Association of South Asian Archaeologists in Western Europe*, ed. Adalbert J. Gail and Gerd J. R. Mevissen, Stuttgart, 1993

Bengali, Kaiser, ed., *The Politics of Managing Water,* Oxford/Islamabad, 2003

Bertsch, Wolfgang, *The Currency of Tibet: A Sourcebook for the Study of Tibetan Coins, Paper Money and other Forms of Currency*, Dharamsala, 2002

Beyer, Stephan, *The Cult of Tara: Magic and Ritual in Tibet*, Berkeley, 1978

Biddulph, C. E., *Afghan Poetry of the Seventeenth Century: Being Selections from the Poems of Khush Hal Khan Khatak*, London, 1890

Biddulph, John, *Tribes of the Hindoo Koosh*, Calcutta, 1880

Bilgrami, Raft Masood, *Religious and Quasi-Religious Departments of the Mughal Period (1556–1707)*, Delhi, 1984

Bolitho, Hector, *Jinnah: Creator of Pakistan*, London, 1954

Bombay, Government of, *Handbook for Passengers from Bombay to Mooltan, Via Kurrachee, Kotree, and Sukkur, By the Steamers of The Bombay Steam Navigation Company, and Steamers of the Indus Flotilla*, Bombay, 1861

Bosworth, Clifford Edmund, *The Ghaznavids: Their Empire in Afghanistan and Eastern Iran 994–1040*, Edinburgh, 1963

Britain, Government of, Foreign Office: General Correspondence from Political and Other Departments, 'Indus Waters Dispute' [National Archives, London: FO 371/92893], 1951

Bryant, Edwin, *The Quest for the Origins of Vedic Culture: The Indo-Aryan Migration Debate*, Oxford/New York, 2002 [2001]

—— with Laurie Patton, eds, *The Indo-Aryan Controversy: Evidence and Inference in Indian History*, London, 2005

Bunbury, E. H., *A History of Ancient Geography Among the Greeks and Romans*, New York, 1959 [1883]

Burnes, Alexander, 'Letter from Captain Burnes to Gen. Ramsay relating to proceedings at Roopur' [Dalhousie Letters, National Archives of Scotland: G45/5/93], 31 October 1831a

—— 'Extracts of Narrative and Journal of a voyage by the Rivers Indus and Punjnud to Lahore by Lieut: Alex. Burnes, Ass. Resident, Cutch, On a Mission to Lahore in 1831' and Memoir on the Indus, and Sinde country by L. Burnes of the Bombay Army. 1831. Addressed to the Bombay Govt.' [Dalhousie Muniments, National Archives of Scotland: G45/5/80], 1831b

—— *Travels in Bokhara: Together with Narrative of A Voyage on the Indus*, London, 1834

—— Holograph Letter written by Capt. Alexander Burnes, 21st Bombay Native Infantry, from 'On the Indus above Moultan' to H.E. John McNeil Minister at the Court of Persia, dated 6 June 1837 [MssEurD1165/2], 1837

Burnes, James, *A Narrative of a Visit to the Court of the Ameers of Sinde*, Edinburgh, 1831

—— 'Letter by James Burnes on the death of his brother' [Wellesley Papers, European Manuscripts Collection, British Library: Add. 37313, Series II, Volume XL], 1842

—— *Correspondence with Lord Palmerston*, London, 1861

Burrard, S. G. and H. H. Hayden, *A Sketch of the Geography and Geology of the Himalaya Mountains and Tibet*, Delhi, 1933

Burton, Richard, *Sindh and the Races that Inhabit the Valley of the Indus: with notices of the topography and history of the province*, London, 1851a

—— *Scinde; or, the Unhappy Valley*, London, 1851b

—— *Sind Revisited: With Notices of The Anglo-Indian Army; Railroads; Past, Present, and Future, Etc.*, London, 1877

—— 'Terminal Essay: Social Conditions: Pederasty', in *A Plain and Literal Translation of the Arabian Nights Entertainments*, Boston, 1919 (X)

—— and J. E. Stocks, 'Notes relative to the population of Sind; and the customs, language, and literature of the people etc.' [*Selections from the Records of the Bombay Government, New Series*, India Office Records, British Library: Fiche no. 1069–70], 1848

Bux, Sufi Huzoor, 'Shah Inayat Shaheed' [monograph in Sindhi], Mirpur Bathoro, 1981

Cacopardo, Albert and Augusto Cacopardo, 'The Kalasha in Southern Chitral', in Elena Bashir and Israr-ud-Din, eds, *Proceedings of the Second International Hindukush Cultural Conference*, Karachi, 1996

Cammann, Schuyler, *Trade Through the Himalayas: The Early British Attempts to Open Tibet*, Princeton, 1951

Carless, T. G., 'Memoir on the delta of the Indus' and 'Report upon portions of the River Indus' [*Selections from the Records of the Bombay Government, New Series*, India Office Records, British Library: V/23/214, Fiche no. 1067–8], 1837

Caroe, Olaf, *The Pathans: 550 B.C. – A.D. 1957*, London, 1958

Carter, G. E. L., 'Religion in Sind', in *Indian Antiquary*, Bombay, September 1917 (XLVI)

—— *The Stone Age in Kashmir* [Memoirs of the Archaeological Survey of Kashmir Series], Amritsar, 1924

Carter, Martha L., 'Dionysiac Aspects of Kushan Art', in *Ars Orientalis: The Arts of Islam and the East*, Ann Arbor, 1968 (VII)

Catlin-Jairazbhoy, Amy and Edward A. Alpers, eds, *Sidis and Scholars: Essays on African Indians*, Trenton, NJ/Delhi, 2004

Cheesman, David, 'The Omnipresent Bania: Rural Moneylenders in Nineteenth-Century Sind', *Modern Asian Studies*, Cambridge, 1982 (XVI:3)

Chowdhury, K. A. and S. S. Ghosh, 'Plant Remains from Harappa 1946', in *Ancient India: Bulletin of the Archaeological Survey of India*, Delhi, January 1951 (VII, pp. 3–19)

Clift, Peter D., 'A Brief History of the Indus River', in *The Tectonic and Climatic Evolution of the Arabian Sea Region*, ed. Peter D. Clift et al., London, 2002

Cloughley, Brian, *A History of the Pakistan Army: Wars and Insurrections* [Second Edition: With a New Chapter on the Kargil Issue], Karachi, 2000

Cohen, Stephen P., *The Indian Army: Its Contribution to the Development of a Nation*, Delhi, 1990 [1971]

—— *The Pakistan Army. 1998 Edition. With a New Foreword and Epilogue*, Oxford, 1999 [1994]

—— *The Idea of Pakistan*, Washington, DC, 2004

Coll, Steve, *Ghost Wars: The Secret History of the CIA, Afghanistan, and bin Laden, from the Soviet Invasion to September 10, 2001*, New York, 2004

Collins, Larry and Dominique Lapierre, *Mountbatten and the Partition of India*, Volume 1: *March 22–August 15, 1947*, Delhi, 1982

Connolly, Arthur, *A Journey over land from Russia to India*, London, 1834

Coomaraswamy, Ananda K., *The Origin of the Buddha Image*, New York, 1927

Cousens, Henry, in *Progress Report of the Archaeological Survey of Western India*, Bombay, for the year ending 30 June 1897

Coverte, Robert, *A true and almost incredible report*, London, 1612

Cunningham, Alexander, *Ladák, Physical, Statistical, and Historical; With Notices of the Surrounding Countries*, London, 1854

Curtis, Gregory, *The Cave Painters: Probing the Mysteries of the First Artists*, New York, 2006

Curtius Rufus, Quintus, *The History of Alexander*, tr. John Yardley, Harmondsworth, 1984

d'Anville, Jean-Baptiste Bourguignon, *Éclaircissemens géographiques sur la carte de l'Inde*, Paris, 1753

Dani, A. H., *Ancient Pakistan*, Peshawar, 1967 (III)

—— *History of Northern Areas of Pakistan (Up to 2000 AD)*, Lahore, 2001

Das, Karashni Narayan, *Shri Sindh Sapt Nad Sadhubela Teerath Mahatamay* [The

Importance of the Seven Rivers of Shri Sindh, Sadhubela Teerath, Anthology of passages about the Indus from Hindu scriptures in Sindhi and Sanskrit], Sukkur, 1922

Dawood, N. J., tr., *The Koran*, London, 2003 [1956]

de Terra, H., 'The Megaliths of Bursahom, Kashmir, a New Prehistoric Civilization from India', in *Proceedings of the American Philosophical Society*, September 1942 (LXXXV:5, pp.483–504)

—— and T. T. Paterson, *Studies on the Ice Age in India and Associated Human Cultures*, Washington, 1939

Defence Journal, Karachi, http://www.defencejournal.com/2000/mar/wagah.htm

Diamond, Jared, *Guns, Germs, and Steel: The Fates of Human Societies*, New York, 1999 [1997]

Doniger O'Flaherty, Wendy, *The Rigveda An Anthology: One hundred and eight hymns, Selected, Translated and Annotated*, Harmondsworth, 1981

Dorst, Jean, *The Migrations of Birds*, tr. Constance D. Sherman, London, 1962 [Paris, 1956]

Duarte, Adrian, *A History of British Relations with Sind 1613–1843*, Karachi, 1976

Duncan, Emma, *Breaking the Curfew: a Political Journey through Pakistan*, London, 1989

Dupree, Nancy Hatch, *An Historical Guide to Afghanistan*, Kabul, 1977 [1970]

During, Jean, 'African Winds and Muslim Djinns. Trance, Healing, and Devotion in Baluchistan', in *Yearbook for Traditional Music*, 1997 (XXIX, pp.39–56)

East India Company, 'Memoranda on the N.W. Frontier of British India and on the importance of the river Indus as connected with its defence, drawn up by the desire of Sir J. Malcolm', 1830 [European Manuscripts Collection, British Library: Add. 21178], 1830

—— 'Abstract of Proceedings Relative to the Trade and Navigation of the Indus, Since the Settlement of the Last Treaty Regarding That River', London, 1837

—— 'Treaty with the Ameers of Sinde, 22nd August, 1809', in *Correspondence Relating to Persia and Affghanistan*, London, 1839

Ehrenberg, Victor, *Alexander and the Greeks*, tr. Ruth Fraenkel von Velsen, Oxford, 1938

Elliot, H. M., *The History of India, as told by its own historians: the Muhammadan period,* ed. John Dowson, London, 1867–77 (II)

Enoki, Kazuo, 'On the Nationality of the Ephthalites', in *Memoirs of the Research Department of the Toyo Bunko (Oriental Library)*, Tokyo, 1959 (XVIII)

Erdosy, G., ed., *The Indo-Aryans of Ancient South Asia: Language, Material Culture and Ethnicity*, Berlin/New York, 1995

Euripides, *Euripides V: The Bacchae,* tr. William Arrowsmith, Chicago, 1959

Fa Hsien, *A Record of Buddhistic Kingdoms: Being an Account by the Chinese Monk Fâ-Hien of His Travels in India and Ceylon (A.D. 399–414) In Search of the Buddhist Books of Discipline*, tr. James Legge, Oxford, 1886

Faccenna, Domenico, *Sculptures from the Sacred Area of Butkara I, Part 2: Plates*, Rome, 1962

—— *A Guide to the Excavations in Swat (Pakistan) 1956–1962*, Rome, 1964

Falk, Harry, 'The Purpose of Rgvedic Ritual', in *Harvard Oriental Series, Opera Minora 2*, Cambridge, Mass., 1997

Feldman, Herbert, *Karachi through a Hundred Years: The Centenary History of the Karachi Chamber of Commerce and Industry 1860–1960*, Karachi, 1960

Ferishta, Muhammad Kasim, *History of the Rise of the Mahomedan Power in India*, tr. J. Briggs, London, 1829 (I)

Foltz, Richard C., *Religions of the Silk Road: Overland Trade and Cultural Exchange from Antiquity to the Fifteenth Century*, London, 1999

Fonia, R. S., 'Ladakh Corridor to Central Asia: An investigative report of prehistoric cultures', in *Journal of Central Asian Studies*, Srinagar, 1994? (IV, pp.35–41)

Forster, George, *Sketches of the mythology and history of the Hindus*, London, 1785

—— *A Journey from Bengal to England*, London, 1798

Foster, William, *The English Factories in India 1634–1636*, Oxford, 1911

—— *The English Factories in India 1637–41*, Oxford, 1912

—— ed., *The Embassy of Sir Thomas Roe to India 1615–1619, As Narrated in his Journal and Correspondence*, London, 1926

Foucher, Alfred, *L'Art Gréco-Bouddhique du Gandhâra*, Paris, 1905–41

—— *La Vieille Route de l'Inde de Bactres à Taxila*, Paris, 1942

Francfort, Henri-Paul, Daniel Klodzinski and Georges Mascle, 'Archaic Petroglyphs of Ladakh and Zanskar', in *Rock Art in the Old World, Papers presented in Symposium A of the AURA Congress, Darwin, Australia, 1988*, ed. Michel Lorblanchet, New Delhi, 1992

Francke, A. H., 'The Eighteen Songs of the Bono-na Festival', in *Indian Antiquary*, Bombay, May 1905, pp.93–110

—— *A History of Western Tibet: one of the unknown empires*, London, 1907a

—— 'The Dards at Khalatse in Western Tibet', in *Memoirs of the Asiatic Society of Bengal*, Calcutta, 1907b (I)

—— *Ten Ancient Historical Songs from Western Tibet*, Bombay, 1909

—— tr., *Ladvags rGyalrabs. The Chronicles of Ladakh, according to Schlagintweit's MS* [from *Journal and Proceedings, Asiatic Society of Bengal*], Calcutta, 1910 (VI:8)

—— *Antiquities of Indian Tibet*, Part 1: *Personal Narrative*, Calcutta, 1914

Freeman-Grenville, G. S. P., 'The Sidi and Swahili', *Bulletin of the British Association of Orientalists*, London, 1971 (VI, pp.3–18)

Friese, Kai, 'The Aryan Handshake: Blood and Belonging in India', *Transition 83: An International Review*, Durham, NC, 2000 (IX:3, pp.4–35)

Fryer, John, *A new account of East-India and Persia, in eight letters*, London, 1698

Gibb, H. A. R., tr., *Ibn Battuta: Travels in Asia and Africa 1325–1354*, New Delhi, 2001 [1929]

Greathed, H. H., *Letters written during the Siege of Delhi*, 1858

Griffith, Ralph, *The Hymns of the Rigveda: Translated with a popular commentary*, Benares, 1889

Grose, John Henry, *A Voyage to the East Indies*, London, 1772

Guha, Ramachandra, 'Could Partition have been made less bloody?', in *The Hindu*, Chennai, 28 August 2005

Gunderson, Lloyd L., *Alexander's Letter to Aristotle about India*, Meisenheim am Glan, 1980

Habib, Irfan, *The Indus Civilization: Including Other Copper Age Cultures and History of Language Change till c. 1500 BC*, New Delhi, 2002

Habib, Mohammad, *Sultan Mahmud of Ghaznin*, Aligarh, 1951 [1927]

Haleem, Muhammad Abdel, *Understanding the Qur'an: Themes and Style*, London, 1999

Hall, J. H. W., *Scenes in A Soldier's Life*, London, 1848

Hallier, Ulrich W., 'Petroglyphen in Nordpakistan: Neuentdeckungen an Gilgit und Yasin', in *Antike Welt*, Mainz, 1991 (XXII, pp.2–20)

Hamilton, Alexander, *A New Account of the East Indies*, Edinburgh, 1727

Hammond, N. G. L., *Sources for Alexander the Great: an Analysis of Plutarch's Life and Arrian's Anabasis Alexandrou*, Cambridge, 1993

Hansard's Parliamentary Debates, London, 1840 (LI)

Harris, Joseph E., *The African Presence in Asia: Consequences of the East African Slave Trade*, Evanston, 1971

Hasan, Arif, 'Another Time, Another Place: A journey through Karachi's pre-British past', in *Herald*, Karachi, August 1986

—— *Understanding Karachi: Planning and Reform for the Future*, Karachi, 1999

—— *The Unplanned Revolution: Observations on the Process of Socio-Economic Change in Pakistan*, Karachi, 2002

—— 'The changing nature of the informal sector in Karachi as a result of global restructuring and liberalization', in *Environment and Urbanization*, London, April 2002 (XIV:1, pp.69–78)

Hasan, Mubashir, *Birds of the Indus*, Karachi, 2001

Hasan, Mushirul, ed., *India Partitioned: The Other Face of Freedom*, New Delhi, 1995

—— 'The Partition Debate – II', in *The Hindu*, Chennai, 3 January 2002

Hauptmann, Harold, ed., *The Indus: Cradle and Crossroads of Civilizations: Pakistan-German Archaeological Research*, Islamabad, 1997

Heddle, J. F., 'Memoir on the River Indus' [*Selections from the Records of the Bombay Government, New Series*, India Office Records, British Library: V/23/214, Fiche no. 1066–7], 1836

Hedin, Sven, *Trans-Himalaya: Discoveries and Adventures in Tibet*, London, 1909

Herodotus, *The Histories*, tr. George Rawlinson, London, 1992 [1910]

Holdsworth, T. W. E. [with a Preface by A. H. Holdsworth], *Campaign of the Indus: In A Series of Letters from an Officer of the Bombay Division*, London, 1840

Hornblower, Simon and Antony Spawforth, *The Oxford Classical Dictionary*, third edition, Oxford, 1999 [1996]

Hotchand, Seth Naomal, *A forgotten chapter of Indian history as described in the memoirs of Seth Naomal Hotchand*, Karachi, 1982 [1915]

Hughes, A. W., *A Gazetteer of the Province of Sindh*, London, 1874

Hultzsch, E., *Inscriptions of Asoka*, Oxford, 1925

Husain, N. et al., 'Depression and Social Stress in Pakistan', in *Psychological Medicine*, March 2000 (XXX:2, pp.395–402)

Husain, Yusuf, *L'Inde Mystique au Moyen Age: Hindous et Musulmans*, Paris, 1929

International Seminar on Kalhora Rule in Sindh, Karachi, 1996

Iran Society, *Al Biruni Commemoration Volume*, Calcutta, 1951

Ismail, Professor M., 'Ghazi Brotha's Effects on Swabi', in *News International*, Karachi, 18 November 1995

—— 'Community Perceptions of Male Child Sexual Abuse in North West Frontier Province, Pakistan', Peshawar: www.crin.org/docs/resources/publications/SexAbuse1.pdf [n.d., *c.* 1997]

Jackson, K. A., *Views in Affghaunistaun, &c. &c. &c. from Sketches taken during the Campaign of the Army of the Indus*, London, 1842

Jalal, Ayesha, *The Sole Spokesman*, Cambridge, 1985

—— and Anil Seal, 'Alternative to Partition: Muslim Politics Between the Wars', *Modern Asian Studies*, 1981 (XV:3)

Jettmar, Karl, 'Ethnological Research in Dardistan 1958', in *Proceedings of the American Philosophical Society*, Philadelphia, February 1961 (CV:1, pp.79–97)

—— ed., *Cultures of the Hindukush: Selected Papers from the Hindu-Kush Cultural Conference Held at Moesgard 1970*, Wiesbaden, 1974

—— *Bolor and Dardistan*, Lahore, 1980

—— 'An Ethnographic Sketch', in Ahmad Hasan Dani, ed., *History of Northern Areas of Pakistan (Up to 2000 AD)*, Lahore, 2001

—— *Beyond the Gorges of the Indus: Archaeology before Excavation*, Karachi, 2002

Jha, Vivekanand, 'Stages in the History of Untouchables', in *Indian Historical Review, Biannual Journal of the Indian Council of Historical Research*, Delhi, July 1975 (II:1, pp.14–31)

Jiao, Ben, *Socio-economic and Cultural Factors Underlying the Contemporary Revival of Fraternal Polyandry in Tibet* [PhD dissertation], Case Western Reserve University, 2001: www.case.edu/affil/tibet/tibetanSociety/documents/BenJiaodissertation.pdf

Jones, Schuyler, *Tibetan Nomads: Environment, Pastoral Economy, and Material Culture*, Copenhagen/London, 1996

Joshi, Jagat Pati and Madhu Bala, 'Manda: A Harappan Site in Jammu and Kashmir', in Gregory L. Possehl, ed., *Harappan Civilization: A Contemporary Perspective*, Warminster, 1982, pp.185–95

Joshi, Rita, *The Afghan Nobility and the Mughals, 1526–1707*, Delhi, 1985

Jotwani, Motilal, *Sufis of Sindh*, Delhi, 1986

Kalhana, *Kalhana's Rajatarangini: A Chronicle of the Kings of Kashmir*, tr. M. A. Stein, London, 1900 (I)

Kantowsky, Detlef and Reinhard Sander, eds, *Recent Research on Ladakh: History, Culture, Sociology, Ecology*, Köln/London, 1983

Kargil, Government of, http://kargil.gov.in/tourism/monastery.htm

Karttunen, K., *India in Early Greek Literature*, Helsinki, 1989

—— *India and the Hellenistic World*, Helsinki, 1997

Kaye, John, *Lives of Indian Officers: Illustrative of the History of the Civil and Military Services in India*, London, 1867

—— *History of the War in Afghanistan*, London, 1874

Kazi, Elsa, *Risalo of Shah Abdul Latif*, Hyderabad, 1996 [1965]

Kazmi, S. Hasan Askari, *The Makers of Muslim Geography: Alberuni*, Delhi, 1995

Keay, John, *The Honourable Company: History of the English East India Company*, London, 1993 [1991]

—— *India: a History*, London, 2000

Kenoyer, Jonathan Mark, *Ancient Cities of the Indus Valley Civilization*, Karachi, 1998

Kepel, Gilles, *Jihad: the Trail of Political Islam*, Cambridge, Mass., 2002 [2000]

Kerr, Ian, *Building the Railways of the Raj: 1850–1900*, Delhi, 1995

Khakee, Gulshan, *The Dasa Avatara of the Satpanthi Ismailis and the Imam Shahis of Indo-Pakistan* [unpublished PhD thesis], Harvard, Cambridge (Mass.), 1972

Khamisani, Amena, *The Risalo of Shah Abdul Latif Bhitai: Translated in Verse*, Hyderabad, 2003

Khan, Adeel, *Politics of Identity: Ethnic Nationalism and the State in Pakistan*, New Delhi/London, 2005

Khan, Ghani, *The Pathans: A Sketch*, Peshawar, 1958

Khan, Gulzar Mohammad, 'Excavations at Zarif Karuna', in *Pakistan Archaeology*, Karachi, 1973 (IX)

Khan, Makin, 'The Tibetan Pilgrim, Urgyan-Pa, also passed through Swat valley in 1250 AD', in *Archaeological Museum Saidu Sharif, Swat: A Guide*, Saidu Sharif, 1997

Khuhro, Hamida, *Sind Through the Centuries*, Karachi, 1981

—— *Mohammed Ayub Khuhro: a Life of Courage in Politics*, Lahore, 1998a

—— 'Masjid Manzilgah 1939–40: Test case for Hindu-Muslim Relations in Sind', in *Modern Asian Studies*, Cambridge, 1998b

Kipling, Rudyard, *Kim*, ed. Alan Sandison, London, 1987 [1901]

Kirpalani, S. K., *Fifty Years with the British*, London, 1993

Knight, E. F., *Where Three Empires Meet*, London, 1893

Kohli, Surindar Singh, *Travels of Guru Nanak*, Chandigarh, 1969

Lafont, Jean-Marie, *Indika: Essays in Indo-French Relations, 1630–1976*, Delhi, 2000

Lambrick, H. T., *Sir Charles Napier and Sind*, Oxford, 1952

Lamotte, Etienne, *History of Indian Buddhism*, Louvain La Neuve, 1988

Lane Fox, Robin, *Alexander the Great*, London, 1973

—— *The Search for Alexander*, London, 1980

Lari, Yasmeen and Mihail S. Lari, *The Dual City: Karachi During the Raj*, Karachi, 1996

Lashari, Kaleem and Asma Ibrahim, 'Mural Paintings of Dadu', in *Archaeological Review 2000–2001*, ed. Asma Ibrahim and Kaleem Lashari, Karachi, 2001, pp.109–16

—— 'Painted Tombs', in *Dawn*, Review section, 15–21 July 2004

Laurie, William A., *Memoir of James Burnes*, Edinburgh, 1850

Lawrence, Bruce, *The Qur'an: A Biography*, London, 2006

Lilienthal, David E., 'Another "Korea" in the Making?', in *Collier's Magazine*, New York, 4 August 1951

Lohuizen de Leeuw, J. E. van, 'New Evidence with Regard to the Origin of the Buddha Image', in *South Asian Archaeology*, ed. Herbert Hartel, Berlin, 1979

Lopez, Donald S., *Buddhism*, London, 2001

Mackenzie, D. N., *Poems from the Divan of Khushal Khan Khattak*, London, 1965

Mahabharata, *Mahabharata: Translated into English prose from the original Sanskrit text*, tr. Kisari Mohan Ganguli, New Delhi, 1993 [1970]

—— *The Mahabharata*, tr. J. A. B. van Buitenen, Chicago, 1973

Manrique, Fray Sebastien, *Travels of Fray Sebastien Manrique 1629–1643: A Translation of the Itinerario de las Missiones Orientales*, Volume II: *China, India, Etc.*, Oxford, 1927

Mansergh, Nicholas, ed., *Transfer of Power: The Mountbatten Viceroyalty*, London, 1982

Mariwalla, C. L., 'The Tri-islets in the Indus', in *Sindhian World*, Karachi, 1940 (I:3)

Markovits, Claude, *The Global World of Indian Merchants, 1750–1947: Traders of Sind from Bukhara to Panama*, Cambridge, 2000

Marshall, John, *A Guide to Taxila*, Calcutta, 1921

—— ed., *Mohenjo-Daro and the Indus Civilization: Being an official account of Archaeological Excavations at Mohenjo-Daro carried out by the Government of India between the years 1922 and 1927*, London, 1931

Masson, Charles, *Narrative of Various Journeys in Balochistan, Afghanistan, and the Panjab, Including a Residence in those Countries from 1826 to 1838*, London, 1842

Max Müller, Friedrich, *The Science of Language: founded on lectures delivered at the Royal Institution in 1861 and 1863*, London, 1891a (I)

—— tr., *Vedic Hymns: Hymns to the Maruts* [Sacred Books of the East], Oxford, 1891b

—— *Collected Works of F. Max Müller*, Volume III: *Anthropological Religion*, London, 1903

Mazhar, Sheikh Mohammad Ahmad, *Sanskrit Traced to Arabic*, Lahore, 1982

McClure, H. Elliott, *Migrations and Survival of the Birds of Asia*, Bangkok, 1998 [1974]

McCrindle, J. W., *Ancient India as Described by Megasthenes and Arrian*, London, 1877

McLeod, W. H., *Guru Nanak and the Sikh Religion*, Delhi, 1996 [1968]

Meadows, Azra and Peter Meadows, eds, *The Indus River: Biodiversity, Resources, Humankind*, Karachi, 1999

Michel, Aloys, *The Indus Rivers: A Study of the Effects of Partition*, New Haven/London, 1967

Mirza, Ilyas and Rachel Jenkins, 'Risk factors, prevalence and treatment of anxiety and depressive disorders in Pakistan: systematic review', *British Medical Journal*, London, 3 April 2004 (328:794)

Mishra, Madhusudan, *The Rgveda in the Indus Inscriptions*, Delhi, 2003

Monbiot, George, 'The freshwater boom is over. Our rivers are starting to run dry', *Guardian*, London, 10 October 2006

Monier-Williams, Monier, *Sanskrit–English Dictionary*, Delhi, 1995 [1899]

Moon, Penderel, *Wavell: The Viceroy's Journal*, London, 1973

—— *Divide and Quit: An Eyewitness Account of the Partition of India*, Delhi, 1998 [1961]

Morgenstierne, Georg, *Report on a Linguistic Mission to North-Western India,* Norway, 1932

Mosley, Leonard, *The Last Days of the British Raj*, London, 1962

Mountbatten, Louis, 'Viceroy's Personal Report No. 17. Plus Appendix I: Summary of the Award of the Punjab and Bengal Boundary Commission and the Radcliffe Report', 16 August 1947 [*Listowel Collection*, India Office Records, British Library: L/PO/6/123]

Muhammad, Ghulam, 'Festivals and Folklore of Gilgit', in *Memoirs of the Asiatic Society of Bengal*, Calcutta, 1907 (I)

Muhammad, Tufail and Naeem Zafar, 'Situational Analysis Report on Prostitution of Boys in Pakistan (Lahore and Peshawar)': www.ecpat.net/eng/publications/ Boy_Prostitution/PDF/Pakistan.pdf, June 2006

Muir, J., *Original Sanskrit Texts on the origin and history of the people of India, their religions and institutions*, London, 1868–73

Murray, Stephen O. and Badruddin Khan, 'Pakistan', in *Sociolegal Control of Homosexuality: a Multi-Nation Comparison*, ed. Donald J. West and Richard Green, New York, 1997, pp.119–26

Mussafir, Muhammad Siddiq, *Ghulami ain Azadi Ja Ibratnak Nazara*, Hyderabad, 1952

—— *Manazil Mussafir, Kuliyat Mussafir*, Hyderabad, 1965 (second edition; text completed 2 October 1952)

Naidu, Uthaya, 'Bible of Aryan Invasions: 1500 BC – 1000 AD', http://www. light1998.com/The-Bible-of-Aryan-Invasions/bibai1.html

Naipaul, V. S., *Among the Believers: an Islamic Journey*, London, 1981

—— *India: a Million Mutinies Now*, London, 1991 [1990]

—— *Beyond Belief: Islamic Excursions among the Converted Peoples,* London, 1998

Napier Papers: 'British Prospectus of North of India, Guzerat, and Indus Commercial Company' [European Manuscripts Collection, British Library: Add. 49115], 1843

Napier, Charles, 'Memorandum on Sind' [1846], in 'Correspondence concerning India' [National Archives, London: PRO/30/12/14/5], 1845–58

—— 'Memorandum by Sir Charles Napier on stream navigation of the Indus and Punjab rivers' [Dalhousie Muniments, National Archives of Scotland: GD45/6/402], 24 July 1849

Napier, W. F. P., *The Conquest of Scinde*, London, 1845

Narain, A. K., ed., *Studies in Buddhist Art of South Asia*, New Delhi, 1985

Nayyar, A. H. and Ahmed Salim, in *The Subtle Subversion: The State of Curricula and Textbooks in Pakistan*, Islamabad, n.d. [c. 2003]

Nazim, Muhammad, *The Life and Times of Sultan Mahmud of Ghazna*, Cambridge, 1931

Norberg Hodge, Helena, *Ancient Futures: Learning from Ladakh*, London, 2000 [1991]

—— *Ancient Futures: Learning from Ladakh*, VHS, 1993

North West Frontier Province (NWFP), Government of, 'Hisbah Bill', Law,

Parliamentary Affairs and Human Rights Department, Government of NWFP, Peshawar, 2005

Oppenheimer, Stephen, *Out of Eden: The Peopling of the World*, London, 2003

Padmanabhan, Manjula, *Getting There*, London, 2000

Pande, B. M., 'Neolithic Hunting Scene on a Stone Slab from Burzahom, Kashmir', in *Asian Perspectives*, Hong Kong, 1971 (XIV)

Pandey, Gyanendra, 'India and Pakistan, 1947–2002: Statistics and Their Meaning', in *Economic and Political Weekly*, Mumbai, 16 March 2002 (XXXVII:11): http://www.sacw.net/partition/gpandey2002.html

Pankhurst, Richard and Shihan de Silva Jayasuriya, eds, *The African Diaspora in the Indian Ocean*, Trenton, NJ, 2003

Parpola, Asko, 'The Coming of the Aryans to Iran and India', in *Studia Orientalia*, Helsinki, 1988 (LXIV, pp.195–302)

Pauwels, Heidi R. M., 'The Great Goddess and Fulfillment in Love: Radha Seen Through a Sixteenth-Century Lens', in *Bulletin of the School of Oriental and African Studies*, London, 1996

Peel Papers, 'General Correspondence of Sir Robert Peel, as First Lord of the Treasury (including alleged letter by Sir Henry Pottinger, condemning Lord Ellenborough's treatment of the princes of Sind)' [European Manuscripts Collection, British Library: Add. 40538], 1844

Peissel, Michel, *The Ants' Gold: The Discovery of the Greek El Dorado in the Himalayas*, London, 1984

Philostratus the Elder, *The Life of Apollonius of Tyana: the Epistles of Apollonius and the Treatise of Eusebius*, tr. F. C. Conybeare, London, 1912

Pollock, Sheldon, 'Ramayana and Political Imagination in India', *Journal of Asian Studies*, Ann Arbor, Michigan, 1993 (LII:2, pp.261–97)

Possehl, Gregory L., ed., *Harappan Civilization: A Recent Perspective*, second revised edition, New Delhi, 1993 [1982]

—— *The Indus Civilization: A Contemporary Perspective*, Oxford, 2002

Prakasa, Sri, *Pakistan: Birth and Early Days*, Meerut/Delhi, 1965

Purewal, Shinder, *Sikh Ethnonationalism and the Political Economy of the Punjab*, New Delhi, 2000

Qamar, R. et al., 'Y-Chromosomal DNA Variation in Pakistan', in *American Journal of Human Genetics*, 2002 (LXX:5, pp.1107–24)

Rahim, Muhammad Abdur, *History of the Afghans in India AD 1545–1631*, Karachi, 1954

Rajaram, N. S., 'Aryan Invasion – History or Politics?': http://www.archaeologyonline.net/artifacts/aryan-invasion-history.html

Rashdi, Sayed Hussamuddin, 'Sufi Shah Inayat Shaheed' and 'Shah Inayat Sufi, the first Agricultural Reformist of Sindh' [both articles taken from his Sindhi work, *Chats about the Folk Villages*], Hyderabad, 1981

Rashid, Ahmed, *Taliban: The Story of the Afghan Warlords* [first edition subtitled *Islam, Oil and the New Great Game in Central Asia*], London, 2001 [2000]

Raverty, H. G., *Selections from the Poetry of the Afghans*, Lahore, 2002 [1862]

Richter-Ushanas, Egbert, *The Indus Script and the Rg-Veda*, Delhi, 1997

Roberston, William, *The History of America*, Dublin, 1777

Rodinson, Maxime, *Mohammed*, tr. Anne Carter, London, 1971

Ross, E. Denison, *An Arabic History of Gujarat*, London, 1910–28 (II)

Russell, William Howard, *My Diary in India in the Year 1858–9*, London, 1860

Saigol, Rubina, 'Curriculum in India and Pakistan', in *South Asian Journal*, October–December 2004: www.southasianmedia.net/magazine/journal/ 6_curriculum_india.htm

Salomon, Richard, *Indian Epigraphy: A Guide to the Study of Inscriptions in Sanskrit, Prakrit, and the Other Indo-Aryan Languages*, Oxford, 1998

—— *Ancient Buddhist Scrolls from Gandhara: The British Library Kharoshti Fragments*, London, 1999

Sanghur, Aziz, 'Pakistan's fishermen cast around for a solution', *Pakistan Fisherfolk Forum*, Karachi, www.pff.org.pk/article.php3?id_article=92, 24 February 2006

Sardar, Badshah, *Buddhist Rock Carvings in the Swat Valley*, Islamabad, 2005

Sarkar, Sumit, *Modern India: 1885–1947*, Delhi, 1985 [1983]

Schildgen, Brenda Deen, 'Dante and the Indus: The Salvation of Pagans', in *Dante and the Orient*, Urbana, *c.* 2002

Schimmel, Annemarie, 'Shah Inayat of Jhok, A Sindhi Mystic', in *Liber Amicorum: Studies in Honor of Professor Dr C. J. Bleeker*, Leiden, 1969

—— *Sindhi Literature,* Wiesbaden, 1974

—— *Pain and Grace: A Study of Two Mystical Writers of Eighteenth Century Muslim India*, Leiden, 1976

—— *Pearls from the Indus*, Jamshoro (Pakistan), 1986

'Scindy Diary' [Lambrick Collection, India Office, British Library: MssEurF208/106], 1 August 1762–31 July 1764

Segal, Ronald, *Islam's Black Slaves: The History of Africa's Other Black Diaspora*, London, 2001

Seth, Mesrovb Jacob, *Armenians in India: From the Earliest Times to the Present Day*, Calcutta, 1937 (quoted in 'Sarmad, A mystic poet beheaded in 1661', on www.crda-france.org/fr/6histoire/par_pays/inde_sarmad1.htm)

Shakir, M. H., tr., *The Holy Qur'an*, University of Virginia Electronic Text Center, 1997: http://etext.lib.virginia.edu/koran.htm

Shamsie, Muneeza, ed., *Leaving Home*, Karachi, 2001

Sharma, Arvind, *Studies in Alberuni's India*, Wiesbaden, 1983

Sharma, M. S. M., *Peeps into Pakistan*, Patna, 1954

Sharma, Sunil, *Persian Poetry at the Indian Frontier*, Delhi, 2000

Shiromani Gurdwara Parbandhak Committee, *The Golden Temple: Its Theo-Political Status* [by Sirdar Kapur Singh], Amritsar, 2002

—— *Sikh Reht Maryada: The Code of Sikh Conduct and Conventions,* Amritsar, 2004

Siddiqa, Ayesha, *Military Inc: Inside Pakistan's Military Economy*, London, 2007

Singer, Isidore and Louis H. Gray, 'Sarmad, Mohammed Sa'id', in *Jewish Encyclopedia*, www.jewishencyclopedia.com/view.jsp?artid+257&letter+S, 2002

Singh, Fauja and Kirpal Singh, *Atlas: Travels of Guru Nanak*, Patiala, 1976

Singh, Khushwant, *A History of the Sikhs*, Volume 1: *1469–1839*, Delhi, 2005 [1963]

—— tr., *Hymns of Guru Nanak*, Bombay, 1978 [1969]

Singh, Maharaja Ranjit, Letter to Alexander Burnes, John Murray archive [now in the National Library of Scotland], n.d.

Smith, Vincent, *The Oxford History of India*, Oxford, 1920

Smyth, J. W., *Gazetteer of the Province of Sind: 'B'*, Volume I: *Karachi District*, Bombay, 1919

—— Volume III: *Sukkur District*, Bombay, 1919

—— Volume II: *Hyderabad District*, Bombay, 1920

Sorley, H. T., *Shah Abdul Latif of Bhit: His Poetry, Life and Times. A Study of Literary, Social and Economic Conditions in Eighteenth Century Sind*, Oxford, 1940

Southgate, Minoo S., tr., *Iskandarnamah: A Persian Medieval Alexander-Romance*, New York, 1978

Stacul, Giorgio, 'Excavation near Ghālīgai (1968) and chronological sequence of protohistorical cultures in the Swāt valley', in *East and West*, Rome, 1969 (XIX)

—— *Prehistoric and Protohistoric Swat, Pakistan (c. 3000 BC–1400 BC)*, Rome, 1987

Stein, Aurel, *On Alexander's Track to the Indus*, London, 1929

Stewart, Dugald, *The Collected Works*, ed. William Hamilton, London, 1854 (IV)

Stoneman, Richard, tr., *The Greek Alexander Romance*, Harmondsworth, 1991

Strabo, *The Geography of Strabo*, tr. Horace Leonard Jones, London, 1923 (II)

Streefland, Pieter, *The Sweepers of Slaughterhouse: Conflict and Survival in a Karachi Neighbourhood*, Assen, The Netherlands, 1979

Stuart, Tristram, *The Bloodless Revolution: Radical Vegetarians and the Discovery of India*, London, 2006

Swami, Praveen, 'Unknown Heroes of Batalik', in *Frontline* [magazine of *The Hindu*], Chennai, 17–30 July 1999 (XVI:15)

Syed, G. M., *Religion and Reality*, Karachi, 1986

Tarn, W. W., *The Greeks in Bactria and India*, Cambridge, 1951

Tavernier, Jean-Baptiste, *Les six voyages de Jean Baptiste Tavernier*, tr. V. Ball, London, 1889 [Paris, 1676–7]

Temple, Sir Richard Carnac, 'A general view of Indian Muslim saints' ['First monograph of author's researches into the nature of Zinda Peer, everliving saint of India': Manuscript and typescript in the archives of the School of Oriental and African Studies, 96086], 1931

Thakur, Naraindas S., *Jai Jhoole Lal Life Story: Amar Uderolal*, Pushkar, n.d.

Thapar, Romila, *Asoka and the Decline of the Mauryas*, Delhi, 1997 [1961]

—— *A History of India*, Harmondsworth, 1966

—— 'Megasthenes: Text and Context', in *The Mauryas Revisited*, Calcutta, 1987

—— *Narratives and the Making of History: Two Lectures*, New Delhi, 2000

Thornton, Edward, *A Gazetteer of the Countries Adjacent to India on the North-West*, London, 1844

Tibet Information Network, *Mining Tibet: Mineral exploitation in Tibetan areas of the PRC*, London, 2002

Toru, Miura and John Edward Philips, eds, *Slave Elites in the Middle East and Africa*, London, 2000

Tsuchiya, Haruko, 'Ancient Routes in Northern Pakistan; 1996 (II) and 1997 (I)', in Maurizio Taddei and Giuseppe de Marco, eds, *South Asian Archaeology 1997*, Rome, 2000, pp.889–902

Tucci, G., *The Religions of Tibet*, London, 1980

Vahia, M. N. et al., 'Astronomical interpretation of a Palaeolithic rock carving found at Sopor, Kashmir', to appear in *Puratatva* [journal of Indian Archaeological Society], 2006, www.tifr.res.in/~vahia/papers.html

—— et al., 'Oldest sky-chart with Supernova record', to appear in *Puratatva* [journal of Indian Archaeological Society], 2006, www.tifr.res.in/~vahia/papers.html

—— et al., 'Analysis of the picture found at Bomai in Sopore area by Mumtaz Ahmed Yatoo of Centre for Central Asian Studies, Srinagar, April 2005' [unpublished], 2006

Vernier, Martin, *Exploration et documentation des pétroglyphes du Ladakh, 1996–2006*, Como, 2007

Vigne, G.T., *A Personal Narrative of a visit to Ghazni, Kabul, and Afghanistan, and of a residence at the court of Dost Mohamed*, London, 1840

—— *Travels in Kashmir, Ladak, Iskardo, the Countries Adjoining the Mountain-Course of the Indus, and the Himalaya, North of the Punjab*, London, 1842

Vohra, Rohit, 'Ethnographic Notes on the Buddhist Dards of Ladakh: The Brog-Pa', in *Zeitschrift für Ethnologie*, Berlin, 1982 (CVII:1, pp.69–94)

—— *An Ethnography: The Buddhist Dards of Ladakh: 'Mythic Lore – Household – Alliance System – Kingship'*, Ettelbruck, 1989a

—— *The Religion of the Dards of Ladakh: Investigations into their pre-Buddhist 'Brog-pa Traditions*, Ettelbruck, 1989b

Wada, Akiko, *Kalasha: Their Life and Tradition*, Lahore, 2003

Waddell, L. Austine, *The Buddhism of Tibet or Lamaism*, Cambridge, 1934 [1895]

Waslekar, Sundeep [Strategic Foresight Group], *The Final Settlement: Restructuring India–Pakistan Relations*, Mumbai, 2005

Wilson, H. H., tr., *Rig-Veda-Sanhita. A Collection of Ancient Hindu Hymns constituting the First Ashtaka, or Book, of the Rig-Veda*, London, 1850–54

Wink, André, *Al-Hind: The Making of the Indo-Islamic World*, Volume 1: *Early Medieval India and the Expansion of Islam 7th–11th centuries*, Oxford, 1999 [1990]

Witzel, Michael and Steve Farmer, 'Horseplay in Harappa', in *Frontline* [magazine of *The Hindu*], Chennai, 2000 (XVII:20), http://www.hinduonnet.com/fline/fl1723/17231220.htm

Wolohojian, Albert Mugrdich, tr., *The Romance of Alexander the Great by Pseudo-Callisthenes*, New York, 1969

Wolpert, Stanley, *Jinnah of Pakistan*, New York/Oxford, 1984

Wood, John, 'Report upon the River Indus' [*Selections from the Records of the Bombay Government*, India Office Records, British Library: V/23/212, Fiche nos. 1068–9, A28–9], 1838a

—— 'Chart of the Indus River from Mittun to Attock', by Lieutenant J. Wood, Indian Navy [India Office Records, British Library: V/23/Fiche A29], 1838b

—— *A Personal Narrative of a Journey to the Source of the River Oxus by the Route of the Indus, Kabul and Badakhshan*, London, 1841

World Tibet Network News, 28 December 1994: http://www.tibet.ca/en/wtnarchive/1994/12/28_1.html

Wriggins, Sally Hovey, *XuanZang: A Buddhist Pilgrim on the Silk Road*, Oxford/Colorado, 1996

Xuanzang, *Si Yu Ki: Buddhist Records of the Western World*, tr. Samuel Beal, London, 2000 [1884]

—— *The Life of Hieun-Tsiang, by the Shamans Hwui Li and Yen-Tsung*, tr. Samuel Beal, London, 1888

Zaidi, Mazhar, Hassan Mujtaba and Farjad Nabi, 'The Last of the Mohanos: Special Report', in *News International*, Karachi, 21 October 1994

Zaidi, Z. H., ed., *Quaid-i-Azam Mohammad Ali Jinnah Papers*, Islamabad, 10 vols, 1993–, Volume VII: *Pakistan: Struggling for Survival, 1 January – 30 September 1948*, 2002

Zerjal, Tatiana et al., 'A Genetic Landscape Reshaped by Recent Events: Y-Chromosomal Insights into Central Asia', in *American Journal of Human Genetics*, Chicago, 2002

Ziring, Lawrence, *Pakistan in the Twentieth Century: A Political History*, Karachi, 1997

Acknowledgements

Towards the end of the four years it took to write this book, I received some prize-money from Michael Holroyd and the Arts Council, via an award administered by the Royal Society of Literature and the Jerwood Charitable Foundation, and this munificent gift funded the entire final year of my travel, research and writing. At the beginning, a grant from the Arts and Humanities Research Board fostered many of the ideas. In between, thank you to my agent, David Godwin, and my editor, Roland Philipps, for their support.

It has been a privilege to write this book, to travel the course of the Indus, and to meet the many people who told me their river's stories and debated its history. My debts are numberless in Pakistan, India, Afghanistan and Tibet, and along with those already mentioned in these twelve chapters, I would like to thank the following people. In Karachi: Kaleem Lashari, Asma Ibrahim, Dr Shershah, Sadiqa Salahuddin, Mirza Alim Baig, Nadra Ahmed, Arif Hasan, Amina Jilani, Parveen Rehman, Abdul Wahid Khan, Ajmal Kamal, Amar Mahboob, Maheen Zia, Taimur Khan, Mahera Omar, Faisal Butt, Kamila Shamsie, Vice-Admiral Syed Iqtidar Husain and Begum Romila Iqtidar, Maqbool Rahimtoola, Kashif Paracha, Taimur Kiddie, and above all, Major Inayat Sher Khan and Shahzadi Inayat. In Ibrahim Hyderi and Thatta: Muhammad Ali Shah and the Pakistan Fisherfolk Forum, especially Gulab Shah, with whom I made many journeys through the Delta. In Badin: the Young Sheedi Welfare Organization, and the matriarch and matriarchs-in-waiting of Bilali house. In Hyderabad: Zafar and Rozina Junejo, Aslam Khwaja, Mallah Muhammad Arab of the Sindh Taraqi Pasand Mallah Tanzeem, Mubarak Ali and the members of Al-Habsh, and in particular Professor G. A. Allana. In Bhitshah, the family of Aijaz Shah; in Umerkot, Mussafir Husain Shah; in Johi, Abdul Fattar

Dahri; in Sehwan Sharif, Saleem Lashari, Farzana Buriro, and others at the Indus Resource Centre; in Shahdadkot, Parveen Magsi and family; in Sukkur, Mian Iqbal Ahmad Qureshi, the faqirs of Khwaja Khizr's shrine, and especially Hasan Ali Khan for the royal hospitality he offered me in Sukkur. In the Punjab: Dr Z. H. Zaidi, Professor Dani, Jamshaid and Sara Niaz, General Husain, Dr Ahsan Wagah, Eric de la Varenne, Manzoor Khaliq, and the lovely Zainab Dar. In NWFP: principally Javed Iqbal and his family, for their Pashtun largesse; also Dhanish, Professor Ismail, Raj Wali Shah Khattak, Wazir Ajmal, Nizamullah, Bushra Gohar, BEFARe, and the family of Mian Salim-ur-Rehman. In Kabul: Hafizullah Ghastalai. In Baluchistan: the wonderful Qazis of Quetta; in Swat: Iqbal Rehman and his family, the staff of Khpal Kor, and Ahsan, Aadil and Arif; in Gilgit: Sajjad Ali Firdous; in Chilas: Sabir Hussain; in Skardu: M. Ismail Khan. In Srinagar: Professor Bandey; in Leh: Dr B. L. Malla and his team from the Indira Gandhi National Centre for the Arts. In Kashgar: Abdulwahab of the Uighur Tour and Travel Centre (abdultour@yahoo.com), whom I would recommend as a first port of call to anybody visiting Xinjiang or western Tibet. As I left Darchen, Tsegar was extending his home into a guesthouse, the Om Coffeehouse, and I imagine there can be no nicer place for visitors to stay.

Abdul Sattar Sheedi arranged for Arif Hussain of Talhar to translate from Sindhi the books of Muhammad Siddiq Mussafir, the Uderolal firman, and articles by various writers on Sufi Shah Inayat. Gian Chand of Sukkur translated from Sindhi two Hindu books about the River Indus and Shri Amar Udero Lal Sahib. Dr Yunus Jaffery translated the letter written in Persian by Maharaja Ranjit Singh to Alexander Burnes, which is quoted in Chapter 5. Wolf Forster translated an article on Indus valley rock art from German.

I also greatly appreciate the guidance of Martin Bemmann of Heidelberger Akademie der Wissenschaften, Felsbilder und Inschriften am Karakorum Highway, and of Professor Peter Robb at the School of Oriental and African Studies.

I used many libraries during the course of my research. Thank you to the archivists and staff of the Pakistan Institute of International Affairs in Karachi, the Laar Museum and Library in Badin, the Sindhology Library at Jamshoro University (Sindh), the Sadhubela Temple Library in Sukkur, the Reference Library of the Golden Temple, the Nehru Memorial Library in Delhi, the Peshawar University Library, the Allama Iqbal University Library in Srinagar, the British Library, the School of Oriental and African Studies Library in London, the National Art Library at the Victoria and Albert Museum, the National Archives at Kew, the John Murray Archive (then in London, now in Edinburgh), the National Library of Scotland, the University Library in Cambridge and the Ancient India and Iran Trust Library in Cambridge. Particular thanks to Rigmor Båtsvik of the Bodleian Library, Oxford University.

Several kind people read the book at various stages. I am particularly grateful to my mother, my brother Jack, S. Gautham and Tahmima Anam for their annotations and observations. Daniel Wilson, Naomi Goulder, Sharifa Rhodes-Pitts, Jenny Bangham, Syed Mazhar Zaidi, Farjad Nabi and Patrick French also commented on individual chapters. During the publishing process, I was much obliged to Rowan Yapp, Howard Davies, Thomas Abraham and Sophie Hoult for their help. Along the way, the houses of friends provided writing space; thanks especially to Charlotte Brodie in Edinburgh; Debjani Sengupta and Ritwik Saha in Delhi; and John, Louise and Rose Dargue in Dufton.

From the time that I lived in Delhi and throughout my travels along the River Indus, this book has been influenced in different ways by the conversations, notions or writings of certain people: above all Shuddhabrata Sengupta; Kai Friese; Usman Qazi (for which I have to thank Rustom Vania, one-time neighbour and colleague in Delhi); Declan Walsh, ebullient host; and the exact, encyclopaedic Irfan Khan. Nothing would have been possible without Tristram Stuart, this book's first editor and my own true love.

Finally, while several people I know were born during the writing of this book, I also lost some friends. Mr Bazmi, son of the Sheedi author Mussafir, died of a brain tumour on 22 April 2007. Nausheen Jaffery, whom I have known since we were teenagers when she took me to Gandhi's memorial and the Jama Masjid, died in 2004, aged 32.

My father died many years before this book was even dreamt of, and it is dedicated to him.

Index

Abul-Fazl, 132, 136
Achilles (Greek hero), 207, 209, 212
Adi Granth (Sikh holy book), 111, 120
Advani, L. K., 270–1
Afghanistan: British embassy established, 36; first British campaign and defeat in (1838–41), 41–3; second British force invades (1842), 43; Mujahideen activities, 106; raids Punjab, 116; Mughals and, 131–3; American presence in, 142–3, 144, 157; riots over story of violated Qur'an, 153; Buddhism in, 173; Taliban return to, 179; Alexander the Great in, 180–2; Indus Valley Civilization trades with, 244
Afghans: attitudes to Pakistanis, 174–5
Africa: slaves in Sindh and India, 53–9, 64–5, 67–70; Islam in, 56; cultural influences on Sheedis, 70
Aga Khan, 234, 238
Agni (Vedic god), 219, 241–2
Agra: East India Company depot closed, 32
ahl-al-kitab (people of the book), 3
Ahmedabad, 32
Akbar, Mughal emperor, 58, 114, 118–19, 131–2, 136
Akora Khattak (village), 148–9
Aksai Chin desert, 284–5
Alberuni, Abu Raihan, 137–8, 263
Alchi monastery, Ladakh, 277
Alexander the Great: historians on, xvi; reaches and crosses Indus, 33, 39–40, 102, 177, 179, 200, 214–15;

in Swat, 165, 184; influence on Ashoka, 170; death and division of empire, 177, 214; conquests and campaigns, 178, 181–2; in Afghanistan, 180–2; journey to Pirsar, 186–91, 194, 197, 199, 201, 203, 206–8; admires oxen, 193; follows Greek myth, 207, 209, 212; at Taxila, 208; in Punjab, 208–11; battle and peace with Puru, 209–10; irrational longings (*pothos*), 211–12; reluctant return from India, 212–14; posthumous reputation, 214; in Qur'an, 215
Alexander Romance, 33, 46, 101, 214
Ali Peza pass, 188
Ali (Shiquanhe or Senge Khabab), Tibet, 284–5, 287–9, 291–2, 301
Ali (son-in-law of the Prophet Muhammad), 95; connection with Vishnu, 99–100; Sufi role, 15; sons killed, 225
Allahabad (Prayag), 114, 221
Amazai, 193
Ambar, Malik, 58
Ambhi (or Taxiles), King, 208
Amritsar: granted to India at Partition, 110; Golden Temple (Harmandir), 113, 116, 119, 121–2; water purification system, 122–3
Amrohi, Kamal, 62
Anandpal, Punjabi king, 139
Andrew, W. P., 46
antiquities: smuggling and exploitation, 175, 224, 229
Anville, Jean-Baptiste d', 34